Morning
by Morning

A Prayer Journey with Tommy Hays

Written in real time from real life by Tommy Hays every morning to start each day in contemplative prayer, centered on Jesus, filled with the Holy Spirit, and embraced by the love of the Father

---

Tommy Hays
Spiritual Director and Founder

Messiah Ministries
2800 Tates Creek Rd.
Lexington, Kentucky 40502
www.messiah-ministries.org
MessiahMin@aol.com

Morning by Morning,
A Prayer Journey with Tommy Hays

Requests for information should be addressed to:

Tommy Hays
Messiah Ministries
2800 Tates Creek Road
Lexington, Kentucky 40502
859-422-1794
www.messiah-ministries.org
messiahmin@aol.com

ISBN: 978-159858-692-3

Endorsements for *Morning by Morning*

"Tommy Hays' daily devotionals have spoken to me directly on so many occasions. They speak out of a deep reservoir of passion and desire to know God more fully and to walk in obedience to His call. This collection will become a valuable resource for those of us seeking a deeper spiritual life."

—Sandra C. Gray, Ph.D.
President, Asbury College

"In his insightful, thought-provoking, biblically-based way, Tommy Hays leads many of us to the altar of worship and praise daily with his affirmation of "Good Morning, Lord Jesus." By allowing the Holy Spirit to guide him, Tommy is a conduit of scriptural truth emphasizing God's love, mercy and grace morning by morning, day by day. By setting aside a few minutes each day you will be encouraged and enabled to take Jesus into your day of service for Him."

—W. David Hagar, M.D.
The Focus on the Family Physicians Resource Council;
Advisory Board, The Medical Institute;
Author of: *Women at Risk; Stress and the Woman's Body;*
As Jesus Cared for Women; and *The Reproduction Revolution*

"Tommy Hays, like David, has a heart after God. I count it a privilege to call him my brother and friend. Most mornings, I begin my day sharing his devotionals 'Morning by Morning.' I am always blessed. Tommy demonstrates intimacy with God by being transparent and vulnerable in his conversations with the Lord. Participating in these devotionals leads me into a more personal, intimate and transparent relationship with God! I am grateful that these devotionals are being made available to a wider audience."

—Rev. Gary L. Moore, Executive Director
Aldersgate Renewal Ministries,
an affiliate ministry of The Upper Room, General Board of Discipleship of
The United Methodist Church

"Grounded in the Scriptures, *Morning by Morning* has been God's gentle whisper of reassurance, guidance and love and to me over and over again. Tommy's vulnerability and transparency reflect a level of intimacy with God for which I long. *Morning by Morning* models a daily faith walk of humility and submission to Jesus Christ and challenges me to go deeper with God."

—Jonathan Dow, Associate Executive Director
Aldersgate Renewal Ministries

Preface

"Good morning, Lord Jesus." Since January of 2004, I've begun every morning with these first words on my heart and first words on my lips. They've become my centering thought and my call to prayer, to start off each day centered on Jesus, filled afresh with the Holy Spirit, and embraced by the love of my Father in Heaven. For many years I had been growing in the hunger and passion of prayer, but at the same time, never really being consistent in a daily time set apart for devotion and prayer with God alone.

One of my spiritual mentor, Margaret Therkelsen, who taught me most of what I really know about personal devotion in prayer, had been teaching our weekly prayer group how to wait on the Lord in the silence and to be focused on Him first before beginning to pray. I was finding in the silence a deeper surrender and hunger for the presence of God and intimacy with Him through the communion of prayer.

So at the beginning of the year in 2004, I sensed an overwhelming desire to get up a little earlier and to simply listen for the Lord's leading. I found myself with a desire to journal my thoughts as they came in prayer, without any preconceived direction, outline, or agenda—to literally wait and see what the Lord had for me that day. I had no idea how long I could continue or if there might be mornings where nothing would seem to come at all. But God has been faithful to meet me morning by morning, as I have waited on Him with the simple invitation for Him to come and lead in my time alone with Him. Now for over four years, spending morning by morning with Jesus, what an adventure it's been! So I welcome you to come along with me in this daily journey of prayer, seeking His face, listening for His voice, and welcoming His presence. This first volume that we have published in book form contains my prayers for the year 2006.

As I wrote my prayer each day, I would send them out to my email list of readers who joined me in the journey; and in time, I began to post them on my blog at: http://www.morningbymonrning.blogspot.com/. You'll find a pattern of prayer that emerged over time, where after my first words to Jesus and simple focusing prayer, I would write " ... " Those three dots mean I was waiting on the Lord to begin to lead however He chose—most often with a Scripture, but sometimes with a phrase, a picture, a thought, a verse of a familiar song, or sometimes even a new song He was writing fresh on my heart that morning. Then I would simply journal my words and His, usually for the next hour or sometimes two, depending on any extra time I had that day, but almost always giving Him at least an hour of prayer in communion with Him.

Occasionally, I would not be able to write out my prayer because of time constraints, travel, or something unexpected. In this first year that we are publishing in book form, my good friend Mary Margaret Adams has graciously given her time to edit my prayers for publication and has included her own prayers for the days I missed. You will enjoy hearing her heart for God as well in her own style in her own journey into deeper levels of trust and intimacy with Him. These days are marked with an " * " after the title and signed with her name at the bottom. I'm deeply grateful for her countless hours and sacrifice of time to help me make these prayers available to you.

Though I have chosen to begin each prayer each day directed to Jesus, mostly written a form of personal conversation with Him, you will see from my prayers that I fully embrace the Oneness of God, revealed in every dimension of His Being of Father, Son, and Holy Spirit. I could have begun each day saying, "Good morning, Heavenly Father" or "Come Holy Spirit;" and I often address God in prayer in many various ways throughout my day, but these are the words I believe the Lord gave me to center my thoughts and begin my morning prayer for this season of my life. And I have begun to see the transforming power of the spiritual principle of 2 Corinthians 3:18 take place in my life through these contemplative, centering prayers, simply looking to Jesus:

"Now the Lord is the Spirit, and where the Spirit of the Lord is, there is freedom. And all of us, with unveiled faces, seeing the glory of the Lord as though reflected in a mirror, are being transformed into the same image from one degree of glory to another; for this comes from the Lord, the Spirit" (2 Corinthians 3:17-18).

We become like the One we worship. And it is my prayer and my belief that as I behold Jesus in these morning prayers, I become more like Him, "being transformed into (His) image from one degree of glory to another" morning by morning. I pray the same for you as you join me in this journey toward Christ-likeness, through these prayers of simple devotion and trusting surrender to Him.

The title the Lord gave me for this prayer devotional is "Morning by Morning," inspired by the words of a familiar hymn written by another Methodist minister from the rolling bluegrass hills of Kentucky that have become my home as well:

"Great is Thy faithfulness
Great is Thy faithfulness
Morning by morning
New mercies I see

All I have needed
Thy hand hath provided
Great is Thy faithfulness
Lord unto me"

-- from *Great is Thy Faithfulness*, written by Rev. Thomas O. Chisholm, 1923

May you be encouraged with new mercies of God, morning by morning, each day!

In the Love of Jesus,
Tommy Hays
Lexington, Kentucky
March 31, 2008

"Everything has become New"

Good morning, Lord Jesus. Happy New Year! I begin this new day of this New Year with You. ...

"So if anyone is in Christ, there is a new creation: everything old has passed away; see, everything has become new!" (2 Corinthians 5:17)

The first day of a new year speaks of the joy and freedom of a clean slate and a fresh start. Some see it as a day to enter into new commitments and resolutions, to try harder and do better in this year in ways that couldn't be done last year and the years before. But in Christ, neither the shame or regrets of the sins of the past nor the temptation to rest in the complacency of victories and success has any hold upon what You can do in me and through me in this day and every day ahead. By the power of the blood of Jesus, old things have passed away and everything has become new.

Paul asked, "Do you not know that a little yeast leavens the whole batch of dough? Clean out the old yeast so that you may be a new batch, as you really are unleavened. For our paschal lamb, Christ has been sacrificed. Therefore let us celebrate the festival, not with the old yeast, the yeast of malice and evil, but with the unleavened bread of sincerity and truth" (1 Corinthians 5:6-8).

In this day of celebration, I praise You for cleaning out the yeast of flesh and sin, shame and regret, disappointments and failures by the blood of the Lamb. Rather than enter into any form of bondage of resolutions that are not likely to be kept in the power of human strength and will, I celebrate my freedom from the past and the anticipation of my future in You. I entrust the whole batch of the dough of my heart to the kneading of Your hands and the filling of the yeast of Your Holy Spirit. Arise in my soul my Lord. Like fresh hot bread, let my life be a pleasing aroma to You through this new year and in every year to come. In Jesus' name I pray, Amen.

Be encouraged today! In the Love of Jesus, *Tommy Hays*

Aroma of Christ

Good morning, Lord Jesus. Abide in me as I abide in You, I pray. ...

We prayed in my Sunday School class yesterday that this year would be a year of deliberately drawing nearer to You than ever before. In this year, let every veil that separates us become thinner by the day—the veil between heaven and earth, between the supernatural and the natural, between how things should be and how they are. Let wishful thinking become fulfilled obedience. Let hope deferred become dreams come true, as You increasingly invade the realm of earth with the presence of heaven.

Then, Tricia and I were taking a little Sunday afternoon nap on our day of rest—she in one end of the house and I in the other. We both woke to the strong aroma of fresh hot bread—but there was no bread in the natural realm. Then we both remembered that was the very phrase You had given me in prayer on New Year's Day about living our lives this year as a pleasing aroma to You. We are convinced this was a simple sign of confirmation that there will be an increase of the awareness of Your Presence with us and with the body of Christ this year. Praise You, Jesus! Come Holy Spirit!

"Very truly, I tell you, whoever believes has eternal life. I Am the Bread of Life. Your ancestors ate the manna in the wilderness and they died. This is the Bread that comes down from heaven, so that one may eat of it and not die. I Am the Living Bread that came down from heaven. Whoever eats of this Bread will live forever; and the Bread that I will give for the life of this world is My Flesh" (John 6:47-51).

Lord Jesus, You are the Bread of Life who comes down from heaven to live in us by Your Spirit. "For we are the aroma of Christ to God;" and in You, we are "a fragrance from life to life" (2 Corinthians 2:15-16). This year and every year, please keep filling my home and my heart with the aroma of Your Presence and let others be drawn to the Bread of Life living in me. In Jesus' name I pray, Amen.

Be encouraged today! In the Love of Jesus, *Tommy Hays*

Third Day

Good morning, Lord Jesus. Take me by the hand and lead me by the heart into Your will for my life this day. ...

> *Take me by the hand,*
> *Lead me by the heart.*
> *Let the world around me know,*
> *Just how great Thou art.*
>
> *You're my Savior and my Lord,*
> *My soon and coming King.*
> *I rise to follow You,*
> *Wherever You will lead.*

This is the third day of the New Year, which speaks of the resurrection power of God to arise and fulfill the destiny and calling of our lives. This is the promise and power of God, "that Christ died for our sins in accordance with the Scriptures, and that He was buried, and that He was raised on the third day in accordance with the Scriptures" (1 Corinthians 15:3-4). The same Holy Spirit that raised You from the dead on that third day is now living in me to lead me into my destiny and my calling. "If the Spirit of Him who raised Christ from the dead dwells in you, He who raised Christ from the dead will give life to your mortal bodies also through His Spirit that dwells in you" (Romans 8:11). This third day, I rise to follow You, wherever You will lead. In Jesus' name I pray, Amen.

Be encouraged today! In the Love of Jesus, *Tommy Hays*

"Be Holy"

Good morning, Lord Jesus. You perfectly reveal the heart of my Father. Father, You and Your Son abide in my heart by Your Holy Spirit. Holy Spirit, You are always turning my heart to Jesus, who is always perfectly revealing the heart of my Father. Lord, You are One and You are holy. Make me more like You each day as I become more one with You each day. ...

"His divine power has given us everything needed for life and godliness, through the knowledge of Him who called us by His own glory and goodness. Thus He has given us, through these things, His precious and very great promises, so that through them you may escape from the corruption that is in the world because of lust, and may become participants of the divine nature" (2 Peter 1:3-5). "As He who has called you is holy, be holy yourselves in all your conduct; for it is written, 'You shall be holy, for I am holy' " (1 Peter 1:15-16).

Lord, give me courage and grace to embrace Your "divine power" to become a participant of Your "divine nature" in the humility of surrender and in the faith of commitment to which You are calling me by Your Word. You are everything I need "for life and godliness." I want to grow in holiness of heart and life. I want my nature to become more like Your nature. Though I have so far to go, this is the journey I choose by Your grace. In Jesus' name I pray, Amen.

Be encouraged today! In the Love of Jesus, *Tommy Hays*

False Fears of Mephibosheth

Good morning, Lord Jesus. My eyes are on You, Lord. …

Mephibosheth was the crippled grandson of Saul and the son of Jonathan. He must have been living in fear of his life after David became king of Israel in Saul's place. When David sent for him, he "fell on his face and did obeisance" trembling in fear before David, probably expecting the worst for himself and the worst from the king. But David's heart was one of mercy and grace, not wrath and revenge, saying, "Do not be afraid, for I will show you kindness for the sake of your father Jonathan; I will restore to you all the land of your grandfather Saul, and you yourself shall eat at my table always" (2 Samuel 9:1-7).

How many times do we fear the worst when You desire for us only Your best? How many times do we tremble in fear of what we think is going to happen or what we think someone thinks of us? We fear a reality that is not reality at all. Someone taught me long ago that "F-E-A-R" is "False Evidence Appearing Real."

But Mephibosheth was not only crippled in his body, he was crippled in his spirit as well. Even in light of the mercy and kindness of the king, he was still bound by his wounded and distorted self-image. He responded to David, "What is your servant, that you should look upon a dead dog such as I?" (verse 9:8) But the king backed up his promise with his power, and honored him with favor, restoring and redeeming all that was lost. "Mephibosheth ate at David's table, like one of the king's sons" (verse 9:11).

Lord, deliver me from the oppression of fears that will never come to pass, that are based on assumptions of the experiences of the past, but are not founded upon Your promises of my future. Heal me from the wounds of rejection or shame that try to cripple my identity and my destiny. Give me the humility and the courage to receive the gift of Your grace and Your favor. You have not created me and called me to eat from the scraps under the table, but instead to sit at the place You have prepared for me at Your table as a son of the King. In Jesus' name I pray, Amen.

Be encouraged today! In the Love of Jesus, *Tommy Hays*

Remember Your Roots

Good morning, Lord Jesus. You are the Vine and I am one of Your branches. Let the Life in You flow through me as I abide in You and You abide in me. ...

It's good to remember your roots and the dirt where you were planted. The dirt out here is mostly red sand in the cotton fields and cattle ranches of west Texas, where I've come home for a few days to see my family and work on a book. I suppose remembering where we're from helps us to understand a little better where we are and where we're going. It has a way of humbling our pride and adjusting our perspective, maybe even reminding us of what's important and the ones who inspired us to begin the journey in the first place.

"Remember the long way that the Lord your God has led you these forty years in the wilderness, in order to humble you, testing you to know what is in your heart, whether or not you would keep His commandments. He humbled you by letting you hunger, then feeding you with manna, with which you nor your ancestors were acquainted, in order to make you understand that one does not live by bread alone, but by every word that comes from the mouth of the Lord" (Deuteronomy 8:2-3).

I've been on the journey through the wilderness of this world for forty-four years now. In my lawyer days many years ago, I remember one of my adversaries reminding me of my roots from the other side of his fancy conference room table in his downtown Houston office, "You're a long way from Lamesa, boy." He was right. Along the way, I've spent time in the slums of sin where I should have never been; and by Your grace, I've spent time in the heights of the heavens where even angels fear to tread. But through the times when I was bound-up back in Egypt and the times when I crossed over into Jordan, You were with me, sustaining me and leading me—whether I knew it or not—by Your Word and Your Spirit.

I had the gift of a family, as broken as we were, who loved me and disciplined me, trying to ground me in Your Word and Your ways out here in this country where everything that's not rooted and grounded gets blown away in the sandstorms that will strip the paint right off of your pickup. As they say, hard country makes for hearty people. As I look back and remember, I thank You for the struggles that made me stronger, for the brokenness that made me more humble, and for the discipline that made me Your son. Keep leading me through this wilderness and giving me grace to keep following. In Jesus' name I pray, Amen.

Be encouraged today! In the Love of Jesus, *Tommy Hays*

Through Many Tribulations

Good morning, Lord Jesus. I entrust my life and this day to You. ...

"We must always give thanks to God for you, brothers and sisters, as is right, because your faith is growing abundantly, and the love of everyone of you for one another is increasing. Therefore we ourselves boast of you among the churches of God for your steadfastness and faith during all your persecutions and the afflictions that you are enduring" (2 Thessalonians 1:3-4).

The faith and love of the believers at Thessalonica were growing abundantly and increasing, despite persecutions and afflictions. They were steadfast and unwavering in their commitment to press through every challenge as they continued to look out for one another in their bond of love. In their afflictions, Paul encouraged them by reminding them that God was not the sources of their pain and that "the righteous judgment of God" would come with "vengeance" upon those who were (verse 1:5-8). Even so, God would not be wasting a moment of their suffering as they continued to look to Him in faith and stand by one another in love through every challenge. God used the opportunity of their suffering to make them "worthy of the kingdom of God" (verse 1:5).

Lord, use the challenges of my life to make me worthy of Your kingdom. Though I have not yet faced anything like the persecutions and afflictions that they endured in Paul's day and that many more endure in our day, I pray You would use these that I do face to prepare me for those that may come. Teach me how to be steadfast in the faith. Give me grace to look to You in the midst of every struggle, no matter how small or large, as you are making me worthy for the kingdom. "We must through many tribulations enter the kingdom of God" (Acts 14:22, NKJV). Let me not waste any of my tribulations, but see every challenge as an opportunity to advance in Your kingdom, by Your grace. In Jesus' name I pray, Amen.

Be encouraged today! In the Love of Jesus, *Tommy Hays*

"Listen to Him in the Temple"

Good morning, Lord Jesus. I lift up the eyes of my heart to seek You and open the ears of my spirit to hear You, watching and waiting for Your leading. ...

"And all the people would get up early in the morning to listen to Him in the temple" (Luke 21:38).

My body is a temple of Your Holy Spirit. As Your Word says, "Do you not know that you are God's temple and that God's Spirit dwells in you? If anyone destroys God's temple, God will destroy that person. For God's temple is holy, and you are that temple" (1 Corinthians 3:16-17). So I welcome You into Your temple to listen for Your voice, as You teach me and lead me, now and throughout my day. ...

It seems You are saying, "Seek to have My thoughts. Seek to have My desires. Believe by faith that I am answering your prayers, for I am. This is My will and you are asking as I lead you to ask in accordance with My will, so it will come to pass. Only believe."

Yes, Lord. Now You are leading me to Your written Word to confirm the living word You have spoken into my spirit: "And this is the boldness we have in Him, that if we asking anything according to His will, He hears us. And if we know that He hears us in whatever we ask, we know that we have obtained the requests made of Him" (1 John 5:14-15).

Seeking to have Your thoughts and Your desires is according to Your will. So I know that I have obtained the answer to my prayers, as I ask believing in faith that I have received it. I know this is a process—the process of Your transformation of my soul as You are renewing of my mind. "Do not be conformed to this world, but be transformed by the renewing of your minds, so that you may discern what is the will of God—what is good and acceptable and perfect" (Romans 12:2). Continue Your process of my transformation, as You continue to fill Your temple with Your Spirit. Continue to speak, Lord, for your servant is listening. In Jesus' name I pray, Amen.

Be encouraged today! In the Love of Jesus, *Tommy Hays*

"A Lamp to My Feet"

Good morning, Lord Jesus. Saturate my mind in Your Word and fill my heart with Your Spirit, as I narrow my thoughts upon You alone. ...

"Your Word is a lamp to my feet and a light to my path" (Psalm 119:105).

Let Your Word become the way that I think, let it be the guide for the choices I make in the twists and forks in the paths before me. Let Your Holy Spirit bring it to life with wisdom and understanding, with discernment and truth. I pray for the "spirit of wisdom and revelation" that comes from knowing You, spending time with You, and listening to You as Your Spirit reveals Your Word. In Jesus' name I pray, Amen.

Be encouraged today! In the Love of Jesus, *Tommy Hays*

"Sing to God"

Good morning, Lord Jesus. You are the song in my heart and the joy in my spirit. ...

"Sing to God, sing praises to His name; lift up a song to Him who rides upon the clouds—His name is the Lord—be exultant before Him!" (Psalm 68:4).

My grandfather Hays—we call him PaPa—will turn ninety-seven this week. It's been good to see him on my trip out west. We've been very concerned about him since he almost died last summer from continual bouts with pneumonia.   Amazingly, he has adjusted to receiving his meals through a tube by a hole in his belly going directly into his stomach. He's not very active anymore, spending most of his time sitting in his recliner; but he still desires to live every day, one day at a time. I think he has it in his mind that he wants to live to be one hundred.

He used to lead the singing in the little country church near their farm in west Texas, back in the days when "worship leader" mostly meant that you sang a little louder from your hymn book than everybody else. He can't hear very well or talk very well these days, but I bought him some headphones and a CD player, with some old gospel songs I knew he had sung a million times. When I left him yesterday morning, he had a broad smile across his face, with the volume turned up on his headphones about as high as it goes, waiving his arms in the air like a music conductor. We could barely hear, but we could make out the song of praise being released from his heart—"This is my story, this is my song, praising my Savior, all the day long..."

Thank you, Lord. There is no telling what happens in the spiritual realm when a ninety-six year old man, barely alive on a feeding tube, is still singing praises to Your name. Heaven must rejoice and hell must tremble as they behold the sight of a frail human still praising You to the end of our final breaths. Like PaPa, give me the grace to never take the gift of my breath and the songs of the Lord in my heart for granted. In Jesus' name I pray, Amen.

Be encouraged today! In the Love of Jesus, *Tommy Hays*

Available to You Today

Good morning, Lord Jesus. Like the old hymn says, "This is my story, this is my song, praising my Savior, all the day long." Let the story of my life today be a song of praise to You. Let me begin this day well, that I may finish it well— walking with You all the day long. ...

Some old friends invited me to have lunch at their cafe up on the mountain in Alto, New Mexico yesterday. They probably have the best chicken-fried-steak, mashed potatoes, and gravy anywhere outside of Texas. Pete and Cheryl are the real thing. You've taken the pain and struggles of their past, cleansed it all in Your blood, and given them a joy to share Your love and grace with everybody who wanders into their cafe. On Thursday nights they serve a free meal and a message of hope to anybody who will come, eat, and listen. And many do.

Sitting at the counter, Pete was telling me how they try to start every day saying, "I'm available to You today, Lord. Use me however You see fit." He said it's a really dangerous prayer, because that's just what happens. How thrilling it was to hear some of the stories of salvation and deliverance since the last time I saw them, as You answered their prayers. What an adventure to just give every day to You and see what You do with it!

Lord, give me the courage and grace to be available to You every day. "Or do you not know that your body is a temple of the Holy Spirit within you, which you have from God, and that you are not your own? For you were bought with a price; therefore glorify God in your body" (1 Corinthians 6:19-20). I belong to You, Lord. May the story of my life today glorify You. In Jesus' name I pray, Amen.

Be encouraged today! In the Love of Jesus, *Tommy Hays*

"Where Righteousness is at Home"

Good morning, Lord Jesus. Thank You for the gift of Your constant presence. ...

"But, in accordance with His promise, we wait for new heavens and a new earth, where righteousness is at home. Therefore, beloved, while you are waiting for these things, strive to be found by Him at peace, without spot or blemish, and regard the patience of our Lord as salvation. So also our brother Paul wrote to You according to the wisdom given him, speaking of this as he does in all his letters" (2 Peter 3:13-16).

This week, You have called me to get away from my daily duties and write down some spiritual principles and stories of Your healing love in the lives You have touched through our ministry. May all that I write be according to the wisdom You have given me. As I write, I continue to see how every story of Your healing and deliverance in someone's life, including my own, is a story of striving to be found by You at peace, without spot or blemish.

Healing is wholeness, and wholeness becomes the holiness of heart and life in our spirit and soul and body, where righteousness is at home (1 Thessalonians 5:23). This is the experience of the kingdom of God in our hearts and souls being manifested in our bodies and relationships. This is the fullness of our salvation in You, as we watch and wait for the fullness of Your kingdom to be established here on earth as it is in heaven. Continue to teach me Your Word and Your ways that I may continue to live and serve others in Your healing love and power, according to the wisdom You give me. In Jesus' name I pray, Amen.

Be encouraged today! In the Love of Jesus, *Tommy Hays*

Renewed and Restored

Good morning, Lord Jesus. As best as I can and all by Your grace, I embrace Your purpose and plan for my life this day. ...

"For surely you have heard about Him and were taught in Him, as truth is in Jesus. You were taught to put away your former way of life, your old self, corrupt and deluded by its lusts, and to be renewed in the spirit of your minds, and to clothe yourselves with the new self, created according to the likeness of God in true righteousness and holiness" (Ephesians 4:21-24).

At home, I have an old, handmade rocking chair where I come to meet You morning by morning in the communion of prayer. It used to be painted white when it was sitting in the living room of dear friends, Greg and Connie. Greg was one of the pastors at our home church before You called them to ministry in Cambodia last year. Before they left, they gave away most of what they owned. This old rocker seemed to fit me just right, so it's where I always sat when we went to their home.

A few days before they left for Cambodia, they brought it over and gave it to me. But it wasn't painted white anymore. Greg had stripped away all the layers of paint, sanded it down, varnished it, and restored it to its natural beauty of solid oak. Connie said it took Greg a long time, especially sanding away all the tight places around the carved spindles on the back. But he said it was a labor of love and we were all thrilled to see what beauty was hidden beneath all that paint. What a gift!

Thank You, Lord, for Your labor of love. It hurts at times, as You strip away all the layers of the old self that people have put on us and we have received onto ourselves—our pride and ego, our insecurities and fears, and all the other ways we've allowed ourselves to become somebody different than who we really are inside. But in Your patience and love, You take time with us, even in the places where we make it the hardest to reach. You renew us and restore us into the true self You created us to be—according to Your likeness, but in a uniqueness of beauty made by Your hands, like no one else in the world. What a gift! In Jesus' name I pray, Amen.

Be encouraged today! In the Love of Jesus, *Tommy Hays*

More Than Words Can Say

Good morning, Lord Jesus. I thank You for the grace and mercy through the blood of Your sacrifice that allows me to come into Your presence in the communion of prayer, despite all the sinful things of my past. Let me never take that for granted. ...

"He Himself bore our sins in His body on the cross, so that, free from sins, we might live for righteousness; by His wounds you have been healed. For you were going astray like sheep, but now you have returned to the Shepherd and Guardian of your souls" (1 Peter 2:24-25).

For some reason, I remembered some of those sinful things of my past in a restless night last night, and for a moment I started to linger on regret. But then, You moved in my heart to get up early and come spend some time with You in prayer. Little by little, You have been lifting from me the thoughts of regret and shame, and somehow in Your grace and Your power, You are bringing me a sense of peace and actually a measure of joy—joy to know the depths of Your mercy and forgiveness and love. Not joy that I sinned, but joy that even though I sinned, You wanted to forgive me when Your love convicted me, and You wanted me to receive the fullness of Your forgiveness. You gave me the choice to receive it or not. And through the years, You have taught me how to receive it with a thankful and grateful heart. You have taught me how much it breaks Your heart in the times when I don't. This is the freedom You sacrificed so much—more than words can say—for me to have.

You can't get that in a book or a bar, not anywhere in the world, not even in a church, unless you get that in your heart. Thank You, Lord, for getting that in my heart. Thank You, Lord, for reminding me of Your mercy, as You welcome me into Your presence again today, forgiven and free. ... I can't really put this into words. It seems like more than words can say. So I won't try. I'll just sit here for a while and receive Your undeserved mercy and Your unbelievable love. ... In Jesus' name I pray, Amen.

Be encouraged today! In the Love of Jesus, *Tommy Hays*

Think Snow!

Good morning, Lord Jesus. I love You, Lord, and I thank You, for loving me. ...

Last night, I saw a sign outside a lodge in this little mountain town that said, "Think Snow!" Up here, snow is good for business and good for the soul. There's something about crisp, clean snow that seems refreshing and pure, as it covers everything in white. Everything seems fresh and new when the sun shines on a fresh blanket of snow. I love to hear my kids squeal with delight as they run out to play.

In the spirit, the snow speaks to me of the cleansing of the sins of the past and the brisk, fresh air of the freedom and joy of Your mercy. David said, "Purge me with hyssop, and I shall be clean; wash me, and I shall be whiter than snow" (Psalm 51:7). You said through Isaiah, "Though your sins are like scarlet, they shall be as white as snow" (Isaiah 1:18, NKJV).

Thank You for blanketing my soul in Your mercy and filling my spirit with the brisk, fresh air of Your Holy Spirit. Let me squeal with delight in the faith and joy of a little child. "Everything old has passed away; see, everything has become new!" (2 Corinthians 5:17) In Jesus' name I pray, Amen.

Be encouraged today! In the Love of Jesus, *Tommy Hays*

Pray the Psalms

Good morning, Lord Jesus. You are the Word of God. Speak Your Word to my heart and give life to my spirit today. ...

The Psalmist writes out his prayer from the depths of his soul in the experiences of his life, saying, "Let this be recorded for a generation to come, so that a people yet unborn may praise the Lord" (Psalm 102:18).

The Psalms of Your Word are the cries of the heart of Your people— sometimes they are cries of pain and sometimes cries of joy. But they are always cries to You. We have come to You with our sorrows and struggles, our celebrations and thanksgivings throughout the ages. We need You. We are lost and alone without You.

One of my mentors in prayer was Maxie Dunnam. He only taught one class while I was at Asbury Seminary and he was President for a season. I made sure I was in it, as he shared from his heart of the lessons he learned in ministry. One of those lessons was to "pray the Psalms." He would start with one and read through the songs and prayers until he came to one that touched the place of his soul where he was living at the moment. I find myself doing that often. There is always one that touches the place of my soul where I'm living at the moment.

Thank You, Lord, for the generations of Your people who wrote of their pain and their joy, that the generations yet unborn might praise the Lord. And thank You for our fathers and mothers in the faith who have taught us to come to You in the communion of prayer with all of our soul. You are faithful and You are true. And as John Wesley said in his dying words, "The best of all, You are with us." You are with us in Your Word and in Your Spirit. Thank You for being with me in the depths of my soul today. In Jesus' name I pray, Amen.

Be encouraged today! In the Love of Jesus, *Tommy Hays*

The Work of Your Hands

Good morning, Lord Jesus. I call upon Your name and commit my life to You today. ...

"The heavens are telling the glory of God; and the firmament proclaims His handiwork. Day to day pours forth speech, and night to night declares knowledge. There is no speech, nor are there words; their voice is not heard, yet their voice goes out through all the earth, and their words to the end of the world" (Psalm 19:1-4).

All creation speaks of Your glory by its very existence. So it is with us. We are Your creation and even though we may not speak a word, our lives speak a message. Let the message of my life be a good message today. Let it tell of the glory of God. Remind me throughout the encounters of my day that the world is watching— watching to see who the God of creation has made me to be. My life is my voice. By Your mercy and grace, let my voice be an offering of praise to You. "The Lord will fulfill His purpose for me; Your steadfast love, O Lord, endures forever. Do not forsake the work of Your hands" (Psalm 138:7). In Jesus' name I pray, Amen.

Be encouraged today! In the Love of Jesus, *Tommy Hays*

"Listen to Him!"

Good morning, Lord Jesus. I look to Your face and seek the leading of Your voice. Your sheep know Your voice. I am one of Your sheep and You are my Shepherd. ...

You led Peter, James, and John "up a high mountain apart, by themselves" and You were "transfigured before them" (Mark 9:2). They saw "Elijah with Moses, who were talking with Jesus." Peter said something, but really "did not know what to say, for they were terrified." Then the voice of God the Father spoke to them from the midst of the cloud that came down and overshadowed them, "This is My beloved Son; listen to Him! Suddenly when they looked around, they saw no one with them anymore, but only Jesus" (Mark 9:4-8).

Yes, Father. You speak to my spirit from the cloud of the Spirit of Your Presence covering the mountain of prayer. In this place apart with You, let the fear of God come upon me to humble me in the silence of surrender before You. The words of Your law and the words of Your prophets are perfectly fulfilled in Jesus the Christ, Your beloved Son and my beloved Lord. He is Your Word. Give me the wisdom and humility to obey Your command and "listen to Him." As I do, Your Spirit will focus the eyes of my heart to see no one else, "but only Jesus." In Jesus' name I pray, Amen.

Be encouraged today! In the Love of Jesus, *Tommy Hays*

Life or Death; Blessings or Curses

Good morning, Lord Jesus. You are the Alpha and the Omega. You are the Soon and Coming King. Come into Your kingdom in my heart today. ...

"For whatever was written in former days was written for our instruction, so that by steadfastness and by the encouragement of the Scriptures we might have hope" (Romans 15:4).

Hope is the purpose of the Scriptures—even those that speak of the judgment and curses of God upon rebellion and disobedience. Because even Your judgments are for the purpose of turning our hearts back to You in repentance and faith to receive Your mercy once again. It seems You have led me to read again Your words of blessings and curses which set in place the spiritual principles that would govern the lives of Your people in the land of Your promises (Deuteronomy 27-30).

Regardless of how literally we may believe they apply to us—personally, as a people, or corporately, as a nation—there is, at the very least, the spiritual principle that obedience subjects us to the blessing of Your protection and provision, while disobedience subjects us to the lack of it—if they are to mean anything to us at all. How can we read these passages, even in the light of the Word of God revealed and fulfilled in the love of Christ, without a measure of the fear of God coming upon our hearts? Your judgments are severe, but so is Your mercy—all dependent upon our heart of submission and surrender or disobedience and rebellion toward You.

"See, I have set before you life and prosperity, death and adversity. If you obey the commandments of the Lord your God that I am commanding you today, by loving the Lord your God, walking in His ways, and observing His commandments, decrees, and ordinances, then you shall live and become numerous, and the Lord your God will bless you in the land that you are entering to possess. But if your heart turns away and you do not enter, but are led astray to bow down to other gods and serve them, I declare today that you shall perish; you shall not live long in the land that you are crossing the Jordan to enter and possess. I call heaven and earth to witness against you today that I have set before you life and death, blessings and curses. Choose life so that you and your descendants may live, loving the Lord your God, obeying Him and holding fast to Him; for that means life to you and length of days, so that you may live in the land the Lord your God swore to give to your ancestors, to Abraham, to Isaac, and to Jacob" (Deuteronomy 30:15-20).

"The Scripture says, 'No one who believes in Him will be put to shame.' For there is no distinction between Jew and Greek; the same Lord is Lord of all and is generous to all who call on Him. For, 'Everyone who calls on the name of the Lord will be saved.' (Romans 10:11-13). "Note then the kindness and the severity of God" (Romans 11:22).

By Your grace, I receive the blessing of the fear of God. By Your grace, I turn my heart to You in repentance of the sin of not fully loving You, not fully obeying You, and not fully holding fast to You. And by Your grace, I receive Your mercy and ask You to restore Your protection and Your provision. I pray this for myself, for my family, for my community, for my people, and for my nation— as far as Your grace will go. Whether it offends us or not, Your spiritual principles apply to our lives. Our choices determine mercy or judgment, life or death, blessings or curses. As for me and my house, I choose the Lord. In Jesus' name I pray, Amen.

Be encouraged today! In the Love of Jesus, *Tommy Hays*

War in the Spirit

Good morning, Lord Jesus. I bow low, that You may lift me high. I choose to follow, that You may lead. I draw near, that You may draw me nearer. ...

"For You deliver a humble people, but the haughty eyes You bring down. It is You who light my lamp; the Lord my God lights up my darkness. By You I can crush a troop, and by My God I can leap over a wall. This God—His way is perfect; the promise of the Lord proves true; He is a shield for all who take refuge in Him" (Psalm 18:27-30).

As we humble ourselves before You, You cleanse us and forgive us, You strengthen us and encourage us, You fill us and empower us. Then You send us forth into battle to war in the spirit in Your power. Our battle is not against flesh and blood, but against the spiritual forces of wickedness of this present darkness, who come to steal and kill and destroy in our lives, our families, our communities, and our nations (Ephesians 6:12). But through our repentance and Your forgiveness, our enemies' power is weakened and his plans are exposed. His defenses are breached and his strongholds crumble. And You send us in like a flood to fight for the freedom of Your people.

Forgiven and free, I choose to take up the sword of Your Spirit, the very Word of God. At Your command I will advance, taking my position to stand firm and to fight in the whole armor of God (Ephesians 6:13). You have "trained my hands for war"—this war in the spirit for the souls of those I love and for the people You've called me to defend (Psalm 18:34). Though the enemy may come in like a flood, You raise the banner of the cross to turn back the tide and enforce Your victory in the power of Your blood. There may be casualties and the grief of loss because the battles are real and the stakes are high, but the ultimate victory is secure. For the battle belongs to the Lord. I choose to fight in the battles where You lead, with the courage You have placed in my heart and the weapons You have placed in my hands. In Jesus name I pray, Amen.

Be encouraged today! In the Love of Jesus, *Tommy Hays*

"Victory Belongs to the Lord"

Good morning, Lord Jesus. "I love You, O Lord, my strength. You are my rock, my fortress, and my deliverer, my God, my rock, in whom I take refuge, my shield and the horn of my salvation, my stronghold. I call upon the Lord, who is worthy to be praised, so I shall be saved from my enemies" (from Psalm 18:1-3). ...

Terror has no power unless I allow it to make me afraid. Deception has no effect unless I allow my mind to doubt the truth and believe the lies. Death has lost its sting if I am already dead to the holds of this world and alive to the calling of Christ. Life or death, heaven or earth, I stand secure and victorious in You. And in You, I stand firm against the forces of terror and deception and death.

"For You girded me with strength for the battle; You made my assailants sink under me. You made my enemies turn their backs to me, and those who hated me I destroyed" (Psalm 18:39-40). This is a spiritual battle, won and fought on spiritual ground with spiritual weapons. And in the Spirit, the victory is won.

"The wicked put on a bold face, but the upright give thought to their ways. No wisdom, no understanding, no counsel, can avail against the Lord. The horse is made ready for the day of battle, but the victory belongs to the Lord" (Proverbs 21:29-31). Lord, make me ready for battle—ready to stand firm in my faith in You; ready to fight with the weapons of our warfare that others may be secured in the stronghold of the faith that is not shaken by even the shaking of the earth itself. Make me ready to look with my eyes and behold Your victory—the victory of the cross through the blood of the Lamb. By this, we shall overcome (Revelation 12:11). In Jesus' name I pray, Amen.

Be encouraged today! In the Love of Jesus, *Tommy Hays*

"I am the Gate"

Good morning, Lord Jesus. I seek You with all my heart; I welcome You into all my life. ...

"I am the Gate. Whoever enters by Me will be saved, and will come in and go out and find pasture" (John 10:9).

You spoke to us last night at The Fountain. As we gathered in Your name alone from many different churches and traditions from across our community, as we lifted Your name in our praises and prayers, You drew us near and filled us with Your Spirit. You set before us a choice to rejoice in You—to turn to You or to turn to our troubles and our past. You spoke into our hearts Your words of Spirit and Life. And You continue to release Your word as a call to arise and enter into the fullness of Your provision through the gate of Your presence.

You are saying to all who will come, "I am the Gate. Enter into the fullness of My plans and My provision. Enter into My yoke alone; come under My burden alone. Rest in Me; trust in Me; find your fulfillment in Me. Leave behind the bondage of the past. Arise into newness of life. I am your life. In Me, you are a new creation. Old things have passed away. Behold, all things have become new. Arise and enter in, press in, to the fullness of My plans and My provision for your life."

"Go through, go through the gates, prepare the way for the people; build up, build up the highway, clear it of stones, lift up a banner over the peoples. The Lord has proclaimed to the end of the earth: Say to daughter Zion, 'See, your salvation comes; His reward is with Him, and His recompense before Him.' They shall be called, 'The Holy People, The Redeemed of the Lord"; and you shall be called, 'Sought Out, A City Not Forsaken.' "(Isaiah 62:10-12).

Yes, Lord. I choose to rejoice in You. I choose to enter into the fullness of Your plans and Your provision. You are the Gate of life. I choose for You to be my Way, my Truth, and my Life. In Jesus' name I pray, Amen.

Be encouraged today! In the Love of Jesus, *Tommy Hays*

Good Stewards

Good morning, Lord Jesus. I am available to You today. ...

"Like good stewards of the manifold grace of God, serve one another with whatever gift each of you has received. Whoever speaks must do so as one speaking the very words of God; whoever serves must do so with the strength that God supplies, so that God may be glorified in all things through Jesus Christ. To Him belong the glory and the power forever and ever" (1 Peter 4:10-11).

We are the body of Christ, filled with the Spirit of Christ. All that You are doing on earth in this season between the first and second coming of Christ, You are doing through us. You are making us one with You, one with each other, and one in ministry to the entire world. Let us speak and serve in Your power and strength for the glory of Your name. Keep us from the false humility and confusion that would keep us from receiving our authority; keep us from the disobedience and passivity that would keep us from our responsibility.

Lord, I want to be a good steward of the gifts and graces You have given me. Teach me what they are, disciple me in how to use them, and empower me to use them well. I have a part in the body of Christ. You desire every part to be strong and in shape. I pray that for myself and for every part of Your body. In Jesus' name I pray, Amen.

Be encouraged today! In the Love of Jesus, *Tommy Hays*

"A Strong Tower"

Good morning, Lord Jesus. I call upon Your name and I choose to be called by Your name—"Christian," one who follows Christ. ...

"The name of the Lord is a strong tower; the righteous run into it and are safe. The wealth of the rich is their strong city; in their imagination it is like a high wall. Before destruction one's heart is haughty, but humility goes before honor" (Proverbs 18:10-12).

There is safety, provision, and protection in Your name. Your name speaks of Your nature—"Jesus" from the Greek, "Yeshua" from the Hebrew—The Salvation of Yaweh. "There is salvation in no one else, for there is no other name under heaven given among mortals by which we must be saved" (Acts 4:12). Salvation is living in fullness the life You have given each of us to live, eternally—now and forever. Not just now, but forever. Not just forever, but also now. To be alive to Christ and the fullness of this life for which we were created is to be dead to our own desires apart from You. To the degree we are, the world, the flesh, and the devil have no power over us. To the degree we are, we trust not in earthly riches or power or security, but in the heavenly name of the One who holds our lives in His hands—now and forever.

As best I can and all by Your grace, I choose to humble myself before You, to desperately depend upon You alone as my safety, my provision, and my protection. Here in the strong tower of Your name, I am safe and I am saved—no matter what happens. Earth has no power over me, for I belong to Heaven. I will not fear man, but fear the Lord my God; I will not trust in my riches of my own strength or wisdom, but trust in the Lord alone (Luke 12:4-7). In Jesus' name I pray, Amen.

Be encouraged today! In the Love of Jesus, *Tommy Hays*

Word Made Flesh

Good morning, Lord Jesus. I open my heart to Your Spirit and open my mind to Your Word. Come, Lord Jesus, come. ...

"And the Word became flesh and lived among us, and we have seen His glory, the glory as of a father's only son, full of grace and truth" (John 1:14).

Your Word reveals Your will and Your nature, for You are the Word of God made flesh. Your Word and Your will are already done in heaven, and they are in the process of being done on earth as they are in heaven. Your kingdom comes and Your will is done in the hearts of those who embrace Your kingdom and Your will. Today I join my words in agreement with Your Word and I join my will in agreement with Your will, as best as I can and all by Your grace. Let Your kingdom come and Your will be done here in my heart and here on earth as it already is in heaven (Matthew 6:10).

In heaven, Your Word and Your will is for our protection and security. I agree with Your Word of Psalm 91, revealing Your will for those who love You and call upon Your name:

"You who live in the shelter of the Most High, who abide in the shadow of the Almighty, will say to the Lord, 'My refuge and my fortress, My God in whom I trust.' For He will deliver you from the snare of the fowler and from the deadly pestilence; He will cover you with His pinions, and under His wings you will find refuge; His faithfulness is a shield and buckler. You will not fear the terror of the night, or the arrow that flies by day, or the pestilence that stalks in darkness, or the destruction that wastes at noonday."

"A thousand may fall at your side, ten thousand at your right hand, but it will not come near you. You will only look with your eyes and see the punishment of the wicked. Because you have made the Lord your refuge, the Most High your dwelling place, no evil shall befall you, no scourge come near your tent."

"For He will command His angels concerning you to guard you in all your ways. On their hands they will bear you up, so that you will not dash your foot against a stone. You will tread on the lion and the adder, the young lion and the serpent you will trample under foot."

"Those who love Me, I will deliver; I will protect those who know My name. When they call to Me, I will answer them; I will be with them in trouble, I will rescue them and honor them. With long life I will satisfy them, and show them My salvation" (Psalm 91).

Lord, let it be so on earth as it is in heaven—here in my life and family and community, and as far as Your grace will go. Let Your Word be made flesh in my heart and in my prayers today. In Jesus' name I pray, Amen.

Be encouraged today! In the Love of Jesus, *Tommy Hays*

Found Favor

Good morning, Lord Jesus. I need Your wisdom and I need Your grace. I need You. As best as I can, I give You all my heart and mind and soul and strength. I ask for the peace that comes from trusting You with all I have and all I am. ...

"The Lord saw the wickedness of humankind was great in the earth, and that every inclination of the thoughts of their hearts was only evil continually... But Noah found favor in the sight of the Lord" (Genesis 6:5-8).

Lord, purge the wickedness from my soul—the wickedness of self-centeredness and self-pity, the wickedness of trusting in my own power and strength instead of humbling myself to desperately depend upon You, the wickedness of my pride that causes me to be in control instead of entrusting control to You. Deliver me from the evil inclinations of my thoughts and the unholy desires of my heart that are drawn to the sin of the culture around me, rather than boldly shining as a light in the midst of the darkness.

Purify me and sanctify me by "the washing of water by the Word" (Ephesians 5:26). Let a flood of Your Spirit wash through my soul, and draw me up into the ark of Your presence. Let me find favor in Your sight. You favor those who seek Your wisdom with wisdom and You favor those who seek Your grace with grace. Noah found favor in the sight of the Lord because "Noah walked with God" (Genesis 6:9). I want to walk with You, Lord. Guide my steps in the path of Your presence. In Jesus' name I pray, Amen.

Be encouraged today! In the Love of Jesus, *Tommy Hays*

Worship on Eagle's Wings

Good morning, Lord Jesus. In these first moments of the morning, I watch for Your leading and wait in the silence of surrender before You. Come make me to lie down in Your green pastures as You lead me beside Your still waters. Restore my soul—bring my body into submission to my soul, my soul into submission to my spirit, and my spirit into submission to Your Holy Spirit. Let my cup be filled in these moments of worship and prayer with the fullness of Your presence that You may pour me out as You will throughout this day. ...

A friend coming for spiritual direction gave me a tape of simple, but powerful, songs of worship, and Your Spirit keeps singing one of them in my spirit. This song of worship called "Eagle's Wings" is my prayer of willing submission and trusting surrender in the intimacy of true worship to You—my Lord, my Shepherd, and my Best Friend:

"Here I am waiting. Abide in me I pray. Here I am longing for You.
Hide me in Your love. Bring me to my knees. May I know Jesus more and more.
Come live in me, all my life. Take over. Come breathe in me. And I will rise on eagle's wings" (by Reuben Morgan).

Yes, Lord. This is my worship; this is my prayer. Let me know You more and more every day—as I watch and wait for Your presence, then rise and follow Your lead. "But those who wait for the Lord shall renew their strength, they shall mount up with wings like eagles, they shall run and not be weary, they shall walk and not faint" (Isaiah 40:31). In Jesus' name I pray, Amen.

Be encouraged today! In the Love of Jesus, *Tommy Hays*

Prepared and Protected

Good morning, Lord Jesus. Help me focus on Your face and listen for Your leading. ...

You see the end from the beginning. All time and space throughout the past and the future is present and eternal to You. You know every decision that will be made, every consequence of every action—both good and evil, both those in obedience to Your will and those in rebellion against Your will. And You are there. You are working in ways we do not see in Your persistent, unfailing love to redeem all that happens for our good and Your glory as we entrust it to You.

Before the days of the flood, You commanded Noah to be prepared. You knew his heart and You knew he would choose to obey. "And Noah did all that the Lord had commanded him" (Genesis 7:5). Through his obedience, You prepared a place of protection for all who would hear and receive Your call to come into the ark of Your presence.

In these days, not many will seek You, not many will obey You, and not many will be prepared. But Lord, I want to be among those who will. Help me to hear what the Spirit is saying to Your people in this hour. Let me not only be a hearer of Your word, but also a doer. Give me Your grace to do my part in our generation to be prepared. There is no greater preparation than to make provision for Your presence in our hearts through humble obedience to Your call and trusting faith in Your love. In Jesus' name I pray, Amen.

Be encouraged today! In the Love of Jesus, *Tommy Hays*

Paradise of Your Presence

Good morning, Lord Jesus. You are the King of the kingdom of God. You are the "King of kings and the Lord of lords" (Revelation 19:16). You are my King. You are my Lord. Come into Your kingdom in my heart this day. ...

One of those crucified with You turned to You in humility and faith, saying, "Jesus, remember me when You come into Your kingdom." You replied, "Truly I tell you, today you will be with Me in Paradise" (Luke 23:42-43).

You come into Your kingdom wherever we bow our hearts to the King of the kingdom of God. Heaven touches earth in our hearts, and we experience a measure of Paradise—the eternal restoration of all things. Let my heart be Your kingdom. Let my body be Your temple. For wherever You are, the kingdom of God has drawn near. The fullness of Your presence in my heart is my Paradise. In Jesus' name I pray, Amen.

Be encouraged today! In the Love of Jesus, *Tommy Hays*

The Throne of Your Glory

Good morning, Lord Jesus. You open the door of heaven and call me up into Your presence through the spirit of worship and prayer (Revelation 4:1). I accept Your invitation and enter into the Holy of Holies of Your presence through the blood of the Lamb. ...

As You drew John up into Your presence through the open door of heaven, You opened his spiritual eyes to see beyond the veil of the earthly realm into the heavenly realm. At the center of all he saw was the "One seated on the throne" (verse 4:2). He saw each of the three dimensions of Your Being—Father, Son, and Holy Spirit. He saw God the Father in the glory of precious jewels and the light of a glorious rainbow (verse 4:3). He saw God the Son as the Lamb of God and the Lion of the tribe of Judah (verse 5:5-6). He saw God the Holy Spirit as the seven flaming torches of the seven-fold Spirit of God (verse 4:5).

Lord God, You are One and You are holy. You are Spirit and those who seek You must seek You in spirit and truth (John 4:24). And in the spirit of worship and prayer, I join with all creation around Your throne to bow low as You lift me high, singing, "You are worthy, our Lord and God, to receive glory and honor and power, for You created all things, and by Your will they existed and were created" (verse 4:11). Thank You for the gift and the invitation of Your open door. You are the open door, Lord Jesus. We enter into this heavenly realm of Your presence and bow before the throne of the glory of God through the sacrifice of the blood of the Lamb. "For everyone who asks receives, and everyone who searches finds, and for everyone who knocks, the door will be opened" (Matthew 7:8).

You may not always pull back the veil and let me see in the spirit into the heavenly realm, but I know You are there and I know You are worthy of my worship and prayer. So I come asking, searching, knocking—knowing I will find You here in all Your glory, welcoming me to come up with You in Your presence through the blood of the Lamb. In Jesus' name I pray, Amen.

Be encouraged today! In the Love of Jesus, *Tommy Hays*

The Sacrifice that Satisfies

Good morning, Lord Jesus. Let the peace of Your presence fill my soul. ...

Let the peace of Your presence fill my soul.
Let the life of Your Spirit make me whole.
Open my ears to hear,
As You come and draw me near.
Come make my heart Your home.

Let the joy of the Lord be my strength,
As I lift my hands and bow my knees.
Open my eyes to behold
The glory of Your throne.
Come live Your life through me.

Let Your Holy Spirit fill me afresh.
I want all of You and nothing less.
Open my spirit to be possessed
By the fullness of Your righteousness.
Come fulfill in me Your promises.

Let my life be hid with You in Christ.
The Spirit must live and my flesh must die.
Open my heart to receive
The full measure of the One who never leaves.
Come lead me in Your path of life.

Yes, Lord. Thank You for these words of surrender and submission Your Spirit is speaking through my heart. Let me die daily the death to self apart from You; let my "life be hidden with Christ in God" (Colossians 3:3). This is the death that leads to life. This is the sacrifice that satisfies the longing of my soul. By Your grace, I offer my life as a sacrifice of praise to You this day. In Jesus' name I pray, Amen.

Be encouraged today! In the Love of Jesus, *Tommy Hays*

Word of Christ

Good morning, Lord Jesus. I embrace You and Your Word. You are Spirit and You are Life. ...

"Let the word of Christ dwell in you richly; teach and admonish one another in all wisdom; and with gratitude in your hearts sing psalms, hymns, and spiritual songs to God" (Colossians 3:16).

As I read Your written Word in the Scripture and listen for Your living word in my spirit, I can choose to let it linger or let it leave. I can receive the teaching and admonitions You speak into my life through the accountability of trusting relationships or not. I can embrace an attitude of gratitude in thanksgiving and praise for Your presence in my life or decide to keep it all to myself, deciding to somehow privately worship You and thank You in the hidden places of my soul.
But if I were silent, even "the stones would shout out" (Luke 19:40).

The Word of God cannot be contained. It will rise up and it will go forth. It will change whatever it touches. Your Word is "alive and active," and it is dwelling in me (Hebrews 4:12). You are the Word of God and You are dwelling in me— changing me, and therefore, changing everything around me. Let my life be a psalm and a song of praise to You today as the Word of Christ dwells in me and changes me today. In Jesus' name I pray, Amen.

Be encouraged today! In the Love of Jesus, *Tommy Hays*

Come Fill Me Afresh

Good morning, Lord Jesus. I worship and adore You. I want to live for You. Come fill me afresh with Your Presence today. ...

> *I worship and adore You,*
> *I want to live for You.*
> *Come fill me afresh with Your Presence today.*
>
> *You are the Father and the Son,*
> *The Spirit of the Holy One.*
> *Come fill me afresh with Your Presence today.*
>
> *You must increase,*
> *And I must decrease.*
> *Come fill me afresh with Your Presence today.*
>
> *I give you my life,*
> *A living sacrifice.*
> *Come fill me afresh with Your Presence today.*
>
> *I am Yours and You are mine,*
> *Let our lives be intertwined.*
> *Come fill me afresh with Your Presence today.*
>
> *Let Your Fire fall from above,*
> *Baptize me in Your love.*
> *Come fill me afresh with Your Presence today.*
>
> *Set me ablaze with the passion*
> *Of the heart You have fashioned.*
> *Come fill me afresh with Your Presence today.*
>
> *May my life tell a story*
> *Of Your power and glory.*
> *Come fill me afresh with Your Presence today.*
>
> *When all is said and done,*
> *I want to be Your faithful son.*
> *Come fill me afresh with Your Presence today.*

Yes, Father. These words of surrender and trust that Your Holy Spirit has written on my heart this morning is my worship and prayer. You have put Your words to the longing of my heart. What more could I want than the fullness of Your Presence in every dimension of my life. In Your grace and by Your power, may I continually "be filled with all the fullness of God" (Ephesians 3:19). In Jesus' name I pray, Amen.

Be encouraged today! In the Love of Jesus, *Tommy Hays*

Costly Grace

Good morning, Lord Jesus. I wait for Your leading and watch for Your appearing. One day, You will appear in Your glory across the skies. Today, I ask You to appear in Your glory in my heart. ...

"If you love Me, you will keep My commandments" (John 14:15). "They who have My commandments and keep them are those who love Me; and those who love Me will be loved by My Father, and I will love them and reveal Myself to them" (John 14:21). "Those who love Me will keep My word, and My Father will love them, and We will come to them and make Our home with them" (John 14:23).

There is a connection between loving You and obeying You. At times we are tempted to give in to the idea of cheap grace—that somehow we can come into relationship with You and then live our lives for ourselves alone, however we desire, as if we had never surrendered our lives to You. But this love You call us to is a love of You and Your ways. To love You is to obey You. This kind of love and this depth of love is impossible apart from Your grace, but Your grace is available to all who will ask and receive.

Someone has said, "Grace is free, but it's not cheap. It will cost you everything You have." Yes, Lord. This is the grace I ask for. This is the grace I receive; the grace of Your power to love You and to obey You, to live my life for You and not for myself. As I lose my life, then I will truly find it. As I die daily to myself apart from relationship with You and obedience to You, to that degree I will truly live the life You have created me to live. To that degree, You and the Father by Your Holy Spirit, will come to me and make Your home in me, according to Your Word (John 14:3).

As You said to Your first disciples, so You say to me and all Your disciples today, "If you keep My commandments, you will abide in My love, just as I have kept My Father's commandments and abide in His love" (John 15:10). Any understanding of grace that does not understand this call to obedience is merely a vain philosophy of the traditions of men. I ask for Your forgiveness for my disobedience and I ask for Your grace to obey You more completely and to love You more deeply—more today than yesterday, more tomorrow than today. I welcome You Father, Son, and Holy Spirit to come make Your home in my heart, abiding in me continually and abounding in me thoroughly—more and more each day. In Jesus' name I pray, Amen.

Be encouraged today! In the Love of Jesus, *Tommy Hays*

Friend of God

Good morning, Lord Jesus. Draw me close to You, as I watch and wait with anticipation in the silence of surrender. ...

"You are My friends if you do what I command you. I do not call you servants any longer, because the servant does not know what the master is doing; but I have called you friends, because I have made know to you everything that I have heard from My Father" (John 15:14-15).

This personal relationship with You is one of both intimacy and obedience. You call me a friend, while You also call me to obedience. You make known to me the depths of the nature and will of my Father, for You and the Father and the Spirit are One, but this is for the purpose of both intimacy and obedience. As You dwell in my heart, You shape my will, and direct my actions. You immerse me in Your nature so that in the fullness of our friendship, Your nature becomes my nature. It is by yielding to Your will as Master that You draw me to Your side as a friend. Give me the humility to obey and the courage to come. In Jesus' name I pray, Amen.

Be encouraged today! In the Love of Jesus, *Tommy Hays*

Delivered for Worship

Good morning, Lord Jesus. I bow my head before You in prayer and lift my heart to You in praise. ...

"Then the Lord said, 'I have observed the misery of My people who are in Egypt; I have heard their cry on account of their taskmasters. Indeed, I know their sufferings, and I have come down to deliver them from the Egyptians, and to bring them up out of that land to a good and broad land, a land flowing with milk and honey...' "(Exodus 3:7-8).

Father, You have observed our misery and You know our sufferings. You hear our cries for deliverance. As You sent Moses to deliver the Hebrew people from the hand of Pharaoh, so You have sent Your Son to deliver us from the oppression of the enemy of our souls. As You confirmed Your word of deliverance to Moses, so You confirm Your word of deliverance to us, saying, "I will be with you; and this shall be a sign for you that it is I who sent you: when you have brought the people out of Egypt, you shall worship God on this mountain" (Exodus 3:12).

We are delivered for worship. Our enemy knows that hearts that are weary and oppressed are too heavy to be lifted up in worship and praise. So he brings every form of misery and suffering to crush our spirits and steal our joy. But You are with us to bind up the brokenhearted and set the captives free. "The Lord is near to brokenhearted and saves the crushed in spirit" (Psalm 34:18). Hearts that are set free are free to worship.

Lord, set me free to worship You. Cast off every spirit of heaviness and cloak me with the garments of praise (Isaiah 61:3). This is the purpose of deliverance— to "worship God" (Exodus 3:12). This is what our enemy hates and fears the most— hearts set free from the chains of oppression and filled with the praise of worship for You. Bring me out of Egypt and into the good and broad land, a land flowing with milk and honey of worship and praise from a heart that is free. In Jesus' name I pray, Amen.

Be encouraged today! In the Love of Jesus, *Tommy Hays*

"More and More"

Good morning, Lord Jesus. Let there be more of You and less of me. Let there be more of Your Spirit and less of my flesh; more of Your will and less of mine. ...

"And this is my prayer, that your love may overflow more and more with knowledge and full insight to help you determine what is best, so that in the day of Christ you may be pure and blameless, having produced the harvest of righteousness that comes through Jesus Christ for the glory and praise of God" (Philippians 1:9).

There is always more. As the worship song says, "More love; more power; more of You in my life." Let me never be satisfied with how much I have grown in spiritual maturity or how far I have come in the journey of faith—there's always more and it's always by Your grace. To be made "pure and blameless" is not a day to mark on the calendar or even a destination along the journey, but a choice of complete surrender and submission—a choice You continually set before me every moment of every day. This is the life through Christ that produces a "harvest of righteousness" and glorifies God. By Your grace, I choose to continually give as much of me as I can and to continually receive as much of You as I can. As I do, Your love and Your power will overflow in me and through me "more and more." In Jesus' name I pray, Amen.

Be encouraged today! In the Love of Jesus, *Tommy Hays*

Unashamed

Good morning, Lord Jesus. I open my heart and lift my hands in worship and praise, in humility and faith, in the trusting surrender of intimate love. ...

"Nevertheless even among the rulers many believed in Him, but because of the Pharisees, they did not confess Him, lest they should be put out of the synagogue; for they loved the praise of men more than the praise of God" (John 12:42-43, NKJV).

Lord, continue to deliver me from the fear of man and continue to impart to me the fear of God. Let me live for Your praise and not theirs, for Your glory and not mine. Convict me of the sin of pride manifested in self-consciousness that is more concerned of what others think of me than what You think of me. Let me not be ashamed to seek Your face and praise Your name, to let my life be a witness of Your love and Your power wherever I am and whoever I am with. As Paul said with words, let me say with my life, "I am not ashamed of the gospel of Christ; it is the power of God to salvation for everyone who believes" (Romans 1:16, NKJV). In Jesus' name I pray, Amen.

Be encouraged today! In the Love of Jesus, *Tommy Hays*

Revival Fire at Asbury

Good morning, Lord Jesus. Kindle the embers of my soul. Let the wind of Your Holy Spirit set my heart ablaze with a fresh passion for You. Let the flames of fire fly and touch everything that is dead and dry in the world around me. Let the rising smoke confirm for all to see that souls are being consumed by the fire of Your glory. ...

"Blessed are those who hunger and thirst for righteousness, for they will be filled" (Matthew 5:6).

Lord, You are moving again in the hearts of the students at Asbury College in Wilmore, Kentucky, about fifteen miles south of Lexington. Your Spirit has set the world ablaze with revival fires that were kindled there several times in the past. But You send fresh fire to fall on the altars prepared through repentance and prayer, worship and praise, hungering to be filled with the fullness of Your presence.

Some students came back from an encounter with You in Kansas City at the International House of Prayer—a furnace of prayer in an atmosphere of worship twenty-four hours a day, seven days a week that began over six years ago with the commitment to continue until You return to gather Your bride. The student-led chapel that began with their simple testimonies on Monday is still continuing. All the angels of heaven rejoiced as six students gave their hearts to You the first day and all who come sense the holiness and majesty of Your presence in Hughes Auditorium. I would say this is a revival more characterized so far by a tremendous hunger and thirst for Your presence, rather than signs and wonders. But really, that is revival— faces turned to seek You and hearts opened to receive You in desperate cries for Your coming and confident faith to believe You will.

You drew me there yesterday morning to join in worship and prayer—to join in hunger and thirst for Your righteousness and to be filled. I sensed that I was not only there to receive but also to stand as a watchman on the wall to watch for the glory of Your coming and to watch for any advance of the enemy. Wherever You are moving in glory, the enemy tries to move as well (Matthew 24:13-30). It amazes me that You recently called us to purchase a home in Wilmore where we went to Asbury Seminary and we will be moving there next week. We will be moving into a revival of Your presence and taking our place on the wall in a very real way.

Lord, awaken Your watchmen to guard the hearts of these students and all who will be touched by these revival fires of Your glory. Continue to pour out Your Spirit to fan into flame these embers of hungry hearts desperate for Your presence. Let this revival become a transformation of our hearts, our families, our communities, and even the nations. Let this not be just a visitation of Your glory, but a habitation of Your presence. Release the anointing to seek You without reservation and to pray without ceasing until Your return in the fullness of Your glory in our hearts and throughout the earth. In Jesus' name I pray, Amen.

Be encouraged today! In the Love of Jesus, *Tommy Hays*

You are I Am

Good morning, Lord Jesus. I worship You in every dimension of Your Being—God the Father, God the Son, God the Holy Spirit. You are One; You are Holy; You are Faithful and True. You are not I was or I will be. You are I AM. ...

"But Moses said to God, 'If I come to the Israelites and say to them, 'The God of your ancestors has sent me to you,' and they ask me, 'What is His name?' What shall I say to them?' God said to Moses, 'I Am Who I Am.' He said further, 'Thus you shall say to the Israelites, 'I Am has sent me to you.' ' God also said to Moses, 'Thus you shall say to the Israelites, 'The Lord, the God of your ancestors, the God of Abraham, the God of Isaac, the God of Jacob, has sent me to you': This is My name forever, and this is My title for all generations' " (Exodus 3:13-15).

Lord God Almighty, You are "the same yesterday and today and forever" (Hebrews 13:8). Your presence is not a relic of the past, as the deists teach. Your power is not a relic of the past as the dispensationalists teach. Wherever You are, so is Your power. You are I Am. Your name is Your nature. Your presence and Your power is for right now and "forever" and "for all generations."

You are sufficient for every need in the moment of my need. You are worthy of my worship in every moment of my life. You are the eternal God who rules and reigns in the power of Your presence throughout all eternity. "For thus says the high and lofty One, who inhabits eternity, whose name is Holy: I dwell in the high and holy place, and also with those who are contrite and humble in spirit, to revive the spirit of the humble, and to revive the heart of the contrite" (Isaiah 57:15).

Though You dwell in the highest heaven, You also dwell in my heart—to the very degree that I come to You and call upon Your name with a humble spirit and a contrite heart. This is the heart You revive and renew in the transformation of the power of Your eternal presence. By Your grace, let this be my heart and my revival this day and every day, forever and for all generations. In Jesus' name I pray, Amen.

Be encouraged today! In the Love of Jesus, *Tommy Hays*

Awakened to Worship

Good morning, Lord Jesus. I worship You, Lord, in spirit and truth. You are the Spirit of Truth and I welcome You here in my heart afresh today. ...

There is an awakening of worship in the land. And what is worship but the willing surrender of our lives into Your hands. It's not only singing songs or praying prayers—no matter how personally, intimately, or prophetically—it is entrusting and abandoning ourselves to You, without hesitation and without limitation. It is a death to self and self-consciousness and life to You and God-consciousness. As the worship song says, it is the place where "the things of earth grow strangely dim in the light of Your glory and grace."

The move of Your Spirit in the revival of hearts at Asbury College is an awakening of worship. There are no famous speakers, no famous worship leaders, no famous prophets, evangelists, pastors, teachers, or apostles. There are just the "blessed" ones—those who are "poor in spirit," who "mourn," who "hunger and thirst for righteousness." They are being "filled" with the fullness of "the kingdom of heaven" (Matthew 5:3-11).

Yesterday morning I joined with the students and those from the community who came to watch and wait in the stillness of Your presence and in the trusting surrender of intimate worship. I spoke with a friend from one of our citywide prayer groups who is a seminary student who came to the revival the night before with an eye infection. A twelve year-old boy who had just been baptized with Your Holy Spirit a couple of nights before prayed for his healing. When he woke up yesterday morning, his eyes were healed! He said You were teaching him there can be a sickness of our souls manifested in our bodies when we spend too much time looking to ourselves. But healing comes as we turn our eyes toward You.

Lord, I choose to take my eyes off of myself and turn my eyes toward You—as best as I can and all by Your grace. I worship You in spirit and truth. As the song says, I turn my eyes upon You and look full in Your wonderful face; and the things of earth grow strangely dim, in the light of Your glory and grace. You have awakened me to worship. In Jesus' name I pray, Amen.

Be encouraged today! In the Love of Jesus, *Tommy Hays*

God is on the Move

Good morning, Lord Jesus. I turn my eyes upon You, as I watch and wait for the leading of Your Spirit and as I rest in the arms of my Father. ...

A revival is a move of God. Father, You are moving in our hearts and communities to fill us with Your Spirit and transform us into the image of Your Son. And wherever You are moving, the enemy will try to move. He will try to squelch Your move through our flesh through whatever means is available—self-centered pride, rigid religion, traditions of men, fear of losing control, envy of the blessing of others, deception and confusion to distort discernment, ignorance of the ways of God, and arrogance that we think we know all the ways of God.

In humility and faith, we must seek Your wisdom and discernment to take our place as watchmen on the walls. From our posts on the walls and at the gates, we must herald the coming of the Lord and be ready for the coming of the enemy (Isaiah 62:6-7). We need supernatural grace to overcome our supernatural foes. When we are tempted to judge one another, we need Your grace to release mercy to one another. When we see our relationships strained with the temptation to turn away from one another, we must seek Your grace to embrace one another in the bonds of love. "Above all, maintain constant love for one another, for love covers a multitude of sins" (1 Peter 4:8).

Revival brings restoration of relationships—both our relationship with You and our relationship with one another. So the enemy, who comes to steal and kill and destroy, will try to attack our relationships. We must guard our hearts and stand guard for the hearts of one another. "And we do this so that we may not be outwitted by Satan; for we are not ignorant of his designs" (2 Corinthians 2:11). Where You are sowing good seeds of life and the unity of the body of Christ, the enemy is sowing evil seeds of death and division to try to cripple and confuse the move of God to destroy or delay the harvest of Your kingdom (Matthew 13:36-43).

Lord, give me the mind of Christ, the Father heart of God, and the discernment of the Holy Spirit. Give me grace to be vigilant, courage to stand, and humility to seek You for Your leading in every moment—not relying on the patterns of the past and not being caught up in the emotions of the moment. You use our emotions and our minds. You honor Your moves of the past and You call us to move with You in the present. Thank You that You are on the move. I want to move with You as You move in me. In Jesus' name I pray, Amen.

Be encouraged today! In the Love of Jesus, *Tommy Hays*

"Tear Open the Heavens"

Good morning, Lord Jesus. Cleanse my heart and soul by the mercy of the blood of the Lamb, as I enter into the holy place of Your presence in worship and prayer this morning. ...

"O that You would tear open the heavens and come down, so that the mountains would quake at Your presence—as when fire kindles brushwood and the fire causes water to boil—to make Your name known to Your adversaries, so that the nations might tremble at Your presence! When You did awesome deeds that we did not expect, You came down, the mountains quaked at Your presence. From ages past no one has heard, no eye has perceived, no eye has seen any God besides You, who works for those who wait for Him" (Isaiah 64:1-4).

Father, You are the God who works for those who wait for You. As we wait for You, we humble ourselves from the striving and straining of our own labors. As we wait for You, a longing for Your presence takes hold in the yearning of our souls. As we wait for You, we begin to desire You—to hunger and thirst for You, to be filled by Your Spirit and the fullness of Your presence.

And when You see hungry hearts yearning for Your presence, crying out to You more than we are crying out for food or entertainment or the praises of others or anything else but You, You tear open the heavens and come down! The mountains quake and the nations tremble at Your presence; the fire of heaven falls and sets our hearts ablaze. Our spirits bubble and burst like boiling water, purified and cleansed by the flame of the fire of Your Spirit. Then the awesome deeds of Your power are released as we embrace Your presence—passion for God, salvation of souls, healing and deliverance of every dimension of our being, holiness of our hearts and lives, and transformation of our communities.

These are the blessings of Your presence. Yet they will not come without a fight. Your adversaries are at work as well to keep heaven from touching earth in our hearts and souls. Your adversaries are our adversaries, doing all they can in the short time they have to keep us from waiting on You and seeking the fullness of Your presence above all else. The distractions and destructions of the spiritual forces of wickedness working through fallen flesh and fallen nature are all strategically intended to keep us from seeking Your face and waiting for Your presence.

Lord, give me grace to press through and press in, to keep my eyes as fixed as the sun on Your face and insisting on the fullness of Your presence. "But as it is written, 'What no eye has seen, nor ear heard, nor the human heart conceived, what God has prepared for those who love Him'—these things God has revealed to us through the Spirit; for the Spirit searches everything, even the depths of God" (1 Corinthians 2:9-10). I love You, Lord, and I am watching and waiting for You—as best as I can and all by Your grace. Tear open the heavens and come down! May I receive the fullness of all You have prepared for me and all those who love You and wait for You. In Jesus' name I pray.

Be encouraged today! In the Love of Jesus, *Tommy Hays*

Awakening a Craving for God

Good morning, Lord Jesus. Thank You for the gift of starting the day with You. Take me by the hand and lead me by the heart, as I awaken and arise to follow You. ...

"So I say to you, ask, and it will be given to you; search, and you will find; knock, and the door will be opened for you. For everyone who asks receives, and everyone who searches finds, and for everyone who knocks, the door will be opened. Is there anyone among you who, if your child asks for a fish, will give a snake instead of a fish? Or if the child asks for an egg, will give a scorpion? If you then, who are evil, know how to give good gifts to your children, how much more will the heavenly Father give the Holy Spirit to those who ask Him!" (Luke 11:9-13)

The meaning of "ask" in this passage carries the idea of craving, desiring, and even requiring. Lord, the revival You are releasing at Asbury and throughout the land is an awakening of a craving for You. You are the gift we long to receive. You are giving us a taste of Your presence—not to become satisfied with an experience of the moment, but to hunger and thirst for even more. Your Spirit is moving in our hearts to keep on asking, to keep on seeking, to keep on knocking. We want more than a flash in the pan of the gold of Your glory, we want the fullness of the presence of Christ conforming us to Your nature and transforming us to our destiny.

Holy Spirit, keep releasing a craving for the presence of God in my soul. Give me the persistence to persevere in prayer, taking hold of You and never letting You go. Let the taste of Your presence only make me hungry for more. By Your grace, I will keep on asking and keep on receiving; I will keep on searching and keep on finding; I will keep on knocking and keep on opening. In Jesus' name I pray, Amen.

Be encouraged today! In the Love of Jesus, *Tommy Hays*

A Day of Love

Good morning, Lord Jesus. As the worship song says, "I'm falling on my knees, offering all of me; Jesus, You're all this heart is living for." I offer as much of me as I can and receive as much of You as I can. Help me offer more of myself today than yesterday, and more tomorrow than today. ...

"And hope does not disappoint us, because God's love has been poured into our hearts through the Holy Spirit that has been given to us" (Romans 5:5).

Today, much of the world will celebrate Valentine's Day as a day of love. Somewhere among the cards and candies and everything else the day has become, we will likely forget it is a day named for a saint who was martyred for his faith in Christ by a Roman Emperor. Valentine was pierced in his heart with a love of God that would not deny his loyalty to You even in the face of death. Perhaps he died, declaring his undying love with his face turned toward heaven, singing to the God of unfailing love, "I'm falling on my knees, offering all of me. Jesus, You're all this heart is living for."

Today I'll say, "I love you" to the one You've given as gift to love me. It's her favorite day. But any love I have to give that is pure and true is only because You have first loved me. You have pierced my heart with Your unfailing love. Thank You, Lord, for pouring Your love into my heart through Your Spirit. Let Your love pour out of me today to my wife and my children and all those You will love through my life today. In Jesus' name I pray, Amen.

Be encouraged today! In the Love of Jesus, *Tommy Hays*

Go

Good morning, Lord Jesus. Let everything else fade away in these first moments of the morning, as I turn my heart and thoughts to You. ...

"Now the Lord said to Abram, 'Go from your country and your kindred and your father's house to the land that I will show you....' So Abram went as the Lord told him" (Genesis 12:1-4).

We became citizens of Wilmore, Kentucky yesterday, purchasing our property and home at the edge of the city that is home to Asbury College and Asbury Theological Seminary, where my wife and I received training for the ministry of the Kingdom of God. With our ministry in Lexington and our home in Wilmore, it seems You are expanding our territory to cover with our hearts and our prayers. With what You are doing in the awakening of a revival in the hearts of the students at Asbury, it seems we are moving into revival and our soon-to-be-born son will be birthed in revival. You are on the move and we're moving with You.

A friend of mine said the other day; the journey with God is not really even day by day, it is step by step. In every moment of every day, I want to learn to hear and obey, to follow wherever You lead. Let me know as much about my mission when I get there as I need to know now. But mostly, it is not what I need to know as much as it is *who* I need to know. Thank You for the grace of knowing You, Lord, in every dimension of Your Being—Father, Son, and Holy Spirit. Help me to know You more deeply and obey You more completely day by day and step by step in this journey of relationship and obedience. In Jesus' name I pray, Amen.

Be encouraged today! In the Love of Jesus, *Tommy Hays*

The Joy of Giving

Good morning, Lord Jesus. You gave Your all for me. As best as I can and all by Your grace, I give my all for You today. ...

Father, You are the ultimate Giver: "For God so loved the world, that He gave His only begotten Son...." (John 3:16). Because You are One as Father, Son, and Holy Spirit, You did not give a sacrifice of someone else for us to be restored in relationship with You; You gave Your very Self in the humility and sacrifice of the cross, in a mystery too deep for us to fully comprehend on this side of heaven. "For you know the generous act of our Lord Jesus Christ, that though He was rich, yet for your sakes He became poor, so that by His poverty you might become rich" (2 Corinthians 8:9).

Today, You are sending me to the Regional Generous Giving Conference in Lexington to learn more of Your principles of giving generously of all I am and all I have for You, because You have given generously of all You are and all You have for me. You call each of us to give of ourselves to You and Your Kingdom in "the privilege of sharing in this ministry" with "eagerness" (verse 8:1-15). This is the "abundant joy" of giving that "overflows in a wealth of generosity" (verse 8:2).

You call each of us to give the same, no matter how much we have— out of the abundance of the gift of life You have given us, "according to what one has— not according to what one does not have" (verse 8:12). You call us each to give our all, as You lead. And all that we have belongs to You anyway. We are blessed to be Your stewards of Your resources to give and to receive as You lead for Your purposes of Your kingdom. "Each of you must give as you have made up your mind, not reluctantly or under compulsion, for God loves a cheerful giver. And God is able to provide you with every blessing in abundance, so that by always having enough of everything, you may share abundantly in every good work" (verse 9:7-8).

Lord, make me a cheerful giver. Remind me of the abundance that You have given me and let that abundance overflow in generosity to others. I want to experience the joy of giving and I want to share abundantly in the ministry of Your kingdom in every good work as You lead. In Jesus' name I pray, Amen.

Be encouraged today! In the Love of Jesus, *Tommy Hays*

"Do Not Forget the Lord"

Good morning, Lord Jesus. I thank You for the gift of Your presence that fills my heart and I thank You for the gift of Your grace that allows You to. ...

"When the Lord your God has brought you into the land that He swore to your ancestors, to Abraham, to Isaac, to Jacob, to give you—a land with fine, large cities that you did not build, houses filled with all sorts of goods that you did not fill, hewn cisterns that you did not hew, vineyards and olive groves that you did not plant—and when you have eaten your fill, take care that you do not forget the Lord, who brought you out of the land of Egypt, out of the house of slavery" (Deuteronomy 6:10-12).

Lord, You have given me so much that I do not deserve, so much I could never earn, so much I could never repay. All that I am and all that I have belongs to You. You have moved ahead of me in the power of Your righteousness and in the principles of Your justice in ways I cannot fully see and ways I cannot fully understand on this side of heaven. Give me the faith to trust You in this, the humility to obey You in this, the courage to follow You in this, the gratitude to thank You in this.

As You bring me into the land of fulfillment of Your promises to me and my generations, let me "not forget the Lord." Let me not forget it's all by Your grace and Your power. When there is opposition to the fulfillment of Your promises, let me press through and press in with persevering faith and a believing heart that sees every challenge as an opportunity to enter into my inheritance in You. In Jesus' name I pray, Amen.

Be encouraged today! In the Love of Jesus, *Tommy Hays*

"Come and See"

Good morning, Lord Jesus. I'm waking up in our new home in our new town this morning. I sense You have called us to a new place, and I'm excited to see where You are leading and what You are doing. Help me to be quiet enough to listen and courageous enough to obey. ...

"The next day John again was standing with two of his disciples, and as he watched Jesus walk by, he exclaimed, 'Look, here is the Lamb of God!' The two disciples heard him say this and they followed Jesus. When Jesus turned and saw them following, He said to them, 'What are you looking for?' They said to Him, 'Rabbi' (which translated means Teacher), 'where are You staying?' He said to them, 'Come and see' "(John 1:35-39).

Lord Jesus, You are the One I'm looking for. Open my eyes to see You and to see where You are moving. Open my ears to hear You, when You say to my spirit, "Come and see." You are my teacher. And the things You want to teach me, I can't find only in a book, not even Your Book alone. I have to learn them in relationship with You. These are the things of life I'll learn only as I come and follow You. A follower of Christ is one who follows You.

I hear Your Spirit singing in my spirit, as I turn the eyes of my heart to seek You:

> "Come and see,
> Come follow Me,
> I will lead the way to life.
>
> Come to know,
> Come and grow,
> I will teach you all you need to know."

Yes, Lord. Here I come as You lead. There is no place I'd rather be, than following You. In Jesus' name I pray, Amen.

Be encouraged today! In the Love of Jesus, *Tommy Hays*

An Everlasting Promise

Good morning, Lord Jesus. Draw me close to You and fill me afresh with the fullness of Your Spirit. ...

"Peter said to them, 'Repent, and be baptized every one of you in the name of Jesus Christ so that your sins may be forgiven; and you will receive the gift of the Holy Spirit. For the promise is for you, for your children, and for all who are far away, everyone whom the Lord our God calls to Him' " (Acts 2:28-29).

A couple of Asbury College students came to speak and pray with us at The Fountain last night, to share what is going on with the revival in Wilmore, Kentucky. Andrew came to the chapel that first morning and stayed past midnight, worshipping and praying as You began to move in power in the hearts of the students. In the atmosphere thick with the fullness of Your presence, he remembered one "far away" who needed You and this gift of Your promise. Andrew called to tell his brother back in Philadelphia, who had been caught in cycles of drugs and alcohol, depression and despair, for over five years. But You touched his heart with a sense of hope he hadn't had in a long time.

He caught the next plane to Lexington and was at the revival the next day. The students surrounded him with encouragement and love. That night, he fell on his face in tears of humility and confessions of repentance, hungering and thirsting for Your righteousness, at the altar with hundreds of others. In desperation and faith, he cried out to You. When he finally stood, he was changed—filled with the faith and hope of Your Spirit, committing his heart and his life to You. Andrew told us that his brother is still "on fire" and those flames are now setting hearts ablaze in Philadelphia. Praise You, Lord! Let the Fire continue to fall and to burn in our hearts as the flames spread to those who are near and those who are far away. In Jesus' name we pray, Amen.

Be encouraged today! In the Love of Jesus, *Tommy Hays*

Galatians 2:20

Good morning, Lord Jesus. Come rule and reign in my heart today. ...

As I write today's date of "2-20" the passage of Galatians 2:20 comes to mind: "I have been crucified with Christ; and it is no longer I who live, but it is Christ who lives in me. And the life I now live in the flesh, I live by the faith of the Son of God, who loved me and gave Himself for me."

This is my desire, my goal, and my commitment. By Your grace, You put this desire in my heart and give me the will to walk it out. My part is to choose the destination, and Your part is to encourage me and empower me to go there. This is the death to self and the life to Christ You call me to choose. I can't do it without Your Spirit and You won't do it without my heart.

Crucifixion is a death that takes time. As my wife knows, I have far to go in the process of the crucifixion of my flesh. But by Your grace, I die a little more each day, as I thirst for Your presence and commit my spirit into Your hand. And every morning, You arise a little higher in Your resurrection glory, as I choose again to turn to You and live my life by the faith of the Son of God. In Jesus' name I pray, Amen.

Be encouraged today! In the Love of Jesus, *Tommy Hays*

God of My Breakthrough

Good morning, Lord Jesus. As the song says, "You are my strength when I am weak, You are the treasure that I seek, You are my all in all." ...

Lord, all around me people are crying out—some in praise and thanksgiving, excitement and anticipation, and others in sickness and pain, discouragement and despair. It's as if the enemy of our souls senses an advance of the kingdom of heaven in the hearts of Your people and is unleashing a preemptive strike from the pit of hell. Many are gravely concerned for our governor, Ernie Fletcher, weary and weakened by unrelenting fevers and a raging infection of e-coli. It seems to speak of an attack of sickness and disease against our spirits and souls and bodies at every level of our relationships in our region and throughout the earth in this hour.

We cry out to You for healing and deliverance, for courage and strength, to perservere in faith through every challenge. Through many tribulations, we enter into the promises of the kingdom of God (Acts 14:22). We lift our eyes to You and we are strengthened and empowered by the resolve of Your gaze. Send the fire of Your Spirit to consume the fevers of infection and disease. Send the water of Your Word to replenish our souls with the peace of Your presence. Draw our focus off of our troubles and awaken our hearts to fix our gaze on the One who delivers our lives from every pit of destruction and despair, sickness and disease, confusion and discouragement. Remind us of Your Word, for Your Word reveals Your will; and Your will for us is good:

> "Bless the Lord, O my soul,
> and all that is within me,
> bless His holy name.
> Bless the Lord, O my soul,
> and do not forget all His benefits --
> who forgives all your iniquity,
> who heals all your diseases,
> who redeems your life from the pit,
> who crowns you with steadfast love and mercy,
> who satisfies you with good as long as you live,
> so that your youth is renewed like the eagle's"
>
> (Psalm 103:1-5).

As I look to You, for myself and for others, let me be honest with my pain, but also honest with Your power. Your power is made perfect in my weakness (2 Corinthians 12:9). I hear a song of Your Spirit rising up to lift my spirit and heart, as I entrust every burden to You:

Blessed are You, Lord
When all around me is pain.
Blessed are You, Lord
When I'm weary and I'm drained.

Blessed are You, Lord
When I call upon Your name.
Blessed are You, Lord
For You are always the same.

I need You now
And I need Your power.
I need You to come breaking through.

Won't You hear me now,
In this very hour?
You're the God of my breakthrough.

Blessed are You, Lord
When the enemy comes in like a flood.
Blessed are You, Lord
For the Living Waters and the Blood.

Blessed are You, Lord
When all around me seems to give way.
Blessed are You, Lord
You're my hope and You're my stay.

I need You now
And I need Your power
I need You to come breaking through.

Won't You hear me now,
In this very hour?
You're the God of my breakthrough.

Yes, Lord. You are the God of my breakthrough. Give me faith to believe it and perseverance to keep pressing through in prayer and praise until I see it—in my life and in the lives of those You have put on my heart. In Jesus' name I pray, Amen.

Be encouraged today! In the Love of Jesus, *Tommy Hays*

Pressing In and Breaking Through

Good morning, Lord Jesus. I lift my heart to You in praise. Praise draws me out of myself and into You; it takes my eyes off of my problems and leads me to Your promises. Prayers of praise fill my heart with thankfulness for the One who is the maker and the keeper of the promises. ...

"The Lord has broken through my enemies before me, like a breakthrough of water" (2 Samuel 5:20, NKJV).

Yesterday morning, You were reminding me that You are the God of the breakthrough. I heard from many who needed Your word of encouragement to keep pressing in and pressing through to the breakthrough for themselves and for others. There has to be breaking for there to be breakthrough—sometimes breaking of the barriers between Your kingdom and Your will on earth as it is in heaven, sometimes breaking of the walls of our pride and self-sufficiency, and sometimes breaking the gates of hell that can't prevail against Your church moving in Your power and Your authority in obedience to Your command to overcome.

When we breakthrough, we break through from one place to another—sometimes from our place of our wilderness into the place of Your promises, sometimes from how things are to how things ought to be, and sometimes from "I can't by my power" to "I will by Your grace." We can't break through unless we have the courage and the will to begin breaking what needs to be broken so we can break through from where we are to where we are going. When we strike one blow and the walls come crumbling down, that's a miracle of the instantaneous power of God. When we strike one blow and then strike another blow and then strike another blow until the cracks become crevices and the rocks become rubble, that's the process of persistence through persevering faith in Your promises. Either way, there is no breakthrough without breaking, and there is no going through unless we are going forward—all by Your grace and all in Your power.

One of those who called me to stand with him and his family to cry out to You for breakthrough was my good friend, Pastor Tim in Indiana. You've touched many souls through his words and healed many bodies through his hands. He is a faithful disciple of Christ and an obedient instrument of Your grace. But yesterday it was not just a pastor's heart, but a father's heart crying out for breakthrough for his little girl, Olivia. A viral infection lapsed into diabetic shock. She went to the emergency room and her daddy went to his knees. Her doctors fought in the natural realm and her daddy fought in the spiritual realm. Both fought for her life as the medical team told her parents she might not make it through the night. But You are the God of the breakthrough, and little Olivia has broken through!

As I write my prayer from her hospital in Indiana this morning, I praise You for her breakthrough as one snatched from the jaws of death to life. Yet we are not satisfied with the promise of life, we keep pressing in and pressing through for breakthrough into Your promise of abundant life. We pray for freedom from every infirmity and healing of every disease, including the diabetes that has been exposed in the failed attempt to destroy her life. And we are pressing in and pressing through in the persistence of prayer for all those who need the power of Your breakthrough.

We can't go in the middle of the night to join the fight for breakthrough in person for everyone who needs a breakthrough, but You can. And You will—as we keep persisting in prayer as You lead and as daddies keep entrusting their little girls into Your arms of love. Sometimes we won't see the breakthrough until the ultimate healing of heaven, but as we persist in the power of prayer, we will see more breakthrough of healing on earth. In Jesus' name we pray, Amen.

Be encouraged today! In the Love of Jesus, *Tommy Hays*

Every Moment Counts

Good morning, Lord Jesus. As best I can and all by Your grace, I entrust my life and this day to You. May I live for You as You live through me today. ...

"Come now, you who say, 'Today or tomorrow we will go to such and such a town and spend a year there, doing business and making money.' Yet you do not even know what tomorrow will bring. What is your life? For you are a mist that appears for a little while and then vanishes. Instead you ought to say, 'If the Lord wishes, we will live and do this or that' " (James 4:13-15).

Like a dusting of snow that melts by mid-afternoon or the morning mist that evaporates with the rising sun, my earthly life is but a moment in the perspective of heaven's eternity. Yet every day matters and every moment counts. Like precious jewels, they are more valuable because they are few in number.

One day I will give an account for how I spent my time in the moments and opportunities of my days (Matthew 12:36; Revelation 20:11-15). You are "the One who judges all people impartially according to their deeds" (1 Peter 1:17 and 4:5). The standard will not be about numbers or wealth. It will be about my obedience to Your will and Your way in my walk with You through the journey of the moments of my life. I want You to do all You have intended in me and through me in these few, precious moments I have. In Jesus' name I pray, Amen.

Be encouraged today! In the Love of Jesus, *Tommy Hays*

Kingdom Come

Good morning, Lord Jesus. I call upon Your name and draw upon Your nature, as I behold You and give myself to You. ...

"Thy kingdom come, Thy will be done...." (Luke 11:2, KJV)

I've heard the phrase "from here to Kingdom Come" all my life, growing up in west Texas and eastern New Mexico. I didn't know it really refers to a little community tucked far away back in the Appalachian Mountains of eastern Kentucky. As they say, "it may not be the end of the earth, but you can see it from here." Yesterday I traveled with a small group of pastors, intercessors, and a mission's leader down the "Kingdom Come Parkway" on behalf of the Kentucky Christian Foundation to see what all the fuss was about. Revival flames have been breaking out in pockets of fire across Kentucky. But rather than brush fires, there seems to be a slow burn building as the fires are fanned into flame through prayer.

We've been hearing about a regional transformation of new hope and abundant life rising up out of the poverty and depression that has dominated the Appalachian region. But You have been preparing the way for this move of Your power in prayers of desperation and faith for generations, that You display Your glory in the fullness of time. The time has come for Kingdom Come and every little community scattered throughout the hills and hollers of this region. The transformation has begun.

Lord, let me be a part of what You are doing in this land. Fresh faith mingled with desperate prayers and new hope prepares the way for transformation by Your power. Give me a burden in my soul to see this region made whole. Remind me of the pain of poverty here in our own backyard of our prosperous nation. And remind me of the joy and life I see rising in the hearts of those You are setting free from the bondage of the past to embrace the destiny of their future. Move my heart in prayer for the fulfillment of the awakening of life You have promised in response to the faithful prayers of desperate generations. In Jesus' name I pray, Amen.

Be encouraged today! In the Love of Jesus, *Tommy Hays*

The Company Store

Good morning, Lord Jesus. In these first moments of the morning, I choose who will have priority of my thoughts and plans for my day. This day, I choose You. ...

Tennessee Ernie Ford used to sing a song of a coal miner's lament, "Sixteen tons and what do you get, another day older and deeper in debt. St. Peter don't you call me 'cause I can't go, I owe my soul to the company store." The other day we saw the company store in the Appalachian Mountains of Lynch, Kentucky. It's boarded up now like a lot of those little towns that served the coal mines and the coal mine companies. When the coal companies left, they took the heart and soul of everything that was bound to them.

But Lord, You have come to bind up the brokenhearted and set the captives free. You use the broken and base things of this world as a means to display Your glory. You love to breathe the life breath of Your Spirit into dry bones, and You are still raising the dead. There is new life in Lynch and Benham and Cumberland and little communities throughout the Appalachian region. You are leading those who will follow beside the still waters and restoring the soul of the people and the land. Desperation and faith are producing hope. Salvation is not in a coal mine company or in continuing to live as victims of what happened when the company left town. Salvation and hope is in You. And You are redeeming and restoring, breathing new life into weary souls.

Lord Jesus, I owe my soul to You. I am "a slave of Christ" who is "bought with a price," no longer a "slave of human masters" (1 Corinthians 7:22-23). Let my life not be controlled by my work or my mortgage, my church or denomination, or my own goals and ambitions apart from You. Let my life be controlled by You. Let me come to Your company store to receive all I need. As You said long ago, "Therefore I counsel you to buy from Me gold refined by fire so that you may be rich" (Revelation 3:18). Let me find my security and riches in You alone, and then I will be free to live my life for You alone, unencumbered by the slavery of this world. In Jesus' name I pray, Amen.

Be encouraged today! In the Love of Jesus, *Tommy Hays*

Walking it Out

Good morning, Lord Jesus. Help me to be still before You in these first moments of the morning to watch and wait for Your leading as I lay my life before You this day. ...

"He took her by the hand and said to her, 'Talitha cum,' which means, 'Little girl, get up!' And immediately the girl got up and began to walk about (she was twelve years of age). At this, they were overcome with amazement" (Mark 5:41-42).

Praise You, Lord, for Your healing power of life over death. Like Jairus' daughter, my friend Tim's little girl, Olivia, was "at the point of death," as both of these fathers came to You in desperation and faith, saying, "Come and lay Your hands on her, so that she may be made well, and live" (verse 5:23). So You came and so You did. That little hospital room was filled with people from their church ministering the healing love of God through their hugs and prayers.

Three days after Olivia was admitted into the emergency room in diabetic shock, nearing a coma that the doctors feared would lead to death that night, Olivia was free to go home! When the nurse came to ask her if she wanted them to carry her out to the car in the little wheelbarrow or the wagon, Olivia said, "No thanks, I'll walk." As her daddy said, that was a prophetic word that by God's grace, she has walked out of this snare of death and will walk out her complete healing from the disease of diabetes in Your power. Lord, we are overcome with amazement and thrilled with joy for Olivia. And we continue to cry out to You in desperation and faith with every mother and father for the healing and abundance of life of their little girls and boys no matter how old and no matter how sick. In Jesus' name we pray, Amen.

Be encouraged today! In the Love of Jesus, *Tommy Hays*

Surrender of the Silence

Good morning, Lord Jesus. Help me decrease as You increase, emptied of myself and filled with You. ...

"For God alone my soul waits in silence, for my hope is from Him. He alone is my rock and my salvation, my fortress; I shall not be shaken. On God rests my deliverance and my honor; my mighty rock, my refuge is in God" (Psalm 62:5-7).

Waiting in the silence before You humbles my soul. I want to speak or plan or worry. Sometimes I want to get up and get on with my day. But Your gentle Sprit draws me to Your side as if to say, "Shhhh.... Be still and know that I am God. Turn your eyes toward Me to seek My face. As you focus on Me for a moment, your heart and your mind is set free from the burdens and pressures of everything else. As you are resting in Me, I am going before you—ordering the steps of your day and lighting the path of My will. Then when you arise to go your way, you will be able to see the steps of the path I have set before you."

Yes, Lord. As I watch and wait for You, You steady me in Your steadfast love and in the security of Your peace. You strengthen me in Your power as my confidence in You settles into my soul. Spending these first moments of the morning in the surrender of silence is the wisest decision of my day. Now every decision I will make and every challenge I will face throughout my day, I will know in the depths of my soul that I do not face them alone. I know I have begun my day by Your grace, entrusting my thoughts and my desires to You in the surrender of the silence. In Jesus' name I pray, Amen.

Be encouraged today! In the Love of Jesus, *Tommy Hays*

Knowing Father, Son, and Holy Spirit

Good morning, Lord Jesus. Good morning, Father. Good morning, Holy Spirit. You are One, yet You reveal Yourself and manifest Yourself in these three interwoven dimensions of Your Being. I want to know You more fully in every dimension. You are my Redeemer, my Creator, and my Sustainer. You are my God, my King, and my Best Friend. I want to fear You and follow You. I want to worship You and adore You. And I welcome You here in my heart and in every dimension of my being again today. ...

Your heart breaks when I suffer or when I sin, as a father's heart breaks for his son or daughter when he sees the pain or shame of their struggles. You are my Father and I am Your son. "For in Christ Jesus you are all children of God through faith" (Galatians 3:26).

You know my temptations and my sufferings, because You faced them all for me as You humbled Yourself to be both Son of God and Son of Man. You walk along side me as an elder Brother, having laid down Your life for me in a sacrifice of love I cannot fully imagine or understand on this side of heaven. "For the One who sanctifies and those who are sanctified all have one Father. For this reason, Jesus is not ashamed to call them brothers and sisters....   Therefore, He had to become like His brothers and sisters in every respect, so that He might be a merciful and faithful high priest in the service of God, to make a sacrifice of atonement for the sins of the people. Because He Himself was tested by what He suffered, He is able to help those who are being tested" (Hebrews 2:11-18).

You never leave me nor forsake me. The very moment I experience anguish or joy, temptation or triumph, You immediately experience it with me as well because You live here within me by Your Holy Spirit. In an amazing mystery human minds can't fully comprehend, the God of all creation has descended to live in my heart and in the hearts of all who believe and entrust their lives to You. "But you are not in the flesh; you are in the Spirit, since the Spirit of God dwells in you. Anyone who does not have the Spirit of Christ does not belong to Him. But if Christ is in you, though the body is dead because of sin, the Spirit is life because of righteousness" (Romans 8:9-10).

You are my Father and my Brother and You have come to make Your home in my heart by Your Spirit. Let me live my life more fully aware of the intimacy of Your presence in the moments of my day. Let it bring the fear of God upon me when I'm tempted to sin and let it bring the comfort of God upon me when I'm wounded by the sins of others. What could be better than the amazing peace and joy of Your constant presence in all the challenges and celebrations of my life? In Jesus' name I pray, Amen.

Be encouraged today! In the Love of Jesus, *Tommy Hays*

Fasting for Fulfillment

Good morning, Lord Jesus. On the morning of this Ash Wednesday, take the ashes of my soul, burned and purified by the fire of Your Spirit, mingle them with the living waters of Your Word, and impose them upon my heart and mind as a mark and seal of Your redemption of my life. I belong to You, and I submit to You in humility and faith as best as I can and all by Your grace. ...

"I humbled my soul with fasting" (from Psalm 69:10).

Many of the spiritual leaders of our generation are calling for a season of fasting between Ash Wednesday and Easter this year—Francis Frangipane, Mike Bickel, Dutch Sheets, and others. Their call bears witness in my spirit. From the beginning of this year, I have had a sense that this would be a year of fulfillment of many hopes and promises that seemed to have been stuck in a wilderness of delay and hindrance. But this is a year of Your favor, a year of fulfillment (Isaiah 61:1-2). And though it is through many tribulations that we must enter into the kingdom of God, we will enter in if we keep pressing through in obedience and faith (Acts 14:22).

Fasting speaks of humility. It is a choice of our will to be emptied of ourselves and to be filled with You, to join in the fellowship and sacrifice of Your sufferings, that we might share in the joy and power of Your resurrection (Philippians 3:10). You purify our souls through obedience to Your call to trusting surrender and desperate dependence upon You alone as the Source and Sustainer of our lives (1 Peter 1:22). "But in your hearts, sanctify Christ as Lord" (verse 3:15).

Fasting in obedience to Your call and in faith for the fulfillment of Your promises humbles the pride of our self-sufficiency and self-centeredness. It causes us to hunger and thirst for You alone—the Bread of Life and the Living Waters which alone can sustain us through the valleys of the shadow of death and into the land of our destiny in Christ. "Humble yourselves therefore under the mighty hand of God, so that He may exalt you in due time" (verse 5:6).

Yes, Lord. I choose to answer Your call to fast and pray in the way You will lead for these forty days, until You bring me through my Jordan and into the Land of Your Promises for me. "Unless a grain of wheat falls into the earth and dies, it remains just a single grain; but if it dies, it bears much fruit" (John 12:24). Let these days of fasting be a death to my flesh that I may arise into the newness of life in the fullness of Your Spirit (Romans 6:4). In Jesus' name I pray, Amen.

Be encouraged today! In the Love of Jesus, *Tommy Hays*

Sacrifice of Surrender

Good morning, Lord Jesus. Let Your name be the first word I speak today. Let Your praise be the first emotions of my soul today. ...

"Through Him, then, let us continually offer a sacrifice of praise to God, that is, the fruit of lips that confess His name. Do not neglect to do good and to share what you have, for such sacrifices are pleasing to God" (Hebrews 13:15-16).

To sacrifice is to surrender—to give up something I have. To pray is to sacrifice my time. To praise is to sacrifice my attention. To fast is to sacrifice my food. As David said, "I will not offer sacrifices to the Lord that cost me nothing" (from 1 Chronicles 21:24). But the ultimate sacrifice is not only to surrender what I have, but to surrender who I am. It is to surrender my life to You more deeply and more completely each day. That's when the praise of Your name on my lips becomes the substance of Your nature in my soul. And it will cost something—everything I am. Give me the courage to keeping trusting You and praising You as I keep surrendering my life to You a little more each day. This is the sacrifice that is "pleasing to God." In Jesus' name I pray, Amen.

Be encouraged today! In the Love of Jesus, *Tommy Hays*

Alpha and Omega

Good morning, Lord Jesus. I entrust my life to You again today. Let me begin and end this day with You. You are my Alpha and Omega. ...

" 'I am the Alpha and the Omega,' says the Lord God, 'who is and who was and who is to come, the Almighty' " (Revelation 1:8). "See, I am coming soon; My reward is with Me, to repay according to everyone's work. I am the Alpha and the Omega, the first and the last, the beginning and the end" (verse 22:12-13).

This weekend, I will help with prayer ministry on the "Holy Spirit Weekend" of our church's Alpha Course. Over one hundred people have joined the course this time for about ten weeks to ask their questions and discuss their views to try to understand You and Your call to surrender our lives to You. Many have never known You before and have never welcomed You into their hearts. Others have, but are coming to a place of deeper trust and deeper surrender.

The group has been learning about God the Father and God the Son. This weekend, they will learn more specifically about God the Holy Spirit. Many will pray to "be filled with the Spirit" as they take a deliberate step of faith to be emptied of themselves and filled with You (Ephesians 5:18). I will be there to minister and pray, but I will also be there to be filled.

By Your Holy Spirit, You are always "coming soon" into the hearts of all who welcome You in. But that's only the beginning. You are not only the Alpha but You are also the Omega, and everything in between. As Father, Son, and Holy Spirit, You are our "all in all" (1 Corinthians 15:28). Let me learn to continually begin and end every moment of every day in You and You in me. In Jesus' name I pray, Amen.

Be encouraged today! In the Love of Jesus, *Tommy Hays*

Is God Approachable?*

"Through the Lord's mercies we are not consumed, because His compassions fail not. They are new every morning; Great is Your faithfulness" (Lamentations 3:22-23, NKJV).

"Because of Christ and our faith in Him, we can now come boldly and confidently into God's presence" (Ephesians 3:12, NLT).

Sundays have always been difficult for me. They seem even more so lately, because my little dog Maxwell is gone. Tonight, I looked out into his favorite spot in the yard and could almost feel him there. The sun broke through the clouds and lit up his little spot as if to say, "I'm not gone forever, I'm just someplace better!"

In that moment, God answered a question of mine that I had been thinking about over the past two weeks: Is God approachable? God said "It's like that time you went to see Phil."

When I was in my twenties, I was struggling a bit. I was jobless and seeing a counselor. At the time, I belonged to a house group with a few "prestigious" members—not that I really fully recognized it at the time! To me they were people—Phil, David, Beverly, and so forth. We were a pretty tight knit group and since I saw them out of the realm of the University, I didn't really assimilate who they were in terms of the community, church, or University.

On one particular day, I was driving home from a session with my counselor and I was quite upset. I had just gotten Maxwell (my scraggly little Cairn terrier in need of much attention and training) and much to my surprise, training him had been more than a little overwhelming for me! After two weeks, I hadn't even made a dent! My counselor had suggested on that particular day that maybe the dog just wasn't good for me and that I might consider giving the dog back!

A terrible sense of hopelessness filled my heart as I drove home that day. I couldn't help thinking, "I can't even take care of a dog! And not just any dog, but a dog God gave me and one that needs me too—a poor, little, homeless dog!"

---

* The following devotional was written by Mary Margaret Adams.

On my ride home, I saw the Vet College up ahead and to my surprise, God told me to go talk to Phil before I went home. I had never been to the Vet school before, but I figured someone would help me find him there.

I went up to what must have been a secretary and said; "I would like to see Phil. Can you please find him for me?" To which she replied, "Dr. Sponenberg?!" like I had somehow been confused. "Yes. Phil Sponenberg!" I replied. "That's *Dr.* Sponenberg. Do you have an appointment?" My answer was a simple "No." Her curt reply was, "You don't just walk up and ask to see Dr. Sponenberg, you know." My reassuring reply was, "Oh, but we are friends and he will see me."

And Phil did! He graciously received me that day in spite of the secretary's objections!

Basically, God was showing me through this example that although God is holy, I can still approach Him, because through His great mercy, He has given me access to Him through Christ. More than that, I can approach Him with confidence and boldness, because I am known by Him and know Him—I have a relationship with Him. And when I approach Him, He receives me as He would a daughter.

Romans 8:15-16 says, "For you did not receive the spirit of bondage again to fear, but you received the Spirit of adoption by whom we cry out, 'Abba, Father.' The Spirit Himself bears witness with our spirit that we are children of God."

All praise and glory be to God! *Mary Margaret Adams*

Walk in the Light You Have

Good morning, Lord Jesus. As the worship song says, "Lord, I give You my heart. I give my soul. I live for You alone. Every breath that I take, every moment I'm awake, Lord have Your way in me." By Your grace, let this be my desire and by Your grace, let this be my way of life. ...

This weekend, You were our Alpha and Omega. Your Holy Spirit met every person where they were and drew them closer to You. Some committed their lives to You for the first time. Some embraced the filling of Your Holy Spirit for the first time. Some released the hard places of their hearts and the bitter places of their souls into Your hands; and some allowed You to touch their hurts and wounds, their burdens and bondages with Your healing hands and living words. Some chose simply to be willing to be willing. But we all encountered the presence of Your light and love in the divine appointments You had for each of us along the way.

It seems I hear You saying, "This is the walk I have for you. Walk in the light as I am in the light, and I will give You more light still. My light is My Word and My Spirit. I open the eyes of all who are willing to seek My light and I empower the steps of all who are willing to walk in the journey with Me."

Yes, Lord. Keep opening my eyes and empowering my steps. I want to go on with You. I want to keep walking in Your light. As I do, I can't help but be changed by Your light for You are the Light (1 John 1:5-7). No matter how much You have changed me, You want to change me more. No matter how far You have brought me, there is always further to go. And while the destination is very important, so is the relationship we build along the way. In Jesus' name I pray, Amen.

Be encouraged today! In the Love of Jesus, *Tommy Hays*

Spiritual Leadership

Good morning, Lord Jesus. No one comes to the Father, but through You. And no one comes to You unless the Spirit draws them. Holy Spirit, I thank You for drawing me to Jesus. Lord Jesus, I thank You for perfectly revealing to me my Father. Heavenly Father, I thank You for welcoming me into the embrace of Your arms as Your son. ...

Today, I'll travel to Corbin, Kentucky to speak with the pastoral staff of one of Your churches on spiritual leadership. In this main-line denominational church, someone spoke a word of prophecy in tongues and someone else interpreted Your message to the church a few Sundays ago. That apparently doesn't happen every Sunday in their church—or mine. But maybe it should. You give us guidelines and principles in Your Word of how to embrace the freedom of Your Spirit and the words You speak to us through the spiritual gifts You have given us as the body of Christ on earth (1 Corinthians 12, 13, and 14). "So my friends, be eager to prophecy, and do not forbid the speaking in tongues; but all things should be done decently and in order" (1 Corinthians 14:39-40).

Though I have so much left to learn, You have been teaching me how to facilitate the flow and ministry of Your Holy Spirit in our ministry's monthly gatherings for prayer, praise, and healing worship at The Fountain. We gather from many different traditions and streams of the body of Christ to seek Your face and welcome Your presence. Every month is a little different because Your move and mercies are always fresh and new, alive with the life of Your Spirit. "The steadfast love of the Lord never ceases. His mercies never come to an end. They are new every morning; great is Your faithfulness" (Lamentations 3:22-23).

Maybe one of the most important principles of spiritual leadership You have taught me is to facilitate the freedom of the Spirit of God moving through one another to encourage and edify us all. It's risky, but it's right. There are mistakes, but there is Your mercy. How can we grow up "to maturity, to the measure of the full stature of Christ" unless we are willing to step out in faith and step into Your presence through a desperate dependence upon You that we can't completely order and control ourselves? Paul expressed this principle of spiritual leadership this way: "My little children, for whom I am again in the pain of childbirth until Christ is formed in you" (Galatians 4:19). Like childbirth, this kind of spiritual leadership can be risky and painful, but it's worth it. It was worth it to You to endure the pain You did to make the mercy of God and the freedom of the Spirit available to us. In Jesus' name I pray, Amen.

Be encouraged today! In the Love of Jesus, *Tommy Hays*

Principalities and Powers Displaced by Unity

Good morning, Lord Jesus. I worship You Lord God Almighty in spirit and truth— Father, Son, and Holy Spirit. ...

"Of this gospel I have become a servant according to the gift of God's grace that was given to me by the working of His power. Although I am the very least of all the saints, this grace was given to me to bring to the Gentiles the good news of the boundless riches of Christ, and to make everyone see what is the plan of the mystery hidden for ages in God who created all things; so that through the church the wisdom of God in its rich variety might now be made known to the rulers and authorities in the heavenly places. This was in accordance with the eternal purpose that He carried out in Christ Jesus our Lord, in whom we have access to God in boldness and confidence through faith in Him" (Ephesians 3:7-12).

Lord, Your church is not one particular place or even the people gathered together in one particular place. Your church is the gathering of all who believe and who are called by Your name throughout all generations. Though we may worship in different ways and even have different understandings of the meaning of Your Word, we are "one body through the cross" (Ephesians 2:16). And when we come together as one church, setting aside our differences to worship You alone and proclaim the glory of Your name alone, Your power and wisdom is "made known to the rulers and authorities in the heavenly places" (Ephesians 3:10). In unity and faith as Your church, we are a witness "to the principalities and powers in the heavenly places" (Ephesians 3:10, NKJV).

Today pastors, ministers, intercessors, watchmen, and saints will gather together as Your church from our region in the mountains of Kentucky at Manchester. From the diverse traditions of Your body, we will pray and proclaim as one, under the covering of Your name and in the power of Your name. As one we are Your church. And as one, we are empowered with the authority of Your name to take our stand for You in our region. The rulers and authorities, the principalities and powers of darkness in the heavenly places over this region will be pushed back by the power of the light of Your glory, as Your name is high and lifted up in the heavenlies.

"God put this power to work in Christ when He raised Him from the dead and seated Him at His right hand in the heavenly places, far above all rule and authority and power and dominion, and above every name that is named, not only in this age but also in the age to come. And He has put all things under His feet and has made Him head over all things for the church, which is His body, the fullness of Him who fills all in all" (Ephesians 1:20-23).

Praise You, Lord God Almighty! Give me humility and faith to join my brothers and sisters of Your body from every tribe and tongue and nation and denomination in our region. When we gather in unity, You command Your blessing for all Your people (Psalm 133). Let the principalities and powers of darkness be pushed back further every time we gather as one church under the one name that is "above every name"—Jesus. In Jesus' name I pray, Amen.

Be encouraged today! In the Love of Jesus, *Tommy Hays*

Our Enemy is Under Our Feet

Good morning, Lord Jesus. I speak out Your name in prayer as the first words from my mouth this day. ...

"The God of peace will shortly crush Satan under your feet. The grace of our Lord Jesus Christ be with you" (Romans 16:20).

As we gathered for prayer and praise as one body at my friend Doug Abner's church in Manchester, Kentucky yesterday, he reminded us of Your call to him and the city-wide spiritual leaders of their community a couple of years ago to take a bold stand for Jesus. Their county had become recognized as the "Painkiller Capitol of the Country" with more people per-capita addicted to painkillers than anywhere in America. They were losing an entire generation to death and suicide by those overwhelmed by addiction and depression. But You called your people to pray. And through prayer, You called your people to march through town with banners declaring Your name and Your power to overcome. As they marched, You crushed Satan under their feet.

You led them to take courage and serve notice on the drug dealers of their community that the united church of Jesus Christ throughout their county was actively and aggressively praying that every one of them would "get saved or get busted." And they did. Several of them stood at our prayer meeting to praise Your name and thank You for Your conviction and grace and deliverance. Now hundreds of families whose lives were being destroyed and whose lives were destroying others are getting the help for recovery and restoration You provide by the power of the blood of Jesus and the love of God through people willing to take a stand of obedience in faith. "Every place that the sole of your foot will tread upon I have given you" (Joshua 1:3).

As Ray Hughes said yesterday, sometimes the pain we're trying to kill is not always because we've hurt our back or stepped on a nail. Sometimes it's because we are overwhelmed by hopelessness and discouragement, having lost our identity and forfeited our destiny through our sins and the sins of others against us throughout the generations. But You are redeeming the generations and You are driving out our enemies before us. Then You call us to take our stand and to march forward under the banner of Your name. "Let God rise up, let His enemies be scattered" (Psalm 68:1). Lord Jesus, arise in my heart and in my community and throughout the earth today, as You crush our enemy under our feet. In Jesus' name I pray, Amen.

Be encouraged today! In the Love of Jesus, *Tommy Hays*

Excited for the Adventure

Good morning, Lord Jesus. Before I think about my day, before I even intercede for others, I turn my eyes and my heart to You. In these first moments, let everything else fade away as I narrow my focus on You alone. ...

As I try to center my thoughts on You this morning, my quiet, contemplative prayer is being interrupted my little boy, Elijah. He's excited and up early because today is "Donuts with Dads" at his preschool at our church. It was the last thought on his mind last night and the first thought this morning— though I'm not sure if he's thinking more about the donuts or about the dads. For him, it's an adventure and he is filled with anticipation and excitement for the day.

Father, fill my heart with anticipation and excitement for the day. Holy Spirit, arise in my spirit to get up early and come running into the throne room of my Dad in prayer to see where You'll take me today with You. Lord Jesus, let me hear Your voice and sense the leading of Your Spirit, as You call me to come and follow You. "Whoever serves Me, must follow Me, and where I am, My servant will be there also. Whoever serves Me, the Father will honor" (John 12:26). Lord, I am Your servant and Your son. I'm excited to serve You and follow You in the adventure You have planned for us today. In Jesus' name I pray, Amen.

Be encouraged today! In the Love of Jesus, *Tommy Hays*

Grow in Grace

Good morning, Lord Jesus. I call You "Lord" because I willingly choose to submit to Your Lordship in every area of my life, as best as I can and all by Your grace. You and my Father are One, and I welcome You to come take charge of my life and fill me afresh with Your life again today. Put Your thoughts in my mind and Your desires in my heart, as I submit my will to Your will and my ways to Your ways. I know it is the process of a lifetime, and I thank You for Your patience and Your grace for me in the process. ...

"But grow in the grace and knowledge of our Lord and Savior Jesus Christ. To Him be the glory both now and to the day of eternity" (2 Peter 3:18).

Lord, I grow in Your grace as I grow in Your knowledge—not knowledge about Jesus, but the knowledge of Jesus. You give grace to the humble but resist the proud (1 Peter 5:5). But as long as I am willing to be teachable and willing to yield my thoughts to Your thoughts and my ways to Your ways, You pour out Your grace upon me to learn and to change. In patience and in love, You are making me more like You each day and I am being "conformed to the image" of the Son of God (Romans 8:29). I have so far to go, but eternity is a long time.

In the beginning of the process, my thoughts are not Your thoughts and my ways are not Your ways (Isaiah 55:8). But that's only the beginning. As You impart Your grace and Your knowledge to me, You are transforming me by the renewing of my mind (Romans 12:2). It is Your will that I "have the mind of Christ"—that Your thoughts become my thoughts and Your ways become my ways. From now until the day of eternity, keep changing my mind and my heart. As the worship song says, "Take my mind, and transform it. Take my heart, and form it. Take my will, conform it—to Yours, to Yours, O Lord. Holiness, Holiness—is what You want from me." That's what I want from You, because You have put that desire in my mind and my heart by Your grace. In Jesus' name I pray, Amen.

Be encouraged today! In the Love of Jesus, *Tommy Hays*

You Hear Me when I Call

Good morning, Lord Jesus. I love You, Lord and I need You, Lord. So I call to You and wait for the answer of Your manifest presence in my heart. ...

When I am weary, You are my strength. When I feel misunderstood, You understand me. When others don't seem to value me, You remind me You created me with purpose and destiny. When I'm rejected, You accept me. When I'm troubled, You are my peace. Let me find my security and my significance in You alone. "But know that the Lord has set apart the faithful for Himself; the Lord hears when I call to Him" (Psalm 4:3).

Lord, keep me faithful to You. Thank You for being faithful to me. In Jesus' name I pray, Amen.

Be encouraged today! In the Love of Jesus, *Tommy Hays*

The Father's Blessing

Good morning, Lord Jesus. You and my Father are One and You dwell in my heart by Your Holy Spirit. Father, I am Your son. I seek the blessing of Your presence and the inheritance of Your provision in every area of my life again today. ...

"By faith Isaac invoked blessings for the future on Jacob and Esau. By faith Jacob, when dying, blessed each of the sons of Joseph, 'bowing in worship over the top of his staff' " (Hebrews 11:20-21).

My oldest son Zachary and I got away for a little time together yesterday. We were playing golf, but the conversations we had were much more important then the shots we made. Zach is fifteen now and this year he has finally achieved one of the goals of his lifetime—to be taller than me. At my height, it doesn't seem like such a lofty goal, but there is something in the heart of sons that tends to cause them to measure themselves by their fathers. And there is something in fathers that tends to make us want our sons to grow taller, run faster, and do better. That's part of what was in Isaac's heart as he blessed his sons and what was in Jacob's heart as he blessed his sons and the sons of his sons.

Part of the Father heart of God that You impart to our hearts is the desire to bless our sons and our daughters, to see them go farther than we could go in our generation. Part of the role and calling of the father is to speak life into the hearts of his sons and daughters, to affirm who they are and who they were created to be, to confirm their gifting and calling and anointing, and to celebrate their life and growth and maturity, so that they can pass it on as a blessing to the next generation.

Father, forgive us when we fail to represent Your Father heart well. Forgive us when we fail to bless our sons and our daughters—with our words, our time, our encouragement, and our resources. Make up the difference of what they lack from us as You pour Your unfailing love into their hearts and bless them with Your holy hands. Let us be aware of the importance of our words and our presence in their lives and let us make them aware of the importance of allowing Your words and Your presence in their lives. In Jesus' name we pray, Amen.

Be encouraged today! In the Love of Jesus, *Tommy Hays*

Arise and Shine

Good morning, Lord Jesus. Be near to me today, as I willingly and deliberately submit my life into Your hands in these first moments of my day. ...

"Again Jesus spoke to them, saying, 'I am the light of the world. Whoever follows Me will never walk in darkness but will have the light of life' " (John 8:12).

Lord, shine Your light into the depths of my soul like the light of the morning sun shining into the depths of dawn. Light my spirit like a candle so that I will shine with Your light today. As You drive the darkness out of me, then I will be like a lighted candle in Your hand as You carry me throughout the day driving out the darkness wherever You take me.

Though my culture and the cultures of the earth are filled with darkness, You have called me to stand out from the darkness and to shine with the light of Your glory in the midst of the darkness. But I can only shine with Your light to the degree that I have embraced Your light and submitted to Your deliverance from the darkness that tries to linger in my soul. By Your grace, I can choose to walk in Your light or linger in the darkness with every decision set before me each day.

"For once you were darkness, but now in the Lord you are light. Live as children of the light—for the fruit of the light is found in all that is good and right and true. Try to find out what is pleasing to the Lord.... but everything exposed by the light becomes visible, for everything that becomes visible is light. Therefore, it says, 'Sleeper, awake! Rise from the dead, and Christ will shine on you' " (Ephesians 4:8-14).

Help me live in Your light as Your light lives in me more each day. "For it is the God who said, 'Let light shine out of darkness,' who has shone in our hearts to give the light of the knowledge of the glory of God in the face of Jesus Christ" (2 Corinthians 4:6). In You, I will "Arise and shine; for my Light has come, and the glory of the Lord has risen upon me" (Isaiah 60:1, personalized). In Jesus' name I pray, Amen.

Be encouraged today! In the Love of Jesus, *Tommy Hays*

"The Battle at the Gate"

Good morning, Lord Jesus. I open the gates of my heart and soul to You this day. I welcome You in as the King of Glory. ...

"In that day the Lord of hosts will be a garland of glory, and a diadem of beauty, to the remnant of His people; and a spirit of justice to the one who sits in judgment, and strength to those who turn back the battle at the gate" (Isaiah 28:5-6).

Lord, I want to be among the remnant of Your people. I want to be counted as one who remains faithful and true by Your grace through every wave of judgment that comes and through every battle that is waged. But free me from the confusion of passivity and passivism that sits back waiting for Your return or waiting for You to do what You have called me to do in the power of Your strength and Spirit. In Your strength, let me take my place to obey Your command to "turn back the battle at the gate" of my city, and my family, and my heart.

This is a spiritual battle, to be fought with the spiritual weapons of faith and courage, truth and justice, humility and grace. We are to wield "the weapons of our warfare"—the name of Jesus, the power of Your blood, the sword of Your Spirit in the Word of God, worship and praise that exalts our God and confuses our enemies (2 Corinthians 10:4). "For we do not wrestle against flesh and blood, but against principalities, against powers, against the rulers of the darkness of this age, against spiritual hosts of wickedness in the heavenly places" (Ephesians 6:12, NKJV). We are not to run in fear or to rest in passivism; we are "to stand" and "to withstand in the evil day" the enemy of our souls (verse 6:13). It is an all-volunteer army, but You are calling us and commanding us to volunteer, to be trained, and to be employed at Your command.

In the name of Jesus, I renounce the passivity of the confused Christian culture of my generation. Though You came the first time as the gentle Lamb of God who takes away the sins of the world, You are coming now with fire in Your eyes, a sword in Your hand, and a robe dipped in blood as You lead the armies of heaven (Revelation 19:11-16). "In righteousness He judges and makes war" (verse 19:11). These battles are fought through the choices we make every day. Be victorious in my heart that You can be victorious through my life to turn back the battle of evil forces and sinful flesh at the gates where You call me to take my stand. In Jesus' name I pray, Amen.

Be encouraged today! In the Love of Jesus, *Tommy Hays*

Led by the Spirit

Good morning, Lord Jesus. Help me listen for Your leading. ...

"The wind blows where it chooses, and you hear the sound of it, but you do not know where it comes from or where it goes. So it is with everyone who is born of the Spirit" (John 3:8). "For all who are led by the Spirit of God are children of God" (Romans 8:14).

Lord, increase my sensitivity to the leading of Your Spirit. And increase my willingness to be flexible and obedient to follow. The ways of the Spirit are not the ways of my flesh. My flesh wants certainty and security and conformity. But Your Spirit comes in ways I don't expect and leads me to places I would not have gone.

Being led by Your Spirit is part of growing into the maturity of relationship with You. I have to take time to know Your voice and listen for Your leading. I am called to have courage to rise and follow You at the prompting and directing of this spiritual Force as unseen as the wind, but just as real. This spiritual Force is a Personhood of Your Being—the Holy Spirit of the Living God—living in me and living through me and all those who are "born of the Spirit" and called by Your name as children of God.

Your life on earth is my example. You were "led up by the Spirit into the wilderness to be tempted by the devil" for forty days as You fasted and prayed (Matthew 4:1). Flesh would not choose that, but the Spirit did. "For those who live according to the flesh set their minds on the things of the flesh, but those who live according to the Spirit set their minds on the things of the Spirit" (Romans 8:5). You are freeing me from the weakness of my flesh, encouraging me each day to rise in the power of Your Spirit and follow the leading of the will of God, which is often so contrary to my natural thoughts and desires. "The Spirit helps us in our weakness" and "the Spirit intercedes for the saints according to the will of God" (Romans 8:26-27).

Thank You for the gift of Your Spirit—the "Spirit of Life in Christ Jesus" (Romans 8:2). Thank You for the grace You are giving me to follow Your Spirit where You lead, even when my flesh does not want to go there. In Jesus' name I pray, Amen.

Be encouraged today! In the Love of Jesus, *Tommy Hays*

Somebody's Praying

Good morning, Lord Jesus. I come into the Holy of Holies in prayer under the Blood of the Lamb. By Your grace, give me clean hands and a pure heart, as I lift my face to You in worship and prayer in the first offering of my day. ...

"For there were many in the assembly who had not sanctified themselves; therefore the Levites had to slaughter the Passover lamb for everyone who was not clean, to make it holy to the Lord. For a multitude of the people ... had not cleansed themselves, yet they ate the Passover other than as prescribed. But Hezekiah prayed for them, saying, 'The good Lord pardon all who set their hearts to seek God, the Lord the God of their ancestors, even though not in accordance with the sanctuary's rules of cleanness.' The Lord heard Hezekiah, and healed the people" (2 Chronicles 30:17-20).

In Your mercy, it is Your heart to pardon and to heal all who set their hearts to seek You. You desire obedience and cleansing from sin. You desire hearts that are sanctified completely and set apart entirely unto You. But even in our disobedience You move on the hearts of others to pray for us for Your pardon and Your grace—a grace that is only available through the Blood of the Passover Lamb. You are "the Lamb of God who takes away the sin of the world" (John 1:29).

Thank You for those who are willing to intercede throughout the generations. Thank You for their prayers in submission to the leading of Your Spirit that open a window of Your grace for us. John Wesley said You do nothing except through prayer. It may be that the only reason any of us ever come to a place of setting our hearts to seek God is because someone has been praying, maybe even many generations before they even knew our names. It reminds of the song, "Somebody's praying ... I can feel it." Thank You for hearing their prayers for me. Thank You for putting those prayers on their hearts to pray. In Jesus' name I pray, Amen.

Be encouraged today! In the Love of Jesus, *Tommy Hays*

"I Die Daily"

Good morning, Lord Jesus. I seek You and I need You. I welcome You into my heart more deeply each day. Let me continually be emptied of myself and filled with You, as the Father and the Son come and make Your home in my heart by Your Holy Spirit (John 14:23). ...

"Then He said to them all, 'If any want to be My followers, let them deny themselves and take up their cross daily and follow Me. For those who want to save their life will lose it, and those who lose their life for my sake will save it. What does it profit them if they gain the whole world, but lose or forfeit themselves? Those who are ashamed of Me and My words, of them the Son of Man will be ashamed when He comes in His glory and the glory of the Father and of the holy angels' " (Luke 9:23-26).

Yes, Lord Jesus. I want to be Your follower. I want to life the live I was created to live and fulfill the fullness of my calling and destiny in this opportunity I have during this sliver of eternity I live in this earthly body. Remind me daily of this eternal perspective. Remind me daily to live for You and not myself. Remind me daily to choose by Your grace to take up my cross and follow You. As I deny myself, I embrace You, as You continue to come in glory into my heart and life.

As Paul said, "I die daily" (1 Corinthians 15:31, NKJV). As John the Baptist said, "You must increase and I must decrease" (John 3:30, personalized). This is a choice You set before me each day—to follow the world or follow You, to live for myself or live for You, to be ashamed of You or glorify You. I choose You again this day. In Jesus' name I pray, Amen.

Be encouraged today! In the Love of Jesus, *Tommy Hays*

Clarity

Good morning, Lord Jesus. I turn my eyes to You. Let the light of Your truth shine into my soul, as I embrace the light of the glory of Your presence here in my heart. ...

Last night at The Fountain, I was praying for a woman with deep faith, struggling to persevere through a hard season of anxiety and stress. As I was praying, You impressed upon me to pray for "clarity"—clarity of thinking, clarity of perspective, clarity of devotion. You seemed to be showing me that her weary mind needed peace and rest from the swirl of activity and chaos that seemed to engulf her. And because of the deep heart of compassion and mercy You have given her, she was drawn to carry all these burdens on herself as the enemy of her soul tried to twist her gift of God and use it against her to weigh her down and crush out her strength and hope.

As I said "clarity" in my prayer, she burst into tears. You had been leading her to pray for "clarity." After we prayed, she showed me a bracelet she recently bought to remind her to pray. It was called "clarity." Part of the purpose of the words of knowledge You give us in prayer is to let us know in a very specific way that You are watching over us and You are with us in the struggles and sufferings we face (1 Corinthians 12:8). You are reminding us that You have the answers because You are the answer. We can trust Your leadings because we can trust You.

Lord, open the eyes of my heart to see You more clearly. Remove the filters and distortions that cloud my thinking and blur my focus. Like sharpening the point of a pencil, narrow my thoughts to the One who knows the answer to every need I have because You are the answer. You are the Word of Knowledge because You are the Word of God (John 1:1). Let me keep growing in the wisdom of Your ways and in the knowledge of who You are. "Now we see things imperfectly as in a poor mirror, but then we will see everything with perfect clarity. All I know now is partial and incomplete, but then I will know everything completely, just as God knows me now" (1 Corinthians 13:12, NLT). In Jesus' name I pray, Amen.

Be encouraged today! In the Love of Jesus, *Tommy Hays*

Obedience Brings Blessing

Good morning, Lord Jesus. I worship You, my Father. I welcome You, Holy Spirit. Teach me the wisdom of Your ways and give me the desire to obey Your will. I watch and wait for Your leading in silent surrender before Your throne. ...

"You shall keep My sabbaths and reverence My sanctuary: I am the Lord. If you follow My statutes and keep My commandments and observe them faithfully, I will give you your rains in their season, and the land shall yield its produce, and the trees of the field shall yield their fruit. Your threshing shall overtake the vintage, and the vintage shall overtake the sowing; you shall eat your bread to the full, and live securely in your land. And I will grant peace in the land, and you shall lie down, and no one shall make you afraid. ... And I will walk among you, and will be your God, and you shall be My people" (Leviticus 26:3-12).

Obedience brings blessing. You desire from me the obedience of a son, not the obedience of a slave or a hired hand. You desire obedience "from the heart" (Romans 6:17). This is the obedience that comes from the desire to please You and to trust You because I believe You love me and You know what is best for me. If I keep Your sabbaths, I will learn to rest in You. If I reverence Your sanctuary, I will know the place of peace in Your presence. If I lie down from the labors of my flesh and rest in the strength of Your Word and Your will, I will experience Your love that casts away all my fears and anxieties and stress. As I continually welcome You to walk with me through the moments of my life, I will know with ever-increasing certainty that You are my God and I am Your son. In Jesus' name I pray, Amen.

Be encouraged today! In the Love of Jesus, *Tommy Hays*

"Go Out to War"

Good morning, Lord Jesus. I prepare my heart for You, as I welcome You to come and prepare me for the battles and adventures of the day. ...

"When you go out to war against your enemies, and see horses and chariots, an army larger than your own, you shall not be afraid of them; for the Lord your God is with you, who brought you up from the land of Egypt. Before you engage in the battle, the priest shall come forward and speak to the troops, and say to them: 'Hear, O Israel! Today you are drawing near to do battle against your enemies. Do not lose heart, or be afraid, or panic, or be in dread of them; for it is the Lord your God who goes with you, to fight for you against your enemies, to give you victory!' " (Deuteronomy 20:1-4).

The wars and battles in the natural realm of the Old Testament speak to us of the wars and battles in the spiritual realm of the New Testament. Our true enemies are not flesh and blood, but the spiritual forces of wickedness of "this present darkness," who often deceive and confuse those of flesh and blood to be the instruments of wickedness and destruction through their words and actions in our lives (Ephesians 6:12). Every day is a new battle.

And in this broken and fallen world cloaked under cover of darkness and deception by "the ruler of this world," we are called to "go out to war" (John 12:31, 14:30, and 16:11). As we do, Your light overcomes the darkness by every choice we make to walk in the truth of Your light rather than bowing to the deception of the darkness. You give us the victory as we enforce the victory of Your cross in the power of Your Spirit. "Now is the judgment of this world; now the ruler of this world will be driven out. And I, when I am lifted up from the earth, will draw all people to Myself" (John 12:31).

Sometimes it seems like I am outnumbered and overwhelmed, but I do not fight alone. In fact, I cannot fight alone. Apart from you I would already be defeated. But You are the Priest who stands before me to encourage me and fill me with courage and faith for the battle. You are the Warrior who rises within in me to give me Your heart and to give me Your victory. I need not fear, for You are with me, and by Your Holy Spirit, You are within me. You do not stand back in the safety of heaven and send me "out to war", You arise in my heart to go out to war through me along with all those who welcome You into their hearts to give us heart for the battles we face on earth. The moment we take our stand in You and allow You to take Your stand in us, our enemy is defeated and the victory is won. "The Lord does not save by sword and spear; for the battle is the Lord's!" (1 Samuel 17:46). In Jesus' name I pray, Amen.

Be encouraged today! In the Love of Jesus, *Tommy Hays*

Forty Days of Fasting

Good morning, Lord Jesus. In these first moments of the morning, I turn my eyes toward You, opening my heart to Your Holy Spirit and resting in the arms of my Father, here in the communion of prayer. ...

"Then Moses went up on the mountain, and the cloud covered the mountain. The glory of the Lord settled on Mount Sinai, and the cloud covered it for six days; on the seventh day He called to Moses out of the cloud. Now the appearance of the glory of the Lord was like a devouring fire on the top of the mountain in the sight of the people of Israel. Moses entered the cloud, and went up on the mountain. Moses was on the mountain for forty day and forty nights" (Exodus 24:15-18).

Lord, You have called me again this year to a season of fasting for forty days from the repentance of Ash Wednesday to the resurrection of Easter Sunday. Thank You for allowing me the grace of juices of fruit and fluids of vitamins to help sustain my strength and health. You are drawing me up to the mountain of Your presence; but the closer I come, the more Your devouring fire is revealing and consuming my flesh—the unsanctified areas of my soul that are not yet like Jesus. Like Isaiah, the more I behold Your glory, the more I find myself crying out in my spirit, "Woe is me! I am lost, for I am a man of unclean lips, and I live among a people of unclean lips; yet my eyes have seen the King, the Lord of hosts!" (Isaiah 6:5).

John Wesley charged his preachers with nineteen questions to affirm their calling and commitment to You before commissioning them as ambassadors of Your gospel. At ordination, I also affirmed those historic vows as a Methodist minister—one of "Mr. Wesley's preachers," but above all, one of Your preachers. Question sixteen affirms the spiritual discipline of fasting as a means of growing in holiness of heart and life: "Will you recommend fasting and abstinence, both by precept and example?"—To teach it and to live it. Fasting speaks of the process of sanctification and spiritual transformation—death to the indulgences of our own desires of the flesh in order to be awakened to a life of the desires of Your Spirit.

"So then, brothers and sisters, we are debtors, not to the flesh, to live according to the flesh— for if you live according to the flesh, you will die; but if by the Spirit you put to death the deeds of the body, you will live. For all who are led by the Spirit of God are children of God ... and if children, then heirs, heirs of God and joint heirs with Christ—if, in fact, we suffer with Him so that we also may be glorified with Him" (Romans 8:12-17).

By grace You have called me to this process, and by grace You are bringing me through it. Morning by morning and day by day, I become more desperate and dependent upon You alone. May this season of fasting be a means of Your grace to join in the struggle of Your suffering, as it becomes a means of Your grace to join the joy of Your resurrection. "He fasted forty days and forty nights, and afterwards He was famished" (Matthew 4:2). Lord, make me more famished still for You, for Your Word, and for Your Spirit. I stand on Your promise by faith, "Blessed are those who hunger and thirst for righteousness, for they will be filled" (verse 5:6). In Jesus' name I pray, Amen.

Be encouraged today! In the Love of Jesus, *Tommy Hays*

Signs of the Times

Good morning, Lord Jesus. I look to You and await Your coming, for You are always coming to those who watch and wait for You. ...

"The Pharisees and Sadducees came, and to test Jesus, they asked Him to show them a sign from heaven. He answered them, 'When it is evening, you say, 'It will be fair weather, for the sky is red.' And in the morning, 'It will be stormy today, for the sky is red and threatening.' You know how to interpret the appearance of the sky, but you cannot interpret the signs of the times. An evil and adulterous generation asks for a sign, but no sign will be given to it except the sign of Jonah'" (Matthew 16:1-3).

The first day of Spring came this week. And then a day of snow came this week. What are the signs of the times? How should we interpret these things? It seems, at the very least, these signs would say that things are not right. Like a fever lets us know that something in the body is not right, so the earth is letting us know that something is not right. "For the creation waits with eager longing for the revealing of the children of God. ... We know that the whole creation has been groaning in labor pains until now; and not only creation, but we ourselves, who have the first fruits of the Spirit, grown inwardly while we wait for adoption, for the redemption of our bodies" (Romans 8:19-23).

It is Your judgment and Your mercy to let us know when things are not right. It is a call to join in the travail of prayer, to awaken us to the reality of the evil and adultery in our generation and in our own hearts. It is a call to repentance—to confess our sin and the sins of our generations so we can turn away from sin and turn to You by the grace of Your love for us. Through repentance, Your "mercy triumphs over judgment" (James 2:13).

Father, open my eyes to the signs of the times. Open my ears to the cry of creation and cry of the Spirit. Give me courage and hope to enter into this season of birth pangs, as Christ is being formed in me and in all who turn to You in repentance and faith. The sign of Jonah was the ark—the only place of safety in the coming days of judgment. You are the Ark. You are the only Place of safety in the coming days of judgment, and You will lift us up into the safety of Your protection. As we turn to You in repentance for ourselves and for our generations, Your mercy will triumph over judgment. This is the redemption of our bodies and the adoption of our souls as the children of God we long to have in the fullness of Your salvation—not only our redemption, but the redemption of all creation. In Jesus' name I pray, Amen.

Be encouraged today! In the Love of Jesus, *Tommy Hays*

Diamond in the Rough

Good morning, Lord Jesus. You are My Lord and Savior, My Healer and Deliverer, My God, My King, and My Best Friend. You are the One who sees my heart and loves me anyway. ...

"He's a diamond in the rough." Those words have always stuck with me. I had grown up on a cotton farm and then in little oil towns around west Texas and eastern New Mexico. I had worked my summers in middle school, high school, and college mostly hauling hay and driving tractors. I even filled in a couple of weeks as a roughneck on an oil rig until the reality of losing a finger or a toe from hauling drill pipe up and out of a greasy derrick really sank in and I went back to hauling hay.

But now I was being considered for position as a trial lawyer in a Dallas law firm where I had worked part of my summer through law school as a law clerk. The lawyer who was pulling for me to be on the list of new hires from the graduating class passed along the summary of how I was seen by the hiring committee—"a diamond in the rough." It felt good and it hurt at the same time. They were willing to see my potential but not fooled by my present and my past.

That's how You are, Lord. With Your Father's heart, You see me as You created me to be. You see me in the fullness of the potential of my purpose and destiny, along with all the gifting, calling, and anointing You have given me and imparted to me by Your grace. But at the same time, You are not fooled by my present and my past. You see the diamond, but You also see the rough. You see my true self that needs to be nurtured and healed as You call forth my true identity and destiny, but You also see the false self that I have created and I have allowed others to create out of my own hurts and wounds, pride and insecurities, that needs to broken off in order to reveal the diamond hidden beneath the rough.

When You called me to the ministry of inner healing—healing from the inside out— You began to remind me of those words and that image from long ago. You began to give me Your Father's heart to see Your sons and daughters as You see them, like a diamond in the rough. You taught me how to confront the "rough" and call the sin for the sin that it was in order to lead a person to confession and repentance in submitting every area of their life to the Lordship of Jesus Christ. You taught me how to help them acknowledge the pain and the shame that was still buried in the hurts and wounds of their past, from the things they had done and the things done to them. You taught me how to help them let Your Holy Spirit release it all to You—step by step and layer by layer, liking pealing the layers of an onion with patience and faith, persistence and truth.

You taught me how to speak life into the dry bones in the power of Your name and call forth their God-given purpose and passion to see and be who You created them to be. You began to teach me how to listen to You and speak Your heart to them, as You called forth the diamond and broke off the rough, through inner healing. And You began to teach me how to take the authority You had given me as Your disciple and Your ambassador over all the power of the enemy of our souls who seeks to keep us bound up in the idolatries and addictions of the bondage of self in our flesh. You were teaching me how to bind up the broken-hearted and set the captives free, as You proclaimed through my prayers the coming of the kingdom of God and the year of the Lord's favor in each person's life (Isaiah 61; Luke 4). Much of it You taught me as You used others to minister this kind of life and healing to me, as You gave me the courage and humility to set aside my pride and fear to receive the ministry of the healing love of God through those You had anointing to be Your healing hands and living words to me, as instruments of Your grace.

You reminded me how when You saw the woman at the well, You went much more deeply than the surface (John 4:1-42). You looked into her past and confronted her shame and her need for love and acceptance. You could have just ministered a miracle, but You ministered inner healing as You exposed her past, so she could release it to You. In her healing, her eyes were opened to see You as her Messiah; and in her joy, she hurried off to tell everyone she knew about the love of the One "who told me everything I have ever done!" (verse 4:29) "Many Samaritans in the city believed in Him because of the woman's testimony" (verse 4:39).

And You reminded me how the friends of the paralyzed man pressed through the crowds and every barrier to bring him to you for healing (Mark 2:1-12). You could have simply worked the miracle and said, "Rise and walk." But instead You looked beneath the surface of the problem to the root of the issue, ministering inner healing from the inside out. You spoke to the sins of his past as well as to the manifestation of that sin in his body; and he was healed. You expressed Your authority through divine insight and revelation knowledge to not only work miracles, but also to expose the root and the source of all that keeps Your people from experiencing the healing and freedom of Your will. " 'But so that you many know that the Son of Man has authority on earth to forgive sins'—He said to the paralytic—'I say to you, stand up, take up your mat and go to your home' " (verse 2:10-11).

Thank You for the ministry of Your healing love. Thank You for the ministry of inner healing and deliverance. In the same way that You have ministered Your healing and deliverance to me, now You have given me the heart and the joy to minister Your healing love to others by the power and authority of Your Spirit living through me. In the same way we are healed and comforted by You, so You send us to be Your heart and hands of healing and comfort to others (2 Corinthians 1:3-4). There is still much to receive and there is still much to give. Freely have I received, now freely am I to give (Matthew 10:8). Lord, thank You for letting others see the diamond in the rough in me, so now I can minister that same Father's heart of Your healing love to others. In Jesus' name I pray, Amen.

Be encouraged today! In the Love of Jesus, *Tommy Hays*

Filled Up and Squeezed Out

Good morning, Lord Jesus. Fill me afresh with Your Spirit today, as I welcome You, God the Father and God the Son, to come abide in me by God the Holy Spirit this day and every day (John 14:18-24). ...

"For in Christ Jesus you are all children of God through faith. As many of you who were baptized into Christ have clothed yourselves with Christ" (Galatians 3:26-27).

Father, continue to baptize me into Christ by Your Sprit through faith, continue to clothe me with Christ. To "baptize" is to saturate, to immerse, and to soak. Like a dry sponge that is soaked in the water, then squeezed out in use, then soaked in the water again, keep soaking me, keep squeezing me, keep using me, and keep soaking me again. Every time You squeeze me to let the Living Waters of Your Life pour out of me, You make room for me to be filled again by "the Spirit of Christ" who is "the Spirit of God" abiding in me by Your Holy Spirit (Romans 8:9).

Every time You squeeze me, the sponge of my heart becomes softer and more tender, more sensitive to Your hand and more able to be filled and squeezed and used in Your service. The hard, crusty places are being soaked and saturated until they are emptied and open, ready to be filled again and filled more fully— but always filled for the purpose of being squeezed out again. As You keep baptizing me into Christ, You keep filling me with Your Holy Spirit (Ephesians 5:18). As You keep filling me up to keep squeezing me out, Your rivers of Living Water will keep flowing in and then flowing out of me (John 7:37-39). Filled up, squeezed out, and filled up again—this is the way I am continually and increasingly "filled with all the fullness of God" (Ephesians 3:19). In Jesus' name I pray, Amen.

Be encouraged today! In the Love of Jesus, *Tommy Hays*

Obedience, Love, and Joy

Good morning, Lord Jesus. I love You, Lord. Help me hear You more clearly and obey You more completely. Open Your Word of truth and life to Me today. ...

"I do as the Father has commanded Me, so that the world may know that I love the Father" (John 14:31). "If you keep My commandments, you will abide in My love, just as I have kept My Father's commandments and abide in His love. I have said these things to you so that My joy may be in you, and that your joy may be complete" (John 15:9-11).

There is a relationship between obedience and love and joy. To abide in the love of God requires obedience to the commands of God. You want me to love You enough to trust Your commands; trusting that You know what is best for me and trusting that You call me to obedience to Your will out of the wisdom of Your love. And to the degree that I abide in Your love in trusting surrender and obedience to Your will, Your joy will abide in me and my joy will be complete. As I do, I will hear in my heart, "Well done, good and faithful servant ... enter into the joy of your Lord" (Matthew 25:21, NKJV). In Jesus' name I pray, Amen.

Be encouraged today! In the Love of Jesus, *Tommy Hays*

Come Speak to Me

Good morning, Lord Jesus. I lift my spirit to seek Your face and open my heart to hear Your voice. ...

"When Moses went into the tent of meeting to speak with the Lord, he would hear the voice speaking to him from above the mercy seat that was on the ark of the covenant from between the two cherubim; thus it spoke to him" (Numbers 7:89).

Word of God, Lord of my heart
Come speak to me.

Word of God, Lord of my heart
Come reign in me.

Word of God, Lord of my heart
Come live Your life through me.

I want to hear You, Lord
To be near You, Lord
Closer than I've ever been.

I want to see Your face
I want to know Your grace
Come lead me deep within.

Voice of God, You're in my heart
Come speak to me.

Voice of God, You're in my heart
Come reign in me.

Voice of God, You're in my heart
Come live Your life through me.

Thank You, Lord, for drawing me into the tent of meeting in the holy place of prayer. Thank You for the voice of Your Spirit singing this song of intimacy and praise through my spirit to You as "deep calls to deep" (Psalm 42:7). Open the eyes of my heart to see You. Open the ears of my heart to hear You. Let me be forever changed and forever changing in Your presence and into Your image, as I behold the glory of Your face and the power of Your voice (2 Corinthians 3:18).

Be encouraged today! In the Love of Jesus, *Tommy Hays*

"Unfailing Treasure"

Good morning, Lord Jesus. I entrust my life to You today, as best as I can and all by Your grace. ...

"Do not be afraid, little flock, for it is your Father's good pleasure to give you the kingdom. Sell your possessions and give alms. Make purses for yourselves that do not wear out, an unfailing treasure in heaven, where no thief comes near and no moth destroys. For where your treasure is, your heart will be also" (Luke 12:32-34).

Today, we will sell our most significant material possession, as we close on the sale of our former home. Thank You, Lord, for the grace of selling it quickly and for leading Tricia to this new home she truly loves. May the peace of Your presence rest on the home we have left and the home we have received. And may the peace of Your presence rest on those who have no home at all, as You remind us daily that our true home is a kingdom not of this earth. "But our citizenship is in heaven, and it is from there that we are expecting a Savior, the Lord Jesus Christ" (Philippians 3:20).

Our new home in Wilmore is a little smaller, with a little less space for our possessions. Thank You, Lord, for the grace of giving, as we have received of the blessing of simplifying our possessions and our hearts. And even then, You have given my wife a gift of making our home a place of simple beauty and welcoming warmth. But while our possessions will wear out and one day our treasures in this world will cease, You will endure and the treasures that are truly worth possessing will last forever.

"So we do not lose heart. Even though our outer nature is wasting away, our inner nature is being renewed day by day. For this slight momentary affliction is preparing for us an eternal weight of glory beyond all measure, because we look not at what can be seen but at what cannot be seen; for what can be seen is temporary, but what cannot be seen is eternal" (2 Corinthians 4:16-18).

Lord, continue to simply my life and help me release my hold on the material possessions and the passing treasures of this world. Remind me every day that all that I have and all that I am belongs to You and is to be used by You in the service of Your kingdom. Continue to open my eyes and my heart to Your eternal perspective. You are my "unfailing treasure." In Jesus' name I pray, Amen.

Be encouraged today! In the Love of Jesus, *Tommy Hays*

"With Eager Longing"

Good morning, Lord Jesus. I seek Your face and welcome the glory of Your presence in my heart and in my world. ...

"I consider that the sufferings of this present time are not worth comparing with the glory about to be revealed to us. For the creation waits with eager longing for the revealing of the children of God" (Romans 8:18-19).

Tricia and I are waiting with eager longing for the revealing of our next son—to be born any day. Some contractions have already begun to prepare the way for birth. We've been praying for him and speaking blessings over him, that he is welcome and honored. We want him to know in the depths of his spirit that he is being received with thanksgiving and joy into his family and into this world, to fulfill his calling and destiny in his generation for Your kingdom. We have prayed "even before his birth he will be filled with the Holy Spirit" (Luke 1:15).

So it is throughout Your creation today. You are moving on the hearts of the spiritual mothers and fathers of the body of Christ to prepare the way with eager longing for the revealing of Your glory in the earth. The earth itself and all who live in Christ are experiencing the stress and strain of contractions to prepare the way of the Lord. One day You will come in glory in the skies (Matthew 24:30; 1 Thessalonians 4:16). But even now, You are coming in glory into the hearts of all who seek You with eager longing and are preparing the way of the Lord in our hearts and souls. As we do, You are revealing the children of God. Soon we will see that the sufferings and struggles of these birth pains and contractions were worth it, to behold the fullness of Your glory in our hearts and throughout the earth. In Jesus' name we pray, Amen.

Be encouraged today! In the Love of Jesus, *Tommy Hays*

King Josiah will Reign

Good morning, Lord Jesus. You are the King of Kings and the King of Glory. Come into the kingdom of Your glory in my heart again this day. ...

"Josiah was eight years old when he began to reign; he reigned thirty-one years in Jerusalem. He did what was right in the sight of the Lord, and walked in the ways of his ancestor David; he did not turn aside to the right or to the left" (2 Chronicles 34:1-2).

A spiritual generation is being birthed in the earth who will begin to reign at an early age in the authority you have given them. They will know who they are in You and they will know who You are in them. They will know their place as "a chosen race, a royal priesthood, a holy nation" to "proclaim the mighty acts" of God throughout the earth (1 Peter 2:9). They will be "saints from every tribe and people and language and nation; You have made them to be a kingdom of priests serving our God, and they will reign on the earth" (Revelation 5:9-10).

The spiritual generation of Elijahs before them has been preparing the way of the Lord through prayer and proclamation, and now this generation of Josiahs will rule and reign with the authority and power of Christ living in them and living through them. This will be a generation of those who are called by Your name and called to Your ministry, who will do the "greater works than these" that You prophesied of long ago (John 14:12).

"For in the eighth year of his reign, while he was still a boy, Josiah began to seek the God of his ancestor David, and in the twelfth year he began to purge Jerusalem and Judah of the high places, the sacred poles, and the carved and cast images. In his presence they pulled down the altar of the Baals; he demolished the incense altars that stood above them. He broke down the sacred poles and the carved and cast images; he made dust of them and scattered it over the graves of those who had sacrificed to them. He also burned the bones of their priests on their altars, and purges Judah and Jerusalem" (2 Chronicles 34:3-5).

In this generation, let us not fear man, nor his false religions, false idols, and false priests. Let us confront them and overcome them with authority and zeal to purge the land and the hearts of Your people. Let us "repair the house of the Lord" and welcome the coming of the King of Glory to take Your place on Your throne in our land and in our hearts (verse 34:8). Let us be a priesthood of kings who rediscover Your Word and renew our covenant of commitment to trust You and obey You with all our hearts and souls for all of the days of our generation (verses 34:29-33). In Jesus' name I pray, Amen.

Be encouraged today! In the Love of Jesus, *Tommy Hays*

The Celebration is worth the Sacrifice

ood morning, Lord Jesus. I quiet my soul to begin this day in the silence of surrender, watching and waiting for the leading of Your Spirit. ...

"Very truly, I tell you, you will weep and mourn, but the world will rejoice; you will have pain, but your pain will turn into joy. When a woman is in labor, she has pain, because her hour has come. But when her child is born, she no longer remembers the anguish because of the joy of having brought a human being into the world. So you have pain now; but I will see you again, and your hearts will rejoice, and no one will take your joy from you" (John 16:20-22).

Tomorrow morning, we have an appointment to have a baby. Our doctor will induce the process of labor for the birth of our child. Already, Tricia's body is experiencing the contractions of birth, as these nine months of preparation will come to a close in a final burst of the intensity and anguish of travail. But as our son breathes his first breath and I hand him into his mother's embrace, all the suffering and struggle of pregnancy will be consumed in the celebration of birth. Tears of pain will turn to tears of joy.

These forty days of preparation for the pain of crucifixion of Good Friday is really preparation for the joy of resurrection of Easter Sunday. "Weeping may linger for the night, but joy comes with the morning" (Psalm 30:5). The celebration is worth the sacrifice. You teach us that lesson through the pain of travail in birth that gives way to the joy of new life. You teach us that lesson through Your journey to the cross that gives way to the joy of eternal life. We look to Jesus, "who for the sake of the joy that was set before Him endured the cross" (Hebrews 12:2).

Give me courage and faith to endure the travails of life, to press through the sufferings of a broken and fallen world, for the sake of the joy that is set before me through life in You. The celebration is worth the sacrifice, as You turn all my tears of pain into tears of joy. In Jesus' name I pray, Amen.

Be encouraged today! In the Love of Jesus, *Tommy Hays*

Christ remains the same[*]

"Jesus Christ is the same yesterday, today, and forever" (Hebrews 13:8).

Lately, there have been so many changes—some good and some not so good. All of the change has produced uneasiness in me. Somehow the changes make me feel less centered and more fearful.

During times like these, it is helpful for me to be reminded that Christ never changes. There's comfort in the thought that He is the same yesterday, today, and forever. Through all the ups and downs, He is our anchor.

Whatever may lie ahead for you and me, let's be reminded that Christ will be with us through it all.

All Praise and Glory be to God! *Mary Margaret Adams*

---

[*] The following devotional was written by Mary Margaret Adams.

It's a Boy! Josiah Benjamin Hays is Born!

Good morning, Lord Jesus. Praise God from whom all blessings flow! Thank you for the birth of my son—Josiah Benjamin Hays—born at 6:11 p.m. on March 31 at 8 pounds, 10 ounces, 21 inches long, with curly blonde hair. Praise You for a healthy mama, a healthy baby, and a happy daddy! ...

"For this child I prayed; and the Lord has granted me the petition that I made to Him. Therefore I have lent him to the Lord; as long as he lives, I have given him to the Lord" (1 Samuel 1:27-28).

The day we found out this baby would be a boy, Tricia and I believe You impressed the name of our son upon our hearts. In Your Word, a person's name speaks of their nature. Every time we call his name, we are calling forth his nature. In the Hebrew of the Old Testament, "Josiah" means "the fire of the Lord" and "Benjamin" means "son of my right hand." Josiah was a king of Israel who ruled with righteousness, authority, and boldness, knowing his calling and destiny from an early age and then living it out in obedience and faith. "He did what was right in the sight of the Lord, and walked in the ways of his ancestor David; he did not turn aside to the right or to the left" (2 Chronicles 34:1-2). You set him ablaze with passion and zeal to purge and purify the land and the people in the holiness of the fire of the Lord. There was great revival throughout the land in the days of the reign of King Josiah.

Benjamin was one of the sons of Jacob, the last born of the twelve tribes of Israel, speaking of the last generation of the sons of men before Your return. At Joseph's table, Benjamin received fives times as much as his brothers and when they were given provisions for the journey, Benjamin again received fives times as much as his brothers, along with a wealth of silver (Genesis 43:34; 45:22). Your glory and grace upon this latter generation will be greater than the former in an exceeding abundance of provision and power than ever seen before. This is a generation of abundance and fulfillment of the purposes and promises of God.

At Josiah's birth, our obstetrician Dr. Owen said, "He's great." This morning, our pediatrician Dr. Wilkes said, "He's perfect." That's a pretty good start and a pretty high calling, but we entrust him to You and to Your calling alone. Father, it seems You are saying, "Josiah Benjamin Hays is a carrier of My fire and a son of My right hand." Lord, You have answered our prayers and we give him to You as long as he lives. With Dr. Owen and the nurses, I held my son in my arms and blessed him, as his mother and I dedicated and consecrated his life to You as holy unto the Lord, in the name of the Father and of the Son and of the Holy Spirit. Lord, let it be so in his life and in our lives and in the lives of the generations who live out their calling and destiny for Your glory and Your kingdom. In Jesus' name I pray, Amen.

Be encouraged today! In the Love of Jesus, *Tommy Hays*

A Child's Prayer*

Henry and I have been very ill with the flu. We were so ill that we couldn't even keep water down! Today is Henry's third day of being sick and my second day of complete misery. As we sat down for lunch—a pealed pear, apple sauce, and some Gatorade, Henry asked to say a prayer. He said:

"Dear Jesus, Thank you that I am going to eat this pear and not throw it up everywhere! Thank you too that you heal me and Calvin and make us well again! In Jesus' name I pray, amen!"

While some people wouldn't be very impressed with such a prayer, I found it to be so uplifting! Although Henry is just 3 ½ years old, he understood God's nature enough to thank Him in advance for what He would do— restore his physical health to him. Also, he had enough faith to pray in the first place! He offered a humble and meaningful prayer with thanksgiving even though he was very weak and ill. I must admit that these weren't the thoughts on my mind as I sat down with him today.

What would it look like for me to have faith, understanding, and thanksgiving like that of my own child? Some verses in Matthew come to mind:

" '...assuredly, I say to you, if you have faith as small as a mustard seed, you will say to this mountain, 'Move from here to there,' and it will move; and nothing will be impossible for you' " (Matthew 17:20).

"Then Jesus called a little child to Him, set him in the midst of them, and said, 'Assuredly, I say to you, unless you are converted and become as little children, you will by no means enter the kingdom of heaven. Therefore whoever humbles himself as this little child is the greatest in the kingdom of heaven. Whoever receives one little child like this in My name, receives Me' " (Matthew 18:2-5).

These verses clearly state what God can accomplish through a humble and faithful "child" who puts his or her trust in Him. Not only will we be able to move mountains through God's power, but it's the only way we will be able to enter into the kingdom of heaven.

While it is tempting for us to waiver in humility, faith, and thanksgiving, Philippians chapter 4, verses 4-7 remind us of all we have to gain when we turn to the Lord. It says: "Rejoice in the Lord always. Again I will say, rejoice! Let your gentleness be known to all men. The Lord is at hand. Be

---

* The follow devotional was written by Mary Margaret Adams.

anxious for nothing, but in everything by prayer and supplication, with thanksgiving, let your requests be made known to God; and the peace of God, which surpasses all understanding, will guard your hearts and minds through Christ Jesus."

Knowing this, let's learn a valuable lesson from a child and humble ourselves in thanksgiving and prayer so we might know God's nearness, peace, and provision.

All praise and glory be to God! *Mary Margaret Adams*

Big Brother

Good morning, Lord Jesus. I look to You and call on Your name with a grateful heart of thanksgiving and praise. ...

Our little boy, Elijah, loves to tell everybody, "I'm the big brother." He's only three years and ten months older than Josiah, but to him it's like another generation. He loves to bend down and kiss his brother's head and makes sure he never misses his turn to hold the baby. The spirit of Cain asks, "Am I my brother's keeper?" (Genesis 4:4), but the spirit of Elijah proclaims, "I'm the big brother!" "He who loves his brother abides in the light, and there is no cause for stumbling in him" (1 John 2:10).

Lord, give us the heart of Elijah to watch over the generation of Josiah. Give us hearts to hold them and love them, to nurture and protect them until they are ready to step into their calling for their generation. Let us be as elder brothers who celebrate the life and destiny of the generations being birthed and entrusted to our nurture and care. Let us be filled with joy and not jealousy, as we bless what You are doing in them and rejoice in what You are doing in us. In Jesus' name I pray, Amen.

Be encouraged today! In the Love of Jesus, *Tommy Hays*

Leaping for Joy!

Good morning, Lord Jesus. Fill me with Your Spirit. As I settle into the peace of Your presence, let my soul leap for Joy that You are near. ...

"When Elizabeth heard Mary's greeting, the child leaped in her womb. And Elizabeth was filled with the Holy Spirit and exclaimed with a loud cry, 'Blessed are you among women, and blessed is the fruit of your womb. And why has this happened to me that the mother of our Lord has come to me? For as soon as I heard the sound of your greeting, the child in my womb leaped for joy. And blessed is she who believed that there would be a fulfillment of what was spoken to her by the Lord' " (Luke 1:41-45).

The delivery nurse assisting our doctor in the birth of our son Josiah was a young woman named Tatianna from Brazil. She, too, was expecting a child. Near the time of Josiah's birth, her eyes grew wide and she stepped back, with her arms wrapped around the baby in her womb. She was saying, "No, baby. Not yet." It seems her baby was thrilled at the coming of our baby, leaping for joy in the womb! But it was not yet the time of fulfillment in birth for her baby. Though my wife carried Josiah and not Jesus in her womb, we also believe that there will be a fulfillment of what was spoken to us by the Lord. This is a child, like every child, of great promise and destiny.

Someone we love and respect as a person and a prophet has said with the birthing of this child will be a birthing of a season of revival in Kentucky, and it will touch the heart of our nation and the hearts of nations. No doubt, there are many such children of destiny being birthed in this season as we pray the promises of fulfillment. And after the birth of Josiah, but while he was very young, a great revival was birthed in Israel (2 Chronicles 34:1-33). Our little Josiah will live his first years in Wilmore, where many famous revivals have been birthed, where many are praying for the re-digging of the ancient wells of revival to spring up from here again, and where there have already been the first contractions of birth again in recent months.

Holy Spirit, in this day, You are birthing a revival of hearts and souls to be set ablaze with a passion for Jesus and to bear our Father's likeness in the remnant of believers throughout the earth. There have been many promises not yet fulfilled of a great harvest of souls at the end of the age (for example, Matthew 13:36-43). Let it begin in my soul. And let my heart leap for joy as I see it being birthed in the hearts of others around me. Let the wells of revival spring up again, in fulfillment of all that You have spoken. In Jesus' name I pray, Amen.

Be encouraged today! In the Love of Jesus, *Tommy Hays*

Generation of Josiah

Good morning, Lord Jesus. You are the King of kings and the Lord of lords (Revelation 17:14 and 19:16). Those who are found in You are "called and chosen and faithful" (verse 17:14). You have called me and chosen me to be faithful to You. At the beginning of a new day, I continue to call upon on Your name and continue to choose You as my King and my Lord. ...

During the reign of King Josiah, he "purged the land and the house" of the Lord that had been defiled by generations of sin and spiritual adultery. Then he began "to repair the house of the Lord his God" (2 Chronicles 34:8). At Josiah's direction, the governmental leaders of the land "came to the high priest" and "delivered the money that had been brought into the house of God." It was then distributed to the workers who had the oversight of the house of the Lord, and the workers who were working in the house of the Lord gave it for repairing and restoring the house." It was given to "the carpenters and the builders" to restore all that the former leaders of the land "had let go to ruin." Certain of the Levites were given spiritual oversight for the rebuilding and restoration. And "other Levites, all skillful with instruments of music, were over the burden bearers and directed all who did work in every kind of service; and some of the Levites were scribes, and officials, and gatekeepers." In all this, "the people did the work faithfully" (verse 34:8-13).

Lord, in this day of the generation of Josiah, raise up those You have anointed with apostolic leadership and kingdom authority to direct the purging of the devastations of many generations and then to direct the rebuilding of the house of the Lord. In this day, Your people are Your house and our hearts are Your temple. Call forth the funds of the kingdom of God into the hands of Your spiritual leaders, to be distributed to the carpenters and builders of Your kingdom, who will see Your plans and execute them faithfully in bearing the burden of restoration. Anoint the worship leaders who will hear the song of the Lord and sing it over the people to encourage them and direct them with prophetic worship and prophetic intercession. Establish in their strategic positions the scribes who will write the words of the Lord, the officials who will execute the commands of the Lord, and the gatekeepers who will open the way of the Lord. In all this, let us each find our place and fulfill our calling, so that we may be found faithful to You in our generation. In Jesus' name we pray, Amen.

Be encouraged today! In the Love of Jesus, *Tommy Hays*

"In His Steps"

Good morning, Lord Jesus. I turn my eyes of my heart to You, as I watch and wait for the leading of Your Spirit in the embrace of my Father. ...

As Josiah is a type of apostolic leader under the Old Testament, so Paul is a type of apostolic leader under the New Testament. One of the marks of a true leader is one who can lead through controversy—pressing through it rather than avoiding it, overcoming it rather than being overwhelmed by it, growing because of it rather than being embittered by it. Even the church at Corinth that Paul birthed and fathered challenged his leadership when he challenged their ways. Yet in affirming his authority of leadership, he didn't point to his position or his educational degrees; he pointed to Your grace in his life to lead and persevere through adversity and affliction:

"We are putting no obstacle in anyone's way, so that no fault may be found with our ministry, but as servants of God we have commended ourselves in every way: through great endurance, in afflictions, hardships, calamites, beatings, imprisonments, riots, labors, sleepless nights, hunger; by purity, knowledge, patience, kindness, holiness of spirit, genuine love, truthful speech, and power of God; with the weapons of righteousness for the right hand and for the left; in honor and dishonor, in ill repute and good repute. We are treated as impostors, yet true; as unknown, and yet are well known; as dying, and see—we are alive; as punished, and yet not killed; as sorrowful, yet always rejoicing; as poor, yet making many rich; as having nothing, and yet possessing everything" (2 Corinthians 6:3-10).

As disciples of Christ, we are called to lead by following You. As Isaiah prophesied of You eight hundred years before You would come as the suffering servant of God, "He is despised and rejected by men, a man of sorrows and acquainted with grief," but at the same time, "the pleasure of the Lord shall prosper in His hand" (Isaiah 53:3, 10). Give me courage to follow You in order to lead others to You, to endure every affliction and hardship with purity and patience in order for You to work into my soul the holiness of spirit and genuine love You desire from me. "For to this you have been called, because Christ also suffered for you, leaving you an example, so that you should follow in his steps" (1 Peter 2:21). In Jesus' name I pray Amen.

Be encouraged today! In the Love of Jesus, *Tommy Hays*

The Ultimate Destination

Good morning, Lord Jesus. Holiness unto the Lord—giving as much of me as I can and receiving as much of You as I can, all by Your grace. This is my desire, because You have put that desire in my heart. You have put this in my heart, because You have led me to ask it of You. So I come and ask; I come and give; I come and receive again this day. ...

"So I say to you, ask, and it will be given to you; search, and you will find; knock, and the door will be opened for you. For everyone who asks receives, and everyone who searches finds, and for everyone who knocks, the door will be opened. Is there any among you who, if your child asks for a fish, will give a snake instead of a fish? Or if the child asks for an egg, will give a scorpion? If you then, who are evil, know how to give good gifts to your children, how much more will the heavenly Father give the Holy Spirit to those who ask Him!" (Luke 11:9-13)

Heavenly Father, I am asking and searching and knocking. I want more of Your manifest presence in my life, more of Your Holy Spirit filling my soul, more of the nature of Christ formed in my heart. Let me never become satisfied or complacent with where I am in my spiritual journey. "Therefore let us go on toward perfection" (Hebrews 6:1). This kind of perfection is the goal of coming to a place of giving as much of me as I can and receiving as much of You as I can, all by Your grace. The more I give, the more I receive. And the more I receive, the more I want to give.

Help me give more of me to You today and receive more of You in me today. Baptize me more deeply in Your Holy Spirit. Release Your gifts more fully in my ministry. Bear Your fruit more abundantly through my life. No matter how far You lead me along this journey, lead me farther. No matter how deeply You fill me with Your Spirit, fill me more deeply. No matter how painfully You crucify my flesh in the death of my self-centeredness and pride, crucify me more. No matter how purely You baptize me in Your refining Fire of holiness, baptize me more purely. This is the greatest purpose of this life of relationship in Your love—that I be conformed into the image of the Son of God—day by day, moment by moment, morning by morning (Romans 8:29). This is the ultimate destination of my spiritual journey. In Jesus' name I pray, Amen.

Be encouraged today! In the Love of Jesus, *Tommy Hays*

International Harvesters

Good morning, Lord Jesus. You are the Lord of the harvest. Let the seeds of life You have sown by Your Spirit in my soul grow up into maturity until the day I am ready for Your reaping. ...

"Do not be deceived; God is not mocked, for you will reap whatever you sow. If you sow to your own flesh, you will reap corruption from the flesh; but if you sow to the Spirit, you will reap eternal life from the Spirit. So let us not grow weary in doing what is right, for we will reap at harvest time, if we do not give up. So then, whenever we have an opportunity, let us work for the good of all, and especially for those of the family of faith" (Galatians 6:7-10).

This is a day of harvest. We've gathered here in the little town of Benham in the mountains of eastern Kentucky with spiritual leaders from across this region of Appalachia. Amazingly, leaders, intercessors, and watchmen have come from Tennessee, Georgia, Minnesota, and even Alaska to join in the launch of this war in the heavenlies for the freedom of this region. Today will begin a prayer assault of worship and praise, prayer and proclamation, declaring the God-given destiny of this land and its people where the thief has come to steal and kill and destroy for generations.

But this is the generation of breakthrough. And as You break through the strongholds of poverty and depression, hopelessness and despair, disease and death, false religion and witchcraft, perversion and impurity, Your power will be made perfect in our weakness. The victory of Your breakthrough will be "made known by the church to the principalities and powers in the heavenly places, according to the eternal purpose which He accomplished in Christ Jesus our Lord, in whom we have access to God in boldness and confidence through faith in Him" (Ephesians 3:10-12).

On the wall of the old Benham schoolhouse now restored to be an inn where we gathered last night, someone has used the incredible gift of Your creativity locked away in the hearts of the people of these mountains to paint a beautiful mural of the life of this region. In a corner is written a slogan from the past, "Benham—the little town that International Harvester built." That was a company that essentially created this little town and stayed as long it was profitable to stay. And when they left, they left with the hope of everyone who had put their faith in a corporation as their creator. Those who trusted in the corporations and coal mines of men for security and salvation rather than God have been deeply disappointed, discouraged, and depressed ever since that trust was broken.

But You are releasing hope in these hills. You are declaring Your redemptive purposes and releasing Your redemptive gifts from the land and the hearts of the people. You are teaching the principle of walking by faith in the opposite Spirit of whatever the enemy has tried to crush us under by doubt and depression and unbelief. You are teaching us to sow to the Spirit and not the flesh, to arise from the weariness and complacency of a victim mentality bound in the cycles of past disappointments into a new day of victory over the darkness and the flesh in the power of Your Spirit.

As Ray Hughes prophesied last night, You will indeed raise up a generation of international harvesters from these hills of Kentucky. You will display the power of Your glory in the very place of our deepest brokenness and darkest bondage. As You said, "My grace is sufficient for you, for My power is made perfect in weakness" (2 Corinthians 12:9). Let the eyes of the nations be turned to Kentucky in these days of our prayer and Your power, as You call forth the hearts of this people of this land to be the international harvesters You have created them to be. Father, we cry out to You as the Lord of the harvest from our hearts to send us out as laborers into Your harvest. For this region, the time of reaping is at hand.

Lord, redeem the sin and shame of my past and that of the generations of my region. Deliver me from every victim mentality and give me the mentality of the victorious. Father, Your love for us and the purpose of Your plan for us overcomes it all through the power of the blood of Jesus that redeems our past and the power of the light of Your Holy Spirit that displaces the darkness of every principality. "But thanks be to God, who gives us the victory through our Lord Jesus Christ" (1 Corinthians 15:57). "No, in all these things we are more than conquerors through Him who loved us" (Romans 8:37). In Jesus' name I pray, Amen.

Be encouraged today! In the Love of Jesus, *Tommy Hays*

Hosanna!

Good morning, Lord Jesus. On this Palm Sunday, I lift my palms and my praise to You. Hosanna! Hosanna in the highest! ...

"The next day the great crowd that had come to the festival heard that Jesus was coming to Jerusalem. So they took branches of palm tress and went out to meet Him, shouting, 'Hosanna! Blessed is the one who comes in the name of the Lord—the King of Israel!' Jesus found a young donkey and sat on it, as it is written: 'Do not be afraid Daughter of Zion. Look, your king is coming, sitting on a donkey's colt' " (John 12:12-15).

Lord Jesus, You are the One who comes in the name of the Lord. You are the Lord, for You and the Father are One (John 10:30). You humbled Yourself on a donkey as You entered Jerusalem for what would become the "Holy Week," just as You humbled Yourself "in human likeness" when You set aside the glory of heaven to enter the struggle of our lives in a broken and fallen world (Philippians 2:5-8). Here You willingly chose to enter the gates of Jerusalem where the same crowds who would shout "Hosanna!" and praises on Palm Sunday would become the crowds who would shout "Crucify Him!" on Good Friday. Yet for the love of each of them and each of us, You "became obedient to the point of death—even death on a cross" (Philippians 2:8).

Forgive me, Lord, for the times I have praised You in one moment and crucified You with my sin in the next. Lord Jesus, humble Yourself to enter again into the gates of my heart today. As I waive the palms of praise, let me follow in Your steps through this Holy Week. As You laid down Your life for me, give me grace to lay down my life for You. Hosanna! Blessed is the One who comes in the name of the Lord—the King of Israel and the King of my heart! In Jesus' name I pray, Amen.

Be encouraged today! In the Love of Jesus, *Tommy Hays*

I Honor You

Good morning, Lord Jesus. As we sang yesterday, "Amazing love, how can it be, that You my King, would die for me? Amazing love, I know it's true, and it's my joy to honor You. In all I do, I honor You." ...

"Beloved, let us love one another, because love is from God; everyone who loves is born of God and knows God. Whoever does not love does not know God, for God is love. God's love was revealed among us in this way: God sent His only Son into the world so that we might live through Him. In this is love, not that we loved God but that He love us and sent His Son to be the atoning sacrifice for our sins. Beloved, since God loved us so much, we also ought to love one another. No one has ever seen God; if we love one another, God lives in us, and His love is perfected in us" (1 John 4:7-12).

I honor You when I love. I honor You by allowing You to live in me. And when You live in me, You love through me, for You are Love. We cannot see You because "God is Spirit" (John 4:24). But You are the Spirit of Love, living in the hearts of all who honor You by allowing You to live and love through us. As others see us love, they see You, the One who is Love, living through us.

"By this we know that we abide in Him and He in us, because He has given us of His Spirit. And we have seen and do testify that the Father has sent His Son as the Savior of the world. God abides in those who confess that Jesus is the Son of God, and they abide in God. So we have known and believe the love that God has for us" (1 John 4:13-16).

As I follow in Your steps through this Holy Week, let me see Your love for me and for this world in every step of love: As You weep over Jerusalem knowing the rejection that will come; as You boldly confront the secular and religious authorities of the day knowing the penalty for speaking the truth in love will be death on a cruel cross; as You gather with Your disciples to give Yourself to them of Your Body and Your Blood to live eternally in communion with You by Your Spirit abiding in them; as You wrestle in the garden with the calling of the ultimate sacrifice of Your life under the burden of all the world's sins and shame and pain, yet willingly choose to surrender to the will of our Father out of the sacrifice of Your perfect love; as You face the mockery and injustice of blasphemy and rebellion as the holy Lamb of God willingly led to the slaughter; as hands that were created to worship You will turn against You to scourge You and nail You to the cross that will become the eternal sign of Your ultimate sacrifice of love for us; and as You rise in the resurrection power of Your glory to display the ultimate victory of Your Love and Your Life over all sin and death.

You have honored me in the sacrifice of Your love in a way that I will not fully comprehend until the day I see You face to face. In Your amazing love, You are my King who died for me. I choose to love You and honor You by embracing Your gift of love for me. Come live and love through me. In all I do, I honor You. In Jesus' name I pray, Amen.

Be encouraged today! In the Love of Jesus, *Tommy Hays*

"Follow Me"

Good morning, Lord Jesus. As best as I can and all by Your grace, I seek You so I can follow You wherever You lead this day. ...

"Jesus answered them, 'The hour has come for the Son of Man to be glorified. Very truly, I tell you, unless a grain of wheat falls to the earth and dies, it remains just a single grain; but if it dies, it bears much fruit. Those who love their life lose it, and those who hate their life in this world will keep it for eternal life. Whoever serves Me must follow Me, and where I am, there will My servant be also. Whoever serves Me, the Father will honor' " (John 12:23-26).

There is a death that leads to glory. Death to my self—to the will of my self apart from Your will—leads to the glory of the life of Your presence living in me. As I die to my will in this world, You awaken in me a will to live for You in this world and throughout eternity. But only as I die in this way, can I truly live. Only as I follow You as Your servant and disciple in Your steps as my Master and Lord, can I truly be with You. It is only those who follow You who remain with You. It is those who remain with You that our Father will honor. This is the honor and glory I desire. Keep giving me the grace to die, that I may have the grace to live. Keep giving me the grace to serve and to follow, that I may have the grace of the glory and honor of Your presence forever. In Jesus' name I pray, Amen.

Be encouraged today! In the Love of Jesus, *Tommy Hays*

The Peace of Christ

Good morning, Lord Jesus. Help me listen; help me trust; help me obey. ...

"Now My soul is troubled. And what should I say—'Father, save Me from this hour?' No, it is for this reason that I have come to this hour. Father, glorify your name. Then a voice came from heaven, 'I have glorified it, and I will glorify it again' " (John 12:27-28).

In the final days of Your life on earth, You were not too proud to confess Your soul was troubled. Though You had the peace of the presence of the Holy Spirit and the power of the affirmation of Your Father in heaven, Your soul was troubled at the same time. You knew Your calling, Your identity, and Your destiny; You knew the will of the Father; and You knew the suffering of the sacrifice of Your love for us that You were choosing to make in the days to come. And though Your soul was troubled, You chose to press on in obedience and trust in fulfillment of Your destiny. This is the heart that glorifies the name of our Father.

We often use the sense of peace as the test of whether we are in the will of God or not. But Your own example shows us that it is not either/or—either we have peace or we don't. Instead, it is a knowing peace deep down in our soul, even though our soul may be troubled at the same time because we are aware of the reality of our circumstances and we are aware of the cost of the sacrifice of our obedience.

Lord, forgive me for the times I have held back from Your will because I said "I don't have a peace about it." Those were the times when I didn't have a peace about the suffering of the sacrifice in obedience to Your will, even though I had the knowing sense of peace of Your purpose despite the sacrifice You were calling me to. Help me be more honest with the truth of my feelings and willing to test and discern the sense of Your leading and calling. Give me grace to trust and obey, that my choices in every hour will glorify Your name. This is true peace—not the peace of the world, but the peace of Christ (John 14:27). In Jesus' name I pray, Amen.

Be encouraged today! In the Love of Jesus, *Tommy Hays*

Two Gardens

Good morning, Lord Jesus. I love You, Lord and I need You, Lord. Come fill my mind with Your thoughts; come fill my heart with Your desires; come fill my soul with Your Spirit. Continue to give me the grace to follow Your steps throughout this Holy Week. ...

" 'Father, if You are willing, remove this cup from Me; yet, not My will but Yours be done.' Then an angel from heaven appeared to Him and gave Him strength. In His anguish He prayed more earnestly, and His sweat became like great drops of blood falling down on the ground" (Luke 22:42-44).

If there was no cross, there would be no empty tomb. And if there was no Garden of Gethsemane, there would be no cross. Though You were the Son of God, You were also the Son of Man as You walked this earth. You set aside the glory of heaven to humble Yourself to come into this world to be "born in human likeness" (Philippians 2:5-8). You are the One who was born to die, "obedient to the point of death—even death on a cross" (Philippians 2:8). Yet, even knowing Your calling, Your identity, and Your purpose, in the moment of trial, even You wrestled with Your will and the Father's will. "Because He himself was tested by what He suffered, He is able to help those who are being tested" (Hebrews 2:18). The test of the Garden of Gethsemane called for the most significant choice ever made in the history of the sons of men—"nevertheless, not My will, but Thine, be done" (Luke 22:44, KJV).

Before that moment in the Garden, the most significant choice of the sons of men took place in another Garden long ago (Genesis 3:1-7). But the choice of the Garden of Gethsemane was to forever redeem the choice of the Garden of Eden. Adam chose disobedience because he did not fully trust the plan and purpose of the Father; but You chose obedience because You completely trusted the plan and purpose of the Father. And You made the hard choice of obedience in submission to the will of the Father, You were strengthened from heaven to pray even "more earnestly." With each choice of obedience in submission to Your will, we are strengthened by grace and empowered in prayer to press through the anguish and the suffering we fear. As we trust You and obey You, every cross of crisis becomes an empty tomb of triumph!

Lord, give me courage in the Gardens of Gethsemane to choice well, to choose Your will. Strengthen me with Your grace from heaven; empower me to earnestly wrestle in prayer as You conform my will to Your will. Keep the joy of resurrection ever before me as I choose each cross of death to my own self will apart from Your perfect will. In Jesus' name I pray, Amen.

Be encouraged today! In the Love of Jesus, *Tommy Hays*

The Day of Sacrifice

Good morning, Lord Jesus. On this Good Friday, the day of Your suffering and sacrifice of love for me, I thank You and I worship You. You are my Passover Lamb— the Lamb of God who takes away the sins of the world, the Lamb of God who has taken away my sins (John 1:29). ...

The prophet Isaiah saw the glory of Your birth and life and death eight hundred years before You came in the flesh. He prophesied of Your willing sacrifice of amazing love for each of us to be restored and reconciled in relationship with You (John 12:41; Matthew 12:17). In Isaiah 53: 1-12, he declared or You:

"Who has believed what we have heard? And to whom has the arm of the Lord been revealed? For he grew up before him like a young plant, and like a root out of dry ground; he had no form or majesty that we should look at him, nothing in his appearance that we should desire him. He was despised and rejected by others; a man of suffering and acquainted with infirmity; as one from whom others hid their faces he was despised, and we held him of no account."

"Surely he has borne our infirmities and carried our diseases; yet we accounted him stricken, struck down by God and afflicted. But he was wounded for our transgressions, crushed for our iniquities; upon him was the punishment that made us whole, and by his bruises we are healed. All we like sheep have gone astray; we have all turned our own way, and the Lord has laid on him the iniquity of us all."

"He was oppressed and He was afflicted, yet he did not open his mouth; like a lamb that is led to the slaughter, and like a sheep that before its shearers is silent, so he did not open his mouth. By a perversion of justice he was taken away. Who could have imagined his future? For he was cut off from the land of the living, stricken for the transgression of my people. They made his grave with the wicked and his tomb with the rich, though he had done no violence, and there was no deceit in his mouth."

"Yet it was the will of God to crush him with pain. When you make his life an offering for sin, he shall see his offspring, and shall prolong his days; through him the will of God shall prosper. Out of his anguish he shall see light; he shall find satisfaction through his knowledge: The righteous one, My servant, shall make many righteous, and he shall bear their iniquities. Therefore I will allot his portion with the great, and he shall divide the spoil with the strong; because he poured out himself to death, and was numbered with the transgressors; yet he bore the sin of many, and made intercession for the transgressors."

Thank You, Lord Jesus, for pouring out Yourself to death for me, for making intercession for me. For I am a transgressor, but in You and through Your sacrifice, You have made me righteous. Though I can't image the depth of this love or this sacrifice, I find joy in knowing You "find satisfaction" in seeing the will of God prosper through Your eternal act of unfailing love. Like all those who now know the love and peace of God because of Your sacrifice of love, I am "looking to Jesus, the pioneer and perfecter of our faith, who for the sake of the joy that was set before Him endured the cross, disregarding its shame, and has taken His seat at the right hand of the throne of God" (Hebrews 12:2). Only in the knowledge of Your joy can I find peace in the sadness and anguish of this day of Your sacrifice. In Jesus' name I pray, Amen.

Be encouraged today! In the Love of Jesus, *Tommy Hays*

The Day of Waiting

Good morning, Lord Jesus. I watch and wait for Your coming in glory, here in my heart and here in my life again today. ...

"When evening had come, and since it was the day of Preparation, that is, the day before the Sabbath, Joseph of Arimathea, a respected member of the council, who was also himself waiting expectantly for the kingdom of God, went boldly to Pilate and asked for the body of Jesus. Then Pilate wondered if He were already dead; and summoning the centurion, he asked him whether He had been dead for some time. When he learned from the centurion that He was dead, he granted the body to Joseph. Then Joseph bought a linen cloth, and taking down the body, wrapped it in the linen cloth, and laid it in a tomb that had been hewn out of the rock. He then rolled a stone against the door of the tomb" (Mark 15:42-46).

This Holy Saturday between Good Friday and Resurrection Sunday is the Sabbath day of rest—the day Your body lay at rest, buried in the tomb behind the stone. What a day of mourning and grief, hopelessness and despair for those who did not remember or did not believe Your words of hope when You walked among them: "The Son of Man is going to be betrayed into human hands, and they will kill Him, and on the third day He will be raised" (Mathew 17:22-23). But this was only the second day—the day to be "waiting expectantly for the kingdom of God," the day to come "boldly" before the throne of grace, asking "for the body of Jesus" to be raised from the dead in Your resurrection of life and glory.

Lord, help me to be honest with my grief and sorrow, but also help me to be hopeful with anticipation of the coming of Your kingdom. Let me be thankful for all You have done for me through the suffering and agony of the cross, but also expectant of all You are doing for me in the glory and power of Your resurrection. Give me faith to believe not only the anguish of Your death, but also the victory of Your resurrection, even in the days when all I can do is rest in You and keep waiting expectantly for Your coming. You are the King of the Kingdom of God, the King of kings and the Lord of lords, my King and my Lord. Death cannot hold You and the devil cannot stop You. "He will reign over the house of Jacob forever, and of His Kingdom there will be no end!" (Luke 1:33) In Jesus' name I pray, Amen.

Be encouraged today! In the Love of Jesus, *Tommy Hays*

The Good News!

Good morning, Lord Jesus. I greet You this Easter morning with the ancient greeting of Christians throughout the generations since that first Resurrection Sunday: "He is risen! He is risen indeed!" Arise in my heart, in my church, in my community, in my land, and in my generation in Your resurrection power this day! ...

"But on the first day of the week, at early dawn, they came to the tomb, taking the spices that they had prepared. They found the stone rolled away from the tomb, but when they went in, they did not find the body. While they were perplexed about this, suddenly two men in dazzling clothes stood beside them. The women were terrified and bowed their faces to the ground, but the men said to them, 'Why do you look for the living among the dead? He is not here, but has risen! Remember how He told you while He was still in Galilee, that the Son of Man must be handed over to sinners, and be crucified, and on the third day rise again.' Then they remembered His words, and returning from the tomb, they told all of this to the eleven and to all the rest" (Luke 24:1-9).

The stone of death is rolled away! The seal of death is broken by the power of life! You are Life—"the Way, the Truth, and the Life" (John 14:6). You are "the Resurrection and the Life;" and in You, I am alive and I "will never die" (John 11:25-26). "If the Spirit of Him who raised Jesus from the dead dwells in you, He who raised Christ from the dead will give life to your mortal bodies also through His Spirit that dwells in you" (Romans 8:11).

"And we bring you the Good News that what God promised to our ancestors He has fulfilled for us, their children, by raising Jesus, as it is written in the second psalm, 'You are My Son, today I have begotten You.' As to His raising Him from the dead, no more to return to corruption, He has spoken in this way, 'I will give You the holy promises made to David.' Therefore He has also said in another psalm, 'You will not let Your Holy One experience corruption.' For David, after he had served the purpose of God in his own generation, died, was laid beside his ancestors, and experienced corruption. Let it be known to you, therefore, my brothers, that through this Man, forgiveness of sins is proclaimed to you; by this Jesus, everyone who believes is set free from all those sins from which you could not be freed by the law of Moses" (Acts 13:34-39).

Praise You, Lord Jesus, for this Good News! Praise You, Father God, for the fulfillment of Your promises. You spoke to me at the beginning of this year that this would be a year of fulfillment. You led me to fast and pray for these forty days from Ash Wednesday to Resurrection Sunday for the fulfillment of Your promises in my life and my generation. And every promise is fulfilled in You. By Your grace, I am emptied of myself, to be filled with the fullness of Your Spirit (Ephesians 3:19). Keep on emptying me and keep on filling me. As the light of Your glory filled the tomb that day, let the light of Your glory fill my soul this day. By Your grace and the mercy of Your love, I rise "in newness of life" to feast on Your presence—my life in You and Your Life in me (Romans 6:4). Christ in me, "the hope of glory" (Colossians 1:27). This is the Good News! He is risen indeed! In Jesus' name I pray, Amen.

Be encouraged today! In the Love of Jesus, *Tommy Hays*

Moving Forward in Power

Good morning, Lord Jesus. In the celebration of Your resurrection, I celebrate the Passover from death to life, from bondage to freedom, from the land of oppression to the land of promise. You are the Passover Lamb who takes away the sins of the world and You are the Resurrection Power who empowers me to live and move and have my being in You. ...

As I watch and wait for the leading of Your Spirit, I see a bright red new car and a set of keys. I don't think this is a promise of things to come—but I will faithfully receive whatever You choose to faithfully give! As I seek Your discernment, it seems You are showing me the blessing of resurrection is like being given a brand new car. "So if anyone is in Christ, there is a new creation: everything old has passed away; see, everything has become new!" (2 Corinthians 5:17) And the red color I believe speaks of the fire and the power of Holy Spirit. In the glory of Your resurrection in me, I am filled up, on fire, and ready to go! And wherever I go I will be revealing my great gift of the grace of Your glory.

It seems You are saying the keys speak of my part. Even though You have given me this incredible gift and want to send me to incredible places of life and ministry in the journey with You, I can't go anywhere unless I take the keys of the kingdom You have given me and engage the ignition. I can't move forward unless I put action to my faith. You are calling me to put my faith into practice and my hands to the wheel, to put this vehicle of Your grace into "drive" and press down on the pedal of Your power and "give it the gas."

You are the gift and You are the source of power, but my part is to take the gift You have given me and move forward. In Christ, I am raised with You in resurrection power, but now by Your grace, I must "walk in newness of life," not just stand here in newness of life (Romans 6:4). You didn't give me this gift and this power to just sit here and let everyone admire my new car. You've given me a gift for the journey to take me somewhere, as I engage my heart with Your power. I'm filled up and ready to go, Lord! In Jesus' name I pray, Amen.

Be encouraged today! In the Love of Jesus, *Tommy Hays*

Breaking Bread, Burning Hearts

Good morning, Lord Jesus. Break the bread of Your Word with me this morning. Come along side me in our journey of prayer together in Your Spirit. ...

Two of Your disciples were walking along the road to Emmaus on the third day after Your death on the cross (Luke 24:13-35). They were discouraged because they did not really believe the promises You had spoken into their spirits or the promises You had revealed in Your Word. But You came alongside them to both confront their sin of doubt and unbelief and also to comfort their troubled hearts and minds with hope and truth: " 'Oh, how foolish you are, and how slow of heart to believe all that the prophets have declared! Was it not necessary that the Messiah should suffer these things and then enter into His glory?' Then beginning with Moses and all the prophets, He interpreted to them things about Himself in all the Scriptures" (verse 24:25-27).

Every promise of every prophet is ultimately fulfilled in You. The Word of God speaks of You "in all the Scriptures" if we have eyes to see it—eyes to see You in the words and prophecies and prayers of every book of the Bible. As You began to open the Word of God to them, their hearts burned within them. As You broke bread with them, their eyes were opened to Your truth and Your presence (verse 24:30-32). You are the Word of God (John 1:1, 14). You are the Bread of Life. "Very truly, I tell you, whoever believes has eternal life. I am the bread of life.... I am the living bread that came down from heaven. Whoever eats of this bread will live forever; and the bread that I will give for the life of this world is My flesh" (John 6:47-51).

May my heart burn within me as You open Your Word and my eyes to Your truth and Your presence. May I eat of Your Word and feast of Your Presence every day, as You build my faith and renew my hope. Let me see You as You are—Father, Son, and Holy Spirit—in all the Scriptures. And let me see You through all the journey in all the circumstances of my life. In Jesus' name I pray, Amen.

Be encouraged today! In the Love of Jesus, *Tommy Hays*

The Roaring Thunder

Good morning, Lord Jesus. "I hear the roaring thunder, my God how great Thou art." Be enthroned on my heart and throughout all the earth this day. ...

Since early this morning, the rumbling of the Your thunder and the flashing of Your lightning have continued to build in intensity and power. It is as if Your voice is speaking to the earth and the wind and the rain in words too deep for me to grasp. Something inside me trembles. You are the God who draws near to us in both the intimacy of Your unfailing love but also in the majesty of Your unfathomable power.

"At this also my heart trembles, and leaps out of its place. Listen, listen to the thunder of His voice and the rumbling that comes from His mouth. Under the whole heaven He lets it loose, and His lightning to the corners of the earth. After it His voice roars; He thunders with His majestic voice, and He does not restrain them when His voice is heard. God thunders wondrously with His voice; He does great things that we cannot comprehend" (Job 37:1-5).

Thank You for the call to intimacy in the embrace of Your arms in prayer, and thank You for reminding me of Your incredible grace that keeps my heart from failing in fear in the face of Your power. Let me never take Your grace for granted, as I behold both "the kindness and the severity of God" (Romans 11:22). I join heaven and earth in bowing before You in trembling awe of the majesty and power of Your presence. In Jesus' name I pray, Amen.

Be encouraged today! In the Love of Jesus, *Tommy Hays*

First Priority

Good morning, Lord Jesus. I turn my eyes to You and open my heart to You with the first thoughts of my day. ...

"They gave themselves first to the Lord" (2 Corinthians 8:5).

As best as I can and all by Your grace, I give You first place in my life. Before anything or anyone else, I give myself first to You. Anything else that finds its way into that place in my life is an idol—even the good things and the important things, even the very things You have given me as the gifts of Your hand. All must find their place in the priorities of my heart beneath my first priority. When I get this priority right, everything else will come into place. "But seek ye first the kingdom of God, and His righteousness; and all these things shall be added unto you" (Matthew 6:33, KJV).

The most loving thing I can do for anyone else is to love You first. The most giving thing I can do for anyone else is to give of myself to You first. I choose to seek You and Your kingdom first. You are my First Priority. In Jesus' name I pray, Amen.

Be encouraged today! In the Love of Jesus, *Tommy Hays*

"Honor Me"

Good morning, Lord Jesus. I love You, Lord, and I call on Your name. Cause Your nature to be formed in my nature; cause Your heart to be formed in my heart. I entrust my life and this day to You. ...

"For those who honor Me I will honor" (1 Samuel 2:30).

These words are the call to prayer for our National Day of Prayer this year on Thursday, May 4. And these words are Your call to prayer for each of us who are called by Your name on every day. The word "honor" in the Hebrew language carries the idea of weightiness, heaviness, and significance. It is from the same root as the word "glory"—the thickness and heaviness of the substance of the presence of God. It is not shallow or superficial; it is a sense of substance and depth of commitment. As we glorify You, we honor You. As we honor You, we welcome the glory of Your presence.

Forgive us for the shallowness of our faith as a people and a nation. Forgive us for honoring You merely with our words or slogans—"God bless America;" "In God we trust;" "One nation under God." Let these be declarations of surrender to Your will and Your ways rather than sanctimonious and self-serving symbols. Forgive us for allowing ourselves to become "lovers of pleasure more than lovers of God, holding to an outward form of godliness but denying its power" (2 Timothy 3:5). We confess our sin and the sin of our nation throughout our generations in the humility of repentance, asking for the mercy of Your grace to renew us and revive us, to re-awaken us to our calling and destiny as a nation under God.

You created us, as You have created each of us, for the greatness of Your glory. And Your glory fills the hearts and the nation of the people who honor You—who honor You not merely with our lips but with our hearts, not only in the privacy of our prayer closets, but in the way we live our lives before the world to see. Restore us as a nation and a people to the depth of commitment and surrender You long to have from the hearts of Your people of every nation. Let us not be ashamed to honor You publicly and proudly. "Those who are ashamed of Me and of My words, of them the Son of Man will be ashamed when He comes in His glory and the glory of the Father and of the holy angels" (Luke 9:26). As for me and my house, as for me and my nation, let us declare this day and every day, "For I am not ashamed of the gospel; it is the power of God for salvation to everyone who has faith" (Romans 1:16). Blessed is the one who honors God. In Jesus' name I pray, Amen.

Be encouraged today! In the Love of Jesus, *Tommy Hays*

Our Great God

Good morning, Lord Jesus. I sing to You how great is our God. ...

A man and his wife gave testimony to Your greatness last night at The Fountain. They were in a horrendous car wreck, he was in a coma, and the doctor said to his wife, "There's nothing there. Let him go." As she persisted in prayer, You did not give her the peace to let him go. Angered by her resistance, the doctor told her, "You are just a selfish old woman, who won't let him go. Even if he were to live, his mind would be destroyed." But those were not the words You were speaking into her spirit. You had not given her the peace of release, but persisted with a burden to pray for healing and life. And last night, her husband stood before us giving praise to Your name and Your victory of life over death. His body is not broken and his mind is not destroyed. He's still teaching students as a professor of philosophy at Asbury College. No doubt his favorite philosophy is "Trust the Word of God, not the words of men."

You are the God who loves to take the shattered pieces of broken lives and heal them in Your hands and hold them in You arms. You love to speak life into the dead places—to bind up the broken-hearted and set the captives free, to restore what is broken and redeem what is destroyed (Isaiah 61). You love to release the power of Your love into our hurting hearts, our wounded spirits, and our broken bodies. You love to fill us with the peace of Your presence and the power of Your love no matter what we face in our journey through this broken, fallen world. How great is our God! "How great are His signs, how mighty His wonders! His kingdom is an everlasting kingdom, and His sovereignty is from generation to generation" (Daniel 4:3). In Jesus' name I pray, Amen.

Be encouraged today! In the Love of Jesus, *Tommy Hays*

God's Blessing[*]

One of my favorite psalms is Psalm 127. It reads as follows:

"Unless the Lord builds the house, they labor in vain who build it; unless the Lord guards the city, the watchman stays awake in vain. It is vain for you to rise up early, to sit up late, to eat the bread of sorrows; for so He gives his beloved sleep."

"Behold, children are a heritage from the Lord, the fruit of the womb is a reward. Like arrows in the hand of a warrior, so are the children of one's youth. Happy is the man who has his quiver full of them; they shall not be ashamed, but shall speak with their enemies in the gate."

At first glance, this particular Psalm looks like a mismatched pair of socks. However, its meaning becomes clearer to me as I reflect deeper on its meaning.

First, the psalmist speaks on the topic of God's blessing. Have you ever asked for God's blessing BEFORE you did something? If we did, it may save ourselves a lot of futile effort and heartache. According to this Psalm, anything we attempt to do that is outside of God's blessing will be futile. Furthermore, we may actually be bringing sorrow upon ourselves if we seek things that are outside of God's will and plan for us.

Some of us may be tempted to feel frustration towards God for not granting us what we deem to be "success." However, God loves us and it is His desire for us to have peace and to receive rest. He definitely does not want us to spend our time on futile efforts that sap us of our energy and bring us sorrow. This means we need to seek God's guidance and ask for God's blessing before going forward with something and then be willing to really trust Him with it afterwards.

Second, the psalmist speaks of children as a special gift and blessing from God. While our culture tends to focus much more on material gains, it's important to remember that children are a very special reward from God.

There was a time when I never thought I would have any children. In fact, for many years, I was dead set against the idea. I was convinced that academic success of any kind would make me happy and that children would bring me sorrow.

---

[*] The following devotional was written by Mary Margaret Adams.

One day, God actually woke me up and told me to think twice before I passed up motherhood. I thought about it briefly, and then discarded the thought as a "bad dream." However, God eventually changed my heart. In a strange turn of events, I actually ended up praying to be able to conceive both of my sons!

I gave up what I valued as "success," but God showed me that when I entrust my dreams and talents to Him, He will be faithful to enable me to use them. Now, I have two beautiful sons and I am much more fulfilled in what I do, because I am living within God's will and blessing for my life.

All praise and glory be to God! *Mary Margaret Adams*

Walk on the Other Side

Good morning, Lord Jesus. Help me listen; help me trust; help me obey. ...

"Now when Jesus saw great crowds around Him, He gave orders to go over to the other side. A scribe then approached and said, 'Teacher, I will follow You wherever You go.' And Jesus said to him, 'Foxes have holes, and birds of the air have nests; but the Son of Man has nowhere to lay His head.' " (Matthew 8:18-20).

Lord, give me courage to follow You and not the crowd. Give me the integrity to walk with You in the truth even when it's on "the other side" of popularity. It can be a lonely place without the security of the approval of the crowds. But let me not pledge with my lips to follow You wherever You go without determining in my heart to follow You when the road is hard and lonely and when the journey leads in a direction that is contrary to culture. A disciple is one who is disciplined to obey, one who is teachable to learn, one who follows freely in the steps of his teacher. "Blessed rather are those who hear the word of God and obey it" (Luke 11:28).

Lord, let me hear You and obey You. Discipline me and disciple me to be willing to follow You wherever You lead without fearing the rejection of the crowds and without living for the approval of others. By Your grace, let me be found faithful and true by Your side—a side that was pierced by the spear of the very ones You died to save (John 19:31-37). Give me the grace to love those who reject me and to pray for those who mock me. Remind me that when I follow You, it's not me they are rejecting. As You said, "Whoever listens to you listens to Me, and whoever rejects you rejects Me, and whoever rejects Me rejects the One who sent Me" (Luke 10:16). In the power and courage of Your name, I renounce the fear of man and I choose to follow the Son of Man. In Jesus' name I pray, Amen.

Be encouraged today! In the Love of Jesus, *Tommy Hays*

The King of the Kingdom of God

Good morning, Lord Jesus. "Lift up your heads, O gates! And be lifted up, O ancient doors! That the King of glory may come in" (Psalm 24:7). Come into Your kingdom in my heart in deeper measure today than yesterday and in deeper measure tomorrow than today. ...

"He said therefore, 'What is the kingdom of God like? And to what shall I compare it? It is like a mustard seed that someone took and sowed in the garden; it grew and became a tree, and the birds of the air made nests in its branches.' And again He said, 'To what should I compare the kingdom of God? It is like yeast that a woman took and mixed with three measures of flour until all of it was leavened' " (Luke 13:18-21).

You are always teaching us about the kingdom of God. And one truth about this kingdom is that it is always growing into maturity, into fullness, into its full expression. Like the seed that grows into a tree and like the yeast that rises to leaven the whole loaf, it is not stagnant and still, but growing and alive. And as we give ourselves to You, You are the King of the kingdom in our hearts in an ever-increasing measure. Your authority and Your rule increases in our lives as we submit to Your will and Your ways. "For, in fact, the kingdom of God is within you" (Luke 17:21).

Lord Jesus, You are the King of kings and the Lord of lords; You are the King of the kingdom of God. You are the King of glory and the King of my heart. Increase as I decrease (John 3:30). Let me grow more each day, as Your kingdom grows in me and in all those who submit to Your Kingdom and Your Lordship, "until all of us come to the unity of the faith and the knowledge of the Son of God, to maturity, to the measure of the full stature of Christ" (Ephesians 4:13). In Jesus' name I pray, Amen.

Be encouraged today! In the Love of Jesus, *Tommy Hays*

Silent Praise

Good morning, Lord Jesus. I lift my eyes to Your promises and away from my problems. I open my heart to Your presence and welcome Your peace. ...

"The heavens are telling the glory of God; and the firmament proclaims His handiwork. Day to day pours forth speech, and night to night declares knowledge. There is no speech, nor are there words; their voice is not heard; yet their voice goes out through all the earth, and their words to the end of the world" (Psalm 19:1-4).

This morning, I speak my words of prayer and praise to You with my heart and hands alone. The grip of some virus seems to be tightening around my throat and silencing my voice. But while Your Spirit arises in my immune system to drive sickness from my body, Your Spirit is arising in my spirit to tell the glory of God and proclaim Your handiwork through all the earth. In a moment I will send these prayers of praise to the end of the world. Sickness will not silence me; infirmity will not stop me. I join with all Your creation throughout heaven and earth to declare Your goodness and glory as You walk with me through every valley and draw near to me through every struggle.

My struggles are nothing compared to others, but even in these, You draw them into Yourself as I release them to You. Day to day, night to night, and morning by morning, I release them all to You and entrust my life into Your hands—hands eternally scarred by the nails of Your sacrifice of suffering and love for me. How could I not trust You, no matter what I endure and struggle through, with You at my side? "Though He slay me, yet will I trust Him" (Job 13:15, NKJV). In Jesus' name I pray, Amen.

Be encouraged today! In the Love of Jesus, *Tommy Hays*

Deliverance from Infirmity

Good morning, Lord Jesus. God of all peace, I entrust my spirit and soul and body to You, asking You to make me sound and blameless by Your healing blood and sanctifying power as You come into every area of my life (1 Thessalonians 5:23). ...

"When Jesus entered Peter's house, he saw his mother-in-law lying in bed with a fever; He touched her hand, and the fever left her, and she got up and began to serve Him. That evening they brought many to Him who were possessed with demons; and He cast out the spirits with a word, and cured all who were sick. This was to fulfill what had been spoken through the prophet Isaiah, 'He took our infirmities and bore our diseases' " (Matthew 8:14-17).

Lord Jesus, You are the Good Shepherd who heals and nurtures His sheep. I welcome You into my house and my heart. You have already taken my infirmities and borne my diseases. Touch my hand with Your nail-scarred hand. Cast out of me and away from me every spirit of infirmity in the power of Your word and for the glory of Your name. Make me whole and free to rise and serve You.

"Surely He has borne our infirmities and carried our diseases; yet we accounted Him stricken, struck down by God and afflicted. But He was wounded for our transgressions, crushed for our iniquities; upon Him was the punishment that made us whole, and by His bruises we are healed" (Isaiah 53:4-5). I receive Your deliverance from infirmity; I receive Your healing from disease. I agree with Your word and Your will of wholeness for me, and I pray the same for all my family and for all who are suffering from any sickness as they call upon Your name in humility and faith. In Jesus' name I pray, Amen.

Be encouraged today! In the Love of Jesus, Tommy Hays

"On Toward Perfection"

Good morning, Lord Jesus. I watch and wait for Your leading in the silence of surrender before You this day. ...

"Therefore let us go on toward perfection, leaving behind the basic teaching about Christ, and not laying again the foundation: repentance from dead works and faith toward God, instruction about baptisms, laying on of hands, resurrection of the dead, and eternal judgment. And we will do this, if God permits" (Hebrews 6:1-3).

Let these basic teachings be firmly established in the foundation of my understanding of Your nature and Your will. But don't let me ever become satisfied or settled in what I have learned and in what I have become. Give me the desire to keep going "on toward perfection" in Your grace and power. Let me be steadily "filled with the knowledge of God's will in all spiritual wisdom and understanding" as I "grow in the knowledge of God" (Colossians 1:9-10). I want to "grow in the grace and knowledge of our Lord and Savior Jesus Christ" (2 Peter 3:18).

Understanding and living out the principles of repentance, faith, baptisms, laying on of hands, resurrection, and eternal judgment are important and essential. But they are foundational. And a foundation is something to be built upon. We are "members of the household of God, built upon the foundation of the apostles and prophets, with Christ Jesus himself as the chief cornerstone. In Him the whole structure is joined together and grows into a holy temple in the Lord; in whom you also are being built together spiritually into a dwelling place for God" (Ephesians 2:19-22). You are joining us together and growing us up into maturity of understanding and nature to be a dwelling place for God. We have no higher calling than this, but we can only reach these heights if we let You keep building in Your power and we keep growing in Your grace—"on toward perfection." In Jesus' name I pray, Amen.

Be encouraged today! In the Love of Jesus, *Tommy Hays*

"We do see Jesus"

Good morning, Lord Jesus. As the song says, "Open the eyes of my heart Lord; I want to see You." ...

"But we do see Jesus, who for a little while was made lower than the angels, now crowned with glory and honor because of the suffering of death, so that by the grace of God He might taste death for everyone" (Hebrews 2:9).

Holy Spirit of God, You are "the Spirit of Truth" who always guides us into truth and always glorifies Jesus (John 16:13-14). Open my eyes to see Jesus. So many of us think we see Jesus, but we do not see Jesus as He truly is. Our vision is often distorted and our minds are often confused by the false images and deceptive thoughts of the world, the flesh, and the devil calculated to keep us from seeing Jesus as He is. "In their case the god of this world has blinded the minds of the unbelievers, to keep them from seeing the light of the gospel of the glory of Christ, who is the image of God" (2 Corinthians 4:4). "Unbelievers" are more than those who do not believe that Jesus Christ is the Son of God. They are those who do not fully see Christ as the image of God, and who do not fully see God as He is in the full light of His glory.

In one sense, we are all unbelievers in one degree or another until we see God face to face and know Him as we are known, because we cannot fully see Him as He truly is on this side of heaven. "For now we see in a mirror, dimly, but then we will see face to face. Now I know only in part; then I will know fully, even as I have been fully known" (1 Corinthians 13:12). Then our faith will become sight, then we will believe without doubt, then we will see Jesus fully as He is.

Come Holy Spirit. Keep opening my eyes to see Jesus more clearly, to love Him more dearly each day. To see Jesus is to see the Father. To believe in Jesus in the full light of His glory, who tasted death for me so that I might live in Him, is to believe in the fullness of the love of God my Father for me. As Jesus said to His first disciples, He continues to say to each of His disciples, "Whoever has seen Me has seen the Father.... Believe Me that I am in My Father and the Father is in Me" (John 14:9-11). By Your grace—Father, Son, and Holy Spirit—I choose to see and I choose to believe. In Jesus' name I pray, Amen.

Be encouraged today! In the Love of Jesus, *Tommy Hays*

Prevenient Grace

Good morning, Lord Jesus. Lead me in Your ways so that as I lead others by Your grace, I am leading them to You. ...

It was the cry of Hannah's heart to have a son, and You answered her prayers. She brought her son Samuel to the temple of the Lord and dedicated him to You. "For this child I prayed; and the Lord has granted me the petition I made to Him. Therefore I have lent him to the Lord; as long as he lives, he is given to the Lord" (1 Samuel 1:27-28).

Today we will bring our youngest son, Josiah Benjamin Hays, before our church and I will baptize him in the name of the Father and of the Son and of the Holy Spirit. As his family and as his church family, we will dedicate him to You and dedicate ourselves to You to teach him and lead him in Your ways. We will love him and lead him by Your "prevenient grace" until the day he will stand before us as a man of his own faith and confirm the dedication of his heart to You. It is an outward symbol of the inward grace that Your Holy Spirit is with us, drawing us to You, leading us in the ways of life in Christ in the community of faith. Josiah was born into this earth in the flesh and he is being born into Your kingdom in the Spirit. "Very truly I tell you, no one can enter the kingdom of God without being born of water and Spirit. What is born of the flesh is flesh, and what is born of the Spirit is spirit" (John 3:5-6).

Let us all live our lives before him in a way that represents Your true nature. Let him always be drawn to You to know You in a personal relationship of deepest intimacy and trust. By Your grace, let my role as his earthly father be to love him and lead him to his heavenly Father. Let us all do the same before the eyes and in the hearts of all our spiritual children being loved and led in the community of faith in Christ. In Jesus' name I pray, Amen.

Be encouraged today! In the Love of Jesus, *Tommy Hays*

Jesus Had a Mother Too

Good morning, Lord Jesus. I thank You for the life You have given me and I welcome Your Spirit to help me live this life by Your grace and for Your glory. ...

It has been good to have my mother here with us for a few days to celebrate the baptism of one son, the birthday of another, the life of each of my five beautiful children, and the blessing of my beautiful wife. My mom loves to love, and one of the ways she loves is by giving abundantly of herself to us and by helping us learn to give abundantly of ourselves to others. I was thinking this morning of how Your mom was the same way:

"On the third day there was a wedding in Cana of Galilee, and the mother of Jesus was there. Jesus and his disciples had also been invited to the wedding. When the wine gave out, the mother of Jesus said to Him, 'They have no wine.' And Jesus said to her, 'Woman, what concern is that to you and to Me? My hour has not yet come' " (John 2:1-4).

Lord Jesus, You had a mother too. Somehow in the mystery of Your humanity and Your divinity, You had a very heavenly Father and a very earthly mother. Mary, the mother of the Son of God, "found favor with God" and conceived You in her womb by the Holy Spirit and bore You as her son—Son of God and Son of Man (Luke 1:26-38). And with the grace of the wisdom of God and the challenges of human thoughts and desires, Mary mothered You.

One thing mothers do is look into the hearts of their sons and daughters to see the calling and destiny of God. By Your grace, they are created and called to see the best in us—to affirm us and nurture us, discipline us and love us, hold us and heal us, until it's time to release us into maturity and ministry in whatever way You lead. So it was with Mary. Even before it was time for Your hour to come, she knew You were the answer to every need. And no matter what we might think of Your humanity and divinity, of Your humility as the Son of Man and Your authority as the Son of God, that day Your mother had her way. By the end of that day the water was turned to wine—whether You told Your mother Your hour had not yet come or not (John 2:5-11).

Thank You for the gift of mothers who see the best in us, because they see You in us. Any good in us is You, because apart from You there truly is no good in us. Apart from You, we can do nothing, but as we abide in You and You abide in us, our lives bear much good fruit (John 15:5). And mothers have the eyes of God to see the fruit we are called to bear long before we see it ourselves. They plant the seeds and nurture the shoots; they water us with Your Word and set us in Your Light, until we grow up to become who You have created us to be. Mothers are a gift of God. And by Your Holy Spirit living in them, our mothers are the hands and heart of God to encourage us as sons and daughters of God to take those steps into our destiny even when we don't yet know our time has come. You had a mother like that. And so do I. Thank You for the gift of my mother and thank You for loving me and mothering me through her. In Jesus' name I pray, Amen.

Be encouraged today! In the Love of Jesus, *Tommy Hays*

Godly Affirmations*

Many years ago, I met a missionary who was visiting my church. He gave a conference based on the book of Ephesians. At the time, I had just gone back to college and I was extremely anxious that I would fail. After listening to his sermon, I went up to him and asked for prayer that I would pass all of my classes. Although I didn't know it at the time, when I approached the missionary with my request, he prayed silently to God to know the true source of my pain. So rather than pray about my classes, he instead asked me if I had ever been abused as a child. I had certainly never before talked to anyone about my past, but this time I said that I had indeed been abused as a child. I trusted him enough in that moment to tell him the truth, but I also told him he should say all he wanted to say on the topic in those few minutes as I had no plans what-so-ever to discuss my past ever again.

I guess God had other plans. After the conference ended, I received a three page, single spaced, typed letter from him. I was more than a little surprised that he even remembered my name, and stunned that he would actually write me a letter! More letters followed over the next two years and all of them were filled with affirmations about who I was in Christ and how much God loved me. Indeed, we corresponded for many years and he helped launch me onto a road of healing and understanding about God that I could never have imagined or expected; a true miracle.

Today, as I sat down to write, I recalled some of the first verses of affirmation that this missionary gave to me: Isaiah 43:1 and John 10:27-30.

"Thus says the Lord who created you, and He who formed you; I have called you by your name; you are mine."

"My sheep hear My voice and I know them, and they follow Me. And I give them eternal life, and they shall never perish, neither shall anyone snatch them out of My hand. My Father, who has given them to Me, is greater than all; and no one is able to snatch them out of My Father's hand. I and my Father are one."

It was good for me to be reminded that God really knows and understands me and that I belong to Him. Also, Christ is an advocate for me and no one will ever be able to snatch me away from Christ or God the Father (who are one).

---

* The following devotional was written by Mary Margaret Adams.

While these affirmations were given specifically for me, there are numerous other affirmations that God has declared for you in the Bible. May you hear His voice today and be blessed by His wonderful affirmations.

All praise and glory be to God! *Mary Margaret Adams*

The Beauty of Brokenness

Good morning, Lord Jesus. Open the eyes of my spirit to see Your hand in the moments of my life. ...

The Palisades are the beautiful cliffs that rise high above the Kentucky River that runs along the edge of our county and down through the heart of Kentucky from Ohio to Tennessee. The fault line of ancient earthquakes runs along the river's bed and these wondrous Palisades are really just the jagged edge of the brokenness of the past.

Even brokenness can be beautiful in Your hands. You love to release the waters of the River of Life along the jagged edges of our past. Sometimes we would like to bury our wounds and cover them up, but You often use those very places of pain or shame to be lifted high for all to see. This is not to hurt us but to heal us, not to shame us but to share us with others in their suffering when they need to see Your power to bring beauty out of brokenness.

You don't waste a moment of our suffering. You don't forget our pain, You redeem it. You don't change our past, You change the effect of our past, as You transform us and then use us to transform others through the redeeming power of Your love. But it's only when we welcome Your living waters to come running through the pain and shame of the past that we can look up and see the beauty of our brokenness. "The Lord is near to the brokenhearted, and saves the crushed in spirit" (Psalm 34:18). "He heals the brokenhearted and binds up their wounds" (Psalm 147:3). As best as I can and all by Your grace, I entrust my wounds and hurts, my shame and sin, my past and my present and my future to You. Lord, bring Your beauty out of my brokenness. In Jesus' name I pray, Amen.

Be encouraged today! In the Love of Jesus, *Tommy Hays*

The Prayers of a Nation

Good morning, Lord Jesus. Good morning, Heavenly Father. Good morning, Holy Spirit of the Living God. I worship You, Lord my God, my Creator, and my King. ...

"You are worthy, our Lord and God, to receive glory and honor and power, for You created all things, and by Your will they existed and were created" (Revelation 4:11).

Today is the National Day of Prayer in America. We will gather at churches and courthouses, capitol steps and convention centers, water coolers and river front stadiums across our nation today to honor You publicly with our prayers and praise. Thank You for the gift of freedom to express our faith and hope in You. Forgive us for our silence on all the other days of the year when we have the same freedom. But even so, we ask that You would pour out Your Holy Spirit upon the hearts of Your people in a special anointing of prayer and praise, repentance and rejoicing, humility and honor, as we lift our eyes from ourselves for a moment and turn our hearts to You.

Not all will call You by name; not all know You yet by name. But there is one God who created heaven and earth, one God who rules and overrules all, one God who holds every nation in His hands, and when we honor the God of all creation, we honor You alone. "To the King of the ages, immortal, invisible, the only God, be honor and glory forever and ever" (1 Timothy 1:17). "God is King over the nations; God sits on His holy throne" (Psalm 47:8).

A nation is the sum of its people, and today many of the people of this nation will take a moment and pray a prayer in humility and faith to honor You. Lord, hear our prayer. "Blessed is the nation whose God is the Lord" (Psalm 33:12, NKJV). Bless the people of this nation and every nation who seek You and worship You as the One worthy to receive all glory and honor and power. And as You bless Your people in these nations, I pray You will bless the nations of Your people through the earth You have created. In Jesus' name I pray, Amen.

Be encouraged today! In the Love of Jesus, *Tommy Hays*

Thankful Hearts

Good morning, Lord Jesus. Be Lord of my heart, Lord of my home, and Lord of my nation. You are Lord of all. ...

"And whatever you do, in word or deed, do everything in the name of the Lord Jesus, giving thanks to God the Father through Him" (Colossians 3:17).

I joined in the prayers of my fellow countrymen for our nation three different times yesterday at morning, noon, and night. Last night I was honored to lead the part of our prayer on behalf of our state as we gathered from across our city and from across the denominational, racial, and economic lines as one in the body of Christ. We proclaimed our prayers freely and boldly at the courthouse plaza from the center gate at the heart of our city. By the grace of the freedom You have given us, we were not ashamed to pray in the power of Your name as we humbled our hearts in repentance and as we lifted our hearts in praise. As one body and one voice in Your Spirit and in Your Name, we honored You on behalf of our city and our nation.

My little boy Elijah wanted to go with me downtown last night. He's not quite four years old and we were concerned he might not make it through a long, public prayer meeting. But when it was my turn to come up and pray, he was there by my side nodding his affirmation of amens and waiving his little hands with authority. On the ride home, he said, "Thank you for taking me to that prayer meeting, Dad." A father loves to hear the thankful heart of his children.

Father, I know yesterday you loved to hear the thankful hearts of Your children. As a nation, we give You thanks for Your faithfulness to us even in the face of our faithlessness to You. Your mercy and love abound in measures we can't even imagine to the people of the nations who draw near to You with thankful and humble hearts. And I pray the joy that filled my heart on the ride home is just a taste of the joy that fills Your heart when Your children give thanks to You. In Jesus' name I pray, Amen.

Be encouraged today! In the Love of Jesus, *Tommy Hays*

The Life of Jesus in Me

Good morning, Lord Jesus. I want to start this day with You. As we begin the journey of the day together, I welcome You to walk with me throughout this day. How can I follow if You don't lead me and how can You lead me if I don't watch and wait for the leading of Your Spirit from the first moments of the morning? ...

As I listen for Your leading, it seems I hear You say, "Be available." "Be ready." "You feel overwhelmed or confused about your sense of direction and purpose when you try to plan out what you will do and where you will go. Rather, look for Me in the relationships and encounters of your day. Welcome My leading by consciously and deliberately choosing to make your mind available to My thoughts and your heart available to My desires. Trust that I am going before you, preparing the way for what I will do through you. As you welcome Me to touch your heart, you are welcoming Me to touch other hearts through you. It is important what you do, but only in relation to who you are—who you are in Me and who you allow Me to be in you. The most important thing I call you to do is to be available to Me."

Yes, Lord. I choose to be available to You this day. Form Your thoughts in my mind and Your desires in my heart. Direct my steps. Open my eyes to see You and see what You are doing in the lives of those I encounter today wherever You lead. Wherever I go, I carry You with me because Your Spirit is within me. I am a jar of clay filled with the treasure of "the life of Jesus," being "made visible" through my body in the encounters and relationships of my day to every degree I make myself available to You and ready for Your purpose through my life (2 Corinthians 4:7-12). This is my purpose and this is my direction. This is Your purpose and Your direction for me this day and every day. Help me do this better, help me live this better, a little more each day as I walk this journey with You. In Jesus' name I pray, Amen.

Be encouraged today! In the Love of Jesus, *Tommy Hays*

Longing for Heaven

Good morning, Lord Jesus. I fix my focus on You. A moment ago I woke from a strange dream that reminded me of the frailty of life on earth and our destiny of security in heaven through You. ...

"For we know that if this earthly tent that we live in is destroyed, we have a building from God, a house not made with hands, eternal in the heavens. For in this tent we groan, longing to be clothed with our heavenly dwelling—if indeed, when we have taken it off we will not be found naked. For while we are still in this tent, we groan under our burden, because we wish not to be clothed but to be further clothed, so that what is mortal may be swallowed up by life. He who has prepared us for this very thing is God, who has given us the Spirit as a guarantee" (2 Corinthians 5:1-5).

Father, You have created me to live forever with You in the house of God, the heavenly temple which speaks of Your eternal presence. You have placed the hope of eternity and the sense of the freedom of forever in my heart. The truth and life of Your Holy Spirit living in me continually lifts my face to the fullness of eternity even while my feet are fixed in the frailty of my earthly journey. My spirit that was created for freedom and longs for fulfillment of my eternal life groans under the burden of my earthly life. For this season of life between heaven and earth, I must live out my life and walk out my journey in both of these worlds—with eternity in my heart and earth in my soul.

But, "He who has prepared us for this very thing is God." You have prepared me by giving me all I need for this journey—the very Spirit of Your very presence "as a guarantee" to constantly affirm to me Your truth and constantly remind me of the coming fulfillment of my destiny in You. My hope and my confidence is in You. "Yes, we do have confidence, and we would rather be away from the body and home with the Lord. So whether we are at home or away, we make it our aim to please Him" (2 Corinthians 5:8-9). Though I may groan with the longing for my heavenly dwelling, keep giving me the grace to live faithfully in this season of eternity in my earthly dwelling. Let my heart and my aim be to please You whether in heaven or on earth. In Jesus' name I pray, Amen.

Be encouraged today! In the Love of Jesus, *Tommy Hays*

Listen and Learn

Good morning, Lord Jesus. Cleanse my heart and purify my mind. Remove everything in me that would keep me from drawing near to You. ...

"Guard your steps when you go to the house of God; to draw near to listen is better than the sacrifice offered by fools; for they do not know how to keep from doing evil. Never be rash with your mouth, nor let your heart be quick to utter a word before God, for God is in heaven, and you upon the earth; therefore let your words be few" (Ecclesiastes 5:1).

Though You continually draw me near to You, though I am created for the very purpose of intimacy in relationship with You, You call me to approach You in reverence and humility. You say "let your words be few" because my words can get in the way of Your words. There is time for me to offer the petitions of my heart, but there is first the time to offer the silence of surrender of my soul. This silence of surrender is better than the sacrifice of service. This relationship of reverence is far better than the rituals of religion. Keep teaching me how to guard my steps in the fear of God in order to know the intimacy of God. Draw me nearer to You each day, as I enter Your house in reverent humility and approach Your throne in trusting faith. In Jesus' name I pray, Amen.

Be encouraged today! In the Love of Jesus, *Tommy Hays*

God Sees the Heart[*]

Not long ago, a friend of mine and I were discussing our particular shapes. She has a beautiful hour glass figure, curvy yet slender. I have an athletic build, somewhat sturdy and muscular. She mentioned that she wished she had my strength and ability. I told her that I wasn't overly fond of my figure, especially my midsection—I never did have a very good waist and two c-sections hadn't helped any! Her reply was that my waist was at most one-third of my total body so at least two-thirds was okay, even by my standards. I laughed, but honestly, I had never thought about it like that before! Regardless of our shape or size we all have positive features that we may be overlooking.

However, physical appearance is not what is truly important in the eyes of God (and He is our ultimate "judge"). All of us need to be reminded that God looks at the heart. For example, when God spoke to Samuel in the Bible about who should be anointed as the next King of Israel He had this to say: "But the Lord said to Samuel, 'Do not look at his appearance or at his physical stature, because I have refused him. For the Lord does not see as man sees; for man looks at outward appearance, but the Lord looks at the heart'" (1 Samuel 16:7). If Samuel had not listened to God, he would have based his decision on his own personal preferences of appearance and he would have anointed the wrong person!

Although our current culture can be particularly hard on women, 1 Peter 3:3-4 reminds us to redirect our energy from outward appearances to our inward person. It goes as follows: "Do not let your adornment be merely outward—arranging the hair, wearing gold, or putting on fine apparel—rather let it be the hidden person of the heart, with the incorruptible beauty of a gentle and quiet spirit, which is very precious in the sight of God."

While we cannot always control what's on the outside—time, age, environment and genetics all play a role—we can be the beautiful person God desires us to be inwardly. While we may be tempted at times to wish for and pursue things of outward beauty, we can be reminded of this famous passage in Isaiah 53 which describes Christ to us.

"For He shall grow up before Him as a tender plant, and as a root out of dry ground. He has no form or comeliness; and when we see Him, there is no beauty that we should desire Him. He is despised and rejected by men, a man of sorrows and acquainted with grief. And we hid, as it were, our faces from Him; He was despised and we did not esteem Him. Surely He has borne our griefs and carried our sorrows; yet we esteemed Him stricken,

[*] The following devotional was written by Mary Margaret Adams.

smitten by God, and afflicted. But He was wounded for our transgressions, He was bruised for our iniquities, the chastisement for our peace was upon Him, and by His stripes we are healed" (verses 2-5).

The people who were drawn to Christ were not drawn by His outward appearance; they were drawn to Him for His inward beauty. Also, there were people who failed to notice Him and even despised Him for His outward appearance. Yet He was the one and only perfect person who ever walked the face of the Earth. He is our greatest example of perfect love and peace. And above all, He is our Savior.

All praise and glory be to God! *Mary Margaret Adams*

Overcoming Deception

Good morning, Lord Jesus. Let Your Word soak into my soul; let Your Spirit arise in my heart. I choose You as my Way, my Truth, and my Life. ...

"Many deceivers have gone out into the world, those who do not confess that Jesus Christ came in the flesh; any such person is the deceiver and the antichrist. Be on your guard, so that you do not lose what we have worked for, but may receive a full reward. Everyone who does not abide in the teaching of Christ, but goes beyond it, does not have God; whoever abides in the teaching has both the Father and the Son" (2 John 5:7-10).

In these days, we are surrounded with lies—deceptions and distortions of the truth. Movies and books that claim to speak facts concerning historical events are filled with deception to bring confusion and doubt of the truth. The enemy of our souls "is a liar and the father of lies" (John 8:44). He is flooding the earth to defile our minds with the deception of his lies. His strategy is the same from the beginning: "Did God really say that?" (from Genesis 3:1).

But You are truth and Your truth shall prevail (John 14:6). Draw me more deeply into the truth of Your Word and Your Spirit. Let me be prepared to discern and diffuse the floodwaters of deception. Help me abide more deeply in You each day, rooted and grounded in Your teaching and Your truth. As I stand in You and You stand in me, I will not be overcome but I will overcome the deception of the deceiver by the grace of Your truth. In Jesus' name I pray, Amen.

Be encouraged today! In the Love of Jesus, *Tommy Hays*

Build a Firm Foundation*

"For no other foundation can anyone lay than that which is laid, which is Jesus Christ. If anyone's work which he has built on it endures, he will receive a reward" (1 Corinthians 3:11, 14).

"But he who heard and did nothing is like a man who built a house on the earth without a foundation, against which the stream beat vehemently; and immediately it fell. And the ruin of that house was great" (Luke 6:49).

First and foremost, Christ must be our foundation. Without a strong foundation in Christ, all of our efforts are futile to resist the storms of life. However, when we submit our will to that of Christ's we are able to build on a firm foundation. More than that, we will receive a reward for our labors.

The difficult part in submitting our will to Christ is that we have to die to ourselves. Maybe it's difficult, because we don't get the glory, or we aren't in complete control. We have to be willing to accept our rightful place with Christ first and our own wills and desires second. However, God is prodding us to go in this direction for our own good. 1 Corinthians 2:9 says: "Eye has not seen, nor ear heard, nor have entered into the heart of man the things which God has prepared for those who love Him." Furthermore, we can count on God; "for the foolishness of God is wiser than men, and the weakness of God is stronger than men" (1 Corinthians 1:25). Knowing these truths, let's be open to building a lasting foundation and building upon that foundation wisely.

All praise and glory be to God! *Mary Margaret Adams*

---

* The following devotional was written by Mary Margaret Adams.

Be still . . .*

On my run this morning, I noticed how rushed and distracted several people were as they hurried off to work. One person was backing out of his driveway onto a very busy street while talking on his cell phone. Another person almost hit me for the very same reason; he was on his cell phone and he ran a stop sign. I was crossing the road with my double-wide jogging stroller and had to sprint out of his way (not an easy feat with two toddlers on board).

At first, I was more than a little annoyed, wondering what people thought was so important that they had to swerve around a mom with two children in a stroller, but later my thoughts turned more to how distracted we all are when it comes to God. Earlier, I had considered skipping some of my devotionals. "Let's face it," I thought "my home is a complete disaster; heaps of laundry some folded and some not, two less than clean bathrooms, floors that resemble the out of doors more than the inside, and now there's a bird living up near the attic." While I pondered where I would start first, I heard God say "Be still, and know that I am God . . ." (Psalm 46:10). Although many of the things in our life are important (we all have responsibilities), what could be more important than quieting myself before God and hearing what He has to say to me today?

Thank you Lord for showing me the importance of quieting myself before You each day.

All praise and glory be to God! *Mary Margaret Adams*

---

* The following devotional was written by Mary Margaret Adams.

Look Up and Look Around

Good morning, Lord Jesus. I lift my eyes from myself and my world to behold You. Broaden my vision and fill my soul with the fullness of the glory of Your presence. ...

"But I tell you, look around you, and see how the fields are ripe for harvesting. The reaper is already receiving wages and is gathering fruit for eternal life, so that sower and reaper may rejoice together" (John 4:35-36).

I spent the last few days rejoicing together with my friends in the MorningStar Fellowship of Ministries. We gather once a year for a time of refreshing and encouragement from our various ministries and churches around the world. I love to hear the stories of what You are doing in the lives and ministries of others in so many different and unique settings. Some are sowing, others are reaping, and all are at work ministering Your grace of eternal life for the final harvest of souls from the fields of the earth.

Sometimes we can get so busy and focused on what You are doing in our midst that we forget to look up and look around in the fields of Your harvest far beyond our own lives, churches, or ministries. But when we do, our hearts are filled afresh with wonder and awe at Your power and grace. We are reminded again how blessed we are to live in this generation of great harvest and to labor in preparation for even greater harvests yet to come. The harvest of the end will touch the ends of the earth. "But the earth will be filled with the knowledge of the glory of the Lord, as the waters cover the sea" (Habakkuk 2:6).

Lord, keep freeing me from isolation and self-focus. Keep giving me a broader perspective, a kingdom perspective, that stretches my vision of Your glory to the ends of the earth. Let me be found faithful to do my part in my generation as I rejoice together in the faithfulness of my fellow laborers of Your harvest. In Jesus' name I pray, Amen.

Be encouraged today! In the Love of Jesus, *Tommy Hays*

A Mother's Heart

Good morning, Lord Jesus. Open my eyes to see You and open my ears to hear You as I watch and wait for the leading of Your Holy Spirit into the presence of my heavenly Father. ...

King Solomon was called to judge between two women who both claimed to be the mother of a newborn son. In the wisdom that You gave him, he tested their hearts to see which one's "compassion for her son burned within her." The one who was willing to surrender the child to the other woman, despite the pain of her sacrifice, rather than see her son harmed was the true mother. Solomon saw her mother's heart and honored her willingness to sacrifice all for the life of her son and decreed, "She is his mother" (1 Kings 3:16-28).

A mother's heart burns with compassion for her child and is willing to sacrifice all for the sake of fulfilling this highest calling. Many have rightly observed that to be a mother is the highest calling and hardest job of all. Yet a true mother can find fulfillment in nothing less. You have created them that way—with Your heart of compassion, Your mind of wisdom, and Your will of determination to sacrifice all for the sake of the lives entrusted to them. To see a mother's heart is to see the heart of God. "As a mother comforts her child, so I will comfort you" (Isaiah 66:13).

Today is both Mother's Day and my son Elijah's birthday. This seems very fitting to honor my wife Tricia on the day she gave birth to our son. She finds her fulfillment in the calling of motherhood. Nothing less would do. This day, we honor the mothers in our lives. And as we bless the mothers with honor, we receive the blessings of God in our lives and in our land (Exodus 20:12). Thank You Lord for the blessing of the mothers among us. We honor them as You honor them this day. In Jesus' name I pray, Amen.

Be encouraged today! In the Love of Jesus, *Tommy Hays*

Peace will Prevail

Good morning, Lord Jesus. Let the peace of Your presence fill my soul as I entrust my life and this day to You. ...

"The God of peace will shortly crush Satan under your feet. The grace of our Lord Jesus Christ be with you" (Romans 16:20).

It is the peace of Your presence in my soul that crushes the satanic power of fear and doubt, worry and stress, confusion and chaos. By Your grace, my enemy is defeated. But You have chosen in Your sovereignty and power to defeat him under my feet. He is defeated as I choose in obedience and faith by Your grace to stand in You and allow You to stand in me. He is crushed as I cast my burdens to You.

This is Your command that allows me to conquer: "Cast all you anxiety on Him, because He cares for you. Discipline yourselves; keep alert. Like a roaring lion your adversary the devil prowls around looking for someone to devour. Resist him, steadfast in your faith, for you know that your brothers and sisters in all the world are undergoing the same kind of suffering" (1 Peter 5:7-9). This is the peace of the power of Your presence that overcomes every strategy and scheme of the one who would steal my place of peace in You. You have done Your part to defeat him; and by Your grace, I must do my part to resist him. As I cast my burdens on You, Your peace will prevail. In Jesus' name I pray, Amen.

Be encouraged today! In the Love of Jesus, *Tommy Hays*

A Season of Graduation

Good morning, Lord Jesus. Help me humble myself to listen in the silence of surrender. And having listened, help me humble myself to obey. ...

"Jesus said to them, 'My food is to do the will of Him who sent Me and to complete His work.' Do you not say, 'Four months more, then comes the harvest'? But I tell you, look around you, and see how the fields are ripe for harvesting' " (John 4:34-35).

May is a season of graduation. Many are coming to the end of a journey of study and training, having brought to completion the work of preparation. It is a season of transition from equipping to releasing, from learning to doing, from listening to speaking, from waiting to advancing. It is time to advance in the will of the One who has prepared us to send us to accomplish our calling in our generation. Now comes the harvest.

We will continue to learn even as we advance. And at times we will advance the most as we are humbled by our mistakes and our need to learn more. But we must not fear to learn as we go, giving and receiving the grace of God through one another as we dare to risk failure in order to risk success. Success is to do the will of Him who sent me.

Graduation is the completion of one journey and the commencement of the next. As I humble myself before You and turn my face toward You, I will continue to advance "from one degree of glory to another"—Your glory being made manifest in my obedience to Your will and my faith in Your nature (2 Corinthians 3:18). You are always faithful to bring to completion all You have begun in me (Philippians 1:6). As You have been faithful in the preparation, so You will be faithful in the harvest. In Jesus' name I pray, Amen.

Be encouraged today! In the Love of Jesus, *Tommy Hays*

Learn to Discern

Good morning, Lord Jesus. Here I am Lord. Open my eyes to see; open my ears to hear; open my heart to receive. In the first moments of the morning, I narrow my focus to You alone. ...

"Do not quench the Spirit. Do not despise the words of prophets, but test everything; hold fast to what is good; abstain from every form of evil" (1 Thessalonians 5:19-22).

Holy Spirit, You are speaking to the church in these days. We are the church, individually and in the community of relationship with one another. Give us ears to hear "what the Spirit is saying to the churches" (Revelation 2:7, 11, 17, 29; 3:6, 13, 22). But teach us how to "test everything" while we "no not quench the Spirit" at the same time (1Thessalonians 5:4). Give us the faith to listen and the humility to submit everything we think we hear from You to the testing of the standard of the Word of God and the nature of God. Only through the process of judgment and discernment will we be able to determine what is good and what is evil, what we must hold fast to and what we must abstain from. In these days of ever-increasing spiritual activity, we must learn to walk in ever-increasing spiritual discernment. "Let the wise also hear and gain in learning, and the discerning acquire skill" (Proverbs 1:5). We acquire skill by looking to You in humility and faith in the challenges of obeying Your command to "test everything."

One of the gifts of the Spirit is "the discernment of spirits" (1 Corinthians 12:10). Not all spiritual activity in our lives and in the community of relationship with one another is the activity of the Holy Spirit. Not every spiritual voice we hear is the voice of the Holy Spirit. Our crafty enemy often "disguises himself as an angel of light" when his unholy spirits attempt to masquerade as the Holy Spirit to gain our trust and ensnare us in deception (2 Corinthians 11:14). So we need Your Word and we need Your Spirit; we need one another to help us learn to discern in both humility and faith.

You created us to long to be led by Your Spirit. "For all who are led by the Spirit of God are children of God" (Romans 8:14). Our enemy knows our nature and our longing, so he looks for ways to satisfy that longing with his deception. The answer is not to quit longing for Spiritual leading or to "despise the words of the prophets." The answer is to learn how to "test everything," to learn to discern. We have much to learn, but You are ready to teach us if we are willing to learn. We learn it by doing it, risking our mistakes, but trusting in Your grace. By Your grace, I'm willing to learn to discern. In Jesus' name I pray, Amen.

Be encouraged today! In the Love of Jesus, *Tommy Hays*

"Well Done, My son"

Good morning, Lord Jesus. Help me humble myself in the silence of surrender before You now—Father, Son, and Holy Ghost. ...

> *Draw me close and hold me tight,*
> *Take my life and make it right.*
> *Forgive my sins and heal my pain,*
> *Set me free from bonds of shame.*
> *Fill me up with Your Holy Spirit,*
> *Speak Your Word and let me hear it.*
> *Let me know that I am Yours,*
> *Whether peaceful seas or troubled shores.*
> *Help me to rest in Your steady hand,*
> *To rise in faith and take my stand.*
> *Teach me to trust and to obey,*
> *Give me Your words to speak and Your heart to pray.*
> *I offer my life a living sacrifice,*
> *I bring my flesh under Your holy knife.*
> *I have so far to go and so much to learn,*
> *But Your grace is sufficient at every turn.*
> *Make me more like You every day,*
> *Give me Your will and teach me Your ways.*
> *Cause Your thoughts to be my thoughts and Your desires mine,*
> *Help me respond more as You would every time.*
> *I need Your peace and seek Your joy,*
> *To need You alone and nothing more.*
> *Little by little and step by step,*
> *I'm growing up with Your Godly help.*
> *Don't let me give up and don't let me turn back,*
> *But keep seeking the things that will always last.*
> *I long for the day I see Your face,*
> *And know You as You are in the fullness of Your grace.*
> *I want to hear those words from the Holiest One,*
> *"Welcome home. Well done, My son."*

Thank You Lord for writing these words on my heart this morning. I offer them to You as my prayer this day. "His Lord said to him, 'Well done, good and faithful servant; you have been faithful over a few things, I will make you ruler over many things. Enter into the joy of your Lord' " (Matthew 25:23). I choose by Your grace to live my life to please my Lord. Keep putting that desire in my heart and keep giving me the grace to live it out. Keep forgiving me when I fail, keep lifting me up when I fall. Keep turning my heart toward my home in You. In Jesus' name I pray, Amen.

Be encouraged today! In the Love of Jesus, *Tommy Hays*

Relationship is Risky

Good morning, Lord Jesus. I open my heart to You as widely as I can—a little more today than yesterday, a little more tomorrow than today—in this life-long journey of growing in the grace of trust and love. ...

"I therefore, the prisoner in the Lord, beg you to lead a life worthy of the calling to which you have been called, with all humility and gentleness, with patience, bearing with one another in love, making every effort to maintain the unity of the Spirit in the bond of peace" (Ephesians 3:1-3).

Relationship is risky and unity requires effort. The bond of peace must be maintained. To love one another means we must work at bearing with one another. None of this comes easy; none of this comes without deliberate choices and committed effort. But this is our calling and this is our life in the Lord. As You said long ago, "This is My commandment, that you love one another as I have loved you.... I am giving you these commands so that you may love one another" (John 15:12-17).

Without love, without risking our hearts in relationship despite all the struggles and disappointments, woundedness and pain of making ourselves vulnerable to one another, there is no true unity of the Spirit and no true bond of peace. Anything else is a shallow illusion of the family of faith. But You have given us Your Holy Spirit to lead us and empower us by Your grace to live out our lives in the community of relationship with one another. And You have given us some keys to live this life that would be impossible without Your grace—humility, gentleness, and patience.

These do not come easily either. Nor were they intended to. They must be worked into our souls through the risks of relationship. But the more we learn to use these keys and walk in this nature, the more rich and true our relationships will become. These are the bonds of unity that cannot be broken. Though it's risky, though it can be painful, keep working Your nature into my nature. Keep calling me to risk loving others as You have loved me. Keep reminding me that the relationship is worth the risk. In Jesus' name I pray, Amen.

Be encouraged today! In the Love of Jesus, *Tommy Hays*

"A Threefold Cord"

Good morning, Lord Jesus. Bind my heart with Your heart, my mind with Your mind, my spirit with Your Spirit in the communion of prayer. ...

"Two are better than one, because they have a good reward for their toil. For if they fall, one will lift up the other; but woe to one who is alone and falls and does not have another to help. Again, if two lie together, they keep warm; but how can one keep warm alone? And though one might prevail against another, two will withstand one. A threefold cord is not quickly broken" (Ecclesiastes 4:9-12).

You have been showing me an image in my spirit this past week. I saw it again last night at The Fountain. It is the image of a climbing rope—a thick rope woven together with many strands that we had in our gym in junior high school.   It would be almost impossible to climb a smaller rope of only one strand, but when the cords of rope are bound together, there is a multiplication of strength and stability that comes.

We need one another. We need the strength and stability that comes when we allow ourselves to be bonded together—together with You and together with one another. A threefold cord is not quickly broken. The sum is greater than the parts. There is a synergy of relationship. You are calling us to climb higher in this season, but there are heights of our calling and destiny we can only reach together. Empower us to be flexible enough and humble enough to be joined together in the strength of Your bonds. "Woe to one who is alone." But blessed are they who are strengthened in the bonds of relationship in You and with one another. As Father, Son, and Holy Spirit, You are a threefold cord. As we are bonded to You and one another, so are we. Give me the wisdom and grace, the humility and flexibility, to be bonded together with You and with others in the threefold cord of Your strength. In Jesus' name I pray, Amen.

Be encouraged today! In the Love of Jesus, *Tommy Hays*

Traveling to meet the Trinity

Good morning, Lord Jesus. I love You Lord, and I come to You in these moments of the morning to linger with You in Your presence alone. ...

"Now Moses used to take the tent and pitch it outside the camp, far off from the camp; he called it the tent of meeting. And everyone who sought the Lord would go out to the tent of meeting, which was outside the camp" (Exodus 33:7).

I'll be traveling far off from the camp today. My pastor and I will travel with a small team to London for a leadership conference on evangelism and small group community life through the Alpha Course. We will meet with leaders and learners from many nations to share experiences and gain insights of reaching the lost and bringing them into lasting relationships in the bonds of community. But mostly, I will be coming to meet with You. Even the name of the church You have used to birth and mature the Alpha Course which will be hosting our conference reminds me of the goal of our travels—Holy Trinity Brompton. It is not man but the Holy Trinity I'm coming to see. It's the Father, Son, and Holy Spirit I'm coming to meet.

You are always with us and You never leave us. But sometimes we need to come outside the camp of our everyday lives and responsibilities to seek Your face and listen for Your voice with renewed focus. Sometimes it helps to get far off for a little while to encounter You again in a fresh way. I pray for a fresh encounter of Your presence as I come outside the camp to meet with You this week. In Jesus' name I pray, Amen.

Be encouraged today! In the Love of Jesus, *Tommy Hays*

Christk; Our Refuge and Strength*

My first thoughts of the day were, "Help me Lord Jesus!" Thankfully, my second thoughts were from Psalm 46; "God is our refuge and strength, a very present help in trouble" (Psalm 46:1). And, "the Lord of Hosts is with us; the God of Jacob is our refuge" (Psalm 46: 7). At first, I wonder if I can do the things God wants me to do today. Then I hear God telling me that I can *if* I allow Him to help me.

Perhaps this is how some of you feel today. It is day one of week one. We want to do God's will. We want to be more positive in our thoughts and actions. We want to present ourselves as living sacrifices to God (see Romans 12:1-2). Our expectations are high, but by 11 AM, I for one, am already feeling tempted to give up or give in. I'm hopeful, yet unsure.

But as I turn to God in prayer, He shows me that I can accomplish His will! I actually feel the stress, anxiety, and expectations fading and being replaced by the peace of knowing that He has it all covered. He knows everything that will or will not happen today and He will give me the strength to see the day through. An old hymn comes to mind: We Shall Not Be Moved (V. O. Fossett).

> Glory hallelujah, I shall not be moved;
> Anchored in Jehovah, I shall not be moved;
> Just like a tree that's planted by the waters,
> I shall not be moved.
>
> I shall not be, I shall not be moved,
> I shall not be, I shall not be moved;
> Just like a tree that's planted by the waters,
> I shall not be moved.
>
> In his love abiding, I shall not be moved;
> And in Him confiding, I shall not be moved;
> I shall not be, I shall not be moved,
> I shall not be, I shall not be moved;
> Just like a tree that's planted by the waters,
> I shall not be moved.
>
> Tho all hell assail me, I shall not be moved;
> Jesus will not fail me, I shall not be moved;
> I shall not be, I shall not be moved,
> I shall not be, I shall not be moved;

---

* The following devotional was written by Mary Margaret Adams.

Just like a tree that's planted by the waters,
I shall not be moved.

Tho the tempest rages, I shall not be moved;
On the Rock of Ages, I shall not be moved;
I shall not be, I shall not be moved,
I shall not be, I shall not be moved;
Just like a tree that's planted by the waters,
I shall not be moved.

All praise and glory be to God! *Mary Margaret Adams*

Maxwell*

"The Lord is close to the brokenhearted; He rescues those whose spirits are crushed" (Psalm 34:18).

Today is a very sad day for my family. Our family dog, Maxwell passed away. He was the sweetest little Cairn terrier and he will be greatly missed. At this particular moment, we cannot even imagine life without him. He went everywhere with us and did everything with us. The house feels so lonely and sad without him, and yet, there are so many reminders of him! The next several days will be bittersweet; we will be reminded of him countless times, yet we will no longer see him while we are here on earth.

Maxwell fell ill a few months ago with kidney disease. No one knew why he had suddenly become ill; it was unexpected for a dog his age. We were shocked and deeply saddened that he would not be with us as long as we had hoped.

On one particular day, I was out for a run when I felt God call me to pray for my little dog. My response was "I can't Lord, because I know he will be gone soon and I can't bear to face the possibility of never seeing him again." You see, I really didn't know what would happen to Maxwell after he left this earth. My only hope was a verse in Ecclesiastes chapter 4 where the wisest man on earth said: "Who knows whether the spirit of the sons of men goes upward, and whether the spirit of the animal goes downward to the earth?"

I went ahead though and prayed for my dog. It was painful, yet soothing; I was finally dealing with my sadness. During my prayer, God spoke to me; He told me to go home and read Psalm 36:6. I thought I was surely going crazy; since when did God give us exact numbers in our heads? However, I ran straight home and found the verse. It goes as follows: "Your righteousness is like the mighty mountains, your judgments are like the great deep; you save humans and animals alike, O Lord."

God clearly spoke these words into my heart. Like He had done on so many other occasions, God told me that He had it all covered; He was going to take care of Maxwell. From that point on, I knew I could put Maxwell in God's hands and we all would be taken care of.

Today, several weeks later, as we said goodbye to Maxwell, I had the peace of knowing that God sees everything and knew all the days of Maxwell's life;

---

* The following devotional was written by Mary Margaret Adams.

even as He knows mine. Maxwell had a purpose and a place and so do I. And, the Lord will be near to us all.

I will end with Psalm 139:1-18.

> O Lord, you have searched me and know me.
> You know when I sit down and when I rise up;
> You discern my thoughts from far away.
> You search out my path and my lying down,
> and are acquainted with all of my ways.
> Even before a word is on my tongue,
> O Lord, You know it completely.
> You hem me in, behind and before,
> And lay Your hand upon me.
> Such knowledge is too wonderful for me;
> It is so high that I cannot attain it.
> Where can I go from Your spirit?
> Or where can I flee from Your presence?
> If I ascend to Heaven, You are there;
> If I make my bed in Sheol, You are there.
> If I take the wings of the morning
> And settle at the farthest limits of the sea,
> Even there Your hand shall lead me,
> And Your right hand shall hold me fast.
> If I say 'surely the darkness shall cover me,
> And the light around me become night,'
> Even the darkness is not dark to You;
> And the night is as bright as the day,
> For darkness is as light to You.
> For it was You who formed my inward parts;
> You knit me together in my mother's womb.
> I praise You for I am fearfully and wonderfully made.
> Wonderful are Your works; that I know very well.
> My frame was not hidden from You,
> When I was being made in secret,
> Intricately woven in the depths of the earth.
> Your eyes beheld my unformed substance.
> In Your book were written all the days that were formed for me,
> When none of them as yet existed.
> How weighty to me are Your thoughts, O God!
> How vast is the sum of them!
> I try to count them—they are more than the sand;
> I come to the end—I am still with You.

All praise and glory be to God! *Mary Margaret Adams*

Cast your cares on Christ*

We are all miserable, because Maxwell is gone. Even Calvin (not even two) is asking about the doggie. He wanted to go back to the vet this morning to pick up Maxwell. Then he got out Maxwell's toy and squeaked it several times to try to get Maxwell to come.

I don't feel like I have any energy to deal with this, although I already cleaned out a couple of closets this morning. More than anything, I need to cast my cares onto Christ. 1 Peter 5:6-7 says: "Therefore humble yourselves under the mighty hand of God, that He may exalt you in due time, casting all your care upon Him, for He cares for you."

No matter how big or small our particular trials may seem today, we know we can cast all our cares on Christ and He will love and sustain us through our trials. I imagine that my heart will ache for some time over Maxwell; he was such a soothing and comforting little dog. Now more than ever, I want to lean on Christ to get me through this time of grief.

I am also reminded of 2 Corinthians 3-4 which says: "Blessed be the God and Father of our Lord Jesus Christ, the Father of mercies and God of all comfort, who comforts us in all our tribulation, that we may be able to comfort those who are in any trouble, with the comfort with which we ourselves are comforted by God." Not only will God comfort us, but he will use all of our sufferings (big or small) for good; especially to help others who may also be suffering or in trouble. Knowing this, I can persist.

All praise and glory be to God! *Mary Margaret Adams*

---

* The following devotional was written by Mary Margaret Adams.

Tears in a Bottle[*]

I have been filled with anxiety and struggling with a number of things lately. This morning, I flopped down, face first onto my bed. I said, "Lord, I really need help today. I need to know that someone really sees me. I can't handle all of this stuff on my own."

I felt God prompt me to read Psalm 56. Instantly, my eyes landed on the following verse!

"You number my wanderings; put my tears into Your bottle; are they not in Your book?" It goes on to say, "When I cry out to You, then my enemies will turn back; this I know, because God is for me." The psalm ends with; "For You have delivered my soul from death. Have You not kept my feet from falling, that I may walk before God in the light of the living?"

Isn't it good to know that God really sees us? More than that, He is for us! And, He will protect our souls from evil and uphold us and provide a wonderful future for us with Him! WOW! That's much beyond what I had hoped for today!

Thank you Lord Jesus for seeing me and knowing me; knowing where I have been and what I am moving towards. Thank You for not only knowing the "bad," but also knowing the ways I have pressed through to become more like you.

"Now, To Him who is able to do exceedingly abundantly above all that we ask or think, according to the power that works in us, to Him be glory in the church by Jesus Christ to all generations, forever and ever. Amen" (Ephesians 3:20-21).

All praise and glory be to God! *Mary Margaret Adams*

---

[*] The following devotional was written by Mary Margaret Adams.

There is a time for everything . . .*

Ecclesiastes 3:1-8 says; "To everything there is a season, a time for every purpose under heaven:"

A time to be born,
And a time to die;
A time to plant,
And a time to pluck what is planted;
A time to kill,
And a time to heal;
A time to break down,
And a time to build up;
A time to weep,
And a time to laugh;
A time to mourn,
And a time to dance;
A time to cast away stones,
And a time to gather stones;
A time to embrace,
And a time to refrain from embracing;
A time to gain,
And a time to lose;
A time to keep,
And a time to throw away;
A time to tear,
And a time to sew;
A time to keep silence,
And a time to speak;
A time to love,
And a time to hate;
A time of war,
And a time of peace.

Have you ever thought about the season of your life? Is God speaking to you today about a particular time?

For some of us, it is definitely a time to heal and to throw away or cast off the things that have been hindering us in our walk with Christ. Today, I feel God calling me to heal, throw away the things that hinder me, and to keep silence (not stir up strife with negative thoughts and words). The only way I can accomplish this is to turn to Christ for help. God has brought to my mind Hebrews 12: 1-2 to be my focus and my prayer:

---

* The following devotional was written by Mary Margaret Adams.

"Therefore we also, since we are surrounded by so great a cloud of witnesses, let us lay aside every weight, and the sin that so easily ensnares us, and let us run with endurance the race that is set before us, looking unto Jesus, the author and finisher of our faith, who for the joy that was set before Him, endured the cross, despising the shame, and has sat down at the right hand of the throne of God."

May this be your prayer as well!

All praise and glory be to God! *Mary Margaret Adams*

Perfection[*]

Have you ever wondered what it would be like to be perfect? What do you think it would be like living around so many "flawed" individuals? What would you feel like doing or saying?

Christ was perfect and full of wisdom, yet He was "full of love and unfailing faithfulness" toward us (John 1:14). Imagine that? John 3:17 tells us that: "God sent His son into the world not to judge the world, but to save the world through Him. There is no judgment against anyone who believes in Him." Rather than judging others, Christ showed them the way, through his words and actions.

Have you ever wondered what God's perfect wisdom looks like? James 3:17-18 gives us some insight into the wisdom of God. It says, "But this wisdom from above is first of all pure. It is also peace loving, gentle at all times, and willing to yield to others. It is full of mercy and good deeds. It shows no favoritism and is always sincere. And those who are peacemakers will plant seeds of peace and reap a harvest of righteousness."

Christ is our perfect example. We are called to be like Him. This means refraining from judgment and gaining the kind of wisdom that allows us to be peace loving, gentle, yielding, full of mercy and good deeds, never showing favoritism and always being sincere toward others.

WOW! How does this square with your original thoughts about perfection? Is this the kind of wisdom and perfection we seek after?

All praise and glory be to God! *Mary Margaret Adams*

---

[*] The following devotional was written by Mary Margaret Adams.

Love covers over[*]

I received an unwanted and harsh comment from someone today and before I knew it, I was on a downward spiral of negative thinking. Although I hadn't retaliated, my own anger had stirred up enough internal strife to completely sour my mood and my day. It took a major mental readjustment before I could do what God wanted me to do: release my anger to Him and pray for the other person and for myself!

God brought a couple of verses to my mind. First, Proverbs 10:12: "Hatred stirs up strife, but love covers all sins." And second, 1 Peter 4:8: "And above all things have fervent love for one another, for 'love will cover a multitude of sins.'"

As difficult as it is for us to do at times, we are called to turn from hatred and anger toward love. This does NOT mean that we avoid the truth about situations or our feelings, but that we do not dwell to the point of causing strife and bringing grief on ourselves, others, and God. The Bible tells us: "Be angry, and do not sin" (Ephesians 4:26); and "Abhor what is evil. Cling to what is good" (Romans 12:9). However, the Bible also says: "do not let the sun go down on your wrath" (Ephesians 4:26). Once we have acknowledged a wrongdoing of some sort, it is best to put it behind us quickly. And, as much as we are able, we are called to love, forgive, and pray for others.

Perhaps Ephesians 4:30-32 sums it up best: "And do not grieve the Holy Spirit of God, by whom you were sealed for the day of redemption. Let all bitterness, wrath, anger, clamor, and evil speaking be put away from you, with all malice. And be kind to one another, tenderhearted, forgiving one another, even as God in Christ forgave you."

All praise and glory be to God! *Mary Margaret Adams*

---

[*] The following devotional was written by Mary Margaret Adams.

"I am the Alpha"

Good morning, Lord Jesus. It's good to be home and find the familiar place where I settle in for my morning moments with You—to seek Your face and listen for Your voice, to follow the leading of Your Spirit as I begin my day with You. ...

" 'I am the Alpha and the Omega,' says the Lord God, who is and who was and who is to come, the Almighty" (Revelation 1:8).

I'm still processing all I experienced in London last week with my pastor and a small team of leaders from our church at the International Alpha Conference. We worshiped and prayed, learned and listened along with delegates from over seventy nations of the one hundred and fifty nations around the world now using the Alpha Course as a means of evangelism and discipleship—a means of providing a safe place for those seeking God in any culture to ask their questions and find the One who is the answer.

You are the Alpha. And living life in You is the course You have set for our lives. You created every heart with a hunger for relationship with You, and we will never be satisfied and never be fulfilled apart from a living relationship with You. But all who seek You will find You (Jeremiah 29:13).

The Alpha Course is a way for people who don't know You, but sense a need to know God, to come and ask their questions, express their frustrations, and begin to experience the kindness of the community of Christ willing to listen to their questions and walk with them in the journey. What an eternal blessing it is for them and for us to see the hunger of their hearts satisfied by the One who is "the Bread of Life" (John 6:35). Thank You for letting me see more of the breadth of this movement that is touching the nations of the earth across all barriers of denominations and traditions—Protestant, Catholic, Orthodox—because You are drawing our eyes to You. You are our Alpha and our Omega, the beginning and the end of all we need and all we were created to believe and to receive. In Jesus' name I pray, Amen.

Be encouraged today! In the Love of Jesus, *Tommy Hays*

In the Steps of Heroes

Good morning, Lord Jesus. I've come to worship You with the offerings of my time and the devotion of my heart. ...

"Be imitators of me, as I am of Christ" (1 Corinthians 11:1).

On May 24, 1738 John Wesley went to the evening worship service at St. Paul's Anglican Cathedral in London, and then walked down to a prayer meeting on Aldersgate Street in London. There his heart was "strangely warmed" as he recorded in his journal that day. A movement was birthed in that divine encounter with the living God, which would become a spiritual and cultural transformation of England, then the frontiers of America, and ultimately the world. Even the secular historians acknowledge that moment as a wellspring of great revival. Those who followed Wesley in this movement were mocked as "Methodists" for their radical and methodical devotion to Christ in daily worship, prayer, and service. Wesley often explained those whose hearts were strangely warmed as his in light of this Scripture: "And hope maketh not ashamed; because the love of God is shed abroad in our hearts by the Holy Ghost which is given unto us" (Romans 5:5, KJV).

On May 24th last week, we went to that same evening service at St. Paul's and followed the steps of John Wesley down Aldersgate Street. The actual place of the historic prayer meeting no longer stands—destroyed by Hitler's campaign of terror against the innocent civilians of London in World War II. But the spirit of revival remains, burning brightly in the spirit of all whose hearts are strangely warmed by the power and presence of Your Holy Spirit. You are still meeting each of us in the divine encounters that transform our lives and the world around each of us who follow after You. Let the love of God be shed abroad in my heart again this day. Encourage me and inspire me to follow those who follow You, to imitate those who imitate You. Let me look to the example and follow in the steps of Your heroes of the faith (1 Peter 2:21). As I do, let my heart be strangely warmed every day by Your love and presence and power. In Jesus' name I pray.

Be encouraged today! In the Love of Jesus, *Tommy Hays*

The Stump and the Shoot

Good morning, Lord Jesus. Fill me afresh with the life of Your Spirit as I open my heart and spirit to You in worship and prayer. ...

"A shoot shall come out from the stump of Jesse, and a branch shall grow out of his roots. The Spirit of the Lord shall rest on him, the Spirit of wisdom and understanding, the Spirit of counsel and might, the Spirit of knowledge and the fear of the Lord" (Isaiah 11:1-2).

As we gathered each day for worship and teaching in the sanctuary of Holy Trinity Brompton in London last week, I was struck by the marriage of ancient and modern. We were surrounded by centuries-old gothic arches, stained glass, and organ pipes; but spiritual life was teaming from every corner from casually-clad worshippers, led by guitars and drums. An ornately carved pulpit with steps leading high above us stood off to the side with the marble baptistery and other antique religious artifacts stacked underneath to make room for expressive worship and extensive times of prayer ministry following the messages.

Across England, most of the old churches are no longer even churches, being used for museums and remodeled as bookstores, boutiques, and bars—drying up and falling away like the lingering stump of a felled tree. As in so many of the main-line traditions and ritualistic religion without living relationships, the generations begin to turn away from church as a relic of the past and turn to culture to try to find the answers to the emptiness of their souls. But You began breathing Your Spirit of Life into the dry bones (Ezekiel 37:1-6). You began speaking to the mountains of lifeless religion and dying tradition to cast them into the sea (Mark 11:23). You began to call forth a fountain to spring up and flow out with Your Living Water to touch the nations (Joel 3:18). Out of the dead and decaying stump rose a tender shoot of new life in Your Spirit. Through the Alpha Course You birthed in this church, generations were drawn back to the ancient wells of truth in welcoming relationships with the safety to ask hard questions and express honest ideas. This movement is now flowing to the nations in every stream and tradition of Your Church as part of Your renewal of resurrection life.

Lord, continue to awake Your New Life in me. Continue to put Your axe to the root of what is dead in me and my church and my tradition, pruning the branches of what bears no fruit so that the life of Your Spirit may draw the hearts of this generation to You. Deliver us from pride and fear and renew us with courage and life. Let this tender shoot rise up from the ancient stump into a Tree of Life that bears fruit for the glory of Your name. In Jesus' name I pray, Amen.

Be encouraged today! In the Love of Jesus, *Tommy Hays*

Preparation for Pentecost

Good morning, Lord Jesus. I watch and wait for the coming of Your Spirit afresh in my heart again today. You are always with me, always within me, but in these moments of deliberate surrender, I am more with You. Help me decrease as You increase more and more each day. ...

"While staying with them, He ordered them not to leave Jerusalem, but to wait there for the promise of the Father. 'This,' He said, 'is what you have heard from Me; for John baptized with water but you will be baptized with the Holy Spirit not many days from now' " (Acts 1:4-5).

There are fifty days of preparation from Passover to Pentecost. These are days of preparation in the seasons of our heart in faith from the crucifixion of our flesh, the cleansing of the blood of the Lamb, and the resurrection of new life at Easter until the fresh filling and baptism of the Holy Spirit at Pentecost. It speaks of the life-long process of spiritual transformation— being sanctified in spirit, soul, and body (1 Thessalonians 5:23). We must continue to decrease as You continue to increase in every area of our lives (John 3:30). As we are continually emptied of ourselves, You are continually filling us with You—baptizing us, immersing us, saturating us in the fullness of Your Holy Spirit to transform us into Your holy nature layer by layer, step by step, "from one degree of glory to another; for this comes from the Lord, the Spirit" (2 Corinthians 3:18).

This coming Sunday, we will join the body of Christ throughout the earth to celebrate the day of Pentecost. Again this year, there is also a call going out to the nations for a Global Day of Prayer. You will be glorified in our prayer and worship so that on this Pentecost Sunday "the earth will be filled with the knowledge of the glory of the Lord, as the waters cover the sea" (Habakkuk 2:14).

But there is a preparation before Pentecost. You continue to call Your disciples "to wait for the promise of the Father." There is something in the waiting that causes us to focus on the One we are waiting for, the One who comes to baptize us with His Holy Spirit not many days from now. In the watching and the waiting, we begin to hunger and thirst in growing anticipation for a fresh encounter of Your living presence where we "may be filled with all the fullness of God" (Ephesians 3:19).

Your first disciples heeded Your call and obeyed Your command. They pulled away from the labors of life and ministry, "constantly devoting themselves to prayer" (Acts 1:14). Prayer is the preparation for Pentecost. Watching and waiting in constant devotion is the attitude of heart You long to fill with the fullness of Your Spirit. Let me sense Your leading and obey

Your commands for the ways You are calling me to watch and wait in constant devotion for a deeper baptism of Your Holy Spirit in my life.

"When the day of Pentecost had come, they were all together in one place. And suddenly from heaven there came a sound like the rush of a violent wind, and it filled the entire house where they were sitting. Divided tongues, as of fire, appeared among them, and a tongue rested on each of them. All of them were filled with the Holy Spirit and began to speak in other languages, as the Spirit gave them ability" (Acts 2:1-4).

On Sunday, let Your people who are called by Your name throughout the earth gather "together in one place"—the place of prayer, the place of surrender, the place of hungering and thirsting for more of You, more of Your nature, more of the fullness of Your presence and power in our lives. "Blessed are those who hunger and thirst for righteousness, for they will be filled" (Matthew 5:6). Let Your mighty rushing Wind come set our hearts ablaze with the Fire of Your Spirit 'til we run out of our own words to praise Your holy name! In Jesus' name I pray, Amen.

Be encouraged today! In the Love of Jesus, *Tommy Hays*

The Omen of 666

Good morning, Lord Jesus. Let the truth and light of Your Holy Spirit shine in my soul. Bind back the darkness and deception of these days and open my eyes to see the One who is the Truth. By Your grace, You are my Way, my Truth, and my Life. ...

"False christs and false prophets will appear and produce signs and omens, to lead astray, if possible, the elect. But be alert; I have already told you everything. But in those days, after that suffering, the sun will be darkened, and the moon will not give its light, and the stars will be falling from heaven, and the powers in the heavens will be shaken. Then they will see 'the Son of Man coming in clouds' with great power and glory. Then He will send out the angels, and gather His elect from the four winds, from the ends of the earth to the ends of heaven" (Mark 13:22-27).

Last week, all the famous "double-decker" buses in London we saw had advertisements pasted on their sides for the movie coming out on 6-6-06 called "The Omen." It is an obvious reference to the antichrist and the mark of the beast "who performs great signs" and "deceives those who dwell on the earth" (Revelation 13:11-18, NKJV). "Let him who has understanding calculate the number of the beast, for it is the number of a man: His number is 666" (verse 13:18). He comes looking "like a lamb" but speaking "like a dragon" (verse 13:11). But You have warned us to hold fast to what is true, to test everything against the truth of Your Word and Your Spirit. "Beware of false prophets, who come to you in sheep's clothing but inwardly are ravenous wolves. You will know them by their fruits" (Matthew 7:15-16).

The enemy of our souls "is a liar and the father of lies" (John 8:44). His fruit is doubt and unbelief, confusion and fear. He is a counterfeiter of the truth. The movies and books in the media of our day are flooded with deception and distortion of the truth. "The DaVinci Code" book and movie present as facts a litany of outrageous lies easily contradicted by even the secular, historical record; yet the faith of many is being shaken by the false appearance of objectivity and supposed revelation of hidden conspiracy. "The Gospel of Judas" has surfaced as an ancient document but also an ancient distortion of the truth in line with the Gnostic philosophies that were asserted in contradiction to the truth of the Gospel. These are days of relentless and accelerating deception. "Then from his mouth the serpent poured water like a river after the woman, to sweep her away with the flood" (Revelation 12:15).

But Your truth will prevail over every counterfeit and deception for those who choose to seek Your face and stand firm in Your Word by Your grace.

"When the enemy comes in like a flood, the Spirit of the Lord will lift up a standard against him" (Isaiah 59:19, NKJV). A counterfeit only has significance because it is a counterfeit of what is real. There are false signs and wonders because there are true signs and wonders. There are false christs and prophets because there is a true Christ and His true prophets. "And many false prophets will arise and lead many astray. And because of the increase of lawlessness, the love of many will grow cold. But the one who endures to the end will be saved" (Mathew 24:11-13).

These are exciting days! The seeds of truth and deception, of good and evil, have grown into maturity for the time of harvest (Matthew 13:36-43). Lord, give me grace to stand firm in the faith. Give me grace to endure to the end. Let the banner of Your cross, the standard of Your Word, and the power of Your Spirit be the true omens of our day. In Jesus' name I pray, Amen.

Be encouraged today! In the Love of Jesus, *Tommy Hays*

Joy in His Presence*

I have been thinking about death a lot lately: not a very cheerful topic. I wondered one day if there really was a Heaven and for several days now, what it would really be like to meet God. In fact, I just wrote a friend not long ago and said I wasn't sure I was looking forward to Heaven, because I just couldn't imagine God being pleased to see me up there!

Somehow I have the faith to believe in Heaven and the work of the cross, but I still can't believe that God would be happy to see me there one day! Common sense might suggest that if God didn't want me in Heaven, He certainly could put me someplace else! So, I decided I should live a very long time, because facing an angry God didn't sound very appealing to me!

Today, I felt very confused about God in general and decided I should read the Bible. I flipped open to Acts and this was what I read!

"For David said concerning Him: 'I foresaw the Lord always before my face, for He is at my right hand, that I may not be shaken. Therefore my heart rejoiced, and my tongue was glad; moreover my flesh also will rest in hope. For You will not leave my soul in Hades, nor will You allow Your Holy One to see corruption. You have made known to me the ways of life; You will make me full of joy in Your presence'" (Acts 2:25-28).

This passage just sums it all up for me! First, the Lord is always before my face and He walks with me. Second, the Lord strengthens me and redeems my life completely. Third, Christ came to earth and was our example and the assurance that we will one day see Heaven. Finally, when we meet God one day, He will make us full of joy in His presence. Not fear, disappointment, or sadness, but joy!

All Praise and Glory be to God! *Mary Margaret Adams*

---

* The following devotional was written by Mary Margaret Adams.

I will not forget you[*]

"Can a woman forget her nursing child, and not have compassion on the son of her womb? Surely they may forget, yet I will not forget you. See, I have inscribed you on the palms of My hands" (Isaiah 49:15-16).

There are times when I feel like the whole world is moving, but I'm just standing still. I cannot help feeling small and rather ill equipped and disappointed by the fact that I am not really accomplishing much with my life. I suppose today was one of those days; I am ill with an infection and unable to complete even the smallest tasks. While every one and every thing around me is bustling with activity; I am simply strolling down the street pushing my two children. When I stop to ask God what happened, His response is: "I will not forget you" (Isaiah 49:15-16).

I am not lost, alone, or lacking direction. In the whirlwind of activity, God hasn't forgotten about me. Jeremiah 29:11 says: "For I know the thoughts that I think toward you, says the Lord, thoughts of peace and not of evil, to give you a future and a hope." Furthermore, Ephesians 2: 10 says: "For we are His workmanship, created in Christ Jesus for good works, which God prepared beforehand that we should walk in them."

Today, let's be encouraged by the truth that God thinks good thoughts toward us, has a future and a hope planned for us in advance, which includes that of good works, and that He will never forget us.

All praise and glory be to God! *Mary Margaret Adams*

---

[*] The following devotional was written by Mary Margaret Adams.

Godly Discipline*

". . . do not despise the chastening of the Lord, Nor detest His correction; For whom the Lord loves, He corrects, Just as a father the son in whom he delights" (Proverbs 3:11-12).

Have you ever received what you knew was "Godly" discipline from someone? Today, I was cruising along and wham! I received one hardy, well deserved rebuke from someone who knows me well. It was very painful, yet for perhaps one of the very first times in my life, quickly healing. Instead of deflecting, running, or striking back, I was silent (I never knew that response was even within my repertoire of responses). I sat there and took what I initially thought was my "punishment." However, something strange happened. I felt God speaking to me loud and clear that this particular event would be cleansing.

Later, I reflected on what had happened. I felt lead to read through most of Proverbs. I came across three really pertinent verses:

"Blows that hurt, cleanse away evil, as do stripes the inner depths of the heart" (Proverbs 20:30).

"Poverty and shame will come to him who disdains correction, but he who regards a rebuke will be honored" (Proverbs 13:18).

"The name of the Lord is a strong tower; the righteous run to it and are safe" (Proverbs 18:10).

God spoke three things to me. First, some painful events are God orchestrated and although they may feel like destructive "blows," they are actually positive events that God uses to cleanse us of evil. Second, I tend to think of discipline or a rebuke as a negative and shameful event which I should try to avoid at all costs, but God's word says the opposite! When I acknowledge and take in a God given rebuke, I will receive honor, not shame. And, finally, no matter what, I can always run to God for safety; sometimes we need that even though we have received "Godly" discipline.

All praise and glory be to God! *Mary Margaret Adams*

---

* The following devotional was written by Mary Margaret Adams.

Away with You

Good morning, Lord Jesus. I have come away from my world for a couple of weeks of vacation, but I don't want to come away from You. Though my mornings may start a little later, I still want to start them with You. ...

"Where can I go from Your Spirit? Or where can I flee from Your presence? If I ascend to heaven, You are there; if I make my bed in Sheol, You are there. If I take the wings of the morning and settle in the farthest limits of the sea, even there Your hand shall lead me, and Your right hand shall hold me fast" (Psalm 139:7-10).

Wherever I go, You are there.   And in a truth that is beyond my comprehension, You are there waiting for me. You are there waiting for each of us to acknowledge Your presence and welcome Your life into our lives. The moment I lift my face to Your glory and open my heart to Your Spirit in worship and prayer, You are there. You have been there all along, but I come to know that truth more surely as I consciously and deliberately direct my thoughts to know and acknowledge Your presence with me.

It's not getting away from work and daily responsibilities on vacation that will bring me the deepest rest. It's having a little more time to linger in Your presence and look more deeply into Your glory that will renew me and refresh me to return home in a fresh power of Your Spirit. As You said to Moses, "My presence will go with you, and I will give you rest" (Exodus 33:14). The last thing I did at "work" was to preach and pray on Pentecost Sunday for all of us to be filled afresh with Your Holy Spirit. Now You are answering my prayers as I have a little more time to pursue Your presence. In Jesus' name I pray, Amen.

Be encouraged today! In the Love of Jesus. *Tommy Hays*

Acceptance*

Several years ago, I got a job working in the credit department of a bank. It was a prestigious job for me; I didn't have a college education at the time and I suppose, not much of a bright future ahead.

On day two of my job, I realized that I was completely under-qualified, but rather than focusing on my grave weaknesses, I worked as hard as ever. I was determined to learn as I went and, hopefully, keep my job.

I had two main duties at the bank. One was to answer all of the incoming calls and direct the majority of the callers to the correct department. There were ten lines on my phone. From the minute the bank opened up, three were constantly lit. If I failed to answer all of the lines within two minutes, the calls would bounce over to the vice president of the bank and you can only imagine how badly I did NOT want that to happen.

When I wasn't frantically answering the phone (and trying to sound pleasant), I was expected to type endless pages of important documents. One error meant I had to redo the entire job, and no, I wasn't allowed to "save" anything.

Most frustrating of all, I wasn't allowed to work late or during breaks. I would sit there during a fifteen minute break wondering how many more piles of papers were hitting my in-box.

By the end of the first two weeks, something amazing happened! I actually had a good day! I typed with fewer mistakes! I answered and transferred calls more smoothly. My in-box was almost empty! I couldn't wait to tell my fiancé (now my husband) that I could do it! I could actually do this job!

However, just before the day ended, I was called into the vice president's office to sign something. I must have looked confused or asked what it was and I will never forget her answer. "As if it isn't obvious enough, we have to let you go. It's painful for me to watch someone work so hard and fail."

Gulp! I was more than a little devastated. Those words stuck with me for many years afterward. Anytime I thought I was accomplishing something I would recall how I thought I had accomplished something there too, yet I had failed. Anytime I tried something new I thought, "What if I can't handle it?" Or worse yet, "What if I think I can handle it, but I am actually making a huge fool out of myself?"

---

* The following devotional was written by Mary Margaret Adams.

Fortunately, when we seek Christ and seek to do His will we know two things. First, that Jesus accepts us "as is" and second, that He works with us to give us life more abundantly. He is the "good shepherd" and the "overseer of our souls" (1 Peter 2:25).

In case we would have any doubt about who is for us and who is against us, John 10:7-11 clears it all up beautifully!

"Then Jesus said to them again, 'Most assuredly, I say to you, I am the door of the sheep. All who ever came before Me are thieves and robbers, but the sheep did not hear them. I am the door. If anyone enters by Me, he will be saved, and will go in and out and find pasture. The thief does not come except to steal, and to kill, and to destroy. I have come that they may have life, and that they may have it more abundantly. I am the good shepherd. The good shepherd gives His life for the sheep."

Satan comes to steal, rob, and destroy, but Jesus is for us. Jesus is the "good shepherd;" He wants good things for us that will heal and restore our souls. Finally, Jesus gives His life for us and our well-being. We are safe with Him and He will never fail us. We can rest assured that when we seek Him, He will save us and lead us out to good pasture.

All praise and glory be to God! *Mary Margaret Adams*

Faithfulness as Firm as the Heavens

Good morning, Lord Jesus. Help me entrust all things to You. ...

"I will sing of Your steadfast love, O Lord, forever; with my mouth I will proclaim Your faithfulness to all generations. I declare that Your steadfast love is established forever; Your faithfulness is as firm as the heavens" (Psalm 89:1-2).

> *Steadfast and steady, faithful and true*
> *I find my rest and security in You.*
>
> *Others may falter and others may fail*
> *But Your goodness and mercy will always prevail.*
>
> *Why do I doubt and why do I fear?*
> *Through every challenge, You're always near.*
>
> *So help me let go and help me to trust*
> *To rest in You and not worry so much.*
>
> *You hold my life in Your hands, from beginning to end*
> *Every hope and dream, every struggle with sin.*
>
> *Keep lifting my eyes to see as You see*
> *Not looking around or looking at me.*
>
> *I give You my burdens and release them to You*
> *I find rest in Your peace as You want me to.*
>
> *There's no better place than the security of Your presence*
> *Your faithfulness to me is as firm as the heavens.*

In Jesus' name I pray, Amen.

Be encouraged today! In the Love of Jesus, *Tommy Hays*

Times of Refreshing

Good morning, Lord Jesus. Awaken my hunger for the fullness of Your presence in my heart again today. ...

"In this way God fulfilled what He had foretold through all the prophets, that His Messiah would suffer. Repent therefore, and turn to God so that your sins may be wiped out, so that times of refreshing may come from the presence of the Lord, and that He may send the Messiah appointed for you, that is, Jesus, who must remain in heaven until the time of universal restoration that God announced long ago through His holy prophets" (Acts 3:18-21).

Times of refreshing come from the presence of the Lord. We prepare the way of the Lord as we repent of our sins and turn to You. So repentance brings refreshing. Returning to You allows You to return to us in the fullness of Your presence, unhindered by sin. May the hunger for Your presence intensify to the time of universal repentance when You send Your Messiah for the time of universal restoration. You long to restore every heart that turns to You in repentance. You long to refresh every heart that longs for Your presence. Father God, send your Messiah. Fulfill the fullness of Your kingdom on earth as it is in heaven.

Come, Holy Spirit. Convict us of our sin. Convince us of our need for the refreshing and restoration that only the coming of our Messiah can bring. Call us to repentance as we turn to our God and cry out in prayer for the presence of the Lord in measures of intensity that touch the heart of heaven. Come, Lord Jesus. Refresh us and restore us with the fullness of Your presence in our hearts and throughout the earth. In Jesus' name I pray, Amen.

Be encouraged today! In the Love of Jesus, *Tommy Hays*

God's Direction*

"A man's heart plans his way, but the Lord directs his steps" (Proverbs 16:9).

Has God ever redirected your steps? Recently, I had planned a particular course of action that seemed rational and right in my own eyes and in the eyes of others. However, at the last minute, God stepped in and changed my direction! Although I'm not completely overjoyed by this new direction, I am joyful, because it is confirmation that God speaks to me, guides me, and cares for me. Also, He isn't going to allow me to wander off in a wrong direction.

However, this new direction will mean going back to and pressing through a difficult situation rather than avoiding it. While I know this is clearly God's will for me, I do not know if I can trust myself as well as others to handle what may arise in a Godly fashion (which was the reason why I thought I would take a detour in the first place)! More than anything, I need to know that grace can and will abound over the sins of the past (both mine and others). God has brought to my mind a few verses to meditate on. First, Romans 5:20-21, which says: "Moreover, the law entered that the offense might abound. But where sin abounded, grace abounded much more." And, second, Romans 8:28: "And we know that all things work together for good to those who love God, to those who are called according to His purpose." God seems to be telling me that He knows and understands all of the sins and mistakes of the past and that His grace will be great enough to overcome the past. And, that He can and will work all things together for good, in spite of how it may look from my perspective.

Is there a particular situation that God is speaking to you about today? Will you join with me in the difficult decision to trust God for grace, guidance, and endurance? Will you allow God to direct your steps?

All praise and glory be to God! *Mary Margaret Adams*

---

* The following devotional was written by Mary Margaret Adams.

More Fruit of Your Spirit

Good morning, Lord Jesus. Put Your desires on my heart and Your thoughts in my mind. Lead me in prayer and throughout my day by Your Spirit. ...

"The fruit of the Spirit is love, peace, joy, patience, kindness, generosity, faithfulness, gentleness, and self-control. There is no law against such things" (Galatians 5:22-23).

Lord, let me see more fruit of Your Spirit in my life. But even as I pray this prayer, I know You will be doing Your part by providing Your power through Your grace, and calling me to do my part by faith and obedience to Your will. Your answer will come as You bring the circumstances into my life that will become the opportunities for me to choose to bear this fruit or not. Your Word calls us each to "live lives worthy of the Lord, fully pleasing to Him, as you bear fruit in every good work as you grow in the knowledge of the Lord" (Colossians 1:10).

It is our choice how we choose to lead our lives, but You are there to provide the desire and the power to live a life that pleases You. You have put this prayer on my heart because You want to bring this answer in my life. It's only possible by Your grace, but Your grace is sufficient for me. In Jesus' name I pray, Amen.

Be encouraged today! In the Love of Jesus, *Tommy Hays*

"Before All Things"

Good morning, Lord Jesus. Let me see You in Your Word and hear You in my spirit. ...

"He is the image of the invisible God, the firstborn of all creation; for in Him all things in heaven and on earth were created, things visible and invisible, whether thrones or dominions or rulers or powers—all things have been created through Him and for Him. He himself is before all things, and in Him all things hold together. He is the head of the body, the church; He is the beginning, the firstborn from the dead, so that He might come to have first place in everything" (Colossians 1:15-16).

Come to "have first place" in my life, Lord Jesus. I know there are still so many areas where I turn to myself and my will before turning to You and Your will. There are still so many times when You come in second—or far worse—on my list of priorities and guiding principles for my decisions. Not only is that sin, it's also foolish, because in You "all things hold together." When things are not holding together well in my life, I know it's time to reorder my priorities, seek the wisdom of Your ways, and look to You and Your leading "before all things." In Jesus' name I pray, Amen.

Be encouraged today! In the Love of Jesus, *Tommy Hays*

The Breath of Your Spirit

Good morning, Lord Jesus. I come away from the world for a moment to seek You alone and wait in the silence to listen for the leading of Your Spirit. ...

"We look not at what can be seen but at what cannot be seen; for what can be seen is temporary, but what cannot be seen is eternal" (2 Corinthians 4:18).

I cannot see the air I breathe, but it is real. And it is essential for my life. I cannot see You, but You are real. And You are essential for my life. If in my pride I were to stubbornly insist that I would not allow air into my lungs because I could not see it and therefore could not believe it was real, I would surely die. Having known the Breath of Life, I know my life would be as dry as a bone and my spirit would surely die if I were to stubbornly refuse to allow the life breath of Your Spirit to fill me afresh every day.

The same Hebrew word for breath is the same word for spirit—ruach. As the worship song says, "You are the Air I breathe. I'm desperate for You." From the very beginning, we have lived by the breath of God alone: "The Lord God formed man from the dust of the ground, and breathed into his nostrils the breath of life, and the man became a living being" (Genesis 2:7). You are Spirit (John 4:24). And Your Spirit brings new life to dry bones and weary souls. "Thus says the Lord God to these bones: I will cause breath to enter you, and you shall live" (Ezekiel 37:5). By Your grace and my faith, I choose to believe and I choose to receive the breath of Your Spirit, the breath of Your Life. Breathe Your life into my spirit afresh and let these bones live for You today. In Jesus' name I pray, Amen.

Be encouraged today! In the Love of Jesus, *Tommy Hays*

Multiply the Moments

Good morning, Lord Jesus. Before the day begins, it's good to come away with You—Father, Son, and Holy Spirit. I give to You my first thoughts, my first emotions, my first words. ...

As I watch and wait for Your leading in the silence of surrender, it seems I hear You say, "Multiply the moments." I think of these moments with my children and family during our time away. Yes, Lord. Multiply the moments—these moments together with one another, set apart from the intensity of our regular daily lives. Multiply the investment of love and time in these moments with my children.

"Then Peter said, 'Look, we have left our homes and followed You.' And He said to them, 'Truly I tell you, there is no one who has left home or wife or brothers or parents or children for the sake of the kingdom of God, who will not get back very much more in this age, and in the age to come eternal life' " (Luke 18:28-30).

These few weeks near the beginning of each summer have become some of the most important weeks of my life. These are the times when I "get back very much more in this age" some of what I seem to have lost "for the sake of the kingdom of God." As those who have known me in the journey of my life and those who have come to know me in the journey of my prayers have found, I share the pain and the joy of both a broken family and a blended family. After my first year of ministry in the transition of my worlds from lawyer to minister and from Texas to Kentucky, my first wife divorced me, despite all the counseling and prayers and offers to return to the our old world. My three older children from that first marriage—Elizabeth, Zachary, and Madison—are only able to be with me part of the time now. So this block of time when I bring them "back home" to see my family out here in Texas and New Mexico and to spend uninterrupted weeks rather than days and hours with them carries significance far beyond a family vacation. These moments of talks and laughs, arguments and prayers— these moments of real life together—are worth their weight in gold.

This year has been a little harder without my two youngest children—Elijah and Josiah—since it seemed a little too early to travel for my wife with our newborn son. But at the same time, it's allowed a little more focused time with my older children in a rare gift we seldom share. Somehow by the power of Your grace and Your love, You have brought us through and are bringing us through the journey of brokenness and healing, blending our old life into our new life—our redeemed life. I have no idea how anyone could try to make it through this kind of journey without You and I'm so glad we have never had to try.

Multiply the moments, Lord. Thank You for putting this prayer of Your will on my heart this morning. Do in these moments what might otherwise take months that we no longer have to give and to share with one another. Thank You for the gift of "very much more." In Jesus' name I pray, Amen.

Be encouraged today! In the Love of Jesus, *Tommy Hays*

"The Present Age"

Good morning, Lord Jesus. The closer I get to You, the closer I want to be. The more I see of Your glory, the more I see how far I fall short of Your glory and how much I need You and Your grace every day. But here You are—answering my need and my desire. ...

"For the grace of God has appeared, bringing salvation to all, training us to renounce impiety and worldly passions, and in the present age to live lives that are self-controlled, upright, and godly, while we wait for the blessed hope and the manifestation of glory of our great God and Savior, Jesus Christ. He it is who gave himself for us that He might redeem us from all iniquity and purify for himself a people of His own who are zealous for good deeds" (Titus 2:11-14).

There is a present age and there is an age to come. While I wait with eager anticipation for the age to come, I don't want to be passive or complacent about my part in my generation of the present age. By Your grace and love, You desire to bring "salvation to all" and then to convict us and redeem us from "all iniquity" as You purify us and empower us to live our lives for Your glory and Your kingdom on earth as it is in heaven. As the body of Christ on earth, being cleansed from our sins and being filled with Your Spirit, we are created and called to be "the manifestation of glory of our great God and Savior, Jesus Christ." We wait for the hope of Your coming, but at the same time, we embrace the coming of Your kingdom and Your nature in our lives now. This is "the riches of the glory of this mystery, which is Christ in you, the hope of glory" (Colossians 1:27).

Thank You, Lord, for saving me and forgiving me. Thank You for purifying me and redeeming me. Thank You for convicting me of my need for Your grace every day. Thank You for calling me and empowering me to keep welcoming the glory of Your presence in my heart and my life a little more each day. Make me more "zealous for good deeds" for Your kingdom to come and Your will to be done in my life and through my life for the hope of Your glory. In Jesus' name I pray, Amen.

Be encouraged today! In the Love of Jesus, *Tommy Hays*

"Rooted and Built Up in Him"

Good morning, Lord Jesus. Fill my spirit with Your Spirit, draw me up into the heavenly dimension of Your presence I pray. ...

"As you therefore have received Christ Jesus the Lord, continue to live your lives in Him, rooted and built up in Him and established in the faith, just as you were taught, abounding in thanksgiving" (Colossians 2:6-7).

We've been staying with my mom in the little village of Ruidoso tucked away in the mountains of central New Mexico. It's a unique setting of rocky mountains covered with tall, cool pines, surrounded on every side by vast desert. This region is ruggedly beautiful, but suffering a severe drought. Though the rocky soil is hot and dry, the pine trees seem to smell just as fresh and stand just as tall as they do every summer when we come out here. They've been built up by the cycles of winter snows, spring rains, and summer droughts for years. Their roots sink deeply into resources of water beneath the surface of current circumstances.

Keep teaching me how to live my life in You, rooted and grounded in the faith, built up in praise and prayer. Teach me how to flourish with the fragrance of Christ even in the dry seasons—"the fragrance that comes from knowing Him" (2 Corinthians 2:14). Teach me how to abound in thanksgiving for the hidden resources of Your Word and Your Spirit that sustain me and empower me to stand firm in the faith through every season until the rains of blessing come again. In Jesus' name I pray, Amen.

Be encouraged today! In the Love of Jesus, *Tommy Hays*

Joy in the Journey

Good morning, Lord Jesus. Thank You for the gift of Your presence. Thank You for the gift of others to join me in the journey of seeking more of Your presence in our lives each day. ...

"For what is our hope or joy or crown of boasting before our Lord Jesus at His coming? Is it not you? Yes, you are our glory and joy! ... How can we thank God enough for you in return for all the joy that we feel before our God because of you" (1 Thessalonians 2:19-3:9).

Thank You, Lord, for the joy of those who have joined with me these past three years in this daily journey of prayer. Except for a small portion, I have not seen most of them face to face, but when I do, it always amazes me how there seems to be a bond of friendship and relationship that can't be explained apart from You. Our relationships with one another in our journeys of faith in You are our glory and joy because we see You and know You in one another, to a large degree.

Nothing can replace our personal relationship with You; and at the same time, nothing can replace our relationships with one another. You have created us that way, intending for us to find the glory of Your presence in the joy of these relationships. You are love. And love is relational. "Beloved, let us love one another, because love is from God; everyone who loves is born of God and knows God. Whoever does not love, does not know God, for God is love" (1 John 4:7-8). Nothing could be more foundational. Nothing could be truer.

Lord God our Father, You are Spirit and we cannot now fully see You. But You have revealed Yourself and Your nature to us in the person of Jesus Christ, and You have come to dwell in our hearts by the Spirit of Christ living within us in Your nature—the nature of Your love. "Beloved, since God loved us so much, we also ought to love one another. No one has ever seen God; if we love one another, God lives in us, and His love is perfected in us. By this we know that we abide in Him and He in us, because He has given us of His Spirit" (1 John 4:11-13). You call us to abide in this love, reminding us, "I have said these things to you so that My joy may be in you, and that your joy may be complete" (John 15:11). By Your Spirit, You are the love that abides within us and lives through us, bringing to us the fullness of Your joy in the glory of Your presence.

Thank You for letting me see You and Your nature in the love of so many in the relationships You've formed along the journey. Help us keep growing in the journey, as we abide in You and welcome You to abide in us a little more each day—morning by morning and day by day. In Jesus' name we pray, Amen.

Be encouraged today! In the Love of Jesus, *Tommy Hays*

Friends of the Bridegroom

Good morning, Lord Jesus. Form Your thoughts in my thoughts, Your desires in my desires. Cleanse me from my sin and fill me with Your Spirit. Make me more like You each day. ...

John the Baptist "grew and became strong in the Spirit, and he was in the wilderness until the day He appeared publicly to Israel" (Luke 1:80). He listened for Your leading and prepared for Your coming. Some thought he was the Messiah, but his calling and ministry was always to point others to the Messiah. Some came to listen to the leading of his voice, but he always called others to listen for the leading of Your voice. He said, " 'I am not the Messiah, but I have been sent ahead of Him.' He who has the bride is the Bridegroom. The friend of the Bridegroom, who stands and hears Him, rejoices greatly at the Bridegroom's voice. For this reason my joy has been fulfilled. He must increase, but I must decrease " (John 3:28-30).

Help me mature and grow in Your Spirit, Lord. Let me be one of Your witnesses preparing for Your coming in my heart and in our land and throughout the earth. Let my voice lead others to Your voice. Let my words lead others to Your Word. You are the Bridegroom coming for Your bride— a bride made "holy by cleansing her with the washing of water by the Word, so as to present the church to Himself in splendor, without a spot or wrinkle or anything of the kind—yes, so that she may be holy and without blemish" (Ephesians 5:25-27). Let me stand and hear You, rejoicing greatly at Your voice. Help me grow in a relationship of trust and obedience to You as a "friend of the Bridegroom."

As I wait this morning for Your leading and the inspiration of Your Spirit, it seems I hear You say: "Awaken, arise. Do not hesitate; do not look back. Look to Me and follow My lead. Be still and listen for my leading, then move quickly at the command of My voice. Many pieces are in place; many more are coming into place. Your part is to make sure your piece is in place. Only I see all the pieces in all their places, but I am opening the eyes of My children to see more than they have ever seen. You will need to see more to see where I am leading in these days. Fear not, and follow Me."

Yes, Lord. Help me stay in a place of stillness in the silence of surrender to listen for Your leading. Help me find my place and do my part as You call others to find their places and do their parts. Fit us together and purify our souls. You are calling Your bride and preparing her for Your coming— coming first in our hearts and one day in the fullness of Your glory to receive the glorious bride You have prepared. Those who will come to follow Your lead and learn Your ways, You call Your "friends" (John 15:15). As we do our part in our generation—all by Your grace and Your Sprit, preparing Your bride for Your coming—we are Your friends; friends of the Bridegroom. "The Spirit and the bride say, 'Come!' " (Revelation 17:17) In Jesus' name I pray, Amen.

Be encouraged today! In the Love of Jesus, *Tommy Hays*

Thankfulness[*]

Do you ever feel like you are in complete control of your life only to discover that you are actually riding in a canoe in the river of life and God is steering and determining the course from behind? Lately, it seems like around every bend God has somehow beaten me there—meaning He placed me, I didn't row there all by myself!

Lately God has been trying to get my attention with the word "thankfulness." It seems everywhere I go and everything I do, I see or hear the word! Just today, I was quite annoyed to glance over and see on a secular psychologist's book something about healthy and happy people being "thankful" people! I wasn't even supposed to be in that section of the bookstore! I knew better than to go to the "self help" section, because, frankly, I didn't feel like getting any help today.

Anyway, in spite of my stubbornness, I had asked God to forgive me several days ago for being so thankless and to remind me to be more thankful. He was just being true to His word, but reminding me at the most peculiar times, like when I was completely miserable with the flu or full of sadness over something. Today in the bookstore was the final straw and I said, "You know God, I'm really not feeling very thankful today. I don't know why it's so hard for the tiniest bit of thankfulness to come forth out of me, but help me to be a bit more thankful." Strangely enough, I felt like a burden had been lifted and like God's love had been poured into me!

Later, God brought several verses to mind. First, God told me to stop running from the truth. Ephesians 5:15-17, 20 says:

"See then that you walk circumspectly, not as fools but as wise, redeeming the time, because the days are evil. Therefore, do not be unwise, but understand what the will of the Lord is . . . giving thanks always for all things to God the Father in the name of our Lord Jesus Christ."

Second, God showed me that His way is gentle, He is close, and He wants to give me peace. Philippians 4:4-7 says:

"Rejoice in the Lord always. Again, I say rejoice! Let your gentleness be known to all men. The Lord is at hand. Be anxious for nothing, but in everything by prayer and supplication, with thanksgiving, let your requests be made known to God; and the peace of God, which surpasses all understanding, will guard your hearts and minds through Jesus Christ."

---

[*] The following devotional was written by Mary Margaret Adams.

Lastly, God reminded me (as He does a lot!) that He is so gracious and good to us when we turn to Him! Psalm 107:21-22 says:

"Oh, that men would give thanks to the Lord for His goodness, and for His wonderful works to the children of men! Let them sacrifice the sacrifices of thanksgiving, and declare His works with rejoicing."

Knowing all of this, let's willingly and whole heartedly give Him thanks and praise.

All praise and glory be to God! *Mary Margaret Adams*

Stay in the Kitchen*

We have all heard the saying, "If you can't stand the heat, then get out of the kitchen!" I have been feeling this way a lot lately. I finally decided maybe it was time to get out of the "kitchen." I had simply had enough of the tough life lessons of God. I thought I needed a break. However, God had something different in mind.

Today, I decided to flip to Zechariah. Has anyone ever read anything there? I figured it was a safe place to "hang out." After all, what could God possibly have to say to me *personally* from this Old Testament book? I couldn't believe it when my eyes fell on the following verse! God says the following:

"I will bring one-third through the fire, will refine them as silver is refined, and test them as gold is tested. They will call on My name, and I will answer them. I will say, 'This is My people'; and each one will say, 'the Lord is my God'" (Zechariah 13:9).

That sounds like something I need to hear! God's desire for me is to "stay in the kitchen" so to speak, so he can refine me. I'm not so sure I like that idea, but I am reminded of another verse from Isaiah which says:

"But now, thus says the Lord, who created you, O Jacob, and He who formed you, O Israel: 'Fear not, for I have called you by your name; you are Mine. When you pass through the waters, I will be with you; and through the rivers, they shall not overflow you. When you walk through the fire, you shall not be burned, nor shall the flame scorch you' " (Isaiah 43:1-2).

Knowing that I belong to God and He will walk with me helps, as does the fact that I will be refined not burned up. A personal example may further help, and there it is in the book of Psalms:

"Oh, bless our God, you peoples! And make the voice of his praise to be heard, who keeps our soul among the living, and does not allow our feet to be moved. For You, O God, have tested us; You have refined us as silver is refined. You brought us into the net; You laid affliction on our backs. You have caused men to ride over our heads; we went through fire and through water; but You brought us out to rich fulfillment" (Psalm 66:8-12).

In all of these verses, God seems to be saying first, that we belong to Him. Second, He wants to refine and purify us. Third, He will walk with us through this process. And, fourth, when we are brought through this

---

* The following devotional was written by Mary Margaret Adams.

process, we will be brought out to a rich fulfillment that will bring forth praise and adoration for our God.

Maybe the kitchen is not such a bad place to be after all!

All praise and glory be to God! *Mary Margaret Adams*

Laborers of the Harvest

Good morning, Lord Jesus. I entrust my life and this day to You—Father, Son, and Holy Spirit. ...

"After this, the Lord appointed seventy others and sent them on ahead of Him in pairs to every town and place where He himself intended to go. He said to them, 'The harvest is plentiful, but the laborers are few; therefore ask the Lord of the harvest to send out laborers into His harvest' " (Luke 10:1-2).

Lord of the harvest, send out laborers into Your harvest. Send us out ahead of You to every town and place where You intend to go. Send us out in pairs, teamed together in relationships of interdependence and trust, complimenting one another's gifts and callings, temperaments and strengths. You don't just tell us to go, You also tell us to pray—to pray for the others who will labor with us in Your harvest. And as we answer Your call, we become the answer to the prayers of others who are asking for Your harvest.

For a great harvest, there must be ripe grain and ready laborers. Lord, let the grain be ripe and let the laborers be ready. Prepare their hearts and prepare ours. Your Word seems to say the harvest is already plentiful, but it is the laborers who are not ready. The laborers are few. This day we pray for the laborers. I pray for those called to labor alongside me, and I pray I would be ready to labor alongside others, as You send us ahead of You into Your harvest. In Jesus' name I pray, Amen.

Be encouraged today! In the Love of Jesus, *Tommy Hays*

The Kingdom is Near

Good morning, Lord Jesus. As I submit and entrust my life to You, let there be more of You and less of me, more of Your nature and less of my nature—morning by morning and day by day. ...

You sent out seventy disciples—not just twelve—into Your harvest of souls, saying, "Go on your way. See, I am sending you out like lambs in the midst of wolves" (Luke 10:1-3). But even though You warned them You were sending them to "the wolves," You told them to begin their ministry to the people by speaking words of peace rather than judgment, first giving people the chance to welcome Your disciples and Your message of hope and life through faith. "Whatever house you enter, first say, 'Peace to this house!' And if anyone is there who shares in peace, your peace will rest on that person; but if not, it will return to you" (Luke 10:5-6).

The peace of Your presence is within us, as Your disciples. As we go to the places You send us, we are not offering people ourselves, we are offering them You. But at the same time, we offer them You through us—through the peace of Your presence living in us and flowing through us by Your Holy Spirit. As we abide in You and allow You to abide in us, our nature becomes more like Your nature, our words become more like Your words, and then the peace we offer is Your peace You are offering through us. It's all about You—but amazingly, You offer Yourself through us—those You have called and discipled and sent to proclaim with authority and to demonstrate with power that "The kingdom of God has come near to you" (Luke 10:8-9). By the grace and the mystery of Your Spirit living in us, You said, "Whoever listens to you listens to Me, and whoever rejects you rejects Me, and whoever rejects Me rejects the One who sent Me" (Luke 10:16).

And there are consequences for our choices—the choices we make to go where You send us and to do what You command us, as well as the choices they make to welcome us or reject us, to share in Your peace or not. There will come a day of Your "judgment" for each of us, based upon the choices we make in the light of Your grace (Luke 10:14).

Lord, give me grace to choose well—first in welcoming and receiving those You send to bring Your peace, and then in going out into Your harvest to share the peace of Your presence I have welcomed into my soul with others—even to "the wolves" You warned me I would encounter along the way. Keep me close to You, starting each day and continuing each day in You, so that it is more and more Your true nature and Your true message that others have a chance to welcome or reject. Let it be Your kingdom and not my kingdom that "has come near" (Luke 10:9 and 10:11). In Jesus' name I pray, Amen.

Be encouraged today! In the Love of Jesus, *Tommy Hays*

Love Casts Out Fear

Good morning, Lord Jesus. By Your grace and in Your power, I choose to depend on You. Be my wisdom, be my strength. Be my Father and my Savior. Be my Lord, my God, and my Best Friend. ...

"For all who are led by the Spirit of God are children of God. For you did not receive a spirit of slavery to fall back into fear, but you have received a spirit of adoption. When we cry, 'Abba! Father!' it is that very Spirit bearing witness with our spirit that we are children of God, and if children, then heirs, heirs of God and joint heirs with Christ—if, in fact, we suffer with Him so that we may also be glorified with Him" (Romans 8:14-17).

It is the spirit of slavery that always tries to draw me back into fear—fear of failure, fear of rejection, fear of trusting. But it is the Spirit of Adoption— the Holy Spirit of the Living God living in me—who is always trying to draw me forward into the fullness of the future to fulfill my calling and destiny in You. I am a son of God, and You are my Father. I am an heir of God and a joint heir with Christ. Your Spirit bears witness with my spirit of the deepest bonds of relationship with You in every dimension of Your Being— Father, Son, and Holy Spirit. By grace, You have chosen to identify Yourself with me; and by faith, I have chosen to identify myself with You— in suffering and in glory, in failure and in success, in this world and in the world to come.

Keep giving me faith to live in this truth. Keep giving me grace to live in this bond of trust by Your love for me as Your child. Faith in Your love for me breaks the power of all fear and delivers me from every spirit of slavery. "Love has been perfected among us in this: that we may have boldness on the day of judgment, because as He is, so are we in this world. There is no fear in love, but perfect love casts out fear" (1 John 4:17-18). Abba, Father! Keep casting out my fear and keep filling me with Your love. As You do, You are casting out every unholy spirit and filling me with Your Holy Spirit, for You are Perfect Love. "God is love, and those who abide in God abide in love, and God abides in them" (1 John 4:16). Lord God—Father, Son, and Holy Spirit—keep abiding in me as I keep abiding in You, all by Your grace and all in Your love. In Jesus' name I pray, Amen.

Be encouraged today! In the Love of Jesus, *Tommy Hays*

Steady as a Rock

Good morning, Lord Jesus. As the old song says, "Rock of Ages, cleft for me, let me hide myself in Thee."...

"I love You, O Lord, my strength. The Lord is my rock, my fortress, and my deliverer, my God, my rock in whom I take refuge, my shield and the horn of my salvation, my stronghold" (Psalm 18:1-2).

Like a solid rock that never moves, You are steadfast and true, unchanging and unmoving. I find my strength in Your strength, my courage in Your courage. As I look to You, my heart is steadied and still. I am comforted and encouraged in the security of the stronghold of Your covenant with me. In You, "I shall not be moved" (Psalm 62:6, NKJV). In You, I take my stand to face with faith whatever comes—steady as a rock, steady in the Rock. In Jesus' name I pray, Amen.

Be encouraged today! In the Love of Jesus, *Tommy Hays*

Power of the Word of God

Good morning, Lord Jesus. You are mighty. You are powerful. You are the King of kings and the Lord of lords. I trust in the might of Your power. I submit to the authority of Your name. ...

In the struggles of ministry, Moses questioned the extent of Your power, and therefore doubted the authority of Your word. But You simply looked at him and loved him, then You resolved to show him the power of Your name and the faithfulness of Your word. "The Lord said to Moses, 'Is the Lord's power limited? Now you shall see whether my word will come true for you or not' " (Numbers 11:23).

Forgive me for the times I question Your power and doubt Your word. Forgive me for the times I look at the struggles longer than I look to You, submitting to their lordship rather than Yours. You are not a weak God, nor a complacent God. You are involved in every area of my life and in the lives of those around me. You are mighty and You are powerful. And every word You have ever spoken to me in my spirit and to me through Your Scripture will come to pass. In Your perfect timing and in Your perfect way, I will see that Your word for me is true. I will see the glory and the power of Your Word and my King. "For the Kingdom of God depends not on talks but on power" (1 Corinthians 4:20). In Jesus' name I pray, Amen.

Be encouraged today! In the Love of Jesus, *Tommy Hays*

Riches of Life

Good morning, Lord Jesus. I call You Lord, because I choose to submit to Your lordship in every area of my life, as best as I can and all by Your grace. You are the King of kings and the Lord of lords. Be my King. Be my Lord. ...

"As for those who in the present age are rich, command them not to be haughty, or to set their hopes on the uncertainty of riches, but rather on God who richly provides us with everything for our enjoyment. They are to do good, to be rich in good works, generous, and ready to share, thus storing up for themselves the treasure of a good foundation for the future, so that they may take hold of the life that really is life" (1 Timothy 6:17-19).

The two richest men in the world recently announced they are giving incredible proportions of their time and their riches to help the lives of others. Whatever their motives or their circumstances, one thing seems clear—they are seeking to find fulfillment in something other than what they have. And they each seem to have so very much.

In the journey of my life, there have been times when I have been rich and times when I have been poor. But You have shown me over and over again the measure of my wealth is not the measure of my joy. My treasure is found in trusting You.   You know just what I need to find fulfillment, peace, and joy. And when I am willing to trust You in that, letting my focus be Your focus and my priorities be Your priorities, You richly provide everything I need for my enjoyment of life—"the life that really is life." That kind of life may be lived out even in the most horrendous circumstances and challenging struggles, but it is a life of the joy of Your presence and Your pleasure that I have found my "good foundation for the future" in the treasure of trusting You. In Jesus' name I pray, Amen.

Be encouraged today! In the Love of Jesus, *Tommy Hays*

Welcome

Good morning, Lord Jesus. Good morning, Father God. Good morning, Holy Spirit. I welcome You, Lord, in every dimension of Your Being here into every dimension of my being this day. ...

"Now when Jesus returned, the crowd welcomed Him, for they were all waiting for Him" (Luke 8:40).

In the original language of this verse, the word "welcomed" means to receive gladly. Every day, I want to be waiting for Your return and every day I want to be receiving You gladly into my life. One day You will return in glory in the skies, and every day between now and then You want to return in glory in our hearts. Your glory is Your manifest presence. Father, Son, and Holy Spirit—come manifest the glory of Your presence in my life today. I wait for You eagerly and welcome You gladly. In Jesus' name I pray, Amen.

Be encouraged today! In the Love of Jesus, *Tommy Hays*

Buildings of Blessing

Good morning, Lord Jesus. Help me get quiet and listen for Your leading as I spend the first moments of this morning with You. ...

Our church needs a new roof. The estimates for repair have been staggering, and the idea of diverting funds from ministry to materials is overwhelming. But as we use the building You have entrusted to us, You are reminding us it is not a building we honor, but You. It's not a building we serve but the people You bring to the building as a place and a means of Your ministry to them. Our building is a blessing only to the degree we use it to bless those outside our building who need to come inside a living and personal relationship with You.

As we were praying about that and the other challenges we face as a church yesterday, the image came to me of another building where You were ministering. That building was an obstacle to ministry for the friends of a paralyzed man who couldn't get in to see You and receive Your healing words and Your healing power. So they tore the roof off of that building (Luke 5:18-19).

Lord, tear the roof off of everything in our lives and our churches that hinder us from our mission of sharing You and Your Word and Your power with all who need You. Remove the false ceilings, break down the barriers, and open up the heavens over our heads—even if You have to tear the roof off to do it. Let this challenge not be a distraction but a means to our destiny. In the ways of Your kingdom, You'll give us a new roof as we pray for open heavens. Long ago, a torn-up roof led to a mighty demonstration of Your power to forgive sins and heal lives. "Amazement seized all of them, and they glorified God and were filled with awe" (Luke 5:26).

We glorify You for Your goodness. We stand amazed in Your presence. We are filled with awe at Your grace to forgive and Your power to heal. Let our lives be Your temple and let our hearts be open to Your heavens, so that our buildings will be blessings for all people. In Jesus' name I pray, Amen.

Be encouraged today! In the Love of Jesus, *Tommy Hays*

The Roaring Thunder

Good morning, Lord Jesus. The unrelenting rumblings of Your thunder and the flashing of Your lightning have woken me early this morning. I receive them as a call to prayer. As the old hymn says, "I hear the roaring thunder...My God, how great Thou art." ...

"At this my heart also trembles, and leaps out of its place. Listen, listen to the thunder of His voice and the rumbling that comes from His mouth. Under the whole heaven He lets it loose, and His lightning to the corners of the earth. After it His voice roars; He thunders with His majestic voice and He does not restrain them when His voice is heard. God thunders wondrously with His voice; He does great things that we cannot comprehend" (Job 37:1-5).

The rumbling and the roaring of thunder builds a sense of anticipation. Is a storm brewing? Will a crash of lighting jar the night? Will the skies be ripped open to poor out a deluge of rain? They say thunder is the explosion of sound when the fiery heat of a bolt of lighting charges the atmosphere in a burst of light and heat. It gets our attention.

Lord, You are rumbling in the heavens to get our attention. You are stirring in our spirits with anticipation. You are opening our eyes to Your light and awakening our ears to Your voice. You are ripping open the heavens to cleanse our souls in a deluge of the power of Your Word. You will not allow us to sleep and slumber away when You are calling us to arise and listen for the leading of Your Spirit. If we will listen, You will not restrain Your voice. But to hear we must listen, and to listen we must awake and arise from our slumber.

The sound of the thunder draws our eyes to the light. Let the sound of Your voice draw our eyes to the light of Your glory. Let the roaring thunders build a sense of anticipation of what the Spirit is saying to the church in this hour and of what the Spirit is saying to each of us in this hour. In Jesus' name I pray, Amen.

Be encouraged today! In the Love of Jesus, *Tommy Hays*

My Life-line

Good morning, Lord Jesus. Before I turn my eyes the challenges of they day, I first turn them to You. Now is when I receive the wisdom and the strength that will carry me through this day. ...

"So if you have been raised with Christ, seek the things that are above, where Christ is, seated at the right hand of God. Set your minds on things that are above, not on things that are on earth, for you have died, and your life is hidden with Christ in God. When Christ who is your life is revealed, then you also will be revealed with Him in glory" (Colossians 3:1-4).

On a popular television game show, the contestants try to give the right answer to the questions in order to keep progressing to the end. When they really get desperate, and no longer think they can make the right choice on their own, they turn to one of their "life-lines" for help.

There have been many times when I have lived my life like that game show— trying to do it on my own until I get desperate enough to ask for help, to use my life-line. But You have been teaching me the peace that comes with desperately depending upon You from the very beginning. You are my Life-line. You are the right answer to every question I will encounter this day. I don't want to even try to answer the questions and meet the challenges I will face today in my own wisdom or strength apart from You. And I don't have to. I turn my face and my heart to You in desperate dependence upon Your help and Your life, for I have chosen for my life to be hidden in Your. In Jesus' name I pray, Amen.

Be encouraged today! In the Love of Jesus, *Tommy Hays*

Vacations*

Rob and I will be taking a big trip to Wisconsin to visit family and will be away for the next several days. I would appreciate prayer for the trip, because it will be stressful. We will be traveling with our two small children and both of our dogs, one of which is little Charlie—only three months old! Children, pets, relatives and tight quarters should make the trip interesting.

A lot of us will be taking "vacations" during this month and the next. Although these are meant to be relaxing and fun times, they can often be stressful. Both children and adults are out of their normal routines, habits, and living spaces. Tensions can rise with long car rides, air travel, and tight quarters.

Fortunately, Colossians tells us how to have the perfect vacation. Colossians 3:12-15 says:

"Therefore, as the elect of God, holy and beloved, put on tender mercies, kindness, humility, meekness, longsuffering; bearing with one another, and forgiving one another, if anyone has a complaint against another; even as Christ forgave you, so you also must do. But above all things put on love, which is the bond of perfection. And let the peace of God rule in your hearts, to which also you were called in one body; and be thankful."

Imagine what a vacation could be like if we possessed the qualities mentioned above? What would it be like if we were full of Godly mercy, kindness, humility, meekness, longsuffering, forgiveness, peace, love, and thankfulness?

This seems like one tall order, one which we don't have a chance of accomplishing unless we abide in Christ. In John 15:5 Jesus tell us: "I am the vine, you are the branches. He who abides in Me, and I in him, bears much fruit; for without Me you can do nothing." He also says in verse seven: "If you abide in Me, and my words abide in you, you will ask what you desire, and it shall be done for you."

As best as we can, we ask God to show us His will for us and we rely on Him to enable us to carry out His will. We ask Him to fill us with His peace and love so we are able to be humble, kind, merciful, longsuffering, and forgiving toward others.

Above all, let us be reminded of God's love and faithfulness toward us. Lamentations 3:22-23 says: "Through the Lord's mercies we are not

---

* The following devotional was written by Mary Margaret Adams.

consumed, because His compassions fail not. They are new every morning; great is Your faithfulness."

All praise and glory be to God! *Mary Margaret Adams*

Belief and Obedience

Good morning, Lord Jesus. I speak Your name and seek Your nature. ...

"The Father loves the Son and has placed all things in His hands. Whoever believes in the Son has eternal life; whoever disobeys the Son will not see life, but must endure God's wrath" (John 3:35-36).

There is an inseparable connection between belief and obedience. We cannot really believe without also obeying and we cannot really obey without believing.   Faith in the Son of God includes both trusting and obeying. Lord, help me trust more, and help me to obey more.

Father, draw me more deeply into Your love of Your Son by Your Spirit. Keep giving me the grace to trust Him and obey Him. As I keep putting my faith in Your Son, His life becomes my life and His nature becomes my nature. And I grow in my understanding of my identity as a son of God— created to endure Your pleasure and not Your wrath. In Jesus' name I pray, Amen.

Be encouraged today! In the Love of Jesus, *Tommy Hays*

Seeing is Believing

Good morning, Lord Jesus. By the Holy Spirit of the Living God living in me, I come to the Father through Jesus the Son. Lord my God—Father, Son, and Holy Spirit—I want to seek You more deeply and find You more completely in the journey of growing in relationship with You. ...

"Then Jesus cried aloud: 'Whoever believes in Me believes not in Me but in Him who sent Me. And whoever sees Me sees Him who sent Me. I have come as light into the world, so that everyone who believes in Me should not remain in the darkness.' " (John 12:44-46).

You have not created me and called me merely to understand You or assent to the doctrines about You, but to seek to see You. And in seeing You, I come to know You and to believe in You. As the old sayings go, "Seeing is believing" and "I'll know it when I see it." But the darkness of this broken, fallen world blinds our eyes to the truth of Your presence and Your nature, keeping us from seeing You and knowing You as You truly are.

Father, You are Spirit, and those who seek to know You and worship You must seek You in spirit and in truth (John 4:24). So You have entered our darkness in the nature of Your Son. As Your Spirit prophesied of Your coming long ago, "The people who walked in darkness have seen a great light; those who lived in a land of deep darkness—on them light has shined" (Isaiah 9:2). Now through Your Spirit, You are pushing back the darkness to open the eyes of our hearts to see You and believe You (Ephesians 1:17-19).

In the nature of Your Son who has lived among us to show us Your face and who is living among us by Your Spirit to seek Your face, You are "the light of the world" (John 8:12). Darkness has to hide by the coming of the glory of Your light.   "For it is the God who said, 'Let light shine out of darkness,' who has shone in our hearts to give the light of the knowledge of the glory of God in the face of Jesus Christ" (2 Corinthians 4:6). Father God, as I see Your Son, I see You. As I see His nature, I know Your nature, for the Father and the Son "are One" (John 10:30). I know You as I see You. And then seeing is believing. In Jesus' name I pray, Amen.

Be encouraged today! In the Love of Jesus, *Tommy Hays*

Birth of a Nation

Good morning, Lord Jesus. You are the ruler of the nations and one day all will walk in Your light and bow to Your glory (Revelation 21:24). All by Your grace, I choose to walk in Your light and bow to Your glory today. ...

"Righteousness exalts a nation, but sin is a reproach to any people" (Proverbs 14:34).

Today we celebrate the birth of our nation on July 4th, 1776 with the signing of the Declaration of Independence. From the recorded journals and writings of those who made history at that time, history cannot deny that You were on their minds. In signing their names and sealing their oaths of independence on that day, they also affirmed their dependence upon You: "And for support of this Declaration, with a firm reliance upon Divine Providence, we mutually pledge to each other our lives, our fortunes, and our sacred honor." You are Divine Providence. And there is no honor that is not sacred honor. Blessed is the nation and blessed are the people who remember to honor You.

"And now, Almighty Father, if it is Thy holy will that we shall obtain a place and name among the nations of the earth, grant that we may be enabled to show our gratitude for Thy goodness by our endeavors to fear and obey Thee. Bless us with Thy wisdom in our counsels, success in battle, and let all our victories be tempered with humanity. Endow, also, our enemies with enlightened minds, that they become sensible of their injustice, and willing to restore our liberty and peace. Grant the petition of Thy servant, for the sake of Him whom Thou hast called Thy beloved Son; nevertheless, not my will, but Thine be done" (General George Washington, private prayer of June 1779 from his headquarters on the Hudson River).

Restore us in Your righteousness; forgive us of our sins; remind us of our calling and destiny as a nation who proclaims liberty, fights for freedom, and lives in honor. Like all people of all nations, we have sinned and fallen short of the glory of God. But You desire Your mercy to triumph over judgment. And You desire to redeem and restore as You remind us of Your hand of Divine Providence that reaches out to every nation who will humble herself to take it. "Blessed is the nation whose God is the Lord" (Psalm 33:12, NKJV). In our celebrations today, may we also remember to humble ourselves to take Your hand and praise Your name for the blessing of our birth and the faithful fulfillment of our destiny. In Jesus' name I pray, Amen.

Be encouraged today! In the Love of Jesus, *Tommy Hays*

"Sound and Blameless"

Good morning, Lord Jesus. Be Lord of my spirit, Lord of my soul, Lord of my body. Be Lord of all. ...

"May the God of peace himself sanctify you entirely; and may your spirit and soul and body be kept sound and blameless at the coming of our Lord Jesus Christ. The One who calls you is faithful, and He will do this" (1 Thessalonians 5:23-24).

You are faithful and You will do this. By Your healing power, You will keep me sound. By Your forgiving grace, You will keep me blameless. As I keep choosing to keep submitting and surrendering my life into Your hands, You keep sanctifying me—purifying my heart and cleansing my soul, preparing me for the coming our Lord Jesus Christ. This is the life-long process of spiritual transformation—conforming my will to Your will and my nature to Your nature. "For this is the will of God, your sanctification" (verse 4:3).

When will You sanctify me, Lord? When will I be sound and blameless before You? Only when I get to heaven? No. Your Word says You desire to sanctify me now—"at the coming of our Lord Jesus Christ." You are a holy God, and You are coming for a holy people, surrendering by Your grace to Your will and submitting by Your grace to Your Lordship in our spirits and souls and bodies. As we choose this, You are faithful and You will do this. "And may He so strengthen your hearts in holiness that you may be blameless before our God and Father at the coming of our Lord Jesus Christ with all His saints" (verse 3:13). Strengthen my heart in holiness today. Keep giving me the desire to be sound and blameless at Your coming. Conform my will to Your will and transform my nature into Your nature more every day—all by Your grace and all in Your power. In Jesus' name I pray, Amen.

Be encouraged today! In the Love of Jesus, *Tommy Hays*

Favored One of God

Good morning, Lord Jesus. I turn to You and call on Your name. I lift my eyes to the heavens and turn my soul to You. I start this day with You so that You will know I welcome You to walk through this day with me. ...

"Remember me, O Lord, when You show favor to Your people; help me when You deliver them; that I may see the prosperity of Your chosen ones, that I may rejoice in the gladness of Your nation, that I may glory in Your heritage" (Psalm 106:4-5).

Your favor is Your hand of grace—Your protection, Your provision, Your power. When I fall far short of Your glory, Your favor lifts me up and presses me on. When I disappoint myself and others, Your favor reminds me to hear Your words of encouragement, that I am still Your child and there is much You have done and much more You will do through my life that others and I can't always see. When I feel confused about the uncertainties of the present and the anxieties for the future, Your favor reminds me that I am one of Your chose ones—those who have chosen to receive Your free offer of grace and love to all—and that You have chosen me to fulfill a purpose and calling and destiny that depends much more on You than on me.

So as best as I can and all by Your grace, in humility and in faith, I ask for and I receive Your favor. I choose to find my glory in Your heritage, to be available to You to use my life as You will. Just keep letting me know that You remember me. Just keep reminding me that You love me. Just keep encouraging me that You have chosen me. Deliver me from all discouragement and doubt. Establish me in the confident hope and unfailing grace of Your favor. You are all the protection, the provision, and the power I will ever need. In You, I am a favored and chosen one of God. In Jesus' name I pray, Amen.

Be encouraged today! In the Love of Jesus, *Tommy Hays*

Voice of the Good Shepherd

Good morning, Lord Jesus. You are the Good Shepherd and Your sheep hear Your voice. You have called me as one of the sheep of Your fold. In these first moments of my morning, help me hear Your voice and Your voice alone. Help me follow You and You alone. ...

"Very truly, I tell you, anyone who does not enter the sheepfold by the gate but climbs in by another way is a thief and a bandit. The one who enters by the gate is the shepherd of the sheep. The gatekeeper opens the gate for him, and the sheep hear his voice. He calls his own sheep by name and leads them out. When he has brought out all of his own, he goes ahead of them, and the sheep follow him because they know his voice. They will not follow a stranger, but they will run from him because they do not know the voice of strangers. ... I am the good shepherd" (John 10:1-5 and 11).

Lord, how do I learn to discern Your voice from the voices of the thieves and bandits who are strangers pretending to be my shepherd and friend? ...

It seems I hear You say: "My sheep know My voice because My sheep know Me. You know Me because You spend time with Me, and in spending time with Me you know My nature. My nature is love and My nature is life. My nature is truth and My nature is peace. My nature is encouragement and My nature is hope. When I come into the gate of your heart, I come to give you life—abundant life. When the thief comes in, he comes to bring discouragement and death, destruction and fear. Test the voice you hear. Know Me, and in knowing Me, you will also recognize your enemy, the thief who comes to steal and kill and destroy."

Yes, Lord. Forgive me for the times I have given in to deception. Forgive me for the times I have failed to test the thoughts and impressions and voices that come pressing in to my heart and soul. Forgive me for times I have confused Your nature with the thief's nature and judged Your ways as his ways. Remind me of Your nature, renew me in our relationship, refresh me in the knowledge of Your love for me and Your purpose for my life. You are my Good Shepherd. And by Your grace, I want to learn and grow to be a more discerning and obedient sheep. Help me hear Your voice and follow Your lead. In Jesus' name I pray, Amen.

Be encouraged today! In the Love of Jesus, *Tommy Hays*

The Champion of My Cause

Good morning, Lord Jesus. I don't know what this day will hold, but You do. So I commit and commend myself and my day to You. ...

There are so many challenges facing so many that I love and pray for. There are so many challenges facing me. Yet You know every challenge. You know every choice we will make in the face of those challenges. You see the end from the beginning. And You long for us to welcome You to step into every challenge and to lead us in every choice.

It seems I hear You say, "I have come to champion your cause. Your cause will fail without a champion. But you are not without a champion. I am your Champion. And I have come to champion your cause."

What is my cause, Lord?

"Your cause is to allow My character to be formed in you. Those who are receiving my character are then used by Me to form My character in others. This is your cause. This is the cause of the children of God. The character of Christ formed in you, the hope of glory. I am the Champion of your cause."

Yes, Lord. Your Holy Spirit is reminding me of the words one of my mentors in the faith used to say to us when You were training me for ministry. Maxie Dunnam would remind us of Your words to him from Colossians 1:27—"Maxie, the secret is simply this—Christ in you, the hope of glory."

This is the secret to face every challenge—to see these challenges as opportunities to see the character of Christ formed in me and formed in those around me. This is my cause because this is the cause for my life. And You are the Champion of my cause. With this perspective, and with You as my Champion, I can face every challenge for myself and for those I love and pray for.

"I am now rejoicing in my sufferings, and in my flesh I am completing what is lacking in Christ's afflictions, for the sake of His body, that is, the church. I became its servant according to God's commission that was given to me for you, to make the word of God fully known, the mystery that has been hidden throughout the ages and generations but has now been revealed to His saints. To them God chose to make known how great among the Gentiles are the riches of the glory of this mystery, which is Christ in you, the hope of glory. It is He whom we proclaim, warning everyone and teaching everyone in all wisdom, so that we may present everyone mature in Christ. For this I toil and struggle with all the energy that He powerfully inspires within me" (Colossians 1:24-29).

Thank You, Lord, for reminding me what I toil and struggle for with all my energy. Thank You for reminding me of my cause and my calling. Thank You for reminding me of my Champion who powerfully inspires me and commissions me to grow into the maturity of Your character through every challenge I face. The character of Christ in me—You are my hope and You are my glory. In Jesus' name I pray, Amen.

Be encouraged today! In the Love of Jesus, *Tommy Hays*

Extravagantly Glorious and Abundant Life

Good morning, Lord Jesus. I've come to Fairview Heights, Illinois to share Your words of truth and life with the people here this morning and over the next few days. So open my heart to hear Your words and open my spirit to receive Your life so that I can share what I receive. ...

"I came that they may have life, and have it abundantly" (John 10:10).

Abundant life is so much more than living on life support. Abundant life is living the fullness of life in the very face of death—in the face of the thief who "comes only to steal and kill and destroy" (verse 10:10a). We don't live life in a vacuum. We live it out day by day, morning by morning, in the midst of a world submitting to the rule of the evil one. But we need not fear, for You have overcome the world and You have defeated the evil one.

Give us courage then to confront death with life, to cast off our artificial means of just surviving and just getting by. Awaken us to live the extravagantly glorious and abundant lives You have created us to live. Like Lazarus, let us cast off our death clothes as You roll away the stones that have sealed our tombs. Release the Spirit of Your resurrection life into every area of our lives as You drive death, our enemy, from our lives (John 11:1-44). In Jesus' name I pray, Amen.

Be encouraged today! In the Love of Jesus, *Tommy Hays*

Bread upon the Waters

Good morning, Lord Jesus. I worship You, Lord, my God—Father, Son, and Holy Spirit. ...

"Send out your bread upon the waters, for after many days you will get it back" (Ecclesiastes 11:1).

You have given me the bread of Your words of life. You have nurtured me and strengthened me; You are growing me into maturity. And every day You send me to share with others what You have given me, even as I learn from others what You have shared with them. In the giving, there is receiving. And the measure we give will be the measure we receive.

As You said, "Do not judge, and you will not be judged; do not condemn, and you will not be condemned. Forgive, and you will be forgiven; give, and it will be given to you. A good measure, pressed down, shaken together, running over, will be put into your lap; for the measure you give will be the measure you get back" (Luke 6:37-38).

Keep teaching me Your ways, keep leading me in Your will, keep transforming me into Your nature—little by little, step by step, day by day. In Jesus' name I pray, Amen.

Be encouraged today! In the Love of Jesus, *Tommy Hays*

Praying in the Spirit

Good morning, Lord Jesus. As best as I can and all by Your grace, I set aside my prayers and wait on You for Your prayers. ...

"Likewise, the Spirit helps us in our weakness; for we do not know how to pray as we ought, but that very Spirit intercedes with sighs too deep for words. And God, who searches the heart, knows what is the mind of the Spirit, because the Spirit intercedes for the saints according to the will of God" (Romans 8:26-27).

I do not know how to pray as I ought. So, I look to You and listen for Your leading. You search my heart and You know my weaknesses and my needs. You search the hearts of those for whom I'm interceding and You know their weaknesses and their needs. And then You intercede through me with sighs too deep for words, with intercession beyond my comprehension, but with prayers according to the will of God.

As You begin to bring people and circumstances to my mind now, I give you my heart and I pray in Your Spirit according to Your will. ...

... As I pray, these are words and sighs in the groaning of the Spirit, yearning for the will of God to be done, for the kingdom of God to come on earth—and in the lives of each person and each need You are bringing to mind—as it is in heaven. I don't know the words You are praying, but the thoughts that come to my mind as I pray in the Spirit are thoughts of freedom ... healing ... breakthrough ... restoration ... hope ... peace ... cleansing ... joy. I agree with Your will to release Your word and Your power into each of these lives by the power of Your Spirit. And I thank You for those who pray for me in the power of Your Spirit when You bring my face to their minds according to Your will. In Jesus' name I pray, Amen.

Be encouraged today! In the Love of Jesus, *Tommy Hays*

"Who am I?"

Good morning, Lord Jesus. Lift me up into the heavenly places where I am seated in Christ with You at the right hand of our Father in Heaven (Ephesians 1:20 and 2:4-7). ...

"Then King David went in and sat before the Lord, and said, 'Who am I, O Lord God, and what is my house, that You have brought me thus far?" (1 Chronicles 17:16).

To have the honor and the privilege to even come and sit before You is incredible. Then to know that You welcome me into Your presence and You even desire to hear my worship and praise and prayers is beyond comprehension. But even as I ask, like David, "Who am I?" it seems I hear You say, "You are My son. You are a child of God. I have brought you this far in the journey of your relationship of intimacy with Me, but I have so much further for you to go. Keep coming to and sitting before Me. Keep welcoming Me into the moments of Your day. This is the heritage of My children. This is the purpose for which I have created you. I am Love. And I have created you for a relationship of love with Me. You are greatly loved and You are always welcome in My presence."

Thank You, Lord. You are my Father and I am Your son. I am a child of God. Keep drawing me nearer. Keep cleansing me of sin and shame and all that would try to hold me back from drawing near to You. Keep reminding me of who You say that I am. Keep reminding me of who You are and who You are to me. In Jesus' name I pray, Amen.

Be encouraged today! In the Love of Jesus, *Tommy Hays*

Burning Heart

Good morning, Lord Jesus. I seek You Lord, my God—Father, Son, and Holy Spirit. Let me know You more completely in every dimension of Your Being and let me receive You more deeply in every dimension of my being. ...

Most every Methodist knows the birth of our movement began on May 24, 1738 when John Wesley went to a Moravian prayer meeting on Aldersgate Street in London. His heart was "strangely warmed" and set ablaze with a passion for You and for others in a depth of intimacy of relationship with You he had never known. Though at the time he even thought he was having an initial salvation experience, it seems to me and many others, from his later writings and the evidence of the fruit of Your Spirit in his life both before and after that encounter, that You baptized him in Your Holy Spirit in that moment of desperate surrender and humble faith (Matthew 3:11; Acts 1:5).

I've come to the annual Aldersgate Conference again this summer to understand and receive a deeper measure of the presence and power of Your Holy Spirit in my life. Help me to drink deeply of Your Living Water through the ministries of teaching, preaching, prayer, and worship. Free me to worship You from the depths of my soul, unhindered and unrestrained by anything but the leading of Your Spirit. Let me catch up with some old friends who have become family. And anoint me to teach and pray with Your power and authority as I give away to others what You have given me.

When I go home, refreshed and renewed from my time with You, let me be like those disciples who encountered You along the way and received a personal touch of Your presence—"Were not our hearts burning within us!" (Luke 24:32). Yes, Lord. Let my heart be strangely warmed at Aldersgate again this year. Baptize me afresh in Your Holy Spirit and set me ablaze with a passion for You and for others in a depth of intimacy of relationship with You I have never known. In Jesus' name I pray, Amen.

Be encouraged today! In the Love of Jesus, *Tommy Hays*

Waves of His Will

Good morning, Lord Jesus. Here in the silence of surrender, I entrust myself to You in these first moments of my morning. Draw me into Your presence as I welcome Your presence in me. You say, "I am the Vine." I say, "I am one of Your branches. I abide in You as I welcome You to abide in me" (from John 15:1-5). ...

When I practiced law in Corpus Christi beside the Gulf of Mexico, I liked to spend some time at the beach every now and then. It was nice to relax in the sun and walk in the sand along the edge of the water. Stress seemed to wash out to sea with every wave. Sometimes I would wade out a little deeper and I could feel the draw of the water back into the sea after every wave would wash onto the beach. As I tried to walk, I would have to almost dig in with my steps to resist the flow of the water trying to draw me out to sea with the waves. So sometimes I would lay back in the water and kick up my feet with no resistance, just to flow with the waves.

These morning times of prayer are kind of like that—the washing of the waves along the shore of my soul. There will be time to walk through the resistance of all the challenges that will come with the day, time to dig in and take a stand, time to press on when everything seems to be flowing the other way. But these first moments of the morning are a time to lay back in Your arms, kick my feet up in trusting surrender to the flow of Your Spirit, and let You draw me out into the deeper waters of Your presence. Let the morning sun of the Son of God shine on my soul, and let the waves of Your Holy Spirit wash away the stress and strain of my own strength. Draw me out into the flow of the will of my Father today, as I abide in You and welcome You to abide in me. In Jesus' name I pray, Amen.

Be encouraged today! In the Love of Jesus, *Tommy Hays*

Out of the Desert Places

Good morning, Lord Jesus. You are the King of kings and the Lord of lords. I bow to You as King of my heart. I submit to You as Lord of my life. Rule and reign in me today. Come let me hear what You are saying to me today. ...

"Some wandered in desert wastes, finding no way to an inhabited town; hungry and thirsty, their soul fainted within them. Then they cried to the Lord in their trouble, and He delivered them from their distress; He led them by a straight way, until they reached an inhabited town. Let them thank the Lord for His steadfast love, for His wonderful works to humankind. For He satisfies the thirsty, and the hungry He fills with good things" (Psalm 107:4-9).

In these days apart to seek Your face and welcome Your Spirit at the Aldersgate Conference, You have released a hunger and a thirst for Your presence and Your power. The more we seek You, the more You surface our need for You. Times of intense worship are followed by times of intense ministry. Like Isaiah, the more we behold Your glory, the more we see how much we are undone and broken, in need of Your tender mercies, healing grace, and mighty power. But as we cry out to You in our troubles, You deliver us from our distress. You are satisfying our thirsting souls and filling our hungry hearts. We are being changed in the power of Your presence.

Lord, what You are doing in us in these days, I pray You would do throughout the earth. Pour out a thirst and a hunger for Your presence and Your power. Lead every wandering soul out of the desert places of loneliness and isolation, out of brokenness and pain, out of anxiety and fear, out of doubt and unbelief, out of sin and shame, and into the place of Your power and Your presence. In Jesus' name I pray, Amen.

Be encouraged today! In the Love of Jesus, *Tommy Hays*

True Freedom[*]

Today was a stressful day for me. I felt very anxious, because I decided to take the kids out to someone else's house and I just haven't gotten out much to other people's houses lately. I never know how my kids are going to behave or what will happen or how things will go for me. I felt very insecure and unsure of myself and extremely anxious.

The visit was fine, except for the typical messes created by children; spilled water, food, sand, and an occasional squabble over a toy. It was sort of a zoo with my puppy also along and he wasn't quite as well behaved; chasing children, chewing shoes, and an accident on my friend's rug!

When I drove away, I felt down, even depressed. I felt empty and worthless. I wondered why I was so stupid as to bring the dog, why I was always so anxious when I did something with someone else (which usually manifests in me talking too much), and why I couldn't be more relaxed with my kids.

Rather than think about it too much, I got ready to take the kids to the dentist. While I was there, I felt so anxious about it. Henry looked scared and I just knew Calvin was going to throw a tantrum. More than that, I was waiting for a lecture from the dentist about something. By the end of the appointment, I couldn't even think straight!

When I finally got home, I had to finish a devotional and I was stuck. I felt like giving up and sinking further into a pit of negative thinking about myself. I was tired too from the hectic day.

I told God that I wasn't sure I would ever be free from feeling worthless and anxious. I figured He probably would agree or maybe even point out a few things I hadn't seen. However, God in His mercy, gave me the following verses:

"There is therefore now no condemnation to those who are in Christ Jesus, who do not walk according to the flesh, but according to the Spirit. For the law of the Spirit of life in Christ Jesus has made me free from the law of sin and death" (Romans 8:1-2).

After reading those words, I chose to release the day's events to God. I felt like a huge burden had been lifted. It was as if God told me that the condemning "voice" I heard wasn't from Him and I needed to stand against it. God was for me. He wasn't standing over me pointing out every flaw.

---

[*] The following devotional was written by Mary Margaret Adams.

There was enough grace for me. I could make different and better choices next time.

Rather than feeling trapped in a pit of anxiety and negativity, I felt hopeful! Maybe I would be less anxious next time or maybe it wasn't so bad being such a devoted dog owner. At the very least, I knew my friend had forgiven me for far worse!

There are many times when I feel like my flaws are laid bare for the world to see. I rarely try to hide them and truth be told, I probably couldn't even if I tried! That sort of transparency is frightening at times. But God, in His mercy has reminded me once again that He will never leave me or forsake me (Hebrews 13:5). He has also said, "My grace is sufficient for you, for My strength is made perfect in weakness" (2 Corinthians 12:9).

While it may be tempting for us at times to desire perfection or the appearance of perfection, we can find rest in the fact that our true freedom comes through Christ and His work on the cross. We have been set free from such standards (ones we could never attain) through the love and power of Christ. There is therefore now no more condemnation for those who are in Christ!

All praise and glory be to God! *Mary Margaret Adams*

"Drenched in God's Holy Spirit"

Good Morning, Lord Jesus. Cleanse my soul in the washing of the water of Your Word. Fill my heart with the fullness of the life of Your Spirit. By Your grace, I choose to begin this day submitted and surrendered to You. ...

"And as I began to speak, the Holy Spirit fell upon them just as it had upon us at the beginning. And I remembered the word of the Lord, how He had said, 'John baptized with water, but you will be baptized with the Holy Spirit' "(Acts 11:15-16).

At the close of prayer ministry time at the Aldersgate conference in Springfield, Illinois Saturday night, a close friend of mine who pastors a church in Indiana brought his family up for us to pray together. His little boy had just come from the youth service and he was still grinning from ear to ear. I asked him what happened to him. He said, "God drenched me with His Holy Spirit!" He told me when one of the youth leaders began to pray for him, he started to cry for a long time, but they were good tears. Then we prayed for his sister to be "drenched in God's Holy Spirit" and little tears started to flow down her face. After a while of gently praying for her, I asked her if they were good tears and she nodded. Then her daddy kneeled down and held her tight for a long time while they cried good tears together—along with all the rest of us.

This was a wonderful picture in the natural realm of what was taking place in the spiritual realm. Lord Jesus, as we seek You and the fullness of Your presence in our hearts, You fill us with Your Holy Spirit and drench us in the love of God, as our heavenly Father holds us tightly in His powerful embrace. "And hope does not disappoint us, because God's love has been poured into our hearts through the Holy Spirit that has been given to us" (Romans 5:5). Keep pouring Your love into our hearts, Lord. Keep drenching us in Your Holy Spirit. In Jesus' name I pray, Amen.

Be encouraged today! In the Love of Jesus, *Tommy Hays*

"All Day Long"

Good morning, Lord Jesus. Before I begin to think about my day, before I even begin to pray for others, I seek You and offer You the first moments of my morning. No matter where this day will lead, I will know I began it here with You. ...

"To You, O Lord, I lift up my soul. O my God, in You I trust; do not let me be put to shame; do not let my enemies exult over me. Do not let those who wait for You be put to shame; let them be ashamed who are wantonly treacherous. Make me to know Your ways, O Lord; teach me Your paths. Lead me in Your truth, and teach me, for You are the God of my salvation; for You I wait all day long" (Psalm 25:1-5).

I can't wait for You "all day long" unless I wait for You now. I can't follow Your leading "all day long" unless I begin to follow You now. These first moments of the morning set in motion the journey of my day. By Your grace, draw me near to You and focus my thoughts on You. Form Your nature in my nature as I willingly choose to submit myself to You. I seek the mind of Christ, the Father heart of God, the anointing of Your Holy Spirit. "To You, O Lord, I lift up my soul"—my mind, will, and emotions. As I do, You will keep teaching me Your paths and leading me in Your truth "all day long." In Jesus' name I pray, Amen.

Be encouraged today! In the Love of Jesus, *Tommy Hays*

Into Your Hands

Good morning, Lord Jesus. I entrust myself and my family to You this day.
...

"In His hand is the life of every living thing and the breath of every human being" (Job 12:10).

My first thoughts were turned to the phone instead of to prayer this morning and now I'm on a flight from Kentucky to Texas. Sometime around 3:00 this morning, I got the call from my grandmother, Nanny, I knew would come one day soon. My ninety-seven year old grandfather, PaPa, is experiencing massive internal bleeding. He seems to be slipping from this earthly life, through the fleeting grip of death, and into the fullness of eternal life. We have chosen to entrust his life completely into Your hands and Your care, with no artificial means of preserving his life on earth—only our faithful prayers in trusting surrender to Your perfect will.

Death is our enemy (1 Corinthians 15:26). And in Jesus' name, we rebuke death from having any say in this matter, and we entrust PaPa into the hands of Life. You are Life and we trust You to snatch him out of the grip of death and deliver him into the hands of his Father in Your perfect timing and in Your perfect way.

I pray You would steady the heart of my grandmother and give her the peace of Your presence. Calm my spirit and focus my thoughts as I travel to join her in these hours of uncertainty and stress. Give me Your words to speak and Your prayers to pray. Father, I pray for Your favor and grace as we make arrangements for the rest of our family to come alongside my grandparents in these sacred moments of time. They have no living children and as the oldest grandson, I will bear much responsibility. Help me to bear these burdens to You and follow the paths of Your leading through these delicate days. Into Your hands I entrust the spirit and soul and body of my grandfather and Your son. In Jesus' name I pray, Amen.

Be encouraged today! In the Love of Jesus, *Tommy Hays*

Each Day

Good morning, Lord Jesus. You are the Prince of Peace. I welcome Your peace in my soul this day. ...

"Then the Lord said to Moses, 'I am going to rain bread from heaven for you, and each day the people shall go out gather enough for that day" (Exodus 16:4).

Thank You for the grace we need each day. Thank You for a peaceful night for PaPa and thank You for the grace of Your peace this morning as we continue to entrust him into Your hands. As one of his favorite old songs goes, "One day at a time." You give us each day our daily bread as we welcome You to walk through each day with us (Luke 11:3). You are "the Bread of Life" that rains down from heaven (John 6:35). You are enough for every day. In Jesus' name we pray, Amen.

Be encouraged today! In the Love of Jesus, *Tommy Hays*

Resting in the Promise of Resurrection

Good morning, Lord Jesus. As I journey through the moments of my life, You are with me. As we begin the journey today, I welcome Your wisdom, I trust in Your truth, and I rest in the promise of Your resurrection power. ...

"Bless the Lord, O my soul, and all that is within me, bless His holy name. Bless the Lord, O my soul, and do not forget all His benefits—Who forgives all your iniquity, Who heals all your diseases, Who redeems your life from the pit, Who crowns you with love and steadfast mercy, Who satisfies you with good as long as you live so that your youth is renewed like the eagle's" (Psalm 103:1-5).

With just a little strength of life left in one lung, my PaPa finds strength in these last steps of the journey in You alone. Amazingly, there is still strength in his hugs and firmness in his handshake. Through ninety-seven years of life, he is a soul who has been blessed with Your goodness as long as he has lived. Thank You for the many blessings seen and the countless blessings unseen. Thank You for the benefits of being a son of God through faith in You—forgiveness, healing, redemption, love, mercy, and fulfillment.

In Your perfect timing and in Your perfect way through the mercy of faith in You, his youth will be renewed in the full measure of Your glory. "Just as we have borne the image of the man of dust, we will also bear the image of the Man of heaven" (1 Corinthians 15:41). Because we trust You and Your Word, we join in faith with PaPa in committing and commending his spirit, soul, and body to You—Father, Son, and Holy Spirit. In Jesus' name we pray, Amen.

Be encouraged today! In the Love of Jesus, *Tommy Hays*

We will run and not be weary[*]

Today, I had a good run. It was the first good run I have had in weeks. My doctor had put me on a medication that made my ankles swell and as a result, my morning runs had become agony. For the first time in my life I had new found understanding for people who do not like to exercise.

Some of you may be wondering why I didn't just stop running. Well, two reasons. First, I knew it would actually make my problem worse if I stopped. And second, I am very, very stubborn!

Have you ever felt this way with regards to your faith? You are trudging along, but each day feels even harder than the last? You know this is the way God wants you to go, but it's painful, to say the least? You wonder if you should just call it quits, although didn't you hear somewhere that you were supposed to try to persevere? God has some great news for you! Isaiah 40: 28-31 says:

"Have you not known? Have you not heard? The everlasting God, the Lord, the Creator of the ends of the earth, neither faints nor is weary. His understanding is unsearchable. He gives power to the weak, and to those who have no might, He increases strength. Even youths shall faint and be weary, and the young men shall utterly fall, but those who wait on the Lord shall renew their strength; they shall mount up with wings like eagles, they shall run and not be weary, they shall walk and not faint."

First, God never grows weary or faint. Second, God gives power and strength to the weak. Third, every human being has times of weariness; we are not alone here (e.g. even runners have times when they cannot run). Fourth, when we wait on the Lord, and this can sometimes mean persevering through something, He will renew our strength! And finally, we will see the results of a faith renewed. Just like I could physically run and not feel faint, God will also make it possible for me to soar spiritually when I turn to Him and am renewed!

All praise and glory be to God! *Mary Margaret Adams*

---

[*] The following devotional was written by Mary Margaret Adams.

PaPa's Song

Good morning, Lord Jesus. My brother Greg and I have been taking turns keeping the night watch over my PaPa as he draws nearer to the fullness of Your glory with each passing breath. As the night watch moves into the morning watch today, I am moved by the sense of Your watch over our lives every night and every morning and every day. ...

"He will also strengthen you to the end, so that you may be blameless on the day of our Lord Jesus Christ. God is faithful; by Him you were called into fellowship of His Son, Jesus Christ our Lord" (1 Corinthians 1:8-9).

Thank You, Lord, for Your persevering faith and unfailing grace that has strengthened PaPa and kept him near to You to the end. In these last days and moments of Your earthly grace, we are not able to see all he sees nor hear all he hears of Your heavenly grace. But in that realm that he is surely now beginning to experience in a measure far beyond what we could ever ask or imagine, I know he is finding deep assurance of Your forgiveness of sin, complete cleansing from shame of any failures or regrets, healing from the brokenness and pain of ninety-seven years of life through a broken and fallen world, and the sense of peace in the final fulfillment of every promise of Your Word to him.

Sometimes You heal us in the power and glory of a moment, sometimes in the process of a journey in the means of grace You choose, and sometime You heal us in the glory of our resurrection into the fullness of Your presence. You are the Healer and Savior of our spirits and souls and bodies, sanctifying us fully in the joy and peace of Your presence (1 Thessalonians 5:23). Life is a journey of faith, "but the one who endures to the end will be saved" (Matthew 24:13). Thank You for holding my PaPa safe and sound in the grip of Your grace to the end.

In the fading strength of his earthly body, PaPa can't pray with words anymore. So I join with him in my prayers to You, spirit to spirit, deep calling to deep, in the strength of Your Spirit. As I include him in my morning prayer today, I seem to sense Your Holy Spirit rising up in his human spirit in a trusting song of peace:

> *You are my Healer*
> *You heal my hurt and pain*
> *You are my Healer*
> *You heal my brokenness and shame.*
>
> *Sometimes You heal in power*
> *Sometimes You heal in glory*

And sometimes You heal in the glory to come.

You are my Savior
You save me from my sins
You are my Savior
You save me through the end.

Sometimes You save in power
Sometimes You save in glory
And Sometimes You save in the glory to come.

So come now and heal me
Heal me in the wholeness of Heaven
So come now and save me
Save me in the fullness of Your glory to come.

In Jesus' name I pray, Amen.

Be encouraged today! In the Love of Jesus, *Tommy Hays*

Resurrected into Life

Good morning, Lord Jesus. You said to Martha in the midst of her grief from the loss of her bother and friend, "I am the Resurrection and the Life. Those who believe in Me, even though they die, will live, and everyone who lives and believes in Me will never die" (John 11:25). I believe in You. So did my PaPa. And in You, we know we will never die, but live forever in the power and the glory of Your resurrection and life. ...

Yesterday morning, as I finished my morning prayer, so did PaPa. After a little while, I realized he had breathed his last breath on earth. He passed effortlessly through the hands of death into the arms of eternal Life. "For this perishable body puts on imperishability, and this mortal body puts on immortality, then the saying that is written will be fulfilled: 'Death has been swallowed up in victory.' 'Where, O death is your victory? Where, O death is your sting?' The sting of death is sin, and the power of sin is the law. But thanks be to God who gives us the victory through our Lord Jesus Christ!" (1 Corinthians 15:53-56).

Nolan Bradford Hays lived out his ninety-seven years on earth with us and now he will live out eternity in heaven with You. Father, You have given him the victory of life over death through our Lord Jesus Christ. Thanks be to God! His lungs no longer strain to breathe. His aged body no longer strains under the weight of this world. He is home and he is free. Like Abraham, he "breathed his last and died in a good old age, an old man and full of years, and was gathered to his people" (Genesis 25:8). Ninety-seven is a pretty good old age. He is now gathered up with that "great cloud of witnesses" cheering us on to live our lives in the fullness of our years for Your kingdom and Your glory, all by Your grace (Hebrews 12:1). Like PaPa, one day we will be resurrected into eternal life; but even now, let the power of Your resurrection Life live on in us. In Jesus' name I pray, Amen.

Be encouraged today! In the Love of Jesus, *Tommy Hays*

Away from the Body

Good morning, Lord Jesus. Fill my mortal body with fresh breath of Your Holy Spirit, as I look to You and listen for the leading of Your voice. ...

"So we know that we are always confident; even though we know that while we are at home in the body we are away from the Lord—for we walk by faith, not by sight. Yes, we do have confidence, and we would rather be away from the body and at home with the Lord.   So whether we are at home or away, we aim to please Him" (2 Corinthians 5:5).

These earthly bodies of flesh and blood are not our true home. They are but dust (Psalm 103:14). And one day, these mortal bodies of dust will return to dust—"the dust returns to the earth as it was, and the breath returns to God who gave it" (Ecclesiastes 12:7). These bodies are Your means for us to live out our earthly lives until the joyful day we come "home with the Lord."

We were never meant to take up permanent residence in these bodies subject to decay and the weight of sin and death in a broken, fallen world. We are not permanent citizens of this world. "But our citizenship is in heaven, and it is from there that we are expecting a Savior, the Lord Jesus Christ. He will transform the body of our humiliation that it may be conformed to the body of His glory, by the power that also enables Him to make all things subject to Himself" (Philippians 3:21-22).

My grandfather's faith has become sight because he is now "away from the body and at home with the Lord." He can now hear and see perfectly, his mind is clear and his heart is pure. He has run his course and fought "the good fight of the faith" (1 Timothy 6:12). He has heard Your words, "Well done, good and faithful servant; you have been faithful over a few things, I will make you ruler over many things. Enter into the joy of your Lord!" (Matthew 25:23). Until that day comes for me, give me grace to keep running my course and fighting my fight, doing all with the aim to please You. In Jesus' name I pray, Amen.

Be encouraged today! In the Love of Jesus, *Tommy Hays*

"Go Rest High"

Good morning, Lord Jesus. You are the Good Shepherd. Your sheep hear Your voice and follow where You lead— from day to day, from one life to the next.

> *Take my hand and I will follow*
> *Speak Your words, I will obey.*
> *Lead me on and I will follow*
> *Every step of every day. ...*

Thank You for that song, Lord. You said it this way in Your Word:

> "The Lord is my Shepherd; I shall not want.
> He makes me to lie down in green pastures;
> He leads me beside the still waters.
> He restores my soul;
> He leads me in the paths of righteousness
> For His name's sake.
> Yea, though I walk through the valley of the shadow of death,
> I will fear no evil;
> For You are with me;
> Your rod and Your staff, they comfort me.
> You prepare a table for me in the presence of my enemies;
> You anoint my head with oil;
> My cup runs over.
> Surely goodness and mercy shall follow me
> All the days of my life;
> And I will dwell in the house of the Lord
> Forever" (Psalm 23, NKJV).

This morning we will return my grandfather's body to the dust. PaPa has no more need of it now. He has heard the voice of His Good Shepherd and he has followed. Now he's resting in Your green pastures, beside Your still waters. You have lead him through the valley of the shadow of death, and he has had no need to fear, for You are with him.

The last few days, I've been thinking of song written by Vince Gil that makes me think of PaPa's passing form this life to the next:

> "Go rest high on that mountain.
> Son your work on earth is done.
> Go to heaven a shoutin'
> Love for the Father and the Son."

Walking with him through this journey of earthly life, through the fleeting grip of death, into Your arms of eternal life has made me realize even more deeply the critical significance of our relationship with You. How else could we face death with peace and even joy? And every day between this day and that one in my own journey, I can come to You in prayer by Your Spirit. Every day in prayer, I can "go rest high on that mountain." Every day in prayer, I can "go to heaven a shoutin' love for the Father and the Son." In Jesus' name I pray, Amen.

Be encouraged today! In the Love of Jesus, *Tommy Hays*

"Protector of Widows"

Good morning, Lord Jesus. I began this day flying home toward the glorious sun rising in the east over the Texas plains. You are the Son of glory and I thank You for the gift of beginning every day flying in my spirit toward You in prayer. ...

"Sing to God, sing praises to His name, lift up a song to Him who rides upon the clouds—His name is the Lord—be exultant before Him. Father of orphans and protector of widows is God in His holy habitation. God gives the desolate a home to live in; He leads out the prisoners to prosperity, but the rebellious live in a parched land" (Psalm 68:4-6).

You are a Father to the fatherless and You are a Husband to the widow. In her time of rejoicing for my grandfather's spiritual healing and in her time of grieving for the loss of his physical presence, I know You are holding my grandmother near in Your strong arms and tender mercies. Nanny is eighty-seven years old and the day before PaPa's funeral was their sixty-eighth anniversary of marriage. You have filled their long lives with much grace and mercy. I pray that Nanny's later years will be even greater than her former years (from Haggai 2:9).

Edna Marie Hays is amazingly active and deeply spiritual woman of God, still full of much life to give. Give her the grace to live out the richness and fullness of these grandest years of her life for Your glory. "And the disgrace of your widowhood you will remember no more. For your Maker is your Husband, the Lord of Hosts is His name, the Holy One of Israel is your Redeemer, the God of the whole earth He is called" (Isaiah 54:4-5). In Jesus' name I pray, Amen.

Be encouraged today! In the Love of Jesus, *Tommy Hays*

Pleasing God, not People

Good morning, Lord Jesus. Form Your thoughts in my mind and Your desires in my heart. Guide my steps in the way that pleases You today. ...

"For to the one who pleases Him, God gives wisdom and knowledge and joy" (Ecclesiastes 2:26).

Show me how to please You with my life today. Let that be my standard and my goal. I need Your wisdom and knowledge; I want to experience Your joy. Let my focus not be pleasing people but pleasing God. As I please You, some people may be pleased and some may not. Give me the grace and the wisdom to know that I will only find joy as I seek to please You above all else. Anything less will only steal my joy.

Disappointed people that I have not made it my aim to please may condemn me, but my heart will not condemn me if I seek to live my life to please You. "Beloved, if our hearts do not condemn us, we have boldness before God; and we receive from Him whatever we ask, because we obey His commandments and do what pleases Him" (1 John 3:21-22). So, we should not make it our aim to please others; "we make it our aim to please Him" (2 Corinthians 5:9). Then let others be pleased that they see me seeking to please You above all else. In Jesus' name I pray, Amen.

Be encouraged today! In the Love of Jesus, *Tommy Hays*

"To Know Christ"

Good morning, Lord Jesus. I want to know You and hear You and follow You. ...

"I want to know Christ and the power of His resurrection and the sharing of His sufferings by becoming like Him in His death, if somehow I may attain the resurrection from the dead" (Philippians 3:10).

To become like You in Your death is the key to knowing the power of Your resurrection—not just resurrection from the dead when I die, but the power of Your resurrection living in me every day. And to become like You in Your death is to be completely submitted in trusting surrender to the will of our Father no matter what the cost. "Let this mind be in you that was in Christ Jesus, who ... humbled Himself and became obedient to the point of death—even death on a cross" (Philippians 2:5-8).

The words of complete submission and trusting surrender are: "Nevertheless not my will, but Yours, be done" (Luke 22:42 NKJV). Help me know You and become more like You every day—in obedience to the will of our Father. As I do, by Your grace, I will know the power of Your resurrection in my life more every day. In Jesus' name I pray, Amen.

Be encouraged today! In the Love of Jesus, *Tommy Hays*

Desert Place of Prayer

Good morning, Lord Jesus. Father, Son, and Holy Spirit, You are One and You are the One I seek in the quiet of the morning and in the desert place of prayer. ...

"In the morning, while it was still very dark, He got up and went out to a deserted place, and there He prayed" (Mark 1:32).

My deserted place for prayer is most often the deserted hours of the early morning, while it is still very dark because no one else is up yet. Here in my prayer chair with my laptop journal and my Bible, You meet me in the communion of prayer. Here I can get quiet in my soul—my mind, my will, and my emotions—and my spirit can rise into the heavenly places of prayer where I am seated with You, by being seated in You through the communion of Your Spirit and in submission to Your Lordship at the right hand of my Father. "But God, who is rich in mercy, out of the great love with which He has loved us, even when we were dead through our trespasses, made us alive together with Christ—by grace you have been saved—and raised us up with Him and seated us with Him in heavenly places in Christ Jesus, so that in the ages to come He might show the immeasurable riches of His grace in kindness toward us in Christ Jesus" (Ephesians 2:4-7).

Out of these desert places of surrender in the silence of prayer as I wait for Your presence and listen for Your leading, Your living waters of life begin to flow. The desert makes me thirsty and desperate for the life of the water of Your words. "For waters shall break forth in the wilderness, and steams in the desert; the burning sand shall become a pool, and the thirsty ground springs of water" (Isaiah 35:6-7).

Here in the wilderness, I watch and wait for You alone. Here in the desert, I thirst for Your words of life and Your will for my life. And here Your living waters break forth. "Blessed are they who hunger and thirst for righteousness for they will be filled" (Matthew 5:6). You are my Righteousness and I thank You for filling me afresh with Your living waters in the desert place of prayer. In Jesus' name I pray, Amen.

Be encouraged today! In the Love of Jesus, *Tommy Hays*

"Peace like a River"

Good morning, Lord Jesus. Draw me into Your presence, my Father. Come, Holy Spirit. Lord God, I seek all of You with all of me—as best as I can and all by Your grace. ...

"Peace like a river." You brought these words to mind to pray into someone's spirit last night during the prayer time of our New Life Community—our gathering of a couple of small groups that meet on Sunday nights from my home church. With these words came an image of a gently flowing river, but the waters were flowing underground in an underground stream. It seemed You were saying, "Beneath the surface of Your life, I am always here, always moving like a steady flow of peace no matter what things look like on the surface. Don't worry. Be anxious for nothing. Receive my peace like a river."

Yes, Lord. "Cast your burden on the Lord, and He will sustain you; He will never permit the righteous to be moved" (Psalm 55:22). "Cast all your anxiety on Him, because He cares for you" (1 Peter 5:7). You are my Peace, Peace like a River flowing through my life—steady and pure, always moving, always there, always ready to carry me through every trouble I face. Help me not resist Your flow, but freely give myself to You in trusting surrender and to flow with You wherever You take me. In Jesus' name I pray, Amen.

Be encouraged today! In the Love of Jesus, *Tommy Hays*

Possessing the Land, Embracing the Kingdom

Good morning, Lord Jesus. Each day is another day of being conformed to the image of Christ by the power of the Holy Spirit in submission to the will of my Father God (from Romans 8:29; 12:1-2). ...

"Do what is right and good in the sight of the Lord, so that it may go well with you, and so that you may go in and occupy the good land that the Lord swore to your ancestors to give you, thrusting out all your enemies from before you, as the Lord has promised" (Deuteronomy 6:18-19).

The literal realities of the events of those living under the Old Covenant also speak of the spiritual encounters of those living under the New Covenant. "These things happened to them to serve as an example, and they were written down to instruct us, on whom the ends of the ages have come" (1 Corinthians 10:11).

Under the New Covenant, my true enemies are not the human beings but the spiritual beings who will be at work to try to hinder and delay, to defile and distort Your purposes in my life today. "For our struggle is not against enemies of blood and flesh, but against the rulers, against the authorities, against the cosmic powers of this present darkness, against the spiritual forces of evil in heavenly places" (Ephesians 6:12). And the true land You have given me to possess is not marked by metes and bounds, rivers and mountains; it is the land of living in the kingdom of God. And Your kingdom comes in the hearts of all who bow to Your will and Your ways as the King of kings and the Lord of lords. "But strive first for the kingdom of God and His righteousness, and all these things will be given to you as well" (Matthew 6:33). "For the kingdom of God is not food and drink but righteousness and peace and joy in the Holy Spirit" (Romans 14:17).

Give me grace to do what is right and good in Your sight today. As I submit my heart and mind to Your will and ways today, let my enemies be scattered and let me enter into the good land of Your promise and provision. To possess the land is to embrace Your kingdom. Then it will go well with me, despite all I may encounter and all I may endure. Your kingdom come, Your will be done, in my life today. In Jesus' name I pray, Amen.

Be encouraged today! In the Love of Jesus, *Tommy Hays*

God at Work

Good morning, Lord Jesus. Good morning, my Father. Good morning, Holy Spirit. I settle my soul to seek Your face and listen for the leading of Your voice. ...

"From ages past no one has heard, no ear has perceived, no eye has seen any God besides You, who works for those who wait for Him" (Isaiah 64:4).

What an amazing thought! My God works for me as I wait for Him. Of course, You are not working for me in the sense that I am Your boss and You are at my command—that would be arrogant blasphemy. But as I wait for You, You are at work; moving in my life, ordering my steps, preparing the path before me for Your purposes. Yet if I fail to wait, I won't leave room for You to work to prepare the way. If I hurry to go my way, it will be my way rather than Your way that I'm going. So give me the grace of patience to wait—to sit in the silence of surrender before You, to humble myself in Your sight, to listen for the leading of Your voice, then to rise and follow in the path You have prepared in Your work for me this day. In Jesus' name I pray, Amen.

Be encouraged today! In the Love of Jesus, *Tommy Hays*

War in the Heavenlies

Good morning, Lord Jesus. You call me to draw near to You in the morning in the intimacy of prayer so I can rise and go forth into the battle of the day in the authority of Your presence. Now is when I listen, so that I will be ready when You call me to speak. Now is when I bow low in humility before You, so that I will be ready to rise and take my stand in faith to follow You. ...

There is war in the heavenlies, and that war is being manifested in the realms of the earth. Israel is ground zero, as You have prophesied in Your Word from the beginning and through the end. Though the nations gather for destruction and war, true peace will come, but only after a false peace comes first. Let us not be deceived and let us not be complacent. Let us be ready and vigilant with our eyes to the heavens and our ears to Your heart to pray and war in the Spirit as You lead.

"For you yourselves know very well that the day of the Lord will come like a thief in the night. When they say, 'There is peace and security,' then sudden destruction will come upon them, as labor pains come upon a pregnant woman, and there will be no escape. But you, beloved, are not in darkness, for that day to surprise you like a thief, for you are all children of light and children of the day, we are not of the night or of darkness. So than let us not fall asleep as others do, but let us keep awake and be sober, for those who sleep, sleep at night, and those who get drunk get drunk at night. But since we belong to the day, let us be sober and put on the breastplate of faith and love, and for a helmet the hope of salvation. For God has destined us not for wrath but for obtaining salvation through our Lord Jesus Christ, who died for us, so that whether we are awake or asleep we may live with Him. Therefore encourage one another and build each other up, as indeed you are doing" (1 Thessalonians 5:2-11).

You are my Breastplate; You are my Helmet. You are my Warrior and my Peace; my Encouragement and my Hope. Let me be awake and alive in You to obey Your command in the war at hand. In Jesus' name I pray, Amen.

Be encouraged today! In the Love of Jesus, *Tommy Hays*

Peace and Power

Good morning, Lord Jesus. You are my Peace and You are my Power. Fill me with Your Power and Your Peace to follow You in Your ways this day. ...

"The Lord goes forth like a soldier, like a warrior He stirs up His fury, He cries out, He shouts aloud, He shows Himself mighty against His foes" (Isaiah 42:10).

You are not a passive God, sitting back waiting for the world to unravel as time unfolds. You are the Lamb that takes away sins of the world, and You are also the Lion of the Tribe of Judah. There are times when You are silent as a Lamb before the shearers and times when the mountains tremble with at roar of a fierce Lion. You abound in mercy, but You are also righteous in judgment. You are the "Prince of Peace" (Isaiah 9:6) and You give us Your peace, but not the peace "as the world gives" (John 14:27). This is not a peace of appeasement or complacency, not the cessation of conflict at any cost, but the peace that comes only from the wisdom of the One who establishes peace with the sword of His Word and the authority of His name. In this way, You said, "Do not think that I have come to bring peace to the earth; I have not come to bring peace, but a sword" (Matthew 10:34).

You have not come to bring the pacifistic peace of the world that chooses the compromise of appeasement rather than risk confrontation and challenge to injustice, persecution, and oppression. We will only know when to lay down our lives and our weapons and know when to stand and fight when we know the One who is our Peace. Then we will be led by Your Spirit rather than our flesh and unholy spirits. "I have said this to you, so that in Me you may have peace. In the world you may face persecution, but take courage; I have conquered the world!" (John 16:33). Yes, Lord. Only in You do we have true peace. Only in You do we have true power. As they say, "No Jesus; No peace. Know Jesus; Know Peace." In Jesus name I pray, Amen.

Be encouraged today! In the Love of Jesus, *Tommy Hays*

Women on the Frontlines

Good morning, Lord Jesus.   I call upon Your name as You call upon my heart. ...

"At that time Deborah, a prophetess, wife of Lappidoth, was judging Israel. ... She sent and summoned Barak ... and said to him, 'The Lord, the God of Israel commands you, 'Go, take possession of Mount Tabor, bringing ten thousand from the tribe of Naphtali and the tribe of Zebulun. I will draw out Sisera, the general of Jabin's army, to meet you by the Wadi Kishon with his chariots and his troops; and I will give him into your hand.' ' Barak said to her, 'If you will go with me, I will go; but if you will not go with me, I will not go.' And she said, 'I will surely go with you; nevertheless the road on which you are going will not lead to your glory, for the Lord will sell Sisera into the hand of a woman' "(Judges 4:4-9).

I'll be going to a conference in Ohio this weekend with my mother-in-law Beverly called "Women on the Frontlines of Battle." Prepare my heart to hear Your Word from Heidi Baker, Jim Goll, and the others You will use to speak Your Truth and impart Your Spirit. In these days, You are humbling the men of Your kingdom to make room for the leadership of Your women. There are battles we need to fight that cannot be won unless we go out with them into battle. There is land You have given to us to possess that we cannot take unless we take both Your sons and Your daughters with us into battle. We have different roles, but our roles are of equal significance and value in Your kingdom. Let them be the roles You have determined rather than those we have determined, by the traditions of men rather than the Word of God. Let our positions be those You have assigned at Your command rather than our own.

The Word of God says, "In these last days it will be, God declares, that I will pour out My Spirit upon all flesh, and your sons and your daughters will prophesy, and your young men will see visions, and your old men shall dream dreams. Even upon My slaves, both men and women, in those days I will pour out My Spirit; and they shall prophesy" (Acts 2:17-18). From the day You poured out Your Holy Spirit upon all flesh—male and female flesh—on the day of Pentecost, these days have been "these last days." You have called "both men and women" to hear and to speak Your Word with Your authority at Your command.   Forgive us where we have misunderstood Your Word, failed to consider the whole counsel of God, heard only what we wanted to hear, and ignored the rest. This road on which we are going will not lead to our glory but to Yours. In Jesus' name I pray, Amen.

Be encouraged today! In the Love of Jesus, *Tommy Hays*

A Giving Spirit[*]

"Give to him who asks you, and from him who wants to borrow from you do not turn away" (Matthew 5:42).

Something interesting happened today. Just as we were about to fire up the grill for our little family cookout, a transient / homeless person knocked on our door. Rob spoke with him first then left to go get something for him. I had mixed feelings as I went out to greet him. I really wanted to help him, but I felt anxious, too! I just didn't know how I was supposed to help him or even if that was something God wanted me to do! So, I offered up a quick prayer: "God, how will I know what to do?" Then I said to the man, "Is there anything I can get for you?" He said he would really appreciate a cold glass of water. I said "Sure," rather excitedly; who couldn't do that? Then I felt like God prompted me to invite him around to the backyard for dinner. I told him that we were just having a quiet cookout and that he could pull up a lawn chair and join us; a good chance to get out of the hot sun and get refreshed. He agreed. I asked him his name, shook his hand and told him my name as we went around back.

It's hard to put into words all that this encounter taught me. During our brief conversation, I felt like I could see this man's pain and anger, but more than anything, I could also see the good in him and his potential. I knew God loved him and that He was watching over him.

The man didn't stay long; I packed him food to take with him, but as he was leaving, he said, "I'm not going to forget you and what you did for me." I really hadn't done much; just packed him a few hotdogs and some potato salad. But maybe that's the point: I gave the meager stuff that I had and God turned it into a blessing. The man isn't going to remember me or my potato salad and hotdogs per say, what he will remember is an afternoon encounter with God.

All praise and glory be to God! *Mary Margaret Adams*

---

[*] The following devotional was written by Mary Margaret Adams.

Clean Hands and a Pure Heart

Good morning, Lord Jesus. Lord I give You my heart, mind, soul, and strength. Help me hold nothing back from You today. ...

Saturday night at the conference, a little child prayed for me at the altar that I would have clean hands and a pure heart before You. Sunday morning, the pastor and the people of the little country church where I stopped to worship on my way home circled around me to pray for me at the altar. As they laid a "mantle" in the form of a prayer shawl across my shoulders, someone prayed that I would have clean hands and a pure heart before You. I receive Your call to holiness of heart and life. By the love of the Father and the blood of Jesus and the fire of the Holy Spirit, cleanse my hands and purify my heart by Your grace and Your power in accordance with Your Word.

"Who will ascend the hill of the Lord? And who shall stand in His holy place? Those who have clean hands and pure hearts, who do not lift up their souls to what is false, and do not swear deceitfully. They will receive blessing from the Lord, and vindication from the God of their salvation. Such is the company of those who seek Him, who seek the face of the God of Jacob" (Psalm 24:3-6).

By Your grace, I seek Your face. By the blood of the Lamb that cleanses my sins and sanctifies my soul, I ascend this hill and come into this place—the place of Your presence—with clean hands and a pure heart. Thank You for this gift of grace beyond words. In Jesus' name I pray, Amen.

Be encouraged today! In the Love of Jesus, *Tommy Hays*

"The Remnant of the Noble"

Good morning, Lord Jesus. Fill my thoughts with Your thoughts and fill my desires with Your desires as I decrease and You increase, as I watch and wait for Your leading and Your command. ...

"Then down to the gates marched the people of the Lord. Awake, awake, Deborah! Awake, awake, utter a song! Arise, Barak, lead away your captives, O son of Abinoam. Then down marched the remnant of the noble; the people of the Lord marched down for Him against the mighty" (Judges 5:11-13).

There are those who are "the mighty," but You are the Almighty! There are those who take their stand against the will of the Lord, but You are the One whose will stands over eternity. Let Your sons and Your daughters hear Your call to awake and to arise! Let us hear Your call to march in the authority of Your Word and the power of Your Name. We are the remnant of the noble, the people of the Lord who refuse to bow down to the enemies of our King—the world, the flesh, and the devil.

These false gods seek our worship and seek our appeasement. Then those around us who give them place and honor in their lives, give them strength and courage to advance against the gates of the kingdom of God. "When new gods were chosen, then war was in the gates" (Judges 5:8). By Your grace, we will not sit back; we will answer Your call. We will arise and march down to the gates—the gates of our hearts and minds, the gates of our thoughts and desires. There we will worship You alone as God and bow before You alone as King. And there our God will arise and our enemies will be scattered (Psalm 68:1). There we will proclaim as the remnant of the noble, "How the mighty have fallen in the midst of battle!" (2 Samuel 1:25). In Jesus' name I pray, Amen.

Be encouraged today! In the Love of Jesus, *Tommy Hays*

You are I AM

Good morning, Lord Jesus. Father, Son, and Holy Spirit—God of Abraham, Isaac, and Jacob—Maker and Master of Heaven and Earth—You are I AM. ...

"But Moses said to God, 'If I come to the Israelites and say to them, 'The God of your ancestors has sent me to you,' and they ask me, 'What is His name?' what shall I say to them?" God said to Moses, 'I AM WHO I AM." Thus you shall say to the Israelites, 'I AM has sent me to you.' " God also said to Moses, 'Thus you shall say to the Israelites, 'The Lord, the God of your ancestors, the God of Abraham, the God of Isaac, and the God of Jacob has sent me to you: This is My name forever, and this is My title for all generation' " (Exodus 3:13-15).

You are all I need. I need all of You. By Your grace, I give all of me to all of You. Open my eyes to see You clearly as You are. Open the eyes of Israel and Islam to see You clearly as You are. Open the eyes of all nations to behold the One who rules all nations. "He calls to the heavens above and the earth, that He may judge His people: 'Gather to Me My faithful ones, who made a covenant with Me by sacrifice!' The heavens declare His righteousness, for God himself is judge. 'Hear, O My people, and I will speak, O Israel, and I will testify against you, I AM God, your God' " (Psalm 50:4-7). Forgive each of us, Lord God, when You call to us and we do not answer, when You come to us and we do not receive You, when You lead us and we do not follow, when You reveal Yourself to us and we do not see You for Who You are. You are I AM.

You said, "For the sake of My servant Jacob, and Israel My chosen, I call you by your name, I surname you, though you do not know Me. I AM the Lord and there is no other; besides Me there is no god. I arm you, though you do not know Me, so that they may know, from the rising of the sun and from the west, that there is no one besides Me; I AM the Lord and there is no other" (Isaiah 45:4-6). By Your grace and mercy, You arm and protect the people of Your covenant and call them by name, though they do not yet know Your Name. You are I AM.

You said: "I AM the Bread of Life" (John 6:35); "I AM the Light of the World" (John 8:12); "I AM from above" (John 8:23); "I AM the Gate" (John 10:9); "I AM the Good Shepherd" (John 10:11); "I AM God's Son" (John 10:36); "I AM the Resurrection and the Life" (John 11:25). To Your first disciples, You said, "You call Me Teacher and Lord—and you are right, for that is what I AM" (John 13:13). To the Samaritan woman at the well who said, "I know Messiah is coming and when He comes He will proclaim all things to us," You said to her, "I AM He, the One Who is speaking to you"

(John 4:25-26). And when the children of Abraham could not see You as the One who was to come to fulfill their hopes through the sacrifice of Your love, You said, "Very truly, I tell you, before Abraham was, I AM" (John 8:58).

Thank You for Your grace that has opened my eyes to see You, my ears to hear You, and my heart to receive You as You are. You are my protection and my provision, my Lord and my Savior, my God and my King. You are All I need. You are my "All in All" (1 Corinthians 15:28). You are I AM. And I pray the eyes of all people of all nations in all generations would be opened to see You as You are. In Jesus' name I pray, Amen.

Be encouraged today! In the Love of Jesus, *Tommy Hays*

The Days of Amos

Good morning, Lord Jesus. I call upon Your name and seek the fullness of Your salvation for myself and for all who need to know Your name. ...

Are these not the beginning of the days seen by Amos long ago? Through Your prophet You declared Your judgments on the nations of the earth to come. "The Lord roars from Zion, and utters His voice from Jerusalem; the pastors of the shepherds mourn, and the top of Carmel withers" (Amos 1:2). I join those You are calling to intercede throughout the earth for salvation of the people of our nations, the people of all nations, and especially the people of these nations and cities You have named by name under Your judgments to come in the fullness of time: Damascus (Amos 1:3), Gaza (1:6), Tyre (1:9), Edom (1:11), Ammon (1:13), Moab (2:1), Judah (2:4), and Israel (2:6).

"Surely the Lord does nothing, without revealing His secret to His servants the prophets. The Lion has roared; who will not fear? The Lord God has spoken; who can but prophesy?" (Amos 3:7-8).

In the fear of the Lord, I pray. In the love of God, I pray. I pray for the blessing of the fear of God to fall upon every heart that brings conviction of sin—especially the sin of hardened, rebellious hearts of doubt, unbelief, and pride that resist the grace and mercy of God available to all through Your unfailing love revealed and released through the blood of Christ. "This is right and is acceptable in the sight of God our Savior, who desires everyone to be saved and to come to the knowledge of the Truth" (1 Timothy 2:3-4). You are the Way, the Truth, and the Life (John 14:6). Through the sacrifice of Your love and Your offer of grace to all, You have prepared the way for each of us to know the truth and live our lives eternally in You. Though judgment will come, Your "mercy triumphs over judgment" for all who will humble themselves in Your sight (James 2:13). "Everyone who calls on the name of the Lord will be saved" (Romans 10:13). I pray for all who need to call on Your name before judgment and even in midst of the judgment to come. Even Your judgments are Your mercy if those with hardened hearts humble themselves and bow rebellious knees to ask for the grace You long to give.

"The Lord is not slow about His promise, as some think of slowness, but is patient with you, not wanting any to perish, but all to come to repentance. But the day of the Lord will come like a thief, and then the heavens will pass away with a loud noise, and the elements will be dissolved with fire, and the earth and everything that is done in it will be disclosed. Since all these things are to be dissolved in this way, what sort of persons ought you to be in leading lives of holiness and godliness, waiting for and hastening the coming of the day of God, because of which the heavens will be set ablaze and dissolved, and the elements will melt with fire? But in accordance with His promise, we wait for new heavens and a new earth, where righteousness is at home" (2 Peter 3:9-13). Come Lord Jesus, be at home in my heart today. Come be at home in every heart who calls on Your name today. In Jesus' name I pray, Amen.

Be encouraged today! In the Love of Jesus, *Tommy Hays*

Promise of Restoration in the Days of Amos

Good morning, Lord Jesus. Help me be quiet so I can hear. Help me listen so You can speak. ...

Though Your Word through Amos speaks of judgment without measure for the people of the nations and for Israel who will not humble themselves in repentance and turn to You in obedience, Your Word also speaks of the healing and restoration that comes through Your mercy for those who do (Amos 9:11-15).   "On that day I will raise up the booth of David that is fallen, and repair its breaches, and raise up its ruins, and rebuild it as in the days of old; in order that they may possess the remnant of Edom and all the nations who are called by My name, says the Lord who does this" (9:11-12).

Lord, raise up the booth of David—the tabernacle of worship and praise and prayer "before the ark of the covenant of the Lord to minister regularly before the ark as each day required" (1 Chronicles 16:37).   Draw Your people before the ark of Your presence. Let us seek You and Your face for Your protection and Your grace as each day requires. Only the power of Your presence will bring peace and protection. Open our eyes and our hearts to seek You and receive You. Rebuild Your tabernacle of prayer and praise in our hearts. Let it be so in Israel and in Islam, in the hearts of all people of all nations who humble themselves to seek Your face, welcome Your presence, and obey Your will. In Jesus' name I pray, Amen.

Be encouraged today! In the Love of Jesus, *Tommy Hays*

Evil Exposed by the Light

Good morning, Lord Jesus. Let the light of Your life shine in my soul and throughout the earth. ...

"Take no part in the unfruitful works of darkness, but instead expose them" (Ephesians 5:11).

Thank You for exposing the plans and schemes of the terrorists who sought to explode ten passenger planes on their way to America. I join in the prayers of Your people throughout the earth that the works of darkness will be exposed and the works of evil will be thwarted.

Terrorism is the enemy's perversion of the fear of God. "Transgression speaks to the wicked deep in their hearts; there is no fear of God before their eyes. They flatter themselves in their own eyes that their iniquity cannot be found out and hated. The words of their mouths are mischief and deceit; they have ceased to act wisely and do good. They plot mischief while on their beds; they are set on a way that is not good; they do not reject evil" (Psalm 36:1-4).

The true fear of God is honor and reverence for You and Your ways. Your ways are life and light, not death and darkness. I pray for the souls of those who are confused and deceived by this false fear, who worship a god who is not God. Open their eyes to see You as You are. Let the true fear of God come upon them that leads to humility and repentance, then Your mercy and grace. "For with You is the fountain of life; in Your light we see light" (Psalm 36:9). In Jesus' name I pray, Amen.

Be encouraged today! In the Love of Jesus, *Tommy Hays*

The Anger of the Lord

Good morning, Lord Jesus. Your name is above every name. At Your name, every knee shall bow and every tongue shall confess that Jesus Christ is Lord to the glory of the Father (Philippians 2:9-11). ...

"But You indeed are awesome! Who can stand before You when once Your anger is roused? From the heavens You uttered judgment; the earth feared and was still when God rose up to establish judgment, to save all the oppressed of the earth" (Psalm 76:7-9).

Yesterday I sensed Your anger was roused in me. I saw the oppressed of the earth face to face and could do nothing about it, and I was angry at those who could. We took my children to a National Park for the day to see Mammoth Cave, and there were people there from many different nations and cultures. Two men were there with their wives, veiled in black clothes from their heads to their feet with only slits for their eyes to see how to walk and take care of their children. My anger rose and my heart broke that a husband could do that to his wife, that a religion could do that its people. So I continued to release my anger to You and let the anger turn to intercession. I continued to remember that our battle is not against flesh and blood, but against the spiritual forces of wickedness who come to deceive and confuse, to oppress and destroy (Ephesians 6:12).

You desire to save "all the oppressed of the earth," whether they know they are oppressed or not. Lord God, let Your anger be roused against the injustice and oppression of our spiritual enemy who comes to deceive and work his destruction through those he has blinded to the truth of Your nature. The gospel of Your truth "is veiled to those who are perishing. In their case the god of this world has blinded the minds of the unbelievers, to keep them from seeing the light of the gospel of the glory of Christ, who is the image of God" (2 Corinthians 4:3-4). Let the earth fear God and be still before You, as You rise to establish Your judgment and justice to save all the oppressed of the earth. "There is salvation in no one else, for there is no other name under heaven given among mortals by which we must be saved" (Acts 4:12). In Jesus' name I pray, Amen.

Be encouraged today! In the Love of Jesus, *Tommy Hays*

Wonderful in Counsel

Good morning, Lord Jesus. Make my ways more like Your ways; make my thoughts more like Your thoughts. I yield my ways and my thoughts to You. ...

"I bless the Lord who gives me counsel; in the night also my heart instructs me. I keep the Lord always before me; because He is at my right hand, I shall not be moved" (Psalm 16:7-8).

They say that even as we sleep, our minds are working. As our bodies rest, our thoughts are developing strategies and solving problems. Our minds are one of Your most amazing creations! Lord, remind me to begin and end each day with You. Let my mind continually look to You and let my heart continually be led by You. Then it will be Your strategies that are developed and Your answers that come, as You counsel me through the day and even through the night. Then I can be steadfast and confident in the wisdom that comes from the wisest One. You are "wonderful in counsel and excellent in wisdom" (Isaiah 28:29). In Jesus' name I pray, Amen.

Be encouraged today! In the Love of Jesus, *Tommy Hays*

Ministry Together

Good morning, Lord Jesus. Help me humble myself to listen for Your leading and wait for Your word. ...

Paul spoke often of those who worked alongside him in the ministry of Your love and power and grace. He spoke of Timothy, who "like a son with a father he has served with me in the work of the gospel," and of Epaphroditus as "my brother and co-worker and fellow soldier" (Philippians 2:19-30). He spoke of Philemon as a "dear friend and co-worker" and of Mark, Aristarchus, Demas, and Luke as "fellow prisoners in Christ Jesus" and "fellow workers" (Philemon 2, 23). He spoke of Titus as "my partner and co-worker" in ministry (2 Corinthians 8:23).

By Your Holy Spirit, You brought Your disciples together in diverse relationships of trust and respect as teams of ministry for various seasons to be "co-workers for the kingdom of God" (Colossians 4:11). Before their season of missionary journeys together, You brought together Paul and Barnabas for ministry together to the people of the church at Antioch. "So it was for an entire year they met with the church and taught a great many people, and it was at Antioch that the disciples were first called 'Christians' " (Acts 11:25-26).

Over these past ten years of ministry, You have brought me alongside many men and women who have been my co-workers for the kingdom of God. We've learned from one another, grown in maturity with one another, fought for one another and at times—I hate to admit—even fought with one another. But You have used it all to strengthen us and encourage us, to equip us and prepare us to fulfill our destiny in our generation for Your glory. And Your Word makes Your will very clear that You do not intend for us to minister in Your kingdom alone. You call us to find our place and affirm the place of others around us in the relationships of trust and respect You are forming for Your purposes in every season. As we do, let our eyes be open to Your vision, let our ears be open to Your leading, let our minds be open to Your wisdom, and let our hearts be open to Your desires. And there we will find that our arms must be open to embrace one another in the risk of relationship and the bonds of trust You are forming for the work of Your ministry of love and power and grace. In Jesus' name I pray, Amen.

Be encouraged today! In the Love of Jesus, *Tommy Hays*

The Hand of the Lord

Good morning, Lord Jesus. You are welcome into my heart and my life again today. ...

"The hand of the Lord was with them, and a great number became believers and turned to the Lord. News of this came to the ears of the church in Jerusalem, and they sent Barnabus to Antioch. When he came and saw the grace of God, he rejoiced, and exhorted them all to remain faithful to the Lord with steadfast devotion; for he was a good man, full of the Holy Spirit and faith. And a great many people were brought to the Lord" (Acts 11:21-24).

Lord, what is "the hand of the Lord?"

It seems I hear You say, "My hand is My favor. In part, it speaks of My authority and My grace resting upon My sons and My daughters to bring others into a relationship of trust and love with Me."

Lord, help me humble myself under Your mighty hand. Use my life to bring others to You—to know You and to know the peace and pleasure of a relationship with You of trusting love. Let Your authority and Your grace rest upon me to bring a great many people to the Lord. Like Barnabus, let me be "full of the Holy Spirit and faith," ever rejoicing in Your grace, exhorting others to seek Your face, and encouraging them to pursue Your presence "with steadfast devotion" and trusting faith. In Jesus' name I pray, Amen.

Be encouraged today! In the Love of Jesus, *Tommy Hays*

Walk in the Will of Your Ways

Good morning, Lord Jesus. Father, Son, and Holy Spirit, make my paths straight in line with Your will for my life today. ...

"For all the peoples walk, each in the name of its god, but we will walk in the name of the Lord our God forever and ever" (Micah 4:5).

By the grace of the faith You have given me, I choose to walk in Your ways and in the nature of Your name. Forgive me when I stumble. Correct me when I get confused. Turn me back around when I turn the wrong way. Strengthen me when I grow weary. Encourage me when I grow faint. Keep reminding me of the way and leading me in the steps that lead to life in You. You are the Way, the Truth, and the Life that I have chosen. Help me keep choosing You every day. Help me walk in the will of Your ways this day. In Jesus' name I pray, Amen.

Be encouraged today! In the Love of Jesus, *Tommy Hays*

Pray for Our Leaders

Good morning, Lord Jesus. Shape my will as I submit my will to Yours. ...

"Joash was seven years old when he began to reign; he reigned forty years in Jerusalem; his mother's name was Zebiah of Beer-Sheba. Joash did what was right in the sight of the Lord all the days of the priest Jehoida" (2 Chronicles 24:1-2).

You positioned Joash in kingly authority to lead the people of Israel. And You positioned Jehoida in priestly authority and to encourage and intercede for the king, as well as the people. Jehoida was a humble and godly priest, who encouraged the people and the king to seek You and obey You (v. 23:16). With the spiritual leadership of Jehoida, King Joash "restored the house of God to its proper condition and strengthened it" (v. 24:13). And King Joash "did what was right in the sight of the Lord," but only "all the days of the priest Jehoida."

After the death of Jehoida, the spiritual leaders compromised their convictions and failed in their devotion to You. Soon their divided hearts were hardened against You, as they turned to the false gods of the cultures around them. The king and priests and people "abandoned the house of the Lord, the God of their ancestors, and served the sacred poles and the idols. And wrath came upon Judah and Jerusalem for this guilt of theirs" (v. 24:18).

Sincere devotion to You alone leaves no room for compromise. And the devotion of those in spiritual authority affects those in governmental authority. So we are to pray "for kings and all who are in high positions, so that we may lead a quiet and peaceable life in all godliness and dignity" (1 Timothy 2:1-2). Every person, weather in positions of authority or not, is responsible for their own actions and their own life of devotion to You. Yet at the same time, our prayers led by Your Spirit affect them and their choices. And their choices affect each of us under the authority of their government. So remind us to pray for our leaders, to encourage them and intercede for them, to speak the truth in love to them, and always to cover them in a blanket of prayer. Then they will do what is right in Your sight and we will lead lives of godliness and dignity. In Jesus' name I pray, Amen.

Be encouraged today! In the Love of Jesus, *Tommy Hays*

Freedom from Fear of Others

Good morning, Lord Jesus. I find my strength and my identity in You. Strengthen me today in the power of Your Word; remind me again who I am in You. ...

"The fear of others lays a snare, but one who trusts in the Lord is secure" (Proverbs 29:25).

By Your grace, I choose to trust in You. I choose to find my security in You. Forgive me for the times I have given into the fear of man, when I have been more concerned with what others thought of me than what You thought of me. Deliver me from insecurity and establish me in the confidence of who I am in You. "So we can say with confidence, 'The Lord is my helper; I will not be afraid. What can anyone do to me?' " (Hebrews 13:6). In Jesus' name I pray, Amen.

Be encouraged today! In the Love of Jesus, *Tommy Hays*

Holy and Wholly Yours

Good morning, Lord Jesus. Father, Son, and Holy Spirit—You are One and You are holy. Help me be wholly Yours. ...

"His divine power has given us everything needed for life and godliness, through the knowledge of Him who called us by His own glory and goodness. Thus He has given us, through these things, His precious and very great promises, so that through them you may escape the corruption that is in the world because of lust, and may become participants of the divine nature" (2 Peter 1:3-4).

Give me faith to call upon Your name and desire to participate in Your nature—all by Your grace and all in Your power. I hear Your Spirit rising up in my spirit to sing a new song of surrender and faith:

> *You are holy.*
> *You are holy.*
> *You are a holy, loving God.*
>
> *And You call me.*
> *And You change me.*
> *More and more every day.*
>
> *And You cleanse me.*
> *And You free me.*
> *You make my holy and wholly Yours.*

Yes, Lord. "For it is written, 'You shall be holy, for I am holy' "(1 Peter 1:16). Though there is nothing good in me apart from You, I am not apart from You. "For our sake, He made Him sin who knew no sin, so that in Him we might become the righteousness of God" (2 Corinthians 5:21).

Let the truth of Your Word settle into my soul. Let the truth of Your calling and Your will for me and my life awaken my soul to arise into newness of life—a life that desires to be holy and wholly Yours—more and more every day. In Jesus' name I pray, Amen.

Be encouraged today! In the Love of Jesus, *Tommy Hays*

Passion to Pursue Righteousness

Good morning, Lord Jesus. Draw me close to You and make me more like You each day. ...

"The way of the wicked is an abomination to the Lord, but He loves the one who pursues righteousness" (Proverbs 15:9).

Build in my spirit a passion to pursue righteousness—to be in right relationship with You, with others, and within myself. Let the encounters of my day expose the wickedness that remains in my heart. Search my heart and reveal the wickedness of my ways (Psalm 139:23-24). Let me see it; let me hate it; let me give it to You. It's not something to fear; it is something to welcome and something to actively and aggressively pursue.

You don't expose my wickedness because You hate me, but because You love me. You want to help me know the peace and joy that comes with the pursuit of righteousness. "For the kingdom of God is ... righteousness and peace and joy in the Holy Spirit. ... Let us then pursue what makes for peace" (Romans 14:17-19). "Whoever pursues righteousness and kindness will find life and honor" (Proverbs 21:21). Let me find life and honor in the pursuit of righteousness this day. In Jesus' name I pray, Amen.

Be encouraged today! In the Love of Jesus, *Tommy Hays*

Prayer Walking

Good morning, Lord Jesus. I proclaim Your name as Lord over my life, my family, my church, and my community. ...

"And the Lord said to Joshua, 'Do not fear them, for I have delivered them into your hand; not a man of them shall stand before you' " (Joshua 10:8).

For the past few weeks, a group of intercessors from our church have been meeting for prayer and then prayer walking through our church and our community. Last night we walked and prayed through the campus of the University of Kentucky as You led us. Everywhere we went, we welcomed Your presence and Your power, we offered thanksgiving and praise, we prayed and prophesied Your will and Your ways. We proclaimed the name of Jesus over the students, teachers, and staff, over the walkways, buildings, and stadiums, over all time and space and every dimension as far as Your grace would go. And You gave us the faith to believe our prayers made a difference.

Along the journey, a curious group of graduate students from Hyderabad, India came near. Before long, we were inviting them to a meal at our Thursday night Alpha Course to ask questions about faith and to join us on Sunday morning for worship. We were amazed at the opportunity to touch the nations just by walking down the street from our local church. We need not fear to share the love of God in Jesus Christ. Your Word and Your Spirit go before us to prepare the way for the message of Your love and offer of Your grace. Prayer pushes back the darkness to let the light of Your love shine through. Thank You for letting the light of Your love shine through us. Let these young men be among many who will come to the light of Your love this year. In Jesus' name we pray, Amen.

Be encouraged today! In the Love of Jesus, *Tommy Hays*

Tenacity of Spirit

Good morning, Lord Jesus. Worries and concerns, disappointments and fears have been coming against my mind, trying to steal my sleep and my peace. But I hear You calling me to rise and come, and to press into the peace of Your presence. ...

"Do not lag in zeal, be ardent in spirit, serve the Lord. Rejoice in hope, be patient in suffering, persevere in prayer" (Romans 12:11-12).

These words are not suggestions, but commands. There is a tenacity of spirit You desire in me—zealous, ardent, persevering. Like a battering ram that continues to pound away until breakthrough comes; like a bulldog that grabs on and doesn't let go until victory comes; like a baby that cries through the night until somebody gets up out of bed to change him and feed him until sleep comes; You call us to press on and press through. Passivity is sin.

When You saw the temple was no longer a house of prayer and saw that ministry was being merchandised, the tenacity of the Spirit rose in You to drive out the money-changers and cleanse the temple. Your first disciples "remembered that it was written, 'Zeal for Your house will consume me' " (John 2:17). When You saw the lame and the blind, You healed them. When You saw the oppressed and the bound, You freed them. When You saw the broken and hurting, You loved them. You were not passive and complacent; You were tenacious and aggressive in obedience to the will of the Father, no matter the cost. When Your spiritual zeal embarrassed the spiritually lazy, You didn't back down, but persistently replied, "My Father is still working, and I am working" (John 5:17). And when Your message was not heard and Your sacrifices were not received, You kept loving and serving and forgiving. The plans and purposes of God prevailed.

So when I am discouraged, I choose to rejoice in hope. When I am suffering, I choose to be patient in endurance. When I am disappointed, I choose to persevere in prayer. It's all by Your grace and all in Your power, but my part is to choose—and to keep on choosing as I press on and press through in obedience and faith. This is the attitude that will prevail even against the gates of hell (Matthew 16:18). You have not given me a spirit of fear, but of love and power and a sound mind (2 Timothy 1:7). Thank You for the gifts of perseverance of faith and tenacity of spirit. Thank You for the peace of Your presence. As I keep trusting in You, You will cause all things to work together for good (Romans 8:28). In Jesus' name I pray, Amen.

Be encouraged today! In the Love of Jesus, *Tommy Hays*

I Lift My Eyes Up

Good morning, Lord Jesus. "I lift up my eyes to the hills—from where will my help come from? My help comes from the Lord, who made heaven and earth" (Psalm 121:1-2). You are my help and my strength. I lift my eyes and seek Your face; I open my heart and receive Your grace. ...

This morning a good friend of mine is coming to town to pray. Leading a prayer ministry, I pray for others every day. And I am thankful for the blessing of this calling. But these times of getting away for the morning with a trusted friend with no plan and no agenda but to seek Your face and receive Your grace, to worship You in spirit and in truth, to watch and wait for Your leading and then to rise in our spirits to follow You in prayer wherever You lead are moments when Your strength fills my soul. These are moments when You renew my vision and encourage my heart. "But you, beloved, build yourselves up on your most holy faith; pray in the Holy Spirit; keep yourselves in the love of God; look forward to the mercy of our Lord Jesus Christ that leads to eternal life" (Jude 20-21).

I look forward to Your mercy today. I look forward to coming to You and calling on Your name and being filled afresh with Your Spirit in prayer with my friend and brother in the Lord. "When they had prayed, the place in which they were gathered together was shaken; and they were all filled with the Holy Spirit and spoke the word of God with boldness" (Acts 4:31). Let us speak Your words of life into one another's spirits with holy boldness and receive the strength and help that comes only from You. Together we will lift our eyes up to the hills and we will ascend the mountain of the Lord. In Jesus' name I pray, Amen.

Be encouraged today! In the Love of Jesus, *Tommy Hays*

Life Hidden in Christ

Good morning, Lord Jesus. I worship You, Lord God my Father. Welcome Holy Spirit of the Living God. ...

Lord, take my thoughts off of myself and turn them to You. Let my life be hidden in Yours today. "For you have died, and your life is hidden with Christ in God.   When Christ who is your life is revealed, then you also will be revealed with Him in glory" (Colossians 3:3-4).

In a moment I'll have a chance to go and share a word of encouragement to Your servants from across our community who are spending their time and their labor to build a home for a family who doesn't have one. Through the ministry of Habitat for Humanity, they are looking beyond themselves and looking to You to serve others.   While they are building a habitat for humanity, You are building a habitat for Your presence in their hearts. Your nature is to love and to serve, and when we are serving in love, Your nature is becoming our nature. "The only thing that counts is faith working through love" (Galatians 5:6).   Let Your life and Your love work to serve others through me today. In Jesus' name I pray, Amen.

Be encouraged today! In the Love of Jesus, *Tommy Hays*

Blessed be Your Name

Good morning, Lord Jesus. This song of praise has been in my spirit for days, "Blessed be the name of the Lord... Blessed be Your glorious name!" ...

"O how abundant is Your goodness that You have laid up for those who fear You, and accomplished for those who take refuge in You, in the sight of everyone! ... Blessed be the Lord, for He has wondrously shown His steadfast love to me when I was beset as a city under siege" (Psalm 31:19-21).

You are a good God. You love me and care for me as I find my refuge in You. You give me faith and courage to press into the place of peace in You. Your part is to do it; my part is to choose it. I can't make it happen, but as I choose to rest in You and the abundant goodness of Your steadfast, unfailing love and power, You make it happen. I am not to sit back in passivity, allowing waves of worry to wash over me, but I am to rise and seek Your face and receive Your grace with thanksgiving and praise for Your power and Your provision for my every need. This is the character of faith and tenacity of spirit You are working in me through every challenge I face. This is the Sabbath rest You have prepared for the people of God. "Let us therefore make every effort to enter that rest" (Hebrews 4:11). Your part is to do it; my part is to choose it—all by Your grace and all in Your power. In Jesus' name I pray, Amen.

Be encouraged today! In the Love of Jesus, *Tommy Hays*

Teammates and Teamwork

Good morning, Lord Jesus. Help me listen for Your leading and go where You send me. ...

"Then one who plants and the one who waters work as a team with the same purpose. Yet they will be rewarded individually, according to their own hard work. We work together as partners who belong to God" (1 Corinthians 3:8-9, NLT).

In a team, each person does their part. We use our uncommon gifts for a common goal. Lord, reveal to me my part and my place in the teams You have called me to for the work and glory of Your kingdom. Reveal to my teammates their part and their place, as we hear Your call and obey Your commands, working together as partners in pursuit of Your common purpose for our lives. We each have a part in this purpose, and each person must do his or her part. And as we do we will find fulfillment of our purposes in You. In Jesus' name I pray, Amen.

Be encouraged today! In the Love of Jesus, *Tommy Hays*

Lamentation in Lexington

Good morning, Lord Jesus. You are the Comforter when it seems there is no comfort. You are the Healer when it seems there is no healing. ...

"Thus says the Lord: A voice is heard in Ramah, lamentation and bitter weeping. Rachel is weeping for her children; she refuses to be comforted for her children, because they are no more" (Jeremiah 31:13).

Our community is in mourning and grief, wailing in sadness and sorrow. Yesterday morning, the six o'clock flight from Lexington to Atlanta crashed in a field not far from the end of the runway. That's a flight many of us have taken many times. Forty-nine people lost their lives; only one survived. A voice is heard in Lexington. There is lamentation and bitter weeping, as our hearts are broken with Yours over the loss of these lives and anguish of their families and friends. These are our neighbors and we join with them in their pain.

In these days of grief and anguish, where there is no comfort, You fill us with compassion and caring for those who are numbed by the pain and dazed by the shock of such wrenching tragedy. Though we are a large city, we love one another like a small town. And every life of our community will be touched by the loss of these lives. Before the recovery efforts began, our emergency workers gathered around the plane to pray. Without prayer, what would we do? Without You, how could we bear the burden of such sadness and sorrow? "My soul melts away for sorrow; strengthen me according to Your word" (Psalm 119:28).

Father, we offer ourselves to You to be as Your arms and Your heart to those who are grieving. Help us be silent when we should not speak, but listen and love. Help us hold them tight when their emotions burst out with no words to express their pain. As You are there through us, let them know You are there for them. Though we live our lives in a broken, fallen world full of tragedy and sorrow, we do not live our lives without love. You are love, and You love through us. "Beloved, let us love one another, because love is from God; everyone who loves is born of God and knows God. Whoever does not love does not know God, for God is love" (1 John 4:7-8). Give us Your love to love our hurting neighbors through our prayers and our presence in their lives this day. In Jesus' name I pray, Amen.

Be encouraged today! In the Love of Jesus, *Tommy Hays*

A Compassionate God

Good morning, Lord Jesus. As the old song says, "The steadfast love of the Lord never ceases. His mercies never come to an end. They are new every morning, new every morning. Great is Your faithfulness, O Lord. Great is Your faithfulness." ...

"For the mountains may depart and the hills be removed, but My steadfast love shall not depart from you, and My covenant of peace shall not be removed, says the Lord who has compassion on you" (Isaiah 54:10).

The eyes of the world seem to be on Kentucky these past few days—not because of the Kentucky Derby or the World Equestrian Games or another National Championship of the UK Basketball Team, but because the world feels our pain and carries a measure of our shock and sadness. The tragedy of this plane crash and loss of forty-nine lives has touched almost everyone in our community in a personal way. As the Mayor of Lexington said, "We not only grieve with the family and friends of those who died; we are the friends and family of those who died."

Yet as the world watches, let them also see our faith, our hope, and our love. Let them see us comforting one another with the comfort that only You can give us. Let them see the compassion of our God whose heart breaks over the brokenness and suffering of this tragic loss of life. And let them see the mercy of our God who will not waste a moment of our suffering to draw others to Him. Everyone who lost a loved one or friend or saw someone else lose a loved one or friend Sunday morning was reminded that any moment could be our last moment. Life is short and time is precious. There is no time to waste in receiving and sharing the grace of Your love revealed in Your Gospel with one another.

Lord, while the prayers of the world are opening the heavens above our community, let us not squander these sacred moments to share Your hope and demonstrate Your love to those who need Your compassion. As they receive Your grace and enter into Your covenant of peace, Your steadfast love shall not depart and Your mercies shall not fail. No matter what the morning brings, Your mercies will be new every morning. In Jesus' name I pray, Amen.

Be encouraged today! In the Love of Jesus, *Tommy Hays*

Why, God?

Good morning, Lord Jesus. I wake this morning to press through in prayer and praise through the heaviness of heart of our community for myself and for them. Yesterday, we celebrated the life and mourned the passing of a young woman in our community who was full of life until the day she died at the end of her battle with cancer. This week the funerals will begin for forty-nine lives whose day began and suddenly ended in the crash of their plane on their way to another day in the journey of their lives. Just a few months have passed since a young mother on her way to work among us was crushed under a falling slab of cement from the parking garage above her, carrying her unborn child in her womb. I bring to You my questions and listen to You for answers, as I entrust to You our heaviness of heart this day. ...

"My God, my God, why have You forsaken me? Why are You so far from helping me, from the words of my groaning?" (Psalm 22:1). "Why, O Lord, do You stand far off? Why do You hide Yourself in times of trouble?" (Psalm 10:1).

Some say we should never ask, "Why?" But that's not my theology. That's not my four year old, Elijah's theology either. "Why, Daddy?" and "Dad, how come?" make up more than half his vocabulary. "Why?" is an expression of the deepest yearnings You have placed in our spirits to know and understand. And as we seek to know and understand the principles and problems, the tragedies and triumphs of our lives, the question of "Why?" ultimately leads to the question of "Who?" It may begin with "Who did this?" and "Who allowed this?", but sooner or later, it leads to "Who will walk with me through this?" Finally, one day—after the journey of shock and denial, anger and pain, forgiveness and healing—it even becomes, "Who will use this in my life and in the lives of others?"

In my own journey through the suffering and brokenness of living in a broken, fallen world in need of a Savior, I have come to find peace in the One Who wrestles with me through the questions and walks with me through the journey.   Thank You for giving me permission to ask the question "Why?". You asked it of our Father as You hung upon the Cross in Your unfailing love for me—"And about three o'clock Jesus cried with a loud voice, 'Eli, Eli, lema sabachthani?' that is, 'My God, My God, why have You forsaken Me?' "(Matthew 27:46). There, You bore upon Yourself for us "our griefs and carried our sorrows" (Isaiah 53:4, NKJV). Then You entrusted Your spirit into the hands of the Father (Luke 23:46). The question of "Why?" led to the Answer of "Who"—to the One Who sees the end from the beginning and causes all things to work together for good—

even the things that break our hearts and Yours. Keep giving me grace to keep asking the question and giving me faith to keep finding my Answer. In Jesus' name I pray, Amen.

Be encouraged today! In the Love of Jesus, *Tommy Hays*

The Mystery of Faith

Good morning, Lord Jesus. I seek Your wisdom. I seek You, for You are Wisdom. ...

"Without any doubt, the mystery of our religion is great: He was revealed in the flesh, vindicated in Spirit, seen by angels, proclaimed among Gentiles, believed in throughout the world, taken up in glory" (1 Timothy 3:16).

At times when we are hurting and we don't understand, the mysteries of our faith drive us to cling closer to You in faith—faith that You are good, faith that You are for us, faith that You are working in ways we cannot see, faith that You are fighting for us in battles we cannot see. We can't hold onto that kind of faith without holding onto the One who is faithful. That kind of faith is found in a Person, not just principles. It is found in the One who is the Word and our Comfort, not just in comforting words.

It is a mystery that Your Kingdom has come but it is not yet fully manifested in the earth. It is a mystery that You are sovereign and in control, yet You set before us each day the choices we must make of our own free will (Joshua 24:14). It is a mystery that You said, "All authority in heaven and on earth has been given to Me;" and at the same time, You referred to the enemy of our souls as "the ruler of this world" (Matthew 28:18; John 14:30). It is a mystery that You came that we might have life in abundance; yet we face a foe who comes to steel and kill and destroy (John 10:10). It is a mystery that You are our "Prince of Peace;" yet we live our lives in a world where disobedience to Your will and Your ways through our generations have opened doors to the wicked and destructive influences of "the prince of the power of the air" (Ephesians 2:1-2, NKJV). It is a mystery that You send Your angels to do Your bidding, but there is opposition from fallen angels fighting to resist and delay Your word and Your will for Your children (Hebrews 1:14; Daniel 10:10-14).

So we must continue to pray for Your Kingdom to come and Your will to be done—here on earth in the brokenness and fallenness of our lives in a broken, fallen world, as it is in heaven where there are no sinful choices and no fallen angels. We must hold onto faith through these mysteries of life, which Your Word calls a "fight of the faith" (1 Timothy 6:12). Give us courage and compassion to step in the ring and fight for one another when the mysteries of life and faith seem to be pummeling them into a corner. As we do, the love and power of Your presence makes our faith less mysterious to us and the God of our faith more real to us. In this way, we are growing in grace to become "servants of Christ and stewards of God's mysteries" (1 Corinthians 4:1). In Jesus' name I pray, Amen.

Be encouraged today! In the Love of Jesus, *Tommy Hays*

I Know My Redeemer Lives

Good morning, Lord Jesus. You are my Comfort and Strength, my Wisdom and Truth, O Lord, my God—Father, Son, and Holy Spirit. ...

When Job's religious "friends" were confused in their theology of suffering, You spoke Your words of truth and life through the young prophet, Elihu, who heard Your voice and knew Your heart: "Bear with me a little, and I will show you, for I have yet something to say on God's behalf. I will bring my knowledge from far away, and ascribe righteousness to my Maker. For truly my words are not false; One who is perfect in knowledge is with you. Surely God is mighty and does not despise any; He is mighty in strength of understanding. ... He delivers the afflicted by their affliction, and opens their ear by adversity. ... See, God is exalted in His power; who is a teacher like Him? Who has prescribed for Him His way, or who can say, 'You have done wrong?' " (from Job 36:1-23).

You do not despise any. You are Love, and You have created each of us for a relationship of love (1 John 4:8). But to truly love, there must be the freedom to choose to receive that love or reject it. If You created us to automatically receive Your love, it wouldn't be love at all. We would be robots and not loved ones with the capacity to love in return. So love requires freedom, and out of that freedom we make choices that affect our lives and the lives of others, in our generation and throughout all generations. Our choices have consequences, so a relationship based on Your nature of love is risky and dangerous, but necessary.

You cannot automatically make us love You and obey You without destroying the potential for a relationship of love. And out of those choices in our lives and in the lives of others, bad things can happen that are completely contrary to Your will for us. Your will is not to harm us, but to help us, to give us "a future with hope" (Jeremiah 29:11). "For I have no pleasure in the death of anyone, says the Lord God. Turn, then, and live" (Ezekiel 18:32). Yet in a broken, fallen world, there is affliction and there is adversity; there is destruction and sadness and death. It breaks our hearts and it breaks Yours. But even so, You do not waste our suffering and You do not leave us alone in our pain. You redeem all things, causing life to rise up out of the ashes of death and healing life to flow out of broken vessels. As Job came to say, "I know that my Redeemer lives" (Job 19:25). "He has redeemed my soul from going down to the Pit, and my life shall see the Light" (v. 33:28).

As we turn to You in our humble weakness and in trusting faith, You deliver the afflicted by our affliction and You open our ears by adversity (from Job 36:15). Whether You intend it or will it or not, affliction can be a means of

Your grace to deliver us from our self-reliance and independence if we allow it to draw us closer to You, even while it breaks Your heart to see us endure it. Adversity can be a means of Your grace to open our ears again to the leading of Your still small voice, speaking quietly to our spirit to lead us into the destiny of our future with a hope. Only in this way can we possibly hear and receive Your word of encouragement that "whenever you face trials of any kind, consider it nothing but joy, because you know that the testing of your faith produces endurance; and let endurance have its full effect, so that you may be mature and complete lacking in nothing" (James 1:2-4). And that joy does not come—nor should it come—overnight, but in Your timing and in Your way as we walk with You through the journey.

We go through life in all of the full range of misery and joy in order to be conformed to the image of Christ (Romans 8:29). And as we learn to turn to You in our suffering and in our rejoicing, we are becoming "mature and complete" until we are "lacking in nothing" (James 1:4). Who is a Teacher like You? You are exalted in power—the power of Your love for us and Your desire to conform us into Your nature in the wisdom of Your ways. "Who can say, 'You have done wrong?' " (Job 36:22-23). With Job and all those who persevere and press through in Your grace to see Your power, we proclaim, "I know my Redeemer lives!" In Jesus' name I pray, Amen.

Be encouraged today! In the Love of Jesus, *Tommy Hays*

Window of Hope[*]

Today was Henry's first day of school! We got ready early and walked the long way around. As we were walking down a particular stretch of road I thought, "Maxwell would have liked today." It made me sad to think of how my little dog had loved going to and from school to pick up Henry; he had passed away at the end of the previous school year and was no longer with us each day.

When we finally reached Henry's little school, Henry jumped out and said, "See you later Mom!" I suppose I had expected a big hug and kiss, but he was off in a flash.

As I walked home without Maxwell or Henry, I felt sad. I thought of other people and the things they were going through and I felt even sadder. I wondered how they were handling life. The thought went through my mind that life seemed like one heartache after another and it didn't even matter how big or small the heartache was—it was still a terrible pain that wouldn't seem to go away. I wondered if it would ever go away or if we all just had to wait for Heaven someday.

Just when that thought had settled, I noticed something unusual in the front window of the house in front of me. In bright glittery letters, someone had written the word "Hope." The minute I saw the word, I knew God was reminding me not to be overwhelmed by sadness and loss, but to look to Him for what I needed—Hope.

God reminded me again of Romans 5:5:

"Now hope does not disappoint, because the love of God has been poured out in our hearts by the Holy Spirit who was given to us."

God also reminded me of 1 Thessalonians 5:8-11:

"But let us who are of the day be sober, putting on the breastplate of faith and love, and as a helmet the hope of salvation. For God did not appoint us to wrath, but to obtain salvation through our Lord Jesus Christ, who died for us, that whether we wake or sleep, we should live together with Him. Therefore comfort each other and edify one another, just as you also are doing."

God wants us to remember that there is a Heaven. He will redeem everything in the past, we will one day be made perfect, and we will be

---

[*] The following devotional was written by Mary Margaret Adams.

reunited with loved ones. Just last night I read Revelations 21! The first seven verses goes as follows:

"Now I saw a new heaven and a new earth, for the first heaven and the first earth had passed away. Also there was no more sea. Then I, John, saw the holy city, New Jerusalem, coming down out of heaven from God, prepared as a bride adorned for her husband. And I heard a loud voice from heaven saying, 'Behold, the tabernacle of God is with men, and He will dwell with them, and they shall be His people. God Himself will be with them and be their God. And God will wipe away every tear from their eyes; there shall be no more death, nor sorrow, nor crying. There shall be no more pain, for the former things have passed away.' Then He sat on the throne and said, 'Behold, I make all things new.' And He said to me, 'Write for these words are true and faithful.' And He said to me, 'It is done! I am the Alpha and the Omega, the Beginning and the End. I will give of the fountain of the water of life freely to him who thirsts. He who overcomes shall inherit all things, and I will be his God and he will be My son.'"

God wants us to know that there is a Heaven. God wants us to know that there is Hope. While there is terrible sadness and loss, God reminds us that there is also Jesus. He has died to redeem us, the earth, and our future. God has given us the Holy Spirit (Christ in us) to remind us of this and enable us to press through and to even help others who need comfort. Most importantly, one day when we have overcome this world with and because of Christ, we will be with God and He will call us sons and daughters. All sorrow and sadness will be replaced with rejoicing.

If sorrow and sadness overwhelm you today, look to your window of Hope!

All praise and glory be to God! *Mary Margaret Adams*

Live Life in the Present

Good morning, Lord Jesus. Awaken my spirit to arise and follow You. ...

"You turn us back to dust, and say, 'Turn back, you mortals.' For a thousand years in Your sight are like yesterday when it is past, or like a watch in the night. You sweep them away; they are like a dream, like grass that is renewed in the morning; in the morning it flourishes and it is renewed; in the evening it fades and withers" (Psalm 90:3-6).

Teach me to live the fullness of life in the present, Lord. I thank You for the past that You have used to make me who I am. I thank You for the future that You will use to shape me into who I will become. And I thank You for today—"This is the day that the Lord has made; let us rejoice and be glad in it" (Psalm 118:24). Remind me to live this day as if it were my last, as if tomorrow I would stand before You and give an account of how I used the talents and the time You gave me. Each day begins fresh and new, but in the evening it fades and withers; it is no more and every opportunity it brought is forever past. By Your grace, teach me to live life fully each day, so that I will not live in regret the next.

Each day may be my last day. So thank You for encouraging me and empowering me to live each day in the fullness of life in the present. "As we work together with Him, we urge you also not to accept the grace of God in vain. For He says, 'At an acceptable time I have listened to you, and on a day of salvation I have helped you.' See now is the acceptable time; see, now is the day of salvation!" (2 Corinthians 6:1-2) In Jesus' name I pray, Amen.

Be encouraged today! In the Love of Jesus, *Tommy Hays*

Eternal Glory in Christ

Good morning, Lord Jesus. Give me grace to see You and hear You and follow You this day. ...

"And after you have suffered for a little while, the God of all grace, who has called you to His eternal glory in Christ, will Himself restore, support, strengthen, and establish you" (1 Peter 5:10).

You have not promised us a world without pain nor a life without suffering. Yet You have promised us that through it all, You would be with us. You never leave us nor forsake us (Hebrews 13:5). As You said to Your people who would follow Joshua through the battles they would encounter in order to establish them in the fullness of Your promises: "It is the Lord who goes before you. He will be with you; He will not fail you or forsake you. Do not fear or be dismayed" (Deuteronomy 31:8).

You are my Joshua. And I will rise and follow You. You go before me and You are with me. I need not fear the battles nor be dismayed by the suffering. You are restoring me, supporting me, strengthening me, and establishing me as I keep my eyes on You and answer Your call to move forward into the fullness of Your promises. It's not in spite of, but because of the endurance of faith through suffering, that You are establishing in me the promise of Your "eternal glory in Christ." In Jesus' name I pray, Amen.

Be encouraged today! In the Love of Jesus, *Tommy Hays*

Courage and Strength

Good morning, Lord Jesus. Before I rise and go to meet the day, I choose to sit and wait to meet my God. ...

"Wait for the Lord; be strong and let your heart take courage; wait for the Lord" (Psalm 27:14).

Courage comes when I know I have waited for Your leading. Strength comes when I depend upon Your power. Your grace is sufficient for me; Your power is made perfect in my weakness—the weakness of my flesh in submission to Your Spirit. "For whenever I am weak"—courageously and desperately dependant upon You in trusting faith—"then I am strong" (2 Corinthians 12:8-10).

 I need Your courage and I need Your strength. Help me wait for Your leading by seeking Your peace and Your power, choosing not to move forward until I have it.   Let insecurity, fear, and pride have no place in my choices and no power in my decisions. As best as I can, I submit my plans to Yours, yielding my will to Yours alone. Sometimes the most courageous act is to stand firm and wait until You give the command to move forward in Your time and in Your way. By Your grace, I choose to stand firm, trusting in You to be my strength. In Jesus' name I pray, Amen.

Be encouraged today! In the Love of Jesus, *Tommy Hays*

Witnesses of Peace

Good morning, Lord Jesus. I love You, Lord, because You first loved me. I praise You, Lord, because You are worthy of all praise. ...

Thank You for the gift of the Tuesday Night Prayer Group—the group of men and women of prayer from all different traditions across our community who gather together for intercession and worship every week at the heart of our city.   Margaret Therkelsen, one of my spiritual mentors and mothers in the faith, has faithfully led this group every week for over twenty years of city-wide prayer.   We'll never know until we get to heaven how this bond of unity in the faith and in prayer has transformed the spiritual atmosphere of our region as instruments of Your grace to open the heavens over the lives of the people You've called us to love and cover in the power of prayer. Though I've not been able to join them in their faithful ministry as often this past year, I am always refreshed and renewed in weightiness of the glory of Your presence as we seek Your face and pray Your grace.

Last night I felt like I needed to be there with my praying family and friends. At the end, as Margaret led us to wait on You for any final leadings of Your Spirit, I heard You say, "Be witnesses of My peace." And You brought to mind the face of my friend Ann who was singing in the choir at our Community Prayer Gathering last week with her face lifted to You in praise the very next day after her daughter Beth's funeral. What a witness she was to me and our community of the peace of Your eternal perspective. As soon as I prayed, You confirmed through my friend Sandy what You had been speaking to her all night, "Peace I leave with you; My peace I give to you. I do not give you as the world gives. Do not let your hearts be troubled, and do not let them be afraid" (John 14:27).

Yes, Lord. By Your grace, empower us to be witnesses of Your peace. Give us Your eternal perspective. Keep lifting our eyes unto the hills from whence cometh our help; our help comes from the Lord who gives us peace in the midst of pain and quiets our souls in the midst of suffering (see Psalm 121). You are our Peace and our Comforter. Let the world around us see the witness of Your Peace and Your Comfort shining through our faces turned to You in trusting faith and highest praise. Let us be encouraged by the witness of others to be witnesses ourselves to the peace and power of Your presence. In Jesus' name I pray, Amen.

Be encouraged today! In the Love of Jesus, *Tommy Hays*

Walk in the Opposite Spirit

Good morning, Lord Jesus. I call on Your name and I ask for Your nature.
...

"Do not be overcome with evil, but overcome evil with good" (Romans 12:21).

Teach me how to walk in the opposite spirit of the spirits that come against me.   Empower me to walk in the Spirit and not in the flesh. Where there is pride, help me walk in humility. Where there is fear, help me walk in faith. Where there is judgment, help me walk in mercy. Where there is bitterness, help me walk in forgiveness. Where there is heaviness, help me walk in praise. Where there is confusion, help me walk in clarity. Where there is doubt, help me walk in wisdom. Where there is anxiety, help me walk in peace. "For You have delivered my soul from death, and my feet from falling, so that I may walk before God in the light of life" (Psalm 56:13).

Possess me with Your Holy Spirit and deliver me from every unholy spirit (Matthew 6:13). Fill me with Your Light and cast out of me all darkness. "For once you were darkness, but now in the Lord you are light. Live as children of light—for the fruit of the light is found in all that is good and right and true" (Ephesians 5:8-9). "It is You who light my lamp; the Lord, my God, lights up my darkness" (Psalm 18:28).

In faith, I ask and by grace, I receive more of Your mind and more of Your heart, as I choose to submit my nature to Your nature and my will to Your will. Help me walk in Your Spirit and not in my flesh. Help me overcome evil with good. Lord Jesus, make me more like You each day. In Jesus' name I pray, Amen.

Be encouraged today! In the Love of Jesus, *Tommy Hays*

Out of the Great Ordeal

Good morning, Lord Jesus. You are the Lamb upon the throne of God. Be enthroned upon my heart this day. ...

"Then one of the elders addressed me, saying, 'Who are these, robed in white, and where have they come from?' ... Then he said to me, 'These are they who have come out of the great ordeal; they have washed their robes and made them white in the blood of the Lamb' " (Revelation 7:13-14).

Last night at church, The Foundry—our "multi-purpose facility"—was filled with people who came for the purpose of coming to ask their questions about You and Your ways in the journey of our Alpha Course over next ten weeks. As our Pastor, David, told them, they will not only come to understand truth, they will come to encounter and experience the One who is Truth.

As they came in, I wondered in my spirit, "Where have they come from?" In one way or another, and in each one's own journey, they have each "come out of the great ordeal"—living life every day in a broken, fallen world where there are no answers and there is no peace apart from knowing You. With my natural eyes, I saw them as they are—questioning, seeking, hurting, skeptical, and some even a little afraid. But with my spiritual eyes, I saw them as they will be—welcomed, forgiven, trusting, peaceful, and free. They were no longer robed in the ways of the world, but robed in the white of the glory of God.

Though most of these would probably not have ever heard this old hymn, I hear it now as a song of Your Spirit releasing them to ask their questions and drawing them to You to find their Answer: "Are you washed ... in the blood ... in the soul-cleansing blood of the Lamb? Are your garments spotless, are they white as snow, are you washed in the blood of the Lamb?" For many, if not most, they are not yet. But it is Your desire and in the grace of Your power, they will be. They will come to trust You enough to entrust their lives to You, as You cleanse them of their sins and fill them with Your Spirit. And then in the fullness of time and the fulfillment of all Truth, "They will hunger no more, and thirst no more; the sun will not strike them, nor any scorching heat; for the Lamb at the center of the throne will be their Shepherd, and He will guide them to springs of the Water of Life, and God will wipe away every tear from their eyes" (Revelation 7:16-17). Lord Jesus, come into their hearts and keep coming into mine; cleanse their souls in the blood of the Lamb and keep cleansing mine. In Jesus' name I pray, Amen.

Be encouraged today! In the Love of Jesus, *Tommy Hays*

Consecrated and Consumed

Good morning, Lord Jesus. Here I am, Lord. Help me yield my will to Your will, laying down my life so that You can live Your life through me this day. ...

"Then Solomon offered up burnt offerings to the Lord on the altar of the Lord ... as the duty of each day required" (2 Chronicles 8:12-13).

I offer my life to You again this day. This is my burnt offering—my flesh consumed in the fire of Your Holy Spirit. I choose to answer Your call: "I appeal to you therefore, brothers and sisters, by the mercies of God, to present your bodies as a living sacrifice, holy and acceptable to God, which is your spiritual worship (Romans 12:1). Consecrated and consumed, "we are the aroma of Christ to God" (2 Corinthians 2:15). Through the prayer of surrender on the altar of my heart, I consecrate my life and this day to You as holy unto the Lord to be consumed in the flames of Your will in the name of the Father and of the Son and of the Holy Spirit, Amen.

Be encouraged today! In the Love of Jesus, *Tommy Hays*

"Seek His Presence Continually"

Good morning, Lord Jesus. By Your grace, I willingly welcome You into my mind and my heart, to shape my thoughts and form my desires. ...

"Seek the Lord and His strength, seek His presence continually" (1 Chronicles 16:11).

To "seek" is to pursue—not passively, but actively; not merely accepting Your strength, but desperately depending upon it; not merely allowing Your presence, but earnestly desiring it. "Continually" means without ceasing, without distraction, without hesitation.

How would my life be different if I truly depended upon Your strength alone throughout every day? How would my words and my actions be different if I deliberately welcomed Your personal presence into every moment of my day?   Often we kind of have a vague sense of Your general presence in our lives, that You are out there somewhere, sometimes listening in or looking into the matters of our lives. And the truth is, we kind of like it that way. There seems to be less accountability and more liberty to live our lives for ourselves instead of for You.

But this call is to seek You continually, not occasionally; to seek You deliberately, not come across You by accident. Lord, put this desire in my heart and this power in my spirit. Give me a holy hunger for more—more of Your strength, more of Your presence—never being fully satisfied, continually seeking more of You in my life. In Jesus' name I pray, Amen.

Be encouraged today! In the Love of Jesus, *Tommy Hays*

What Tomorrow will Bring

Good morning, Lord Jesus. Speak to me Your words of truth and life. Set my feet on the path You have for me to walk today. ...

"Come now, you who say, 'Today or tomorrow we will go to such and such a town and spend a year there, doing business and making money.' Yet you do not even know what tomorrow will bring. What is your life? For you are a mist that appears for a little while and then vanishes" (James 4:13-14).

On this day five years ago, the world changed for the people of my nation. Terror touched home on a scale beyond any proportion we had ever known. Yet You redeem all things. You cause good to come out of even the most vile and wicked acts of evil if we will humble our hearts and turn to You for Your strength and peace to press on. One way You have redeemed the events of 9-11 is that few take the security and peace of our lives for granted any more. We don't know what tomorrow will bring. We don't know what day may be our last. There is more of a sense of living each day in the fullness of that day, not holding on for tomorrow, because we don't know what tomorrow holds.

You have created each of us for significance, with destiny. You have created each one of us with a sense of eternity in our hearts (Ecclesiastes 3:11). Yet we have but "a little while" to make a difference; then our opportunities vanish like the mist of the morning dew.

Lord, give me Your wisdom and grace to live my life fully this day. Let me not waste my opportunities. Let me not wait for tomorrow. Let me live and love and give and serve today. Tomorrow may never come, but by Your grace and in Your power, I can make a difference in someone's life today. Thank You for reminding me that every day is a significant day. Every day, my choices, my actions, and my words carry the significance of eternity (Matthew 12:36 and 25:31-46). Let this be the legacy of 9-11 for me. In Jesus' name I pray, Amen.

Be encouraged today! In the Love of Jesus, *Tommy Hays*

Don't Hold Back

Good morning, Lord Jesus. Lead me as I linger in the stillness before You at the start of this day. ...

"All day long the wicked covet, but the righteous give and do not hold back" (Proverbs 21:26).

In times of uncertainty, the tendency of the flesh is to covet and horde. But the nature of the Spirit is to give even more. The gifts and graces of God are given to us for the very purpose of giving them away to others. Like the waters of the Jordan that flow into the Dead Sea, they grow stagnant and stale unless they continue to flow through our lives and into the lives of others. Then they become part of the flow of Your Spirit as streams of living water, bringing healing and life to all they touch (Ezekiel 47:9). " 'Out of the believer's heart shall flow rivers of living water.' Now He said this about the Spirit, which believers in Him were to receive" (John 7:38-39).

Lord, help me not hold back. Freely have I received, help me freely give (Matthew 10:8). Help me know the gifts You have given me to give away to others. Remind me that the measure I give will be the measure I receive— "a good measure, pressed down, shaken together, running over" (Luke 6:38). My gifts are not exactly the same as anyone else's gifts, but they are the gifts You have given me for the purposes You have called me to reflect Your image and to minister Your love through my life.

"Now there are varieties of gifts, but the same Spirit; and there are varieties of services, but the same Lord; and there are varieties of activities, but the same God who activates all of them in everyone. To each is given the manifestation of the Spirit for the common good" (1 Corinthians 12:4-7). By Your grace and for Your glory, I choose to give and not hold back, to care and not covet. And then by the mystery of faith and the principles of Your Kingdom, I will gain far more than I can ever give. In Jesus' name I pray, Amen.

Be encouraged today! In the Love of Jesus, *Tommy Hays*

I Will Take My Stand

Good morning, Lord Jesus. Open the eyes of my heart to see You and open the ears of my heart to hear You. ...

As I woke this morning, I heard my heart saying, "I will take my stand." Lord, what does this mean?

It seems I hear You say, "Stand in the strength of the Lord. Apart from Me, you cannot stand, you cannot endure. When all is shaken that can be shaken, there will be no security apart from Me. Learn now to stand secure in Me and you always will."

Yes, Lord. No flesh can stand in the presence of a holy God (Exodus 3:5). By Your grace and in the mercy of Your patience, crucify my flesh and uproot my pride. Break away my self-sufficiency on which I am tempted to stand in the illusion of my own strength. I have no strength that will sustain my spirit through the battles of the day and the challenges to come. Teach me how to take my stand in You.

"So also, when you see these things taking place, you know that the kingdom of God is near.... Be on guard that your hearts are not weighed down with dissipation and drunkenness and the worries of this life, and that day does not catch you unexpectedly, like a trap. For it will come upon all who live on the face of the whole earth. Be alert at all times, praying that you may have the strength to escape all these things that will take place, and to stand before the Son of Man" (Luke 21:31-36).

By the love and mercy of God my Father that calls me Your son through repentance and faith, by the blood of Jesus that cleanses my soul and makes me whole, and by the power of the Holy Spirit that strengthens me to stand in the strength of the Lord, I take my stand in You. "As a result, Christ will make your hearts strong, blameless, and holy when you stand before God our Father on that day when our Lord Jesus comes with all those who belong to Him" (1 Thessalonians 3:13). As I learn to stand in You and welcome You to stand in me, You are making my heart "strong, blameless, and holy" in the grace of God. In Jesus' name I pray, Amen.

Be encouraged today! In the Love of Jesus, *Tommy Hays*

Go Tell Your Friends

Good morning, Lord Jesus. Father, Son, and Holy Spirit—You are One and You are good. Thank You for being so good to me. Help me share Your goodness with others today. ...

"As He was getting into the boat, the man who had been possessed by demons begged Him that he might be with Him. But Jesus refused and said to him, 'Go home to your friends, and tell them how much the Lord has done for you, and what mercy He has shown you.' And he went away and began to proclaim in the Decapolis how much Jesus had done for him; and everyone was amazed" (Mark 5:18-20).

Sometimes we want to come away with You in the stillness and quiet of the morning and just stay there. Sometimes we want to think of our faith as intensely personal and we want to think of Your power to heal us and free us of the pain and bondage of our lives as a discreet and private matter. Yet You call us to set aside our vanity and proclaim boldly the goodness of Your mercy and the power of Your love.

Sometimes we object and say to ourselves, "I'm not like that. I'm shy. I'm more introverted. I'm a private person." But in this story of freedom and restoration, You sent the man to share his testimony with his "friends." It's in these relationships of trust where we have credibility and where those around us can literally see the change in our lives by the power of Your love that we are the most effective witnesses of Your glory. So let me be thankful for the times of intimacy with You in the privacy of prayer and also let me be courageous to share the mercy You have shown me with those You have prepared to hear my testimony of Your power and grace. In Jesus' name I pray, Amen.

Be encouraged today! In the Love of Jesus, *Tommy Hays*

Ambassadors of Christ

Good morning, Lord Jesus. Speak, and I will listen. Lead, and I will follow. Send me, and I will go. As best as I can and all by Your grace, I submit my will to Your will, my thoughts to Your thoughts, and my desires to Your desires. ...

"Then Jesus called the twelve together and gave them power and authority over all demons and to cure diseases, and He sent them out to proclaim the kingdom of God and to heal" (Luke 9:1-2).

As You send me out today to proclaim Your kingdom and to heal, Lord Jesus, I pray You would anoint me with Your power and Your authority over demons and diseases. Help me decrease as You increase. Help me be a vessel emptied of myself and filled with You, allowing the living waters of Your love and Your life to flow freely through me (John 7:37-38).

"All this is from God, who reconciled us to Himself through Christ, and has given us this ministry of reconciliation; that is, in Christ God was reconciling the world to Himself, not counting their trespasses against them, and entrusting the message of reconciliation to us. For we are ambassadors for Christ, since God is making His appeal through us; we entreat you on behalf of Christ, be reconciled to God" (2 Corinthians 5:18-20). Send me forth, filled with faith, empowered by Your Spirit, to proclaim Your kingdom in Your power as Your ambassador this day and every day. In Jesus' name I pray, Amen.

Be encouraged today! In the Love of Jesus, *Tommy Hays*

God's Comfort*

Many years ago, someone I knew told me in a rather matter-of-fact way that there was a verse in the Bible that reminded her of me: "O you afflicted one, tossed with tempest, and not comforted . . ." At the time, I shrugged it off and frankly, I never even bothered to try to locate the verse in the Bible. However, this "truth" resonated with me more and more over the years. I was in fact the kind of person who couldn't receive comfort very easily.

Recently, this verse came to mind again as I agonized over something, unable to tell anyone or get any relief. I told God that I just could not be comforted by anyone, not that I even tried. I knew by now that there were just some things that I couldn't explain to anyone, nor would I be able to receive what they had to offer even if I could speak from my heart.

This time though, I felt prompted by God to actually look up the verse. It goes as follows:

"O you afflicted one, tossed with tempest, and not comforted, behold I will lay your stones with colorful gems, and lay your foundations with sapphires" (Isaiah 54:11).

That sounds a bit more cheerful than the original version that I had absorbed and accepted as "truth." Isaiah 54 goes on to say:

"I will make your pinnacles of rubies, your gates of crystal, and all your walls of precious stones. All your children shall be taught by the Lord, and great shall be the peace of your children" (Verses 12-13).

The chapter ends with:

"'This is the heritage of the servants of the Lord, and their righteousness is from Me,' says the Lord" (Verse 17).

God knows and understands already how I feel and why I cannot be comforted. Instead of condemning me for it, He reminds me that He will build a strong and beautiful foundation for me, then pillars, walls; indeed a beautiful "house." More than that, He will teach and bless my children with something I rarely had when I was a child—peace! What an amazing promise! And, He will do this, because this is the heritage of the servants of God.

---

* The following devotional was written by Mary Margaret Adams.

Maybe in the past we did not experience the best life or have the best heritage. Perhaps now we sometimes feel afflicted, tossed, and unable to be comforted. However, we can find and receive true comfort from God. When we turn to Him we discover that God knows and understands all things and promises us hope and a bright future.

All praise and glory be to God! *Mary Margaret Adams*

Hope Deferred*

There is a famous poem by Langston Hughes called "A Dream Deferred." It goes as follows:

> What happens to a dream deferred?
>
> Does it dry up
> like a raisin in the sun?
>
> Or fester like a sore--
> and then run?
>
> Does it stink like rotten meat?
> Or crust and sugar over--
> like a syrupy sweet?
>
> Maybe it just sags
> like a heavy load
>
> Or does it just explode?

I have always loved this piece by Langston Hughes, because it ends with action. While there are many possible negative outcomes of a hope deferred, it may also spark a positive and radical form of action and "explode" into life!

Indeed the Bible also speaks of our hopes and dreams. In Proverbs 13:12, the writer has this to say about hope:

"Hope deferred makes the heart sick, but when the desire comes, it is a tree of life."

While I love the piece by Langston Hughes, the Bible speaks more positively by also telling us what happens when a hope or dream is fulfilled: "it is a tree of life."

The Bible has much more to say about hope. In 1Timothy 1:1, the apostle Paul reminds us that the Lord, Jesus Christ, is "our Hope."

Do you have a dream deferred that weighs heavily on your heart? Will your hopes and dreams crush the life out of you or will they burst forth into

---

* The following devotional was written by Mary Margaret Adams.

positive action?   When Christ is our Hope and when our dreams and desires are grounded in Him, we can be guaranteed of a positive outcome.

Romans 5:5 reminds us that hope put in Christ does not disappoint us, because Christ will always be present with us through the Holy Spirit to lead and guide us toward good:

"Now hope does not disappoint, because the love of God has been poured out in our hearts by the Holy Spirit who was given to us."

Will we put our faith and hope in Christ who does not disappoint or will we put it into something or someone else and follow a possible path of destruction and despair?

All Praise and Glory be to God! *Mary Margaret Adams*

Word Made Flesh

Good morning, Lord Jesus. You are the Word of God. Word of God, speak. Help me to hear and obey. ...

"In the beginning was the Word, and the Word was with God, and the Word was God.... And the Word became flesh and lived among us, and we have seen His glory, the glory as of a father's only son, full of grace and truth" (John 1:1-14).

Lord, let Your Word become flesh in me. Let Your truth become my truth, let Your ways become my ways. Continue to increase in my life, as I decrease—more of Your will and less of mine, more of Your ways and less of mine (John 3:30). Fill me full of Your grace and truth by the glory of Your Spirit living in me. "To them God chose to make known how great among the Gentiles are the riches of the glory of this mystery, which is Christ in you, the hope of glory" (Colossians 1:27).

Spirit of Christ, come live in the flesh in me (Romans 8:9). Word of God, come live in the flesh in me. As best as I can and all by Your grace, I choose to submit my will to Your will and my life to Your life a little more each day—morning by morning, and day by day. In Jesus' name I pray, Amen.

Be encouraged today! In the Love of Jesus, *Tommy Hays*

M*A*S*H Unit

Good morning, Lord Jesus. I offer to You the first-fruits of my thoughts and prayers. Your name is my first thought. Your name is my first word this new day. ...

As I center my thoughts on You and wait in the silence for the leading of Your Spirit, I hear these words: "Strengthen, Establish, Encourage, Comfort."

Yes, Lord. What do You mean?

In my spirit, I see a picture of an old Army tent like the ones the helicopters always flew over at the beginning of the television show M*A*S*H—for Mobile Army Surgical Hospital. It seems I hear You say: "Strengthen the stakes and cords of the tent of Your heart. Establish a safe perimeter in the power and authority I have given you to go where I send you. Encourage those You find there to come into the place of My healing and grace. Comfort them with the comfort I have given you, My son."

Yes, Lord. I think of Your Word in Isaiah 54: "Enlarge the site of your tent, and let the curtains of your habitation be stretched out; do not hold back; lengthen your cords and strengthen your stakes. For you will spread out to the right and to the left, and your descendants will possess the nations and will settle the desolate towns" (54:2-3). And I think of the prayer of Jabez: "Oh, that You would bless me and enlarge my border, and that Your hand might be with me, and that You would keep me from hurt and harm" (1 Chronicles 4:10).

Thank You for establishing me and strengthening me in trusting faith of Your goodness and grace. Thank You for encouraging me and comforting me so that I may be an encouragement and comfort to others whenever You send me into battle to minister Your healing life and transforming power on the front lines of the enemy in a broken, fallen world. "As you have received Christ Jesus the Lord, continue to live your lives in Him, rooted and built up in Him and established in the faith, just as you were taught, abounding in thanksgiving" (Colossian 2:6-7). In Jesus' name I pray, Amen.

Be encouraged today! In the Love of Jesus, *Tommy Hays*

Good Treasure

Good morning, Lord Jesus. Purify my heart, clarify my thoughts, and sanctify my words. ...

"... For out of the abundance of the heart, the mouth speaks. The good person brings good things out of a good treasure, and the evil person brings evil things out of an evil treasure. I tell you on the day of judgment you will have to give an account for every careless word you utter; for by your words you will be justified, and by your words you will be condemned" (Matthew 12:34-37).

Keep changing my heart, O God. Keep creating in me a clean heart (Psalm 51:10).   Keep cleansing my heart from my old nature and transforming me into Your nature. As You promised Your people long ago, "I will sprinkle clean water upon you and you will be clean from all your uncleannesses, and from all your idols I will cleanse you. A new heart I will give you, and a new Spirit I will put within you; and I will remove from your body the heart of stone and give you a heart of flesh (Ezekiel 36:25-26).

By Your grace, let me speak words of life and truth today from the abundance of a heart that is cleansed and yielded to You. Apart from You, there is nothing good in me; but I praise You that I am no longer apart from You. You are with me and Your Holy Spirit is within me, bearing the good fruit from the good treasure You have given me by Your grace. In Jesus' name I pray, Amen.

Be encouraged today! In the Love of Jesus, *Tommy Hays*

"Mighty Warriors"

Good morning, Lord Jesus. Awaken my spirit this day to rise and follow You wherever You lead. ...

"The following are those who came to David at Ziklag ... they were among the mighty warriors who helped him in war.... They helped David against the band of raiders, for they were all warriors and commanders in the army. Indeed from day to day people kept coming to David to help him, until there was a great army, like an army of God" (1 Chronicles 12:1-22).

Peace within and war without— this is to be the constant state of Your disciples in these days. We are to know the peace of Your presence and the favor of Your grace within our hearts even while we are a people at war. We are at war with the ways of the world, the flesh, and the devil. We are at war with this "band of raiders," the spiritual forces of wickedness who seek to steal our peace (Ephesians 6:12). You come to bring us the fullness and abundance of Your life and peace, but we must fight for our peace as "mighty warriors" against our enemy who "comes only to steal and kill and destroy" (John 10:10).

You are the God who "trains my hands for war" (Psalm 18:34). You are the God who calls me to come and take my place in Your "great army, like an army of God." You are "the Word of God" who is "Faithful and True," who "in righteousness", "judges and makes war," followed by Your "armies of heaven" (Revelation 19:11-16). Teach us how to have Your peace within, even as we war without in the army of God in our life-long battle against the spiritual forces of wickedness and against the rebellious flesh of our own souls. In You, we are "mighty warriors." In Jesus' name I pray, Amen.

Be encouraged today! In the Love of Jesus, *Tommy Hays*

God's Will*

"Trust in the Lord, and do good; dwell in the land and feed on His faithfulness. Delight yourself also in the Lord, and He shall give you the desires of your heart" (Psalm 37:3-4).

I have heard it said before that God never forces us to do anything. The problem was that the times I heard that truth it was usually stated in a forceful and unappealing way! It sounded something like this: "God won't force you to do anything you don't want to do so stop being stupid and hurry up and conform and do His will—we are all getting impatient and you don't want your life to be a complete failure!" Never mind that His "will" was something I had no desire to do at the time like counseling hurting and difficult people or speaking from the pulpit. I would feel like I couldn't breathe from the pressure and thoughts of God finding the thing I hated the most and "making" me do it.

What I was missing (and what others sometimes fail to recognize) can be summed up in two parts. First, we are going to want to do God's will if we submit ourselves to Him, because He will change our hearts. Second, when we submit our will to God, He is going to align our "jobs" with the things we enjoy doing or are good at doing. He has created us and given us particular talents that He wants to use for His good purposes.

I think Max Lucado says it simplest and best. In his book *Just Like Jesus*, he says;

"When we submit to God's plans, we can trust our desires. Our assignment is found at the intersection of God's plan and our pleasures. What do you love to do? What brings you joy? What gives you a sense of satisfaction?

Some long to feed the poor. Others enjoy leading in the church . . . Each of us has been made to serve God in a unique way . . .

The longings of your heart, then, are not incidental; they are critical messages. The desires of your heart are not to be ignored; they are to be consulted. As the wind turns the weather vane, so God uses your passions to turn your life. God is too gracious to ask you to do something you hate."

One thing we know for sure: whatever God has planned for us, we can trust that when the time comes for us to carry it through, we will have the "heart" to do it.

All praise and glory be to God! *Mary Margaret Adams*

---

* The following devotional was written by Mary Margaret Adams.

Good and Evil*

"Do not be overcome by evil, but overcome evil with good" (Romans 12:21).

Have you ever felt overrun by evil? Maybe you turned on the evening news and heard something that horrified you or maybe it was a conversation that you had with a particular person. Maybe it's haunting memories from your past that keep resurfacing. Whatever the "trigger" may be, there are times when we may feel undone and out of sorts by what is evil in the world. These times may be frightening and unnerving; we may need to remind ourselves of several truths in order to stand our ground.

First, let's remember that God is good and that good things come from God. There are countless verses in Bible declaring this truth about God. A few verses come to my mind this morning:

"This is the message which we have heard from Him and declare to you, that God is light and in Him is no darkness at all" (1 John 1:5).

"Every good gift and every perfect gift is from above, and comes down from the Father of lights, with whom there is no variation or shadow of turning. Of His own will He brought us forth by the word of truth, that we might be a kind of first-fruits of His creatures" (James 1:17-18).

Second, we must remember the true source of evil: Satan. John 8:44 says that Satan "was a murderer from the beginning, and does not stand in the truth, because there is no truth in him. When he speaks a lie, he speaks from his own resources, for he is a liar and the father of it."

Third, James 1:13 brings us assurance by showing us that God is clearly separated from evil. It says that "...God cannot be tempted by evil, nor does He Himself tempt anyone."

Fourth, instead of being undone or overcome by evil, God wants us to overcome evil with good (Romans 12:21). While this may seem like a daunting task, if we turn to Christ we can accomplish this. In practical terms, this may mean a simple prayer to God where we ask Him to remove our sense of dread and confusion and replace it with His peace. We may have to choose to release a particular person or memory over to Him and ask Him to declare His truth to us. Or we may need to resist a particular temptation. James 4:7 tells us: "Therefore, submit to God. Resist the devil and he will flee from you."

---

* The following devotional was written by Mary Margaret Adams.

Finally, we can rest in the truth that Christ has overcome all evil through His work on the cross. Revelation chapter 21 describes a new heaven and a new earth where there are no more tears, sorrow, death or crying. Also, all evil will have been conquered and removed from us forever. And God says: "I am the Alpha and the Omega, the Beginning and the End. I will give of the fountain of the water of life freely to him who thirsts. He who overcomes shall inherit all things, and I will be his God and he shall be My son (Revelation 21:6-7).

All praise and glory be to God! *Mary Margaret Adams*

Isolation*

"A man who isolates himself seeks his own desire; he rages against all wise judgment" (Proverbs 18:1).

Have you ever been tempted to isolate yourself from others? Maybe it was because you were feeling down or going through a difficult time. Maybe it was because you had been hurt by people in the past. Maybe it was for what you thought were goods reasons; you had been up and down emotionally or you had developed a shorter fuse lately. Whatever the reason, God tells us that isolating ourselves from others will only bring harm upon ourselves. In fact, we actually rage against all wise judgment.

However, if we trust God and others and stay the course, we may have the opportunity to see something amazing. Proverbs 18:24 says: "A man who has friends must himself be friendly, but there is a friend who sticks closer than a brother." We may have the chance to experience a friendship where a person sticks with us through just about anything. Also, we may have the opportunity to be this kind of person for someone else. Furthermore, God calls us to do just that: "Bear one another's burdens" (Galatians 6:2).

All praise and glory be to God! *Mary Margaret Adams*

---

* The following devotional was written by Mary Margaret Adams.

Iron Sharpens Iron

Good morning, Lord Jesus. I welcome You into my heart and my life again this day. ...

"As iron sharpens iron, so a friend sharpens the countenance of his friend" (Proverbs 27:17, NKJV).

What a gift You have given me the past few days away with over eight hundred men opening up their hearts and getting on their knees together at the Rock Eagle Methodist Men's Retreat in North Georgia. You taught us and loved us. You taught through us and loved through us in the shared experiences of our journeys and the shared hope in the journey ahead.

I thank You for the man who came to the praise and healing service I was leading Friday night. I had a message in mind, but didn't get very far into it before he interrupted me and my message with tears flowing down his face and his heart crying out with a desperate yearning that wouldn't let me go on. He cried out in a mixture of brokenness, desperation, determination, and faith in a way I'm not sure I've ever seen: "I need to be filled with God's Holy Spirit and I need Him to fill me now!"

I was going to preach on the blind beggar who stopped Jesus as He was passing by crying out in desperation and faith for healing, "Jesus, Son of David, have mercy on me!" (Mark 10:46-52). Friday night, You stopped and healed the wounded broken spirit of this man crying out to You for mercy in desperate faith as we gathered around him to stretch out our hearts and hands as we pressed in and pressed through on our knees with him before You. You gloriously filled him with the fullness of Your Holy Spirit, as he became Your message to us that night (Acts 1:4-8; Ephesians 5:18). What an amazing countenance of peace and joy was shining from his face the next morning at breakfast! Thank You, Lord God, for Your grace and Your power that You long to pour out in abundance into hungry hearts who humble themselves to desperately cry out to You in trusting faith. Thank You for friends and brothers in the body of Christ who will come along side us like iron sharpening iron to seek Your face and receive Your grace. In Jesus' name I pray, Amen.

Be encouraged today! In the Love of Jesus, *Tommy Hays*

Through Tragedy and Triumph

Good morning, Lord Jesus. I welcome You, Lord, to be with me through the tragedies and triumphs of every moment of my life. ...

"But now thus says the Lord, He who created you O Jacob, He who formed you O Israel: Do not fear for I have redeemed you; I have called you by name, you are mine. When you pass through the waters, I will be with you; and through the rivers, they shall not overwhelm you; when you walk through fire you shall not be burned, and the flame shall not consume you. For I am the Lord your God, the Holy One of Israel, your Savior" (Isaiah 43:1-3).

While I was away this weekend, tragedy struck our community again. Two young women were swept under the flood waters at the edge of the University of Kentucky campus. Their lives on earth are over. When I heard the news, I wondered—as I always do—were their hearts right with you? Will their families and friends have a firm faith to hold onto through the hard days and hard questions ahead?

We are not promised immunity from pain and tragedy in a broken, fallen world longing and groaning for the redemption and restoration of all things and to be "set free from its bondage to decay" (Romans 8:18-25). Instead, You warn us that in the brokenness of this world, there will be waters and rivers and fires that we must pass through. But we need not pass through them alone. And we need not fear even when we face them and endure them if You have redeemed us through our faith in You. You are with us through them all.

Lord, continue to build my faith in You now so that I am ready to endure the floods and fires of a fallen world. Let me face them all with the peace to know You are with me through them all. Though my life on earth may end one day, my life in You will never end. I can live my life free from the fear of death, knowing You are with me now and You will be with me then. By Your grace, I will triumph over tragedy, with my heart and faith secure in You (Psalm 112:7-8). In Jesus' name I pray, Amen.

Be encouraged today! In the Love of Jesus, *Tommy Hays*

My Heart, Your Home

Good morning, Lord Jesus. I call upon Your name and count upon Your nature. As You increase, help me decrease. Conform my will to Your will, my thoughts to Your thoughts, my desires to Your desires. Make me more like You each day. ...

"Jesus answered him, 'Those who love Me will keep My word, and My Father will love them, and We will come to them and make Our home with them. Whoever does not love Me does not love My words; and the word that you hear is not Mine, but is from the Father who sent Me. I have said these things to you while I am still with you. But the Advocate, the Holy Spirit, whom the Father will send in My name, will teach you everything, and remind you of all that I have said to you' " (John 14:23-26).

I love You, Lord, because You first loved me (1 John 4:19). You said my love for You would be revealed in my obedience to keep Your word. And how can I keep Your word, unless I know Your word? Give me a hunger for Your word—for Your written Word and for Your spoken Word. Open my eyes to see it and open my ears to hear it. Then give me the courage to obey it.

Your Word is Your Scripture, "inspired by God" (2 Timothy 3:16). And at the same time, Your Word is so much more than these written, holy words. You are the Word—the Word of the Father, and the Word of Truth (John 1:1). You are the living fulfillment of all Scripture and all Scripture testifies on Your behalf (John 5:39). Now Your Word comes to life for me by living in me by Your Holy Spirit, as my heart becomes Your home. Make me more sensitive to the leading of Your Word living in me every day. "For all who are led by the Spirit of God are children of God" (Romans 8:14).

By Your grace, I am a son of God because the Word of God and the Spirit of God live in me—loving me and leading me in Your will and Your ways. You are conforming my nature to Your nature a little more each day as I choose to yield my life to Your life, living in me. "And it is no longer I who live, but it is Christ who lives in me" (Galatians 2:20). By Your grace, You are making my heart Your home. In Jesus' name I pray, Amen.

Be encouraged today! In the Love of Jesus, *Tommy Hays*

Child of God through Christ

Good morning, Lord Jesus. Father, I welcome the Holy Spirit of Your Son in my heart this day. ...

"But when the fullness of time had come, God sent His Son, born of a woman, born under the law, in order to redeem those who were under the law, so that we might receive adoption as children. And because you are children, God has sent the Spirit of His Son into our hearts, crying, 'Abba! Father!' So you are no longer a slave, but a child, and if a child, then also an heir of God through Christ" (Galatians 4:4-7).

My little boy Josiah woke us up early this morning. He's almost six months old and not yet sleeping through the night. I don't think he was crying out 'Abba!' in Aramaic, but it got his father's attention. It seems You have created us to long to be comforted and to cry out for the presence and the touch of those who love us and have been entrusted with our care. Our need and desire for our earthly parents in the physical realm is a picture of our need and desire for our heavenly Parent in the spiritual realm.

Sometimes we need to get out a good cry. And sometimes You come in to touch us and comfort us, but not always to lift us up out of our circumstances. Those are times when You are teaching us that You never leave us nor forsake us, even when we don't always get what we want or think we need (Hebrews 13:5). We are still Your children, with the Spirit of Your Son in our hearts and all the inheritance of the kingdom of God in our hands, but You help us grow up into maturity in the fullness of Your timing and Your way. You are a wise Father, who loves Your children enough to help us grow into the maturity of our calling and destiny, even if we don't always understand why you let us cry and don't always give us what we want. And in the security of Your presence and the power of Your touch, You continue to promise us, "As a mother comforts her child, so I will comfort you" (Isaiah 66:13). In Jesus' name I pray, Amen.

Be encouraged today! In the Love of Jesus, *Tommy Hays*

Beauty for Ashes, Joy for Mourning

Good morning, Lord Jesus. You are the Anointed One of God, the Word made flesh, now reigning in glory as King of kings and Lord of lords. Come reign in my heart and my life today. ...

"The Spirit of the Lord God is upon Me, because the Lord has anointed Me to preach good tidings to the poor; He has sent Me to heal the broken-hearted, to proclaim liberty to the captives, and the opening of the prison to those who are bound; to proclaim the acceptable year of the Lord, and the day of vengeance of our God; to comfort all who mourn, to console those who mourn in Zion, to give them beauty for ashes, the oil of joy for mourning, the garment of praise for the spirit of heaviness; that they may be called trees of righteousness, the planting of the Lord, that He may be glorified" (Isaiah 61:1-3, NKJV).

Lord Jesus, You fulfilled Isaiah's prophecy of the ministry of the coming Messiah (Luke 4:21). You are the perfect fulfillment of all Scripture (Matthew 5:17). You are the Word of God (John 1:1 and 1:14). And You are "the same yesterday and today and forever" (Hebrews 13:8). By Your Holy Spirit living on in Your disciples of all generations, You continue to fulfill the Word of God in proclamation and power. As the Father sent You, so You send us in the power of Your Spirit in accordance with Your Word (John 20:21-23). We are Your body, filled with Your Spirit, continuing Your ministry, to display Your glory (1 Corinthians 12:27).

Continue Your ministry of love and power through me today. Send me out with all Your disciples throughout all the earth as Your hands with Your heart in Your power to comfort those who mourn, to offer them Your beauty for their ashes, the oil of gladness instead of mourning, a garment of praise instead of the spirit of heaviness. You are still changing lives and displaying the glory of God. Thank You for changing my life, so that my life may bring You glory by Your grace. In Jesus' name I pray, Amen.

Be encouraged today! In the Love of Jesus, *Tommy Hays*

Knowing the True God

Good morning, Lord Jesus. I call You "Lord" because I choose, by the grace You have given me, to surrender every area of my life to Your Lordship. I surrender all. ...

"Not everyone who says to Me, 'Lord, Lord,' will enter the kingdom of heaven, but only the one who does the will of My Father in heaven. On that day many will say to Me, 'Lord, Lord, did we not prophecy in Your name, and cast out demons in Your name, and do many deeds of power in Your name?' Then I will declare to them, 'I never knew you; go away from Me, you evildoers' " (Matthew 7:21-23).

There are those who strap explosives packed with nails to their bodies and walk into markets and onto buses crowded with men, women, and children going about their lives to reap maximum carnage and grab maximum media coverage.   They say it is the will of God and shout "God is great!" as they murder innocent lives and sacrifice their own to a god whose nature is terror, horror, cruelty and fear. They never knew You.

And there are those who prophecy and cast out demons and do all sorts of religious works seemingly in service to others to appease their consciences and labor to earn Your love or try to atone for their sins and failures. They say it is the will of God as they go about working and serving a god whose nature is demanding, oppressive, unforgiving, and stern. They never knew You.

Father, it is Your will to love us and nurture us, to conform us into the nature of Your Son by the indwelling presence of Your Spirit. You patiently teach us Your ways and lovingly correct us when we stray. You created us for a relationship of love with You and with one another. You humbled Yourself in the nature of Your Son to show us the way to live a life in Your love by the power of Your Holy Spirit living in us. You want us to know You; to know the true nature of the true God.   "Beloved, let us love one another, because love is from God; everyone who loves is born of God and knows God. Whoever does not love does not know God, for God is love" (1 John 4:7-8).

Lord Jesus, You perfectly reveal the Father heart of God, for You are in the Father and the Father is in You; You are One, making us one with You, as You abide in us by Your Holy Spirit (John 14:1-31). We come to know You and Your nature as we surrender our will to Your will and allow You to conform our nature to Your nature by Your Spirit living in us. This is the relationship of love with us You desire; this is the relationship of love with You and with one another for which we were created. Anything else and anything less is a distortion and a perversion of Your truth and Your nature. You desire humility, not horror; love, not hatred; self-sacrifice, not murder; life, not death. You desire loving relationship that leads to willing, joyful obedience to offer our lives in love to You and in the service of love to others. This is how Your name and Your nature is glorified in our lives and throughout the earth (John 14:13).

God my Father, help me know You and Your true nature more every day. Lord Jesus, help me surrender more of life to You every day. Holy Spirit of the Living God, come fill me with Your Life and conform me to Your nature more every day. I offer my life as a willing sacrifice of love to God who is love. Use my life to lead others more deeply into a relationship with the God who loves them and longs to know them. In Jesus' name I pray, Amen.

Be encouraged today! In the Love of Jesus, *Tommy Hays*

Sing a New Song

Good morning, Lord Jesus. I speak Your name and sing Your praise here at the beginning of another day. ...

> *Lord Jesus I come to seek Your face,*
> *To hear Your voice and follow Your ways.*
> *I speak Your name and sing Your praise*
> *Here at the beginning of another day.*
>
> *Awaken my spirit and cleanse my soul,*
> *Fill me with Your Light and make me whole.*
> *Teach me Your Word and let me know*
> *Your grace and love forevermore.*

Thank You, Father, for sending Your Holy Spirit to sing this song of praise to Jesus from my heart and soul. "O sing to the Lord a new song; sing to the Lord all the earth. Sing to the Lord, bless His name; tell of His salvation from day to day" (Psalm 96:1-2). Thank You for the fullness of Your salvation. Your mercies are "new every morning" and Your steadfast love endures forever; "great is Your faithfulness" (Lamentations 3:22-24). In Jesus' name I pray, Amen.

Be encouraged today! In the Love of Jesus, *Tommy Hays*

God is Good to Me

Good morning, Lord Jesus. I settle into my familiar place of prayer to watch and wait for You—Father, Son, and Holy Spirit. ...

"The Lord is good to those who wait for Him, to the soul that seeks Him" (Lamentations 3:25).

As I wait on You for the leading of Your Holy Spirit and as I seek You to listen for the leading of Your still, small voice, You fill me with the goodness of Your presence. You assure me of the goodness of Your will and Your plan for my life. You remind me of the goodness of Your nature in Your patience, protection, provision, and power. "For the Lord is good; His steadfast love endures forever, and His faithfulness to all generations" (Psalm 100:5).

Lord, give me patience to wait on You in the surrender of silence before You in these first moments of every day. Focus my thoughts and prepare my heart for the plans and purposes You have for me each day. Let me persist in prayer until Your goodness overtakes me and goes on before me. I want to live every day of my life filled with the peace of the presence of my God who is so good to me. In Jesus' name I pray, Amen.

Be encouraged today! In the Love of Jesus, *Tommy Hays*

Know I Am with You

Good morning, Lord Jesus. I welcome Your presence and remember Your promises, as I entrust my life into Your hands again this day. ...

"Know that I am with you and will keep you wherever you go, and will bring you back to this land; for I will not leave you until I have done what I have promised you" (Genesis 28:15).

When You spoke these words to Jacob, he was still a liar and a thief, running for his life away from the fury and hatred of his brother Esau. And he was running away from one of the most dysfunctional families of all history—the family of Abraham, Isaac, and Jacob. Yet even under what seemed to be a curse of calamity and confusion, he was also under the blessing of Your covenant and the comfort of Your presence. Even while he still held sin in his heart and before he worked out his understanding of Your true identity and nature, You spoke words of life and promise deeply into his spirit: "Know that I am with you."

It would be a long, long time—time that is still unfolding, in fact—before the fullness of "the blessing of Abraham" for Jacob and his children would come to pass (Genesis 28:4). But You encouraged him to look to the covenant and not the circumstances, to the promises and not the problems. "And the Lord stood beside him and said, 'I am the Lord, the God of Abraham your father and the God of Isaac; the land on which you lie I will give to you and to your offspring; and your offspring shall be like the dust of the earth, and you shall spread abroad to the west and to the east and to the north and to the south; and all the families of the earth shall be blessed in you and in your offspring" (v. 28:13-14).

Certainly Jacob had done nothing to merit these great promises or this encounter with Your great presence. And certainly his present circumstances looked like the opposite of all You were promising. Yet there You were, standing beside him, speaking life to his spirit and calling forth his destiny. You were calling him to see with spiritual eyes and an eternal perspective, far bigger and far beyond himself. And his destiny would one day affect my destiny, among "all the families of the earth"—Gentile and Jew, Black and White, Sunni and Shiite, Republican and Democrat, liar and thief—all who would receive the blessings of God through repentance and faith in His Provision of grace.

Through the blood of a Son of Abraham, Isaac, and Jacob who would, one day, willing lay down His life for us through the sacrifice of the cross, despite our sinful ways and selfish hearts, "all the families of the earth shall be blessed." By the blood of the Lamb, You turn our curses into blessings.

"Christ redeemed us from the curse of the law by becoming a curse for us—for it is written, 'Cursed is everyone who hangs on a tree'—in order that in Christ Jesus the blessing of Abraham might come to the Gentiles, so that we might receive the promise of the Spirit through faith" (Galatians 3:13-14). Thank Your for the promise of Your Spirit through faith. Thank You for coming to us and standing by us—especially when we don't deserve it—to remind us of our calling and destiny in Your eternal purposes. In Jesus' name I pray, Amen.

Be encouraged today! In the Love of Jesus, *Tommy Hays*

Heroes, Saints, & Legends

Good morning, Lord Jesus. I turn my face to seek Your face and turn my heart to seek Your heart. ...

"But Jesus called them to Him and said, 'You know that the rulers of the Gentiles lord it over them, and their great ones are tyrants over them. It will not be so among you, but whoever wishes to be great among you will be your servant, and whoever wishes to be first among you must be your slave; just as the Son of Man came not be served but to serve, and to give His life a ransom for many" (Matthew 20:25-28).

Last night we honored my friend, teacher, and fellow prayer warrior Connie Pitman at the annual Heroes, Saints, and Legends dinner in our community. And she is. Connie loves to love people. Out of the abundance of her heart flows rivers of love—that's what everyone says and that's what everyone knows. And Connie loves to tell people the source of all her love— her Lord Jesus.

She reminded us last night of the day in 1979 when she woke up in a hospital bed to hear the news that the doctors removed her breast from cancer. And there You were in the midst of that moment when she needed You the most—standing by her bed, filling her heart with Your love and Your Spirit in a peace and comfort beyond comprehension. What she received from You that day she loves to give away to others. She has not wished to be great among us, but she is. She is a hero, a saint, and a legend—all by the grace You have given her to give her life of love as a ransom for many. You are her hero, and Connie is one of mine. Give me grace to follow her example as she has followed Yours. "Remember your leaders, those who spoke the Word of God to you; consider the outcome of their way of life, and imitate their faith" (Hebrews 13:7). In Jesus' name I pray, Amen.

Be encouraged today! In the Love of Jesus, *Tommy Hays*

Celebrate Recovery

Good morning, Lord Jesus. I celebrate Your goodness and praise Your for Your presence in my heart and my life. ...

"Is there no balm in Gilead? Is there no physician there? Why then has the health of my poor people not been restored? (Jeremiah 8:22).

Last night at my home church, I was overwhelmed with the sense of Your heart for restoration of Your people. First I met with those You are calling to be equipped and empowered to minister Your healing and life at the altar of our church in the Prayer Ministry Team. And then I joined the meeting with those You are calling to come along side those suffering from the addictions and struggles with every form of hurts, habits, and hang-ups in the ministry of Celebrate Recovery. You want Your people healed and whole, free and filled, saved and sanctified. You are the Balm of Gilead. You are the Great Physician. But we have to humble ourselves to acknowledge we need Your healing of our spirits, souls, and bodies, and that we all have hurts, habits, and hang-ups, that we all need recovery and restoration. As You said long ago, "Those who are well have no need of a physician, but those who are sick" (Luke 5:31). Help us humble ourselves to admit our need and then come to You in faith to restore our health in every area of our lives.

Then we can minister to others out of our healed hearts and not our hurts, with fresh faith and not our wounded spirits. Then others will be drawn to the light of Your glory shining through a people who have humble themselves at the foot of Your cross and allowed You to lift us up in Your arms, heal our hurts, break our bondage, and fill us afresh with life of Your Spirit to shine with the light of Your glory. Then we will be a church and a people who display Your glory—not because we were not broken or bound; but because we were and we called on Your name in humility and faith so that You healed us and set us free! Thank You for letting me be part of a church like that. In Jesus' name I pray, Amen.

Be encouraged today! In the Love of Jesus, *Tommy Hays*

Justice, Mercy, and Faith

Good morning, Lord Jesus. I fall so short of Your glory and I am forever in need of Your grace. Help me grow in the knowledge of Your nature and Your ways as You lead me through the steps of this day. ...

"Woe to you, scribes and Pharisees, hypocrites! For you tithe mint, dill, and cummin, and have neglected the weightier matters of the law: justice and mercy and faith. It is these you ought to have practiced without neglecting others. You blind guides! You strain out a gnat but swallow a camel!" (Matthew 23:23-24).

The weightier matters of the law are justice and mercy and faith. These are weighty matters because there are no easy answers. Sometimes we find ourselves in need of justice and sometimes in need of mercy, but always in need of faith to trust You to lead us through the decisions and challenges of our lives. To become legalistic or dogmatic in demanding either justice or mercy without seeking to follow You in faith is to be a blind guide, bound up in rules rather than relationship, subjecting ourselves and others to law without grace or grace without law. But in Your holy ways, You do both. Even in Your judgment, You remember mercy (Habakkuk 3:2).

As both a prayer minister and trial lawyer, I have often found myself wrestling between these two equal, guiding truths and spiritual principles— to seek both Your justice and Your mercy for myself and for others. You call us to "hold fast to love and justice, and wait continually for your God" (Hosea 12:6). This means there are no easy answers in these weighty matters. So faith in Your wisdom and trust in Your nature brings me to my knees to seek Your face and Your leading, spreading each matter as it comes before the throne of Your will in humility and prayer. There You remind me of Your high standards that I can only live out in the power of Your grace: "He has shown you, O man, what is good; and what does the Lord require of you but to do justice, to love mercy, and to walk humbly with your God" (Micah 6:8, NKJV). Help me walk humbly with You, Lord, looking to You in faith and prayer so I can walk before You and others in both justice and mercy as You lead. In Jesus' name I pray, Amen.

Be encouraged today! In the Love of Jesus, *Tommy Hays*

Enforced Insomnia & Sabbath Rest

Good morning, Lord Jesus. It's a little earlier in the morning to join you in prayer than I had hoped, but I take this moment to welcome Your presence into my heart and home again this day. ...

"In the morning, while it was still very dark, He got up and went out to a deserted place, and there He prayed" (Mark 1:35).

The voice of our little "angel"—six month old Josiah Benjamin Hays—has woken me up twice this morning already while it is "still very dark." His mother and I have gone in to comfort him but not to feed him, as he learns to sleep through the night (and as we try to re-learn how to sleep through the night). He's done it three times this week—Praise the Lord!—but not tonight. The Kingdom of God to come is already breaking in, but not yet fully consummated in its fullness! "So then, a sabbath rest still remains for the people of God" (Hebrews 4:9).

I find it hard to get back to sleep after these times of answering the call of our beloved son who is like the voice of one crying out in the wilderness—loudly and persistently until we repent of our sleepy ways and arise from our slumber to sing the song of rest over our little saint, "Hush little baby, don't say a word; Daddy's gonna buy you a mockingbird, etc., etc., ..." So since I can't go off to a deserted place to sleep, I often go ahead and slide into my prayer chair to spend some time with You before I slip back into sleep for a little nap before the dawn of a new day. You seem to be redeeming this season of enforced insomnia to deepen my life of prayer. You don't waste a moment of our suffering, but cause all things to work together for good (Romans 8:28). But even so, Lord, I pray for the day when I can arise to meet You in the morning again—when it is not "still very dark." Let that day come quickly, Lord Jesus, like a thief in the night. In Jesus' name I pray, Amen.

Be encouraged today! In the Love of Jesus, *Tommy Hays*

"Eternal in the Heavens"

 Good morning, Lord Jesus. Before the thoughts of the day come racing
into my mind, I come racing to You to focus my first thoughts of a new day
on You alone. ...

"For we know that if the earthly tent we live in is destroyed, we have a
building from God, a house not made with hands, eternal in the heavens.
For in this tent we groan, longing to be clothed with our heavenly dwelling"
(2 Corinthians 5:1-2).

Though I live out my life on earth in my earthly body, at the same time I
have a heavenly body which is "eternal in the heavens." Today—like all
days past, present, and future—is included in eternity. One day my faith
will become sight, and my eyes will be opened to fully see the substance of
all the reality of Your creation.   But for now, I engage that eternal
dimension of my being through the communion of prayer, as my human
spirit seeks Your Holy Spirit. I long to encounter and experience Your
presence, because You've placed that desire in my heart to be near to Your
heart.

In this earthly dimension, I groan and long for the heavenly dimension of
Your eternity, never satisfied and never fulfilled with anything less. And
that's how You created me—to never be satisfied and never be fulfilled
apart from You.   Thank You for the gift of longing to be who You created
me to be throughout eternity. Thank You for "the hope of eternal life that
God, who never lies, promised before the ages began" (Titus 1:2). In Jesus'
name I pray, Amen.

Be encouraged today! In the Love of Jesus, *Tommy Hays*

I Need Thee Every Hour[*]

"Teach me good judgment and knowledge, for I believe your commandments" (Psalm119:66).

"For the good that I will to do, I do not do; but the evil I will not to do, that I practice. O wretched man that I am! Who will deliver me from this body of death?" (Romans 7:19, 24)

More than anything, I desire to have good judgment and knowledge. I also know though that even when I know right from wrong, there are many times when I choose to do wrong. There is a constant struggle going on within me to live according to the spirit and to die to the flesh. I am reminded today of how much I need Christ to help guide me and transform me. An old hymn written by Annie Hawks comes to mind.

> I need thee every hour, most gracious Lord;
> no tender voice like thine can peace afford.
>
> I need thee, O I need thee;
> every hour I need thee;
> O bless me now, my Savior, I come to thee.
>
> I need thee every hour; stay thou nearby;
> temptations lose their power when thou art nigh.
>
> I need thee, O I need thee;
> every hour I need thee;
> O bless me now, my Savior, I come to thee.
>
> I need thee every hour, in joy or pain;
> come quickly and abide, or life is vain.
>
> I need thee, O I need thee;
> every hour I need thee;
> O bless me now, my Savior, I come to thee.
>
> I need thee every hour; teach me thy will;
> and thy rich promises in me fulfill.
>
> I need thee, O I need thee;
> every hour I need thee;
> O bless me now, my Savior, I come to thee.

[*] The following devotional was written by Mary Margaret Adams.

I need thee every hour, most Holy One;
O make me thine indeed, thou blessed Son.

I need thee, O I need thee;
every hour I need thee;
O bless me now, my Savior, I come to thee.

May this be our constant prayer; to understand our dependence on Christ and to seek Him.

All praise and glory be to God! *Mary Margaret Adams*

"Arise and Eat"

 Good morning, Lord Jesus. Your Word and Your Spirit are my Light and my Strength. ...

We've been studying the stories of Elijah in church. In the wilderness, You touched him and called to him, "Get up and eat, otherwise the journey will be too much for you" (1 Kings 19:7). It seems I hear You saying, "Arise and eat. Come rise into My presence through your spirit in prayer. Come eat of My Word as I meet you there."

Now it seems I hear Your Spirit singing to my spirit:

> *"Arise, My son, arise!*
> *Come rise into My presence through your spirit in prayer.*
> *Arise, My son, arise!*
> *Come eat of My Word as I meet you there.*
>
> *Arise, My son, arise!*
> *Come follow my steps through this day.*
> *Arise, My son, arise!*
> *Come follow Me and I'll show you the way."*

Yes, Lord. You are a God who sings to my spirit with gladness and renews my spirit in love (Zephaniah 3:17). I thank You for the times of rest and renewal, and I thank you for the times of calling and commissioning to send me on in the light of Your Word and the strength of Your Spirit. "One does not live by bread alone, but by every word that comes from the mouth of God" (Matthew 4:4). Thank You for speaking Your words of life and truth to me today. Help me keep listening and obeying as You keep leading throughout this day. In Jesus' name I pray, Amen.

Be encouraged today! In the Love of Jesus, *Tommy Hays*

God's Perspective

Good morning, Lord Jesus. I love You, Lord and I thank You for loving me.
...

"What is impossible from a human perspective is possible with God" (Luke 18:27, NLT).

Like Peter and Your first disciples, I can get caught up and bogged down in the difficulties of the day and the frustrations of the moment. But You want to lift my eyes to You, not ignoring my problems but also seeing beyond them with Your perspective. You reminded Peter as You continue to remind me, there is no challenge I can face and nothing I can lose on this earth that will not be redeemed beyond all human possibilities "in this age and in the age to come" if I keep following You and living my life in Your grace "for the sake of the kingdom of God" (Luke 18:28-30).

Lord, give me Your perspective. My human perspective often gets me focused on the trees instead of the forest, on the tyranny of the trials of the moment instead of on the bigger picture of Your purposes and Your kingdom. Keep opening the eyes of my heart to see You as You are and to see the world around me from Your eternal perspective, as I live out the hope of my calling for the sake of Your kingdom (Ephesians 1:17-19). In Jesus' name I pray, Amen.

Be encouraged today! In the Love of Jesus, *Tommy Hays*

Anointed by the Holy One

Good morning, Lord Jesus. Teach me Your Word and fill me with Your Spirit as I wait in Your presence and watch for Your leading. ...

"But you have been anointed by the Holy One, and all of you have knowledge. I write to you, not because you do not know the truth, but because you know it, and you know that no lie comes from the Truth. Who is a liar but the one who denies that Jesus is the Christ? This is the antichrist, the one who denies the Father and the Son. No one who denies the Son has the Father; everyone who confesses the Son has the Father also. Let what you heard in the beginning abide in you. If what you heard from the beginning abides in you, then you will abide in the Son and in the Father. And this is what He has promised, eternal life" (1 John 2:20-25).

Father, Son, and Holy Spirit—You are the Holy One. You are the Truth and You are the Spirit of Truth (John 15:26). Your truth sets me free of all deception (John 8:32). And Your anointing breaks every yoke of every burden (Isaiah 10:27, KJV). Anoint me with Your Truth, abide in me with Your Spirit, Holy One of God. I confess my trust and surrender my life to You. I embrace the knowledge of Your grace and the fullness of Your promise of eternal life through Jesus the Christ. In Jesus' name I pray, Amen.

Be encouraged today! In the Love of Jesus, *Tommy Hays*

Destined for Glory

Good morning, Lord Jesus. I rise today to follow You. ...

"Christ in you, the hope of glory" (from Colossians 1:27).

"Destined for Glory" were the first words that came to mind as I woke this morning. I went to bed last night thinking about the theme of a week of spiritual renewal I'll be leading in early November in western Kentucky. The pastor asked me to share messages about our calling to holiness of heart and life, and I guess my spirit was at work seeking the leading of Your Spirit as I slept. We are but dust, yet we are destined for glory—Your glory shining through us with Christ in our hearts.

Peter wrote his first letter as an apostle "to the exiles of the Dispersion" throughout that part of the world "who have been chosen and destined by God the Father and sanctified by the Spirit to be obedient to Jesus Christ and sprinkled with His blood" (1 Peter 1:1-2). But those exiles who had been dispersed by the persecution of the early church of mostly Jewish believers who received Jesus as their long-awaited Messiah, were not the only ones who were "chosen and destined by God" to be "sanctified by the Spirit" and "obedient to Jesus Christ." You are "not wanting any to perish, but all to come to repentance" (2 Peter 3:9). Your invitation and promise of grace is always that "whosoever believes" in the Son of God "should not perish but have eternal life" (John 3:16, NKJV). But You were reminding those who were exiled as strangers in a foreign land to remember their destiny despite their dispersion, to remember their calling despite their circumstances.

They were chosen by God and destined for glory. You were reminding them that though they would experience dark days, Your Spirit would arise upon them and shine through them with the light of Your glory. In Christ Jesus their Messiah, they were the fulfillment of the prophecies of Your Word of a people to come who would be sprinkled by the blood of the Lamb as a holy people of God. "Arise, shine, for your Light has come, and the glory of the Lord has risen upon you" (Isaiah 60:1). And Your call to arise and to shine with the light of Your glory has not changed. You choose all who will answer Your call by Your grace to the destiny of Your glory—"Christ in you, the hope of glory."

I choose to keep answering Your call to holiness of heart and life, to be "sanctified by the Spirit" through Your grace. I welcome the light of Your glory, the glory of the manifest presence of God my Father living in me by the Holy Spirit of the Living Christ. "For God has destined us not for wrath but for obtaining salvation through our Lord Jesus Christ, who died for us, so that whether we are awake or asleep we may live in Him." Thank You for waking me from my sleep to remind me again that though I am a stranger living in a foreign land in this broken, fallen world, my "citizenship is in heaven." From there, my Lord and Savior comes that I "may be conformed to the body of His glory" (Philippians 3:20-21). By Your grace, I am sprinkled by Your blood, sanctified by the Spirit, and destined for glory. In Jesus' name I pray, Amen.

Be encouraged today! In the Love of Jesus, *Tommy Hays*

Brokenness to Breakthrough

Good morning, Lord Jesus. Anoint me with Your presence and Your power to teach Your Word and minister Your love today. ...

"David inquired of God, 'Shall I go up against the Philistines? Will you give them into my hand? The Lord said to him, 'Go up, and I will give them into your hand.' So he went up to Baal-parazim, and David defeated them there. David said, 'God has burst out against my enemies by my hand, like a bursting flood' " (1 Chronicles 14:10-11).

You are the God who bursts out against our enemies—the God of the breakthrough. Our battle is not against flesh and blood, but against the spiritual forces of wickedness (Ephesians 6:12). Our Philistines are the places where the enemy of our souls seeks to hold us in bondage to the past and break our spirits from walking in the authority and victory of the fullness of life You long for us to have (John 10:10). But You come to bind-up the broken-hearted; You come to set the captives free. You heal our brokenness and breakthrough against our enemies.

And You do it all by Your grace and power. The battle belongs to the Lord. But You also choose to do it through us—You give our enemies into our hands. We have a part to play and a stand to take. We must be active and not passive, choosing to press though and press on in the power of You grace, as You burst out against our enemies in response to our choices and our prayers that You lay on our hearts. You lead us from brokenness to breakthrough. In Jesus' name I pray, Amen.

Be encouraged today! In the Love of Jesus, *Tommy Hays*

Running out of Gas*

I once heard a sermon called "running out of gas," and it seemed to describe me perfectly! I would start something God wanted me to do with excitement, enthusiasm, hard work and dedication only to find after weeks or months that I was slowly losing steam. I would reach the point where I was sputtering along, feeling exhausted and looking rather silly and think "I ought to just give up! I should have known I wouldn't be able to do this."

Lately, I am more tired and busier, so I have begun to wonder if I am going to start "running out of gas." Romans 12:1-2 gives us a clue how we can avoid this. It reads as follows:

"I beseech you therefore brethren, by the mercies of God, that you present your bodies as a living sacrifice, holy, acceptable to God, which is your reasonable service. And do not be conformed to this world, but be transformed by the renewing of your mind, that you may prove what is that good and acceptable and perfect will of God."

First, we read that God wants us to live holy lives and that this request is "reasonable." This seems to imply that we are capable of doing what God asks of us. Second, we see that the only way we can be transformed into the kind of person who can live this way is through the renewing of our minds. We must continually put God first and rely on Him for our strength and guidance.

In Matthew chapter 11, Jesus says: "Come to me, all you who labor and are heavy laden, and I will give you rest. Take my yoke upon you and learn from Me, for I am gentle and lowly in heart, and you will find rest for your souls. For My yoke is easy and My burden is light" (verses 28-30).

We know that we are equipped to do His work as long as we know His will and are working with Him to accomplish His will. Anything we do on our own will end up being a burden that we are unable to bear. In order to know His will, we must know Him! This means spending time in prayer, Bible reading, and listening for the voice and will of God.

All praise and glory be to God! *Mary Margaret Adams*

---

* The following devotional was written by Mary Margaret Adams.

Thanksgiving*

Today is a beautiful day. The temperature is just right and there is a nice breeze blowing; a good morning to be outside with my sons. I couldn't help but to praise God for such a beautiful day and for my sons, who are quite adorable playing outside. Psalm 100 came to mind:

"Make a joyful shout to the Lord, all you lands! Serve the Lord with gladness; come before His presence with singing. Know that the Lord, He is God. It is He who has made us, and not we ourselves; we are His people and the sheep of His pasture. Enter into His gates with thanksgiving, and into His courts with praise. Be thankful to Him, and bless His name. For the Lord is good; His mercy is everlasting, and his truth endures to all generations."

There are so many reasons to praise God! He is our Creator and our Shepard. He is good and His mercy and truth are everlasting. He sent His son to save us (John 3:16). And, He loves us. 1 John 4:9-10 says: "In this the love of God was manifested toward us, that God has sent His only begotten Son into the world, that we might live through Him. In this is love, not that we loved God, but that He loved us and sent His Son to be the propitiation for our sins."

Let's take a moment today to praise God for all of His wonderful works and for His goodness toward us!

All praise and Glory be to God! *Mary Margaret Adams*

---

* The following devotional was written by Mary Margaret Adams.

Trials, O Joy!

Good morning, Lord Jesus. I seek Your face and call on Your name as I begin this day. ...

"My brothers and sisters, whenever you face trials of any kind, consider it nothing but joy, because you know that the testing of your faith produces endurance, and let endurance have its full effect, so that you may be mature and complete, lacking in nothing" (James 1:2-4).

Trials—O joy! Tribulation—O joy! Counter-attacks of the kingdom of darkness against every act of faithful obedience—O joy! Lord, sometimes it is really hard to hold on to Your Kingdom perspective that is so different from our worldly perspective. In Your Kingdom, the last shall be first, the greatest of all must be the servant of all, to live we must die, etc., etc., etc. You turn the principles of this world on its head and inside out. But if we keep our eyes on You and listen for the leading of Your voice, You turn even our trials and tribulations into a means of Your grace to draw us nearer to You and to grow us up in spiritual maturity. "We must through many tribulations enter the Kingdom of God" (Acts 14:22, NKJV).

Thank You for the power of Your healing presence throughout the day and evening at our inner healing conference Saturday, "From Brokenness to Breakthrough." You touched us deeply to free us from the hidden and unhealed wounds of the past to free us to fulfill our destiny in Christ. I praise You for the testimonies of Your power and grace we've already heard and I praise You for the ones to come as You are faithful to bring to completion all that You have begun.

And You gave me many opportunities to practice what I preach—trying to press through Friday evening and Saturday with aches and chills, hoping to spend Sunday in bed to rest and heal, but then being called away for a family crisis out of town for two days, finally making it home late last night.

On the outside, I still feel wrung out and tired, but inside I choose to keep looking to You. "So if you have been raised with Christ, seek the things that are above where Christ is, seated at the right hand of God. Set you mind on things that are above, not on things that are on earth, for you have died and your life is hidden with Christ in God" (Colossians 3:1-3). Yes, Lord. Give me grace to practice what I preach and give me faith to walk where I call others to follow, looking to the One who redeems my brokenness into breakthrough. In Jesus' name I pray, Amen.

Be encouraged today! In the Love of Jesus, *Tommy Hays*

Steps Made Firm

Good morning, Lord Jesus. I need You and I choose to be desperately dependent upon You this day and every day. ...

"Our steps are made firm by the Lord, when He delights in our way; though we stumble, we shall not fall headlong, for the Lord holds us by the hand" (Psalm 37:23-24).

Lord, I want You to delight in my way so that You may make firm my steps along the journey of this day. You delight in my way as I commit my way to Your way and my will to Your will. You know what is best because You know what is to come. Help me trust You and Your leading as I entrust myself to Your way and Your will for my life this day. "I delight in Your will, O my God; Your law is within my heart" (Psalm 40:8). Then even if I stumble over the stones of the struggles of this day, I will not fall because You will be with me, holding me by the hand. In Jesus' name I pray, Amen.

Be encouraged today! In the Love of Jesus, *Tommy Hays*

I Become as I Think

Good morning, Lord Jesus. I seek Your face and call on Your name. I open my spirit to be filled afresh with Your Spirit. ...

"For as he thinks in his heart, so is he" (Proverbs 23:7, NKJV).

Lord, cause the thoughts of my heart to line up with Your truth. Let me see You as You are. Let me see myself as You see me and see others as You see them. Bring my mind and my heart into agreement with Your will and Your ways. Transform me by the renewing of my mind (Romans 12:2). Continue to mature my thinking as You patiently form in me "the mind of Christ" (1 Corinthians 2:16). Cause my thoughts to become more like Your thoughts and cause my desires to become more like Your desires.

"When I was a child, I spoke like a child, I thought like a child, I reasoned as a child; when I became an adult I put an end to childish ways" (1 Corinthians 13:11). As I go on in the journey with You, I'm asking You to make me more like You each day. As I think in my heart, so I will become. Let Your nature become my nature as I willingly entrust my mind and my heart to Your will and Your ways. In Jesus' name I pray, Amen.

Be encouraged today! In the Love of Jesus, *Tommy Hays*

Signs of Good News

Good morning, Lord Jesus. I love You Lord, and I choose to begin this new day with my first thoughts on You. ...

"And they went out and proclaimed the good news everywhere, while the Lord worked with them and confirmed the message by the signs that accompanied it" (Mark 16:20).

Lord, You are faithful and gracious and good. You send us out in obedience to Your call and in the authority of Your name to proclaim the good news of the Kingdom of God everywhere we go. You take our brokenness and our limitations of human flesh and blood and let the light of Your glory shine through us as we lead others to You. When we are weak, You are strong; and Your power is made perfect in our weakness (2 Corinthians 12:9). According to Your Word, You humble Yourself to work with us and to work through us in Your ministry of love.

Every day this week, I've seen or heard from someone who came to our Brokenness to Breakthrough conference last Saturday. You have been confirming Your message with Your signs of changed hearts and transformed lives. The steady process of healing and restoration of our lives into Your order is continuing to take place. Your kingdom is coming and Your will is being done in our hearts and in our lives as You continue to bring us from brokenness to breakthrough in the power of Your love. Some have been instantaneous and miraculous like the woman who immediately felt an incredible lifting of her burdens and the settling in of Your peace as we prayed. Most are sensing the steady and sure process of transformation through the healing and freedom You continue to bring step by step and day by day as they walk out the truth of Your Word in the power of Your love.

And at the same time, there was a lady who has not yet been able to receive the good news of Your love and grace who said God was not with us or even in the building that day. I especially pray for her, that You would continue to go to the root and source of her pain and disappointment with You and Your messengers to draw out her pain and pour in Your love until she is free from the bondage of the past and experiences the fullness of the grace of God. Help this lady and each of us continue to turn to You to hear and receive the good news of Your Kingdom being made manifest in our lives every day. "The time is fulfilled, and the Kingdom of God has come near; repent and believe in the good news!" (Mark 1:15). Yes, Lord, I do. In Jesus' name I pray, Amen.

Be encouraged today! In the Love of Jesus, *Tommy Hays*

Charlie*

"Every good and every perfect gift is from above, and comes down from the Father of lights, with whom there is no variation or shadow of turning" (James 1:17).

We all made the big trip to Ohio to pick up our new puppy Charlie. We had to split up the trip due to the distance (Henry has been known to get car sickness). The boys had a great time swimming in the hotel pool and sleeping in the big bed at the hotel.

It seemed like forever before we could get our little puppy! We finally got him and he was absolutely perfect! He has a sweet disposition and loves to follow me around everywhere. He is healthy, rambunctious, and full of life!

While Charlie is a lot of work, he brings so much joy for me. I don't really mind getting up two times each night to let him out to go potty or watching him all day to make sure he's not chewing on something or doing other "naughty" puppy things.

More than anything, I know that Charlie is a special gift from God. I prayed about him before I purchased him and I knew that I was supposed to get this particular dog. Even though there seemed to be certain obstacles, everything worked out smoothly in the end.

We often hear about how God uses our bad experiences and suffering to grow us, but sometimes we forget that God also puts positive experiences in our lives and gives us "good" gifts. Good gifts and positive experiences can heal us and grow our faith (every bit as much as "bad" ones). Ultimately, God desires good for us and He uses all things to lead us to Him; even good things, like a new puppy.

All praise and glory be to God! *Mary Margaret Adams*

---

* The following devotional was written by Mary Margaret Adams.

"Filled with Joy and the Holy Spirit"

Good morning, Lord Jesus. Good morning, Heavenly Father. Good morning, Holy Spirit. Lord, You are One and You are Holy. Help me know You and embrace You in every Dimension of Your Being more fully each day as my Lord and my God. ...

"And the disciples were filled with joy and with the Holy Spirit" (Acts 13:52).

This weekend was our "Holy Spirit Weekend" on the Alpha Course we run at our church to teach the foundational principles of our faith to lead people into a relationship with Christ—either a new relationship or a deeper relationship. On this weekend we get away to learn more specifically about the nature and ministry of the Your Holy Spirit and many prayed for the first time to be filled and refreshed and renewed in the love and peace and joy of Your infilling presence.

Thank You for Your desire to fill us with Your presence and conform us to Your nature. Thank You for giving us a hunger and thirst for more of You. "Blessed are those who hunger and thirst for righteousness, for they shall be filled" (Matthew 5:6). Lord, keep filling me afresh every day with Your Holy Spirit. This is a deep part of the joy in the journey with You. Thank You for the gift of helping lead others along in the joy of the journey together. In Jesus' name I pray, Amen.

Be encouraged today! In the Love of Jesus, *Tommy Hays*

"Your Steadfast Love in the Morning"

Good morning, Lord Jesus. I watch and wait for You and welcome Your Spirit and Your Word in my heart and throughout my day. ...

"Let me hear of Your steadfast love in the morning, for in You I put my trust. Teach me the way I should go, for to You I lift up my soul" (Psalm 143:8).

I was speaking with a woman who has walked in faith through many adversities and afflictions throughout her life. We were sharing with one another how important we have found it to be for us to begin our days with our thoughts and hearts turned to You before anything else. She begins each day by speaking out these words of dedication and trust to You from Psalm 143.

Yes, Lord. As I choose to put my trust in You each morning, You speak to me of Your steadfast love. As I choose to lift up my soul to You each day, You teach me the way I should go. As I wait for Your manifest presence and watch for Your faithful leading, You are my Teacher and Guide. As I lift my eyes to Your face, You open my eyes to see You. As I open my ears to Your voice, You open my ears to hear You. "Your Teacher will not hide himself any more, but your eyes shall see your Teacher. And when you turn to the right or turn to the left, your ears shall hear a word behind you, 'This is the way, walk in it'" (Isaiah 30:20-21). In Jesus' name I pray, Amen.

Be encouraged today! In the Love of Jesus, *Tommy Hays*

Transformation from Humiliation to Glory

Good morning, Lord Jesus. As a worship song of trusting surrender says, "Take my heart and form it; take my mind, transform it; take my will, conform it ... to Yours, to Yours, O Lord." ...

"But our citizenship is in heaven, and it is from there that we are expecting a Savior, the Lord Jesus Christ. He will transform the body of our humiliation that it may be conformed to the body of His glory, by the power that enables Him to make all things subject to Himself. Therefore, my brothers and sisters, whom I love and long for, my joy and crown, stand firm in the Lord in this way, my beloved" (Philippians 3:20-4:1).

Transformation is the steady process of conformation into the image of Christ. As I continue to stand firm in You by grace through faith, You stand firm in me. From humiliation to glory, You are changing me—my thoughts, my desires, my will, and my ways—little by little and day by day as I look to You and yield to Your nature. "And all of us, with unveiled faces, seeing the glory of the Lord as though reflected in a mirror, are being transformed into the same image from one degree of glory to another; for this comes from the Lord, the Spirit" (2 Corinthians 3:18). Lord, in Your power, keep transforming me, keep conforming me, as You make all things—including my heart and soul—subject to Yourself. In Jesus' name I pray, Amen.

Be encouraged today! In the Love of Jesus, *Tommy Hays*

Politicians or Prophets

Good morning, Lord Jesus. You are the "King of kings and the Lord of lords" (Revelation 19:16). Be my King and be my Lord this day. ...

"Samuel said to all Israel, 'I have listened to you in all you have said to me, and have set a king over you. See, it is the king who leads you now; I am old and gray but my sons are with you. I have led you from my youth until this day" (1 Samuel 12:1-2).

This is the season of politics in our country, with national and local elections in just a couple of weeks. I'm reminded of the pleading of Israel to be led by a politician rather than a prophet, by an earthly king rather than the heavenly King. The prophet Samuel declared to the people, "You shall know and see that the wickedness you have done in the sight of the Lord is great in demanding a king for yourselves" (1 Samuel 12:17). Their demand for the leadership of a king was a rejection of the leadership of God. "But today you have rejected your God, who saves you from all your calamities and distresses; and you have said, 'No, but set a king over us' " (1 Samuel 10:19). Their choice set in motion a pattern of politics and government that has continued in one form or another throughout the generations to this day.

Though it broke Your heart to know all that would come to pass as the hearts of Your people turned to their king to be their savior and deliverer rather than the Lord their God, You honored the choice of their will. But even so, You did not abandon them or reject them. Even in their sin of choosing a king to lead them rather than the voice of the Lord through Your prophet, You gave them grace to cover their sin if they and their king would seek Your face and obey Your voice. "If you will fear the Lord and serve Him and heed His voice and not rebel against the commandment of the Lord, and if both you and the king who reigns over you will follow the Lord, it will be well; but if you will not heed the voice of the Lord, but rebel against the commandment of the Lord, then the hand of the Lord will be against you and your king" (1 Samuel 12:14-15).

Lord, I pray for those who have been given authority to reign over us. Though we may call them senators, representatives, mayors, governors, presidents, or prime ministers rather than kings, they have been entrusted to rule and reign in the governance of our lives. The voices they heed and the decisions they make affect us all. Though this was not Your first choice of government for Your people, You meet us where we are in the choices we have made throughout the generations, giving us grace as we seek to follow You in the system of government we have. "Let every person be subject to the governing authorities; for there is no authority except from God, and those authorities that exist have been instituted by God" (Romans 13:1). So we are to pray "for kings and all who are in high positions, so that we may lead a quiet and peaceable life in all godliness and dignity" (1 Timothy 2:1-2).

Lord, establish those in authority who will seek Your face and obey Your voice.   And remove those who will not. Purge and cleanse from our governments those who will not lead us in "all godliness and dignity" by heeding the voice of the Lord. Give us humility to seek and courage to obey Your will and Your ways in the choices we make about the kings we anoint with authority to reign in our lives. Only as we follow You—both ourselves and our kings—will it "be well" with us. In Jesus' name I pray, Amen.

Be encouraged today! In the Love of Jesus, *Tommy Hays*

Two Become One

Good morning, Lord Jesus. Abide in me as I abide in You—Father, Son, and Holy Spirit. ...

"Then the Lord God said, 'It is not good that the man should be alone; I will make him a helper as his partner' " (Genesis 2:18).

In the beginning, You created the heavens and the earth and all that dwell within them. You looked upon all You had made and said "it was very good" (Genesis 1:31). Yet even in the sinless perfection of creation, undefiled before the fall of man through sin, You looked and saw that it was "not good" for man to be alone. You created us to need You and also to need a partner. Even when we might say, "God is all I need," that does not mean that we don't also need one another. You love us directly, and at the same time, You love us through one another. So from the foundations of the earth, You have created us to experience life with a helper as our partner in the journey. "Therefore a man leaves his father and mother and clings to his wife, and they become one flesh" (Genesis 2:24).

Last night I ministered the covenant of marriage to a young couple I've come to know and love through their ministry of healing and love in leading others in worship of You. They've walked their journeys alone, until last night, in the fullness of time and the perfection of Your timing, You joined the two as one. One gifted with passion, one gifted with perseverance; one gifted with tenderness and mercy; one gifted with boldness and strength—You knitted their hearts and lives together as helpers and partners of one another. You sealed their lives and destinies together eternally in the holy covenant of marriage, bound together in the power of the bond of Your unfailing love. "Set me as a seal upon your heart, as a seal upon your arm; for love is strong as death, passion fierce as the grave. It's flashes are flashes of fire, a raging flame. Many waters cannot quench love, neither can floods drown it" (Song of Solomon 8:6-7). "So they are no longer two, but one flesh. Therefore what God has joined together, let no one separate" (Matthew 19:6). Lord, bless them and all of Your children with the helper and partner You have chosen for the joy of the journey together. In Jesus' name I pray, Amen.

Be encouraged today! In the Love of Jesus, *Tommy Hays*

Our Spiritual War

Good morning, Lord Jesus. Through the victory of the cross and the glory of the resurrection, You said, "All authority in heaven and on earth has been given to Me" (Matthew 28:18). I willingly submit in trusting surrender to Your authority in my life again this day. ...

"For who is God except the Lord? And who is a Rock besides our God?—the God who girded me with strength, and made my way safe. He made my feet like the feet of a deer, and set me secure on the heights. He trains my hands for war, so that my arms can bend a bow of bronze. You have given me the shield of Your salvation, and Your right hand has supported me; Your help has made me great. You gave me a wide place for my steps under me, and my feet did not slip. I pursued my enemies and overtook them; and did not turn back until they were consumed. I struck them down, so that they were not able to rise; they fell under my feet. For You girded me with strength for the battle; You made my assailants sink under me. You made my enemies turn their backs to me, and those who hated me I destroyed. They cried for help but there was no one to save them. I beat them fine like dust before the wind; I cast them out like the mire of the streets" (Psalm 18:31-34).

By Your Spirit, I taught on spiritual warfare at our Alpha Course at church last night. Our faith is not a feeble faith, and the battles of our faith are not won through passivity, complacency, or ignorance in denial of spiritual truth. We have a real enemy who is like a roaring lion seeking to devour our souls; he is the ancient serpent who comes to "make war" against the children of God who "hold the testimony of Jesus" (1 Peter 5:8-9; Revelation 12:17). But we are commanded to confront him and his kingdom of darkness in the authority of Your name and in the power of Your blood, steadfast in our faith to overcome the enemy of our souls (Matthew 10:7-8; Revelation 12:11). As we do, the gates of hell cannot prevail against You and Your people who fight for the freedom of those who were bound by the darkness but are set free in Your light (Matthew 16:18; Colossians 1:11-14).

Our enemies are not flesh and blood; they are the spiritual forces of wickedness of this present darkness (Ephesians 6:12). But they are defeated by the victory of the cross, and You call us to enforce that victory in every area of our lives in the lives of others in the power and authority of Your name (Colossians 2:8-15). This is "the good fight of the faith" we are called and empowered to wage as we pursue our spiritual enemies without mercy until they are beaten fine like dust and crushed under our feet in the name of Jesus, before whom all things must bow and submit to Your Lordship and Your authority (1 Timothy 6:12; Philippians 2:9-11). As we do, You have promised, "The God of peace will shortly crush Satan under your feet. The grace of our Lord Jesus Christ be with you" (Romans 16:20). Thanks be to God! In Jesus' name I pray, Amen.

Be encouraged today! In the Love of Jesus, *Tommy Hays*

Called in Righteousness; Sent in Power

Good morning, Lord Jesus. Give me humility to stop and wait for Your leading and give me courage to rise and follow where You lead. ...

"I am the Lord, I have called you in righteousness, I have taken you by the hand and kept you; I give you as a covenant to the people, a light to the nations, to open the eyes that are blind, to bring out the prisoners from the dungeon, from the prison those who sit in darkness. I am the Lord, that is My name; My glory I give to no other, nor My praise to idols" (Isaiah 42:6-8).

Yes, Lord. I give all glory and honor and praise to You alone. You are righteous and holy, worthy of all worship and praise. And You have called me and all those who would answer Your call to a life of righteousness in You. Apart from You, there is nothing good in me, but I am not apart from You. You have taken me by the hand; You have kept me in You arms, all by Your mercy and grace out of Your unbelievable love for me and all Your children. Then You send me to shine Your light by Your grace to heal the blind and free the bound in the power of Your name. "So we are ambassadors of Christ, since God is making His appeal through us; we entreat you on behalf of Christ, be reconciled to God. For our sake He made Him sin who knew no sin, so that in Him we might become the righteousness of God" (2 Corinthians 5:20-21).

These are amazing words and amazing promises, but they are true and they are for me and all Your children. I receive them by faith as I rise today to follow You and join in the ministry of Your love and power to others by Your grace. You have called me to Your righteousness to send me in Your power—all for the glory and honor and praise of Your name. In Jesus' name I pray, Amen.

Be encouraged today! In the Love of Jesus, *Tommy Hays*

Fall Back, Enemies of God

Good morning, Lord Jesus. I lift my eyes to Your face and call on Your name. ...

"On the day when the Lord gave the Amorites over to the Israelites, Joshua spoke to the Lord; and he said in the sight of Israel, 'Sun, stand still at Gibeon, and Moon, in the valley of Aijalon.' And the sun stood still, and the moon stopped, until the nation took vengeance on their enemies" (Joshua 10:12-13).

Today is the day we "fall back" and turn back our clocks for one extra hour of daylight. In a sense, the sun and the moon stand still for an hour today, as in the days of Joshua. On that day, You went before Your people and handed all their enemies into the hands of "the fighting force" with Joshua, "all the mighty warriors" (Joshua 10:7-8).

Today, let our enemies fall back and be consumed at Your hand in this hour when time stands still. Our enemies are not flesh and blood; they are the spiritual forces of wickedness who seek to resist Your promises and purposes in our lives (Ephesians 6:12). "For it is indeed just of God to repay with affliction those who afflict you, and to give relief to the afflicted as well as to us, when the Lord Jesus is revealed from heaven with His mighty angels in flaming fire, inflicting vengeance on those who do not know God and on those who do not obey the gospel of our Lord Jesus. These will suffer the punishment of eternal destruction, separated from the presence of the Lord and from the glory of His might, when He comes to be glorified by His saints and marveled at on that day among all who have believed, because our testimony to you was believed. To this end we always pray for you, asking that our God will make you worthy of His call and will fulfill by His power every good resolve and work of faith, so that the name of our Lord Jesus may be glorified in you, and you in Him, according to the grace of our God and the Lord Jesus Christ" (2 Thessalonians 1:6-12).

When I see how the enemies of our souls seek to distort our image of God and defile the image we have of ourselves through unspeakable cruelty— when I see them laugh and mock at the love and glory of my Lord—when I see them terrorize and torment little children in inhuman abuse and each of us at the most vulnerable times of our lives—I am ready to see the power and vengeance of God poured out in wrath until every evil spirit is utterly destroyed and consumed by Your flaming fire. "Out of the brightness before Him there broke through His clouds hailstones and coals of fire. The Lord also thundered in the heavens, and the Most High uttered His voice" (Psalm 18:12-13).

Come Lord Jesus, and consume our spiritual enemies this day, warring against them until they are utterly consumed and their power over our lives is broken by the power of Your love for us. "The Son of God was revealed for this purpose, to destroy the works of the devil" (1 John 3:8). Let the devil and the demons of his kingdom of darkness fall back today, as You destroy his works in our lives and throughout the earth. In Jesus' name I pray, Amen.

Be encouraged today! In the Love of Jesus, *Tommy Hays*

God's Rest[*]

I am tired and ill and just plain sick of me. I have spent most of my life feeling anxious, restless, and out of sorts. I wasted countless hours worrying about things that were out of my control. I spent a good bit of time envying other people too, only to discover that those I envied weren't any better off than I was!

Hebrews 3:4 says, "For every house is built by someone, but He who built all things is God." Ultimately, all things come from God. Some of us possess more talents, but that's only out of God's grace. Some of us lead and guide, some of us barely creep along, but we are all equal in the sense that God owns everything and can give and take away anything at any time.

I was never that talented, and I figured out pretty early on that I couldn't build a "house" for myself (career, life, achievements, and so forth). It took me a bit longer to realize that I definitely cannot build a spiritual house. Here, I will finally say everything belongs to God and if He wants to enable me to build a house, that's good. If He wants to provide one for me through His mercy and grace, that's good. I can't build this house or find any peace within; however, I choose not to worry about it anymore. I am simply tired of being tossed to and fro (James 1:5-6 says, "If any of you lack wisdom, let him ask of God, who gives to all liberally and without reproach, and it will be given to him. But let him ask in faith, with no doubting, for he who doubts is like a wave of the sea driven and tossed by the wind."). Here and now I will ask God to build this "house" as He so chooses and I will finally enter into His rest.

Hebrews chapter three has much to say about God's rest. The verses that spoke to me go as follows:

"Therefore, as the Holy Spirit says: 'Today if you will hear His voice, do not harden your hearts as in the rebellion, in the day of trial in the wilderness, where your fathers tested Me, and saw my works forty years. Therefore, I was angry with that generation, and said, 'They always go astray in their heart, and they have not known My ways.' So I swore in My wrath, 'They shall not enter My rest' " (Hebrews 3:7-11).

"And to whom did He swear that they would not enter His rest, but to those who did not obey? So we see that they could not enter in because of unbelief" (Hebrews 3:18-19).

---

[*] The following devotional was written by Mary Margaret Adams.

Do I want to wander around in the wilderness for 40 years and then die there, because I am still unable to trust and believe in God? Do I want to wait until the next life to find some peace for my wounded soul? NO! I have had enough. From this day forth, I am completely sold out for Jesus and I will do whatever He requires of me; even live in a cardboard box. I give all I have and all I am (as meager as it is) back to God and boldly ask Him to build this house!

A great Christian hymn has been on my mind for days now. During all of the weariness I have heard it ringing in my ears. It's called "Sweet Will of God," written by Leila N. Morris. Let me end with this great hymn and may this be your desire and prayer also.

> My Stubborn will at last hath yielded;
> I would be Thine and Thine alone;
> And this the pray my lips are bringing,
> Lord, let in me Thy will be done.
>
> Sweet will of God, Still fold me closer,
> `Til I am wholly lost in Thee.
>
> I'm tired of sin, footsore and weary,
> The darksome path hath dreary grown;
> But now a light has risen to cheer me;
> I find in Thee my Star, my Sun.
>
> Thy precious will, O conquering Savior,
> Doth now embrace and compass me;
> All discords hushed, my peace a river,
> My soul a prisoned bird set free.
>
> Shut in Thee, O Lord, Forever,
> My wayward feet no more to roam;
> What power from Thee my soul can sever?
> The center of God's will my home.

All praise and glory be to God! Amen! *Mary Margaret Adams*

"The Lord Who Heals You"

Good morning, Lord Jesus. I turn my eyes toward You and entrust my spirit, soul, and body into Your care again this day. ...

"I am the Lord who heals you" (Exodus 15:26).

You are a healing God. Sometimes You heal instantaneously in the moment of a miracle, when heaven meets earth in display of Your power for all to see. Sometimes You heal in the steady process of restoration to wholeness—little by little and step by step. Sometimes You heal through the help of other people and other means of Your creation You bring into our lives to come along side us in Your healing process. Sometimes You heal by giving us the grace to persevere in faith no matter what we face. And sometimes You heal through the resurrection into the body of glory You have prepared for us in eternity.

Sunday, I felt progressively worse until the doctor identified that I had contracted strep throat. Though You have used doctors and medicine and rest, You are the source of my healing for You are the Lord who heals me. You have "borne our infirmities and carried our diseases" (Isaiah 53:4; Matthew 8:17). By Your cross and through Your blood, You have taken our sins and shame, our sickness and pain, calling us to release them to You in agreement with Your will to live our lives whole and free. "He himself bore our sins in His body on the cross, so that, free from sins, we might live for righteousness; by His wounds you have been healed" (1 Peter 2:24). As I rise today in newness of life, I thank You for the power of Your healing love to me. You are the Lord who heals me. In Jesus' name I pray, Amen.

Be encouraged today! In the Love of Jesus, *Tommy Hays*

Father Heart of God

Good morning, Lord Jesus. You perfectly reveal the Father heart of God, for You and the Father are One, and You come to abide in my heart by Your Spirit (John 14:1-31). Come Holy Spirit, I pray. Cause my heart to be more like the heart of my Father; cause my mind to be more like the mind of Christ; cause my human spirit to more like Your Holy Spirit. ...

"When Israel was a child, I loved him, and out of Egypt I called My son. The more I called them, the more they went from Me; they kept sacrificing to the Baals, and offering incense to idols. Yet it was I who taught Ephraim to walk, I took them up in My arms; but they did not know that I healed them. I led them with cords of human kindness, with bands of love. I was to them like those who lift infants to their cheeks. I bent down to them and fed them (Hosea 11:1-4).

Father God, as You have loved Israel, so You love us all (Ephesians 2:11-22; Galatians 3:14). And as Israel has not always seen Your heart of love and Your hand of mercy as a perfect Father to a wayward child, neither have we. Yet You have been there all along, protecting us and healing us and fighting for us in ways we could not see. You have often loved us and led us through "cords of human kindness" when we didn't realize it was You who moved their human hearts to minister Your healing love even in the times we turned to idols instead of to You. And we often forget that a perfect Father "disciplines those whom He loves, and chastises every child whom He accepts" so that we will turn again to Your arms and Your ways with nothing separating us from Your love and grace (Hebrews 12:5-11).

Even when we don't deserve it, You bend down to us and lift us to Your cheeks to hold us in Your arms and feed us Your Words of Truth and Life to our hungering souls. Yet as tender as You are with our hearts, You are just as stern with our sin. And though it breaks Your heart to see us suffer the consequences of our rebellion, You allow our suffering to surface our need for our Father's love and our Father's care. And there You are—never leaving us and never forsaking us, always calling us to return to You (Hosea 11:10-11 and 14:1-3). This is the blessing of both "the kindness and the severity of God," as Your severity in the discipline of Your love leads us back into the arms of Your kindness (Romans 11:22). By Your grace, You help us renounce our pride and surrender our control to more fully trust Your unfailing love in every area of our lives. And in Your arms, we find the fullness of Your healing and restoration of our calling and destiny, for You are our God and we are Your people (Hosea 14:4-7).

Thank You, Father—for loving us when we fail to fully receive Your love, for bending down to us when we are not reaching up to You, for being faithful to us when we are not always faithful to You. You are the One who answers our prayers and satisfies our hearts, as Your Father's heart covers us "like an evergreen cypress" that restores us to faithfulness and obedience in the surrender of trusting love through the grace You freely give to the children of God (Hosea 14:8). "Those who are wise understand these things; those who are discerning know them" (v. 14:9). Lord, help me keep growing in wisdom and discernment of Your will and Your ways revealed in Your Father heart. In Jesus' name I pray, Amen.

Be encouraged today! In the Love of Jesus, *Tommy Hays*

God Who Reveals Mysteries

Good morning, Lord Jesus. Father, Son, and Holy Spirit—You are One and You are Holy. You are my Healer and Deliverer, my Savior and Lord, my God and King. ...

"There is a God in heaven who reveals mysteries" (Daniel 2:28).

Lord, You hold all time in Your hands. You see the end from the beginning. You see every choice we will ever make and every consequence thereof. And You see the choices and consequences of others that affect our lives and all creation throughout all generations. You see the wounds and sins of our past, the bondage and struggles of our present, and the certain hope and eternal redemption of our future, as we learn to entrust every area of lives to You in humble surrender and trusting faith. To You, all hearts are open and all thoughts are known. No mystery is a mystery to You. Nothing remains hidden beyond Your sight; nothing remains in darkness beyond Your light.

I was moved last night by the testimony of a friend who received the ministry of Your healing love into the hidden places of her soul. There were areas of hurt hidden deeply in her heart that she couldn't see. They were a mystery to her and to me, but You are the God who reveals mysteries, who brings all things out of the darkness, into Your light, and under Your blood, in the power of Your love (2 Corinthians 4:6; Colossians 1:11-14). She experienced Your ministry of inner healing—healing from the inside out as we welcome the light of Your truth and the glory of Your presence in the wounded and bound places of our soul to receive the love and grace of God into every area of our lives. With my friend and her family, I give You all glory and honor and praise for Your Father heart and Your healing hand.

And with such joy she shared with me how You explained to her this experience of healing with You by the confirmation of Your Word from the prayer of Daniel: "Blessed be the name of God from age to age, for wisdom and power are His. He changes times and seasons, deposes kings and sets up kings; He gives wisdom to the wise and knowledge to those who have understanding. He reveals deep and hidden things; He knows what is in the darkness, and light dwells with Him. To You, O God of my ancestors, I give thanks and praise, for You have given me wisdom and power, and you have now revealed to me what we asked of You, for You have revealed to us what the king ordered" (Daniel 2:20-23).

Thank You, Lord, for loving us so much that You leave nothing hidden from the light of Your truth and the glory of Your presence in the depths of our soul. In Your time and in Your way, as You give us grace to yield to Your will and entrust ourselves to Your care, You heal us and free us to truly love You and receive Your love —with all our heart, all our soul, all our mind, and all our strength. Then we are free to love others as ourselves and love ourselves as You have called us to by Your grace. Then the hidden places of our hearts no longer condemn us and we are restored to intimacy of relationship with You (1 John 3:18-24). You are the God who reveals the mysteries of our souls; and You are the God who heals us and makes us whole in the power of Your love (Exodus 15:26; Isaiah 53:4-5; Luke 4:16-21). I praise Your holy name; and I worship You, Lord—my healing God—in spirit and in truth. In Jesus' name I pray, Amen.

Be encouraged today! In the Love of Jesus, *Tommy Hays*

Seeing You as You are

Good morning, Lord Jesus. I speak out Your name and listen for the leading of Your Spirit in the silence of surrender before You. ...

"I tell you, there is joy in the presence of the angels of God over one sinner who repents" (Luke 15:10).

We rejoiced with Your angels yesterday, Lord! One who had become hardened to You through the hurts of her life cried out to You in a step of repentance and faith. You opened her eyes to see You more clearly as You are. She had been rejecting an image of God that wasn't God at all. "The god of this world has blinded the minds of the unbelievers, to keep them from seeing the light of the glory of Christ, who is the image of God" (2 Corinthians 4:4).

But as she chose by Your grace to humble herself before You enough to let You shine the light of the glory of Your truth and presence into the dark places of her soul and the dark moments of her past, she began to see You as You truly are. Then she began to see herself more clearly as she truly is—as You see her. And the angels rejoiced. "For it is God who said, 'Let light shine out of darkness,' who has shone in our hearts to give the light of the knowledge of the glory of God in the face of Jesus Christ" (2 Corinthians 4:6).

Who could see You as You truly are and still reject You? Lord, remove the blinders from our minds and heal the hardness of our hearts. This is the work of the devil, but I praise You that "the Son of God was revealed for this purpose, to destroy the works of the devil" (1 John 3:8). "Let the heavens be glad, and let the earth rejoice!" (Psalm 96:7). In Jesus' name I pray, Amen.

Be encouraged today! In the Love of Jesus, *Tommy Hays*

Secret Sins Exposed

Good morning, Lord Jesus. As best as I can and all by Your grace, I open my heart and every area of my life to You. Let Your light shine in to purify my soul. ...

"Let no one deceive you with empty words, for because of these things the wrath of God comes on those who are disobedient. Therefore do not be associated with them. For once you were darkness, but now in the Lord you are light. Live as children of light—for the fruit of the light is found in all that is good and right and true. Try to find out what is pleasing to the Lord. Take no part in the unfruitful works of darkness, but instead expose them. For it is shameful even to mention what such people do secretly; but everything exposed by the light becomes visible, for everything that becomes visible is light. Therefore it says, 'Sleeper, awake! Rise from the dead, and Christ will shine on you' (Ephesians 5:6-14).

We've just heard news of the secret sins of another Christian leader at the national level being exposed. And we recently heard the same news of Christian leaders here at our local level as well. We live in a broken, fallen world. We are all surrounded by the influences of the world, the flesh, and the devil. "All have sinned and fall short of the glory of God" (Romans 3:23). But "to set the mind on the things of the flesh is death" (Romans 8:6). And as sin takes root, it grows more each day—growing stronger in its snare of destruction and deadening our conscience to its nature and its power a little more each day.

But to You, all hearts are open and all thoughts are known. And though we are drawn by sinful nature to the works of darkness, You love us enough to bring all things out of darkness and into Your light. Though we would prefer to keep our sins secret, with no accountability and no consequences, You shine Your light and expose the darkness with conviction intended to lead to repentance, so that repentance can lead the way to restoration and mercy. "For nothing is hidden that will not be disclosed, nor is anything secret that will not become known and come to the light" (Luke 8:17).

So keep us accountable, Lord. Keep us in close relationship with one another—confessing our sins and admitting our struggles with a few trusted ones You've placed in our lives for that very purpose. Do not let our consciences grow dull and the fire of holiness in our hearts grow dim. Let iron sharpen iron, as we expose our hearts to You and to one another in bonds of accountability and prayer (Proverbs 27:17). And when there is falling and failure from Your light through sin in response to the influence from the darkness and death around us in a broken, fallen world, give us Your wisdom and Your heart to speak the truth in love (Ephesians 4:15).

"My friends, if anyone is detected in transgression, you who have received the Spirit should restore such a one in a spirit of gentleness" (Galatians 6:1).

Yes, Lord. "In Your wrath, may You remember mercy" (Habakkuk 3:2). We all have need of a Savior—a Savior from our sins and our sinful nature who responds to humble repentance and trusting faith. And we all have need of mercy. In Jesus' name I pray, Amen.

Be encouraged today! In the Love of Jesus, *Tommy Hays*

Living Sacrifices, Holy Fire

Good morning, Lord Jesus. Help me see with Your eyes and hear with Your ears, as You continue to transform me by the renewing of my mind (Romans 12:2). ...

"I appeal to you therefore, brothers and sisters, by the mercies of God, to present your bodies as a living sacrifice, holy and acceptable to God, which is your spiritual worship" (Romans 12:1).

Yes, Lord. As best as I can and all by Your grace, I choose to present my body to You as a living sacrifice. May I die to the desires of my flesh and be resurrected into the desires of Your Spirit. Consume me in Your holy fire and set me ablaze with a passion to worship You and live for You, trusting in Your wisdom and Your ways for my life. Let me be "crucified with Christ" a little more each day until "it is no longer I who live, but Christ who lives in me" (Galatians 2:19-20).

You have sent me to the people of Madisonville, Kentucky who are hungry for revival and spiritual renewal. Increase our hunger for You and Your presence until we cannot bear to take another breath that is not infused with the very breath of God. "Blessed are those who hunger and thirst for righteousness, for they will be filled" (Matthew 5:6). You are our Righteousness. You are the One for whom our souls hunger and thirst. Come and fill us with Your presence and purify us with Your power. Revive us and renew us as we present our bodies to You as living sacrifices—"holy and acceptable" to You because You have made us holy in the fire You have sent from heaven upon the altars of our hearts. In Jesus' name I pray, Amen.

Be encouraged today! In the Love of Jesus, *Tommy Hays*

"They will see God"

Good morning, Lord Jesus. As the song of worship says, "Open the eyes of my heart, Lord; I want to see You." ...

"Blessed are the pure in heart, for they will see God" (Matthew 5:8).

Purify my heart and sanctify my soul. Open the eyes of my heart to see You in the radiance of Your glory. Remove the veils from my face and the blinders from my eyes. Your glory is Your presence—the manifest presence of God. And You desire to manifest Your presence in our lives, to fill us with the fullness Your presence and conform us into the fullness of Your nature. Though it is hard for us to grasp with our finite, human minds, You call us to "be filled with all the fullness of God" (Ephesians 3:19).

"No one has ever seen God; if we love one another, God lives in us, and His love is perfected in us. By this we know that we abide in Him and He in us, because He has given us of His Spirit" (1 John 4:12-13). Open my eyes to see You living in me and to see You living in those around me who have received of Your Spirit, who You are filling with all the fullness of God. We cannot fully see You as You are until we stand amazed in Your presence in our glorified and resurrected bodies in the day to come, but we do see You in how You have revealed Yourself and Your nature to us in Jesus Christ. "But we do see Jesus, who for a little while was made lower than the angels, now crowned with glory and honor because of the suffering of death, so that by the grace of God He might taste death for everyone" (Hebrews 2:9).

Unlike the new age movement that calls us to say in pride we are each our own god, You call us to surrender and submit our lives to You in humility so that the One true God may abide in our hearts by the Spirit of Your love. Your Spirit is holy and pure, making us holy and pure by Your grace as we worship You and You fill us with the presence of Your glory (2 Corinthians 3:18). This is the mystery of the presence of God living in all who are called by Your name and filled with Your love—"Christ in you, the hope of glory" (Colossians 1:27). In Jesus' name I pray, Amen.

Be encouraged today! In the Love of Jesus, *Tommy Hays*

Choose Well this Election Day

Good morning, Lord Jesus. Conform my nature to Your nature a little more each day (2 Peter 1:4). Reveal Your will and teach me Your ways, then give me the courage to obey. ...

"When you have come into the land that the Lord your God is giving you, and have taken possession of it and settled in it, and you say, 'I will set a king over me, like all the nations that are around me,' you may indeed set over you a king whom the Lord your God will choose.... When he has taken the throne of his kingdom, he shall have a copy of this law written for him in the presence of the levitical priests. It shall remain with him and he shall read it all the days of his life, so that he may learn to fear the Lord his God, diligently observing all the words of this law and these statutes" (Deuteronomy 17:14-19).

Today is an election day in America. Let us choose the men and women that You have chosen. Let us seek Your face and listen for Your voice, allowing You to place Your thoughts in our minds and Your desires in our hearts. Let us not be deceived by outward appearances and self-promotion. Let us see their hearts with Your eyes, "for the Lord does not see as mortals see; they look on the outward appearance, but the Lord looks on the heart" (1 Samuel 16:7).

Lead us to the leaders who have learned to fear the Lord as God, who carry Your Word in their hearts all the days of their lives and diligently seek to know and obey Your will and Your ways in the choices they make in the authority they have. "There is no authority except from God, and those authorities that exist have been instituted by God" (Romans 13:1). As we willingly submit our wills to Your will, guide our thoughts and decisions to institute the men and women in the seats of authority You choose for Your purposes and our good. "Who are they that fear the Lord? He will teach them the way that they should choose" (Psalm 25:12). Teach us Your way that we may choose well this day. In Jesus' name I pray, Amen.

Be encouraged today! In the Love of Jesus, *Tommy Hays*

Pursue Holiness

Good morning, Lord Jesus. I lift up my eyes unto the hills, from where my help comes from. My help comes from You, the Maker of heaven and earth—my Lord, my God, my King— Father, Son, and Holy Spirit. ...

"Pursue peace with everyone, and the holiness without which no one will see the Lord" (Hebrews 12:14).

To "pursue" is to seek after, to run hard after, to press in and press on with tenacity and perseverance, to settle for nothing less. You call me to pursue peace and to pursue holiness if I am to see You. You give me the grace to desire it and You give me the grace to do it, but ultimately I must make the choice to pursue or not. You are my Peace—my "Prince of Peace" (Isaiah 9:6). You are my Holiness—"majestic in holiness, awesome in splendor" (Exodus 15:11).

Holy One of God, I pursue You, I run hard after You, "looking to Jesus, the pioneer and perfecter of our faith" (Hebrews 12:1-2). Cleanse my heart in the peace of Your presence, that I may be made holy and pure in Your sight by "the blood of Christ" (Hebrews 9:14). Through this mystery of faith in Christ who takes away my sins as I pursue Your peace and Your holiness, I "become the righteousness of God" by Your grace (2 Corinthians 5:21). You make me pure in heart as I "go on toward perfection" in You (Hebrews 6:1). "Blessed are the pure in heart, for they will see God" (Matthew 5:8). And I do yearn to see You, Lord—to see You as You are and to begin to see myself as You see me in Christ. In Jesus' name I pray, Amen.

Be encouraged today! In the Love of Jesus, *Tommy Hays*

Rivers of Living Water

Good morning, Lord Jesus. I am Yours and You are mine. Abide in me, I pray. ...

"Let anyone who is thirsty come to Me, and let the one who believes in Me drink. As the Scripture has said, 'Out of the believer's heart shall flow rivers of living water.' Now He said this about the Spirit, which believers in Him were to receive; for as yet the Spirit had not been given, because Jesus was not yet glorified" (John 3:37-39).

I am thirsty, Lord. I thirst for more of You. As best as I can and all by Your grace, I give as much of me to You as I can; and I receive as much of You in me as I can. Fill me, soak me, immerse me, baptize me in Your Holy Spirit more every day (Matthew 3:11). Your Holy Spirit is "the Spirit of Christ", who lives in me (Romans 8:9). You are the Living Waters that fill me up as I thirst for You and they flow out of me as I give my life to You as a vessel for Your purposes and Your kingdom (John 4:10). "Blessed are those who hunger and thirst for Righteousness for they will be filled" (Matthew 5:6). You are the River of Life that flows through Your people to touch the nations, bringing life to all Your waters touch (Ezekiel 47:1-12; Revelation 22:1-2). Flow, river, flow. In Jesus' name I pray, Amen.

Be encouraged today! In the Love of Jesus, *Tommy Hays*

Slave to Sin or Slave to Christ?*

was walking through my kitchen the other day and these words came to mind: "You are a slave to your weight." At first glance, that doesn't seem to make sense. To others, I appear to be healthy and of a normal weight and I am! The problem is that no matter how well I eat or how much I exercise, I'm never satisfied with the results. Maybe I don't have an eating disorder, per say, but I am still a slave in the sense that my physical size dictates how I feel about myself. The struggle to get to that magic number (or just back to where I used to be) has left me deflated and miserable. Just today, I thought, "I wish someone could just love me the way I am—I am so sick of trying to look good and be slim."

The funny thing is that someone does: Christ! And, He provides the remedy for my problem. In John 8:34-36, Jesus says:

"'Most assuredly, I say to you, whoever commits sin is a slave of sin. And a slave does not abide in the house forever, but a son abides forever. Therefore, if the Son makes you free, you shall be free indeed.'"

I know I have become a slave to sin—that sin being my obsession with weight. My weight currently dictates how I feel (worthless) not Christ. Earlier in the chapter, I catch a glimpse of what I can do to get myself out of this rut I am in.

In verses 31-32 Jesus says, "If you abide in My word, you are my disciples indeed. And you shall know the truth and the truth shall make you free.'"

So what does Christ's word say? What is His truth? Here are several verses that come to mind!

"God demonstrates His own love toward us, in that while we were still sinners, Christ died for us" (Romans 5:8).

"Moreover the law entered that the offense might abound. But where sin abounded, grace abounded much more, so that as sin reigned in death, even so grace might reign through righteousness to eternal life through Jesus Christ our Lord" (Romans 20-21).

"I have been crucified with Christ; it is no longer I who live, but Christ lives in me; and the life which I now live in the flesh I live by faith in the Son of God, who loved me and gave Himself for me" (Galatians 2:20).

---

* The following devotional was written by Mary Margaret Adams.

"I say then: Walk in the Spirit, and you shall not fulfill the lusts of the flesh" (Galatians 5:16).

"Stand fast therefore in the liberty by which Christ has made us free, and do not be entangled again with a yoke of bondage" (Galatians 5:1).

First, Christ loves us and accepts us as we are and demonstrated His love for us by death on a cross. Second, when we try to live by anything except His grace, sin abounds, but His grace is greater than any of our sins. Third, for believers in Christ, we need to remind ourselves that our sinful nature has been crucified with Christ; therefore it IS now possible for us to live as we ought to (and not as slaves to sin). Fourth, we can live the way God wants us to and be free from sin when we submit our will to Christ's and live by the Spirit rather than the flesh. Lastly, we know that we can be forgiven for our mistakes and sin because 1 John 1:9 says, "If we confess our sins, He is faithful and just to forgive us our sins and to cleanse us from all unrighteousness.

Ultimately, we need to decide who we want to serve: self and sinful desires, which lead to death OR Christ which leads to freedom.

All praise and glory be to God! *Mary Margaret Adams*

His Eyes are always upon us[*]

"I will lift up my eyes to the hills—from whence comes my help? My help comes from the Lord, who made heaven and earth. He will not allow your foot to be moved; He who keeps you will not slumber. Behold, He who keeps Israel shall neither slumber nor sleep. The Lord is your keeper; the Lord is your shade at your right hand. The sun shall not strike you by day, nor the moon by night. The Lord shall preserve you from all evil; He shall preserve your soul. The Lord shall preserve your going out and your coming in from this time forth, and even forever more" (Psalm 121).

There are times when I have felt small and almost invisible. During one of those times, I felt like God told me that His eyes were always upon me. Even if others did not notice or see me, He did! More than just seeing me, He was watching over me, protecting me, and preserving me. I did not have to feel alone or afraid.

There's a great song by Stephen Curtis Chapman called *His Eyes* that sums up the heart of Christ. It goes as followed:

> Sometimes His eyes were gentle
> And filled with laughter
> And sometimes they cried
> Sometimes there was a fire
> Of holy anger
> In Jesus' eyes
> But the eyes that saw hope in the hopeless
> That saw through the fault to the need
> Are the same eyes that look down from heaven
> Into the deepest part of you and me
>
> His eyes are always upon us
> His eyes never close in sleep
> And no matter where you go
> You will always be in His eyes, in His eyes
>
> Sometimes His voice comes calling
> Like rolling thunder
> Or like driving rain
> And sometimes His voice is quiet
> And we start to wonder
> If He knows our pain
> But He who spoke peace to the water

---

[*] The following devotional was written by Mary Margaret Adams.

Cares more for our heart than the waves
And the voice that once said "You're forgiven"
Still says "You're forgiven" today

Sometimes I look above me when stars are shinning
And I feel so small
How could the God of heaven and all creation
Know I'm here at all
But then in the silence He whispers
"My child, I created you too
And you're my most precious creation
I even gave my Son for you"

His eyes are always upon you
His eyes never close in sleep
And no matter where you go
You will always be in His eyes

All praise and glory be to God! *Mary Margaret Adams*

The End of the Earth*

I went to a Bible study not long ago and I became very anxious as people talked about the end of the earth and the return of Christ. The more certain people went on (and on), the more fearful and anxious I grew.

Later that night, I prayed and told God that I was afraid and worried. As irrational as this may sound, I was afraid that if Christ returned while I was still alive, He may forget to collect me! Other irrational thoughts followed: What if I wasn't ready upon His return? What if I died before His return and I had missed some crucial "truth" and I woke up in a place more like hell than heaven?

As I worried and fretted, I noticed several verses in Thessalonians in a paper I was editing. 1 Thessalonians chapter 5 says:

"For you yourselves know perfectly that the day of the Lord so comes as a thief in the night. For when they say, 'Peace and safety!' then sudden destruction comes upon them, as labor pains upon a pregnant woman. But you, brethren, are not in the darkness, so that this day should overtake you as a thief. You are all sons of light and sons of the day. We are not of the night nor of darkness. . . . "But let us who are of the day be sober, putting on the breastplate of faith and love, and as a helmet the hope of salvation. For God did not appoint us to wrath, but to obtain salvation through our Lord Jesus Christ, who died for us, that whether we wake or sleep, we should live together with Him" (verses 2-5, 8-11).

Initially, there IS a scary part about how Christ's return will be unexpected for many. However, for the brethren—those who are in Christ, it clearly states that this day should not overtake us like a thief, but instead we are to be aware—expecting His return, and ready. Part of being ready is to put on the breastplate of faith and love and the helmet of salvation. Rather than being fearful, God wants me to protect my heart and soul with the faith and love of Christ and my mind with the helmet of salvation. This means that I need to understand to the depths of my soul how much Christ loves and cares for me, understand that He died for me, and believe that He will save me here on earth and especially in our life to come. Also, those who are in Christ are not in darkness and should not fear, because whether we wake or sleep Christ will be with us to save us and we will live with Him. This implies that we are never really apart from Christ—certainly not here on earth nor once we leave this earth to be with Him in heaven. These are comforting words.

All praise and glory be to God! *Mary Margaret Adams*

---

* The following devotional was written by Mary Margaret Adams.

Let God Arise and Our Enemies be Scattered

Good morning, Lord Jesus. I seek Your face; I need Your grace; I welcome Your embrace. ...

"But my eyes are turned toward You, O God, my Lord; in You I seek refuge" (Psalm 141:8).

I have been so honored and blessed to be a minister of Your healing and freedom among Your people tucked away in a retreat in the beautiful woods and hills of eastern Pennsylvania these past few days. We gathered from churches from this region to worship You in spirit and truth, to listen for Your words of life, and receive healing and freedom from the power of Your hand. You are the God who answers when we call—sometimes dramatically in the miracle of a moment and sometimes little by little and step by step as we can handle it—but always answering when we call in Your perfect timing and in Your perfect way.

From the first night you gave me an image from my recent journey with my family through Mammoth Cave in Kentucky. There are places where there is a low ceiling and you have to bend over as you walk. It seemed You were speaking of a low ceiling of depression and discouragement over this region, trying to keep the people bowed down under a crushing weight. As we gathered for refreshing and renewed in this sanctuary of healing and peace in Your presence, there were many coming as those "utterly spent and crushed," groaning under the burdens of life and ministry under a heaviness of spirit.

But You were speaking to us, "The Lord is near to the brokenhearted and saves the crushed in spirit" (Psalm 34:18). You called us to arise and shine for our Light had come and the glory of the Lord was upon us—though deep darkness covered us, the light of the glory of God within us was rising up in our praises and prayers to push back the darkness and shine for Your light in our hearts and throughout the region (Isaiah 60:1-3). You arose within us and our enemies of discouragement and depression were scattered.

"Let God rise up, let His enemies be scattered; let those who hate Him flee before Him. As smoke is driven away; as wax melts before the fire, let the wicked perish before God. But let the righteous be joyful; let them exalt before God; let them be jubilant with joy!" (Psalm 68:1-3). You are a good God who defeats our enemies before our eyes and fills our hearts with joy. Rise up with us and drive our enemies from us in our hearts, our churches, our cities, and our regions throughout the earth for the glory of Your name. Praise Your holy name! In Jesus' name I pray, Amen.

Be encouraged today! In the Love of Jesus, *Tommy Hays*

Created in Christ for Good Works

Good morning, Lord Jesus. Thank You for this new day. Let me live it well as I live it in You. ...

"For we are what He has made us, created in Christ Jesus for good works, which God prepared beforehand to be our way of life" (Ephesians 2:10).

Lord God, my Father, from before the foundations of the earth, You willed in Your heart that I would live my life for You in Christ. I am what You have made me to be as You have given me grace to choose to embrace Your will and Your way for my life. As I live my life in Christ, let Your ways become my ways, Your will become my will, and Your nature become my nature. As You led me to teach my children to pray at the beginning of each new day, "Lord Jesus, make me more like You each day."

You set before me the good works of Your good pleasure for Your purposes through my life. Open my eyes to see them and direct my desires to do them by Your grace and in Your power and for Your glory this day. Let Your will be my way of life. In Jesus' name I pray, Amen.

Be encouraged today! In the Love of Jesus, *Tommy Hays*

Verses to the King

Good morning, Lord Jesus. All that I am and all that I have, I entrust to You alone—my Lord, my God, and my King—Father, Son, and Holy Spirit. ...

"My heart overflows with a goodly theme; I address my verses to the King; my tongue is like the pen of a ready scribe" (Psalm 45:1).

> *All that I am and all that I have,*
> *I entrust to You alone.*
> *My thoughts and desires, all my waking hours*
> *I give You my heart and soul.*
>
> *In You there's no lack, so I hold nothing back.*
> *I lay my life in Your hands.*
> *You are worthy of my trust and the loyalty of my love,*
> *I give You all that I have and all that I am.*

Yes, Lord. Thank You for putting these new verses on my heart to express my commitment of surrender to You again this day. Help me commit more of myself to You each day than the day before. Help me receive more of You each day than I received the day before. Keep increasing as I keep decreasing (John 3:30). Help me keep my eyes on You, beholding Your glory, as I am "being transformed into the same image from glory to glory, just as by the Spirit of the Lord" (2 Corinthians 3:18, NKJV). In Jesus' name I pray, Amen.

Be encouraged today! In the Love of Jesus, *Tommy Hays*

Renewed Day by Day

Good morning, Lord Jesus. Good morning, Heavenly Father. Good morning, Holy Spirit. ...

"So we do not lose heart. Even though our outer nature is wasting away, our inner nature is being renewed day by day" (2 Corinthians 4:16).

Thank You, Lord, for "the water of rebirth and renewal by the Holy Spirit" (Titus 3:5). Day by day, morning by morning, moment by moment, renew me, Holy Spirit, I pray. Fill me afresh with Your breath of life. Refresh and renew the inner nature of my human spirit by conforming me to the holy nature of Your Holy Spirit. You are the "Spirit of Truth" (John 14:17), the "Spirit of Life" (Romans 8:2), the "Spirit of Holiness" (Romans 1:4), the "Spirit of Jesus" (Acts 16:7), the "Spirit of Christ" (Romans 8:9), the "Spirit of the Lord" (Acts 5:9), the "Spirit of God" (Romans 8:9), and the "Spirit of the Living God" (2 Corinthians 3:3).

As we pray in the song of worship and surrender, "Spirit of the Living God, fall afresh on me...." Thank You for this daily gift of "the new life of the Spirit" as You lead me to entrust You with my life every day (Romans 7:6). You are a good Father who gives good gifts to Your children, giving us the good gift of Your Holy Spirit day by day to all who ask (Luke 11:13). So by Your grace, I ask; and by Your grace, I receive, as You renew my inner nature by Your Spirit this day. In Jesus' name I pray, Amen.

Be encouraged today! In the Love of Jesus, *Tommy Hays*

"Jesus Christ is Lord"

Good morning, Lord Jesus. Be exalted in the heavens and exalted in my heart. ...

"On His robe and on His thigh He has a name inscribed, 'King of kings and Lord of lords' " (Revelation 19:16).

Lord Jesus, You are the King of kings and the Lord of lords. Your name "is the name that is above every name, so that at the name of Jesus, every knee should bow ... and every tongue should confess that Jesus Christ is Lord, to the glory of God the Father" (Philippians 2:9-11). I bow my knees before You this day and confess before heaven and earth that You are Lord and You are my Lord, You are King and You are my King.

As Your first disciples bowed their knees before You in worship before You ascended into heaven, You declared, "All authority in heaven and on earth has been given to Me. Go therefore and make disciples of all nations, baptizing them in the name of the Father and of the Son and of the Holy Spirit, and teaching them to obey all that I have commanded you. And remember I am with you always, to the end of the age" (Matthew 28:16-20). In trusting faith, I submit to Your authority and seek to obey Your command—to do my part in my generation to go and make disciples of all nations.

We each have our part by the grace of the gifts You have given each of us to lead others to You and teach them all You have taught us. Then they will bow their knees before You and confess with their tongues before others that You are Lord. "And this good news of the kingdom will be proclaimed throughout the world, as a testimony to all the nations; and then the end will come" (Matthew 24:14). As we go and make disciples and as we proclaim the coming of Your kingdom, You will be with us always—by the Spirit of Christ within us—to the end of the age (Romans 8:9; Colossians 1:27). To God "be glory in the church and in Christ Jesus to all generations, forever and ever, Amen" (Ephesians 3:20-21). In Jesus' name I pray, Amen.

Be encouraged today! In the Love of Jesus, *Tommy Hays*

Wisdom*

Have you ever been on the verge of doing something stupid and before you could plunge ahead you decided to stop for thirty seconds and ask God first? I can be a bit impulsive at times and it's difficult for me to put on the brakes and turn to God first. God in His mercy told me not long ago that I wouldn't be rebuked for going to Him with an idea or plan that I would later figure out was a bad idea. Instead, He wanted me to approach Him and ask for wisdom in order to be spared the pain and consequences of a bad idea that turns into an action. For our actions are so much harder to undo.

Once we understand who God is and what we have to gain by finding wisdom, we will no longer be tempted to avoiding God or think of Him as a potential spoiler of our "good" plans. Proverbs chapter three has this to say about wisdom:

"Happy is the man who finds wisdom, and the man who gains understanding; for her proceeds are better than the profits of silver, and her gain than fine gold. She is more precious than rubies, and all the things you may desire cannot compare with her. Length of days is in her right hand, in her left hand, riches and honor. Her ways are ways of pleasantness, and all of her paths are peace. She is a tree of life to those who take hold of her, and happy are all who retain her" (Proverbs 3:13-18).

And where does this wisdom come from? It comes from our Lord. For Proverbs 3; 19-20 says:

"The Lord by wisdom founded the earth; by understanding He established the Heavens; by His knowledge the depths were broken up, and the clouds drop down the dew."

In case we forgot, God created the Heavens, earth and everything in it: this of course includes us! Even the wisest person is no match for God. In 1 Corinthians 1:19 God says "I will destroy the wisdom of the wise, and bring to nothing the understanding of the prudent." And verse 25 says: "the foolishness of God is wiser than men."

Wisdom comes from God. However, He isn't holding it over our heads. It's amazing, but true that God wants us to have His wisdom free of charge! All we have to do is turn to Him and ask! James 1:5 tells us: "If any of you lacks wisdom, let him ask of God, who gives to all liberally and without reproach, and it will be given to him."

---

* The following devotional was written by Mary Margaret Adams.

Finally, once we have found wisdom, God wants us to hold onto it for the sake of our minds, physical bodies, and souls. Proverbs 3: 21-24 urges us to: "Keep sound wisdom and discretion; so they will be life to your soul and grace to your neck. Then you will walk safely in your way, and your foot will not stumble. When you lie down, you will not be afraid; yes, you will lie down and your sleep will be sweet."

All praise and glory be to God! *Mary Margaret Adams*

Children of God*

" 'Let the little children come to Me, and do not forbid them; for of such is the kingdom of God'" (Luke 18:16).

Today I went to church to pick up my son from Bible school. Since I arrived early, I decided to sit in the back pew with my two-year-old son, Calvin, and listen in for a few minutes. All of the children were in the sanctuary singing their Bible songs. It was very uplifting to hear the children sing and sitting there, I could really feel how much Jesus loves children.

Sometimes I have wished I was a child again, because I somehow absorbed a false belief that Jesus loves children, but not adults! But John, a disciple of Jesus, tells us the following:

"But as many as received Him, to them He gave the right to become children of God, to those who believe in His name: who were born, not of blood, nor of the will of the flesh, nor of the will of man, but of God" (John 1:12-13).

Even as adults, we are still "children of God." Just as Jesus received children, He will receive all those who call on His name. Romans 10:11-13 says, "For the scripture says, 'Whoever believes on Him will not be put to shame.' For there is no distinction between Jew and Greek, for the same Lord over all is rich to all who call upon Him. For 'whoever calls on the name of the Lord shall be saved.'"

Perhaps some of us falsely believe that there is a special distinction for certain persons; young or old, male or female, or based on race, class, or our line of work. However, with God there is absolutely no favoritism and He loves all of us equally; those who are young and those who are old, those who are men and those who are women, those who are of all different cultures and races, and that includes you!

Knowing this truth, we can take comfort in the fact that we can always go to God in both good and bad times, and as His child. Psalm 116:1-2 paints a lovely visual picture of how God receives us as His children. It goes as followed:

"I love the Lord, because He has heard my voice and my supplications. Because he has inclined His ear to me, therefore I will call upon Him as long as I live."

---

* The following devotional was written by Mary Margaret Adams.

Not only does God hear us, but He inclines His ear to us—a picture that reminds me of how I am with my small children. When they come to me, I get down on their level and incline my ear to them to show them that they are loved and important and that I am listening to them. This is exactly the way God will receive us, when we go to Him.

All praise and glory be to God! *Mary Margaret Adams*

Give Thanks to the Lord

Good morning, Lord Jesus. I set apart these first moments of my morning to watch and wait for the leading of Your Spirit in the communion of prayer. ...

"O give thanks to the Lord, for He is good; His steadfast love endures forever!" (Psalm 118:1).

We give thanks because You are good, because You love us, and because Your love endures forever. Some say we should give thanks to You for all circumstances, but I believe we should give thanks to You "in every circumstance" (1 Thessalonians 5:18). There is a difference. Not everything that happens to us in this broken, fallen world is Your will, where human beings and spiritual beings have the freedom to rebel and resist Your will for our lives and others. You do not will or cause evil. You desire the abundance of life for us, while the thief comes to steal, kill, and destroy through whatever means he can (John 10:10). But even then, You are with us—fighting for us, walking with us, even causing all that we endure to work together for our good out of Your love (Romans 8:28).

So I thank You, Lord. Though I go through the valleys, I will fear no evil, for You are with me (Psalm 23). Though I go through the waters and rivers and fires of hard circumstances in a broken, fallen world, they shall not overwhelm me nor consume, for You are with me (Isaiah 43). Thank You for the steadfastness of Your love; thank You for Your power to redeem all things in my life for my good and Your glory. In Jesus' name I pray, amen.

Be encouraged today! In the Love of Jesus, *Tommy Hays*

Christ and Food*

A few days ago, I was picking out a few bags of carrots when the man next to me said; "Don't you know carrots are bad?" There had been several studies done that labeled carrots as "bad," because of their high sugar content. I reflected on this for a split second then replied: "Have you ever overeaten on carrots? Because I know I haven't!" He nodded and said, "You have a point there."

People will have all sorts of advice on what you should and shouldn't eat, do or be in life. If we spend too much time listening to the well-meaning advice of others, we can get confused. Ultimately, God has all of the answers. With food, for example, Jesus knew when to feast and when to fast. He didn't just fast all of the time, nor did He continually feast, but instead, He had "perfect" balance when it came to food.

When we read through the gospels we can pick up on a few things Jesus knew about food.

First, He understood that "man shall not live by bread alone, but by every word that proceeds from the mouth of God" (Matthew 4:4). More simply stated, He knows that we need more that food to survive and thrive; we need a relationship with God.

Second, He understood that food was and is a big concern for people. In Matthew chapter 6 He tells us, "Therefore I say to you, do not worry about your life, what you will eat or what you will drink; nor about your body, what you will put on. Is not life more than food and the body more than clothing? Look at the birds of the air, for they neither sow nor reap nor gather into barns; yet your heavenly father feeds them. Are you not of more value than they?" (verses 25-26).

Third, He performed miracles centered on food and celebrations. In Matthew chapter 14, He miraculously feeds 5,000 people. In Luke chapter 5, He calls forth a disciple through enabling him to catch a boat full of fish. In John chapter 2, He turned water into wine. In John chapter 4, He brings about a miraculous change in a Samaritan woman by asking her for a drink of water. And, Jesus instituted the Lord's Supper right before his death so we will remember Him and His work on the cross through bread and wine.

The bottom line is that we need to put Christ first in our lives and be more other-centered (as opposed to self-centered). Also, we do not need to worry

---

* The following devotional was written by Mary Margaret Adams.

or be obsessed with food or other basic needs, because God knows we have them and will help supply all of our needs. If we entrust our lives to Him, He will give us true freedom from worries and concerns; our own and those of well meaning and sometimes not so well-meaning others.

All praise and glory be to God! *Mary Margaret Adams*

"Fount of Every Blessing"

Good morning, Lord Jesus. On the eve of Thanksgiving, I come to You this morning with a thankful heart—Father, Son, and Holy Spirit. ...

"How precious is Your steadfast love, O God! All people may take refuge in the shadow of Your wings. They feast on the abundance of Your house, and You give them drink from the river of Your delights. For with You is the fountain of life; in Your light we see light" (Psalm 36:7-9).

I hear the words of the old hymn in my spirit this morning—"Come thou Fount of every blessing, tune my heart to sing Thy grace. Streams of mercy, never ceasing, call for songs of loudest praise." You are the Fount of every blessing; You are the Fountain of Life. As we gather tomorrow to feast on Thanksgiving Day, let us remember that You are the source of our feast. Every good and perfect gift is from You (James 1:17).

Thank You, Lord, for the gift of Your goodness and the abundance of Your steadfast love. You are my Father and I am Your son. Thank You for the gift of salvation through the blood of the Lamb, Jesus Christ my Lord and Savior. Thank You for the gift of Your abiding presence through the Holy Spirit of the Living God living in me. I sing to You my songs of loudest praise! In Jesus' name I pray, Amen.

Be encouraged today! In the Love of Jesus, *Tommy Hays*

Thankful Hearts

Good morning, Lord Jesus. I give You thanks and praise as I lift up my heart to You. ...

"As He entered a village, ten lepers approached Him. Keeping their distance, they called out, saying, 'Jesus, Master, have mercy on us!' When He saw them He said to them, 'Go and show yourselves to the priest.' And as they went, they were made clean. Then one of them, when he saw that he was healed, turned back, praising God with a loud voice. He prostrated himself at Jesus' feet and thanked Him. And he was a Samaritan" (Luke 17:12-16).

On this Thanksgiving Day, I choose to be one who turns to You in worship and praise with a thankful heart. You are my Savior and Healer. You have cleansed me from sin and shame. You are the One who answers when I call. Sometimes the answer comes immediately in the miracle of a moment, but most of the time the answer comes as I go forth in obedience like the lepers who were healed as they went. Thank You for the countless mercies of Your grace in my life that have come and are yet to come in my journey of faith. With a grateful heart, every day is a happy day of thanksgiving in You. In Jesus' name I pray, Amen.

Be encouraged today! In the Love of Jesus, *Tommy Hays*

Anticipating the Coming of Christ

Good morning, Lord Jesus. Let Your light shine in my heart and throughout the earth this day. ...

"The light shines in the darkness and the darkness did not overcome it. There was a man sent from God, whose name was John. He came as a witness to testify to the light, so that all might believe through him. He himself was not the light, but he came to testify to the light. The true light, which enlightens everyone, was coming into the world" (John 1:5-9).

In this season as we turn our hearts from Thanksgiving to Christmas, we look toward the Light who is coming into the world. This is the season of Advent—the season of the anticipation of the coming of Christ. Those who long awaited Your first coming through the prophesies of the coming Messiah, longed for the light to step down into darkness. It would be said of them, "The people who walked in darkness have seen a great light; those who lived in a land of deep darkness—on them light has shined" (Isaiah 9:2, fulfilled in Matthew 4:16).

As we begin this season of anticipation to celebrate Your first coming, let us also continue in this season of hope longing for Your second coming. Step down into the darkness of our souls and the darkness of this broken, fallen world. As the prophets spoke of Your first coming, so they also proclaimed Your second. "Sing and rejoice, O daughter Zion! For lo, I will come and dwell in your midst, says the Lord. Many nations shall join themselves to the Lord on that day, and shall be My people; and I will dwell in your midst. And you shall know that the Lord of Hosts has sent me to you. The Lord will inherit Judah as His portion in the Holy Land, and will again choose Jerusalem" (Zechariah 2:10-12). Come, Lord Jesus.   You are "the Alpha and the Omega," the One "who is and who was and who is to come," "the Almighty" (Revelation 1:8). In Jesus' name I pray, Amen.

Be encouraged today! In the Love of Jesus, *Tommy Hays*

"At All Times"

Good morning, Lord Jesus. As I begin this day with You, I choose by Your grace, to actively and simply seek You and worship You while I wait for You in the silence of surrender. ...

"I will bless the Lord at all times; His praise shall continually be in my mouth.   My soul makes its boast in the Lord; let the humble hear and be glad. O magnify the Lord with me, and let us exult His name together" (Psalm 34:1-3).

Teach me, Lord, how to keep my eyes fixed on You, while at the same time, fully seeing the reality of the circumstances before me. Teach me how to bless You with my praises and honor You with my trust, while also submitting to Your discipline and yielding to Your correction. Because I know You are with me, because I know You care for me, because I know in the end You will cause all things to work together for my good as I keep my face set toward You, I can bless You "at all times." This is how, by Your grace and in Your power, I can "rejoice always, pray without ceasing, give thanks in all circumstances" (1 Thessalonians 5:16). Be magnified and exalted in my heart and throughout the moments of my days. In Jesus' name I pray, Amen.

Be encouraged today! In the Love of Jesus, *Tommy Hays*

King of Glory Come In

Good morning, Lord Jesus. Here I am, Lord—watching and waiting for Your leading, as I offer to You the first-fruits of my thoughts and desires this day. ...

"Lift up your heads, O gates! And be lifted up, O ancient doors! That the King of glory may come in. Who is this King of glory? The Lord of hosts, He is this King of glory" (Psalm 24:9-10).

To You, O Lord, I lift up my head and open up my heart. You are the King of glory. You are the King of kings and Lord of lords. You are the King and Lord of my heart and soul, and I welcome You to continue to come in and establish Your Kingdom in my life. As I behold You in the trusting surrender of worship and yield to Your will and Your ways in the communion of prayer, You are changing me into Your image one day at a time (2 Corinthians 3:18). "Look to Him, and be radiant; so your faces shall never be ashamed" (Psalm 34:5). Thank You for Your blood that cleanses my sin. Thank You for Your fire that purifies my soul. Thank You for Your grace that enables me to lift my head and open my heart that the King of glory may come in. In Jesus' name I pray, Amen.

Be encouraged today! In the Love of Jesus, *Tommy Hays*

Fear Him and Seek Him

Good morning, Lord Jesus. Lead me in the paths of Your righteousness today. ...

"The angel of the Lord encamps around those who fear Him, and delivers them. O taste and see that the Lord is good; happy are those who take refuge in Him. O fear the Lord, you His holy ones, for those who fear Him have no want. The young lions suffer want and hunger, but those who seek the Lord lack no good thing" (Psalm 34:7-10).

You call me to seek You and to fear You at the same time. Teach me Your ways, Lord. Let Your ways become my ways, a little more each day. ...

It seems I hear You say, "My son, there are those who seek the blessings of My hands without seeking the glory of My face. There are those who want to know Me for what I can do for them, not really desiring to know Me for who I am to them. This is not the fear of the Lord. To fear Me is to honor Me for who I am without regard to what I can do for you. I am the Lord your God. Seek Me first and My righteousness. Then all these things will be added unto you. When you seek Me in this way, you honor Me, you fear Me, and you welcome Me to encamp around you."

Yes, Lord. As someone has said, I choose to seek Your face before Your hands. By Your grace, I seek You first (Matthew 6:33). As You have said in the wisdom of Your Word, "I love those who love Me, and those who seek Me diligently find Me" (Proverbs 8:17). Help me continue to learn how to walk this journey of faith in both the fear of the Lord and the intimacy of the Lord, as You teach me to seek You and to honor You for who You are. In Jesus' name I pray, Amen.

Be encouraged today! In the Love of Jesus, *Tommy Hays*

Fire from Heaven

Good morning, Lord Jesus. In these first moments of the morning in contemplative prayer, let me hear no voice but Your voice, think no thoughts but Your thoughts, have no desires but Your desires. I watch and wait for You alone—Father, Son, and Holy Spirit. ...

"Now, O my God, let Your eyes be open and Your ears attentive to prayer from this place.... When Solomon had ended his prayer, fire came down from heaven and consumed the burnt offerings and the sacrifices; and the glory of the Lord filled the temple" (2 Chronicles 6:40-7:1).

Solomon built a temple for You; and by Your grace, You have built a temple in me. Through the sacrifice of the blood of the Lamb of God who takes away the sins of the world, my body is now "a temple of the Holy Spirit" (1 Corinthians 6:19). As I offer to You in prayer the burnt offerings of my heart and soul with the sacrifices of my thoughts and desires, let Your fire come down from heaven. Consume my flesh and fill me afresh with the glory of Your presence living in me. "Do you not know that you are God's temple and that God's Spirit dwells in you? If anyone destroys God's temple, God will destroy that person. For God's temple is holy, and you are that temple" (1 Corinthians 3:16). In Jesus' name I pray, Amen.

Be encouraged today! In the Love of Jesus, *Tommy Hays*

Flesh and Blood

Good morning, Lord Jesus. Before I think of what I have to do today, before I even begin to pray for others or myself, I turn my heart and soul to You. ...

"So Jesus said to them, 'Very truly, I tell you, unless you eat the flesh of the Son of Man and drink His blood, you have no Life in you. Those who eat My flesh and drink My blood have eternal life and I will raise them up on the last day; for My flesh is true food and My blood is true drink. Those who eat My flesh and drink My blood abide in Me, and I in them....' When many of His disciples heard it, they said, 'This teaching is difficult, who can accept it?' ... Because of this many of His disciples turned back and no longer went about with Him" (John 6:53-66).

Lord, help me hear all Your words and receive them all as "spirit and life"—even the hard words and difficult teachings (John 6:63). Give me faith to keep pressing in and courage to keep pressing on, never turning back and never holding back. You are the Word of God and You became flesh to dwell among us (John 1:14). You poured out the blood of Your life to cleanse me from my sins, heal me of my wounds, and free me from my bondage. By Your grace, I choose to abide in You and welcome You to abide in me. I choose to eat of the flesh of Your Word and drink of the blood of Your Life. In the mystery of faith, make me one with You, one with the others of Your body throughout the nations and generations, and one in ministry to all the world. Where You lead me, I will follow—knowing You go with me and You live within me, all the way. In Jesus' name I pray, Amen.

Be encouraged today! In the Love of Jesus, *Tommy Hays*

"Give to Everyone Who Begs from You"

Good morning, Lord Jesus. Good morning, Holy Spirit. Good morning, Heavenly Father. Lord God Almighty, I enter into the Holy of Holies of Your presence in prayer through the blood of the Lamb. ...

"You do well if you really fulfill the royal law according to the Scripture, 'You shall love your neighbor as yourself.' But if you show partiality, you commit sin and are convicted by the law as transgressors.... So speak and so act as those who are to be judged by the law of liberty. For judgment will be without mercy to anyone who has shown no mercy; mercy triumphs over judgment" (James 2:8-13).

Yesterday a man asked me for money to buy some food. It may be the changing season or the changing culture, but that seems to be happening more and more. I have to admit those times make me uncomfortable as I find myself trying to judge the person's heart, motives, needs, and circumstances. Then I find myself judging my own. But this time, as soon as my mind started to go down that road, I heard very clearly in my spirit, "Give to everyone who begs from you." So that made it easy. But as the man walked away, I remembered the many times I have not given to everyone who begs from me, despite the teaching of Your Word (Matthew 5:42). I remembered the times I've tried to find comfort leaning instead toward another teaching of Your Word, "Anyone unwilling to work should not eat" (2 Thessalonians 3:11).

It just reminded me how impossible it would be to try to sort out the heart and circumstances of every person in every encounter, without the leading of Your Holy Spirit. And it seems that is the answer to showing no partiality—with every encounter with every person in every circumstance, I need to listen for the leading of Your Holy Spirit, I need to seek the mind of Christ, I need to choose the path of the Father Heart of God. I need to begin my days entrusting the encounters of that day to You, so I can be ready to make choices out of constant communion with You. Otherwise, I'll always be tempted to look upon the outward appearance and judge from my limited discernment, when You always look at the heart and only You truly know a person's heart. "For the Lord does not see as mortals see; they look on the outward appearance, but the Lord looks on the heart" (1 Samuel 16:7).

Lord, forgive me for the times I have shown partiality by relying on my own wisdom and whims rather than seeking Your will and ways. Forgive me for my judgments that were not sanctified by Your judgment and all the times I have not loved my neighbor as myself, in violation of Your royal law. I am guilty under the law of Your judgment, and I need Your mercy. Thank You for making Your mercy available for my sins when I commit them to You. Thank You that Your "mercy triumphs over judgment." Judgment is real and so are the consequences—now in this age and in the age to come—but so is Your mercy. Thank You for the mercy that freely comes to a repentant heart by the blood of the Lamb in the grace of God. In Jesus' name I pray, Amen.

Be encouraged today! In the Love of Jesus, *Tommy Hays*

Finding the Lost Coin of Peace

Good morning, Lord Jesus. You are my Lord and Savior. I entrust my life and this day to You. ...

"Or what woman having ten silver coins, if she loses one of them, does not light a lamp, sweep the house, and search carefully until she finds it? When she has found it, she calls together her friends and neighbors, saying, 'Rejoice with me, for I have found the coin that I had lost.' Just so I tell you there is joy in the presence of the angels of God over one sinner who repents" (Luke 15:8-10).

Last night, I was one of the "friends and neighbors" who rejoiced in the presence of the angels of God with a young wife and mother who entrusted her life to You fully for the first time. Your Holy Spirit led her, through a friend, to come join us for our Alpha Course at church. Throughout those ten weeks, she was searching for the peace she felt she had lost somewhere along the way. But when she chose to open her heart to You—"Whoom!" as she said—You filled her heart with a Peace that she had never known—the Peace that only comes with Your Presence.   And all the angels rejoiced! Praise You, Lord Jesus! In Jesus' name I pray, Amen.

Be encouraged today! In the Love of Jesus, *Tommy Hays*

"In the Love of Jesus"

Good morning, Lord Jesus. I love You, Lord, and I lift my voice to worship You. ...

"For the whole law is summed up in a single commandment, 'You shall love your neighbor as yourself'" (Galatians 5:14).

As I have sent out these morning prayers for almost three years now, I have felt Your leading to sign them off with the note "In the Love of Jesus, Tommy Hays." Recently the thoughts were coming to me that I shouldn't do that—that it's not manly enough, too awkward, it might make people feel uncomfortable, and on and on. But You began to show me the source of those thoughts, and that the source is not You. You are love, and love is to be at the heart of my relationship with You and with others. "Whoever does not love does not know God, God is love" (1 John 4:8).

The cultures of our world want to make love seem weak and foolish, even unnecessary and unattainable. You warned us that in these last days "the love of many will grow cold" (Matthew 24:12). That's because the enemy of our souls hates love and hates You, because You are love. And love overcomes our enemy. To grow in spiritual maturity is to grow in love—love for You and love for one another. We cannot grow without growing in love. So give me grace to keep loving You and loving others. Give me courage to "declare Your steadfast love in the morning" (Psalm 92:2). In Jesus' name I pray, Amen.

Be encouraged today! In the Love of Jesus, *Tommy Hays*

Pondering God's Words

Good morning, Lord Jesus. Help me settle down into the stillness of the morning to wait and listen for the leading of Your Spirit. ...

"But Mary treasured all these words and pondered them in her heart" (Luke 2:19).

Lord, I want to treasure the words You speak to me. I want to ponder them in my heart. Your words "are spirit and life" (John 6:63). Let them soak me and seep into me until they become truth to me. "Every word of God proves true; He is a shield to those who take refuge in them" (Proverbs 30:5). Let me hear Your words and believe them, then let me obey them and live them. In Jesus' name I pray, Amen.

Be encouraged today! In the Love of Jesus, *Tommy Hays*

Now is the Day of Salvation

Good morning, Lord Jesus. I turn to You and call on Your name. ...

"As we work together with Him, we urge you also not to accept the grace of God in vain. For He says, 'At an acceptable time I have listened to you, and on a day of salvation I have helped you.' See, now is the acceptable time; see, now is the day of salvation" (2 Corinthians 6:1-2)!

Salvation is the fullness of life You give us by the grace of Your love—now in this age and in the age to come, throughout eternity. It includes eternal life, and eternal life includes today. Each moment of each day is the time to choose by Your grace to embrace Your salvation and the fullness of life in Christ or not—lest we have received it in vain. "Now I would remind you, brothers and sisters, of the good news that I proclaimed to you, which you in turn received, in which you also stand, through which you also are being saved, if you hold firmly to the message that I proclaimed to you—unless you have come to believe in vain" (1 Corinthians 15:1-2).

I embrace the grace of this day of salvation. Each day is a new day in the journey of faith. So I choose this day to stand in faith on Your promises, holding firmly to the message of the good news of Your unfailing love and incredible mercy as I am "being saved" by Your grace. As You said to Your first disciples, "The one who endures to the end will be saved" (Matthew 10:22 and 24:13). Throughout the moments of this day, let me call upon Your name with every breath, trusting in You alone and trusting in You continually for my peace and provision. "For, 'Everyone who calls on the name of the Lord will be saved' " (Romans 10:13). In Jesus' name I pray, Amen.

Be encouraged today! In the Love of Jesus, *Tommy Hays*

"Extraordinary Miracles"

Good morning, Lord Jesus. I offer my life a sacrifice. Fill me with Your Spirit, lead me in Your ways, send me in Your will. ...

"God did extraordinary miracles through Paul" (Acts 19:11).

Paul was just a man, made of flesh and blood. Yet he came to the place of trusting faith, brokenness and humility, delivered from pride of self, until he was "crucified with Christ" (Galatians 2:19). Then his life truly became a living sacrifice. Then he could truly say, "It is no longer I who live, but it is Christ who lives in me" (Galatians 2:20). The more he was conformed to the nature of Christ, the more he was entrusted with the authority of Christ. Not Paul's authority, but Your authority being released through him as he learned to abide in You and allow You to abide in him. Then he saw You do extraordinary miracles. You did the miracles, but You did them through Paul—a yielded vessel, an obedient instrument of Your grace and Your power made perfect through his weakness. In humility and in faith, Paul knew the source of the power being released through his life, as he acknowledged before heaven and earth, "I will boast all the more gladly of my weaknesses, so that the power of Christ may dwell in me" (2 Corinthians 12:9).

Lord, I pray You would continue to break my pride and crucify my flesh. Conform me to Your nature. Teach me to abide in You and allow You to abide in me, more and more every day. I am just a man of flesh and blood, but so was Paul. I want to be part of the body of Christ who is so filled with the Spirit of Christ that we see the fulfillment of Your promise in our day: "Very truly, I tell you, the one who believes in Me will also do the works that I do and, in fact, will do greater works than these, because I am going to the Father. I will do whatever you ask in My name, so that the Father may be glorified in the Son" (John 14:12-13). I am asking to see Your extraordinary miracles released through my life for Your glory. In Jesus' name I pray, Amen.

Be encouraged today! In the Love of Jesus, *Tommy Hays*

Tender Sapling to Mighty Oak

Good morning, Lord Jesus. Thank You for the gift of this new day to live my life for You—Father, Son, and Holy Spirit. ...

"Blessed are those who trust in the Lord, whose trust is the Lord. They shall be like a tree planted by water, sending out its roots by the stream. It shall not fear when heat comes, and its leaves shall stay green; in the year of drought it is not anxious, and it does not cease to bear fruit" (Jeremiah 17:7-8).

Heaven welcomed another soul into the kingdom of God yesterday afternoon at our church. She's had many questions along her journey, not willing to accept any of the truths of our faith at face value until they became true to her. It seems You have created her with a gift of steadfast, unwavering faith that the enemy has feared ever coming to light and has tried to cover up all her life with doubt, unbelief, skepticism, rationalism, and humanism. Above all, our enemy fears the soul who finds who they are in Christ, who Christ is in them, what their gifting is, and then begin to walk in it for the glory of the kingdom of God. She has had such a battle of the mind because You have gifted her with a mind to be filled with the wisdom of God, grounded in faith and matured in truth, to share Your wisdom and steadfast faith with others as she grows in her calling and identity in Christ.

As You delivered her from her enemies and freed her to receive Your truth in Your power, You showed me an image of a tender sapling growing into a mighty oak. Though in the spirit, she is as a tiny seedling in these first steps of faith, she will grow by Your grace into a mighty oak of righteousness. Thank You for planting the seeds of truth and life in her spirit through many along the path of her journey of faith. And thank you for guarding and protecting this tender plant who will now grow in grace to stand firm in the faith as a witness to many. "They will be called oaks of righteousness to display His glory" (from Isaiah 61:3). In Jesus' name I pray, Amen.

Be encouraged today! In the Love of Jesus, *Tommy Hays*

Divine Jealousy

Good morning, Lord Jesus. You are faithful and true. Help me be faithful to You. ...

"Do not follow other gods, any of the gods of the peoples who are all around you, because the Lord your God, who is present with you, is a jealous God" (Deuteronomy 6:14-15).

Thank You for loving me with a divine jealousy—unwilling to allow me to share my heart with any god but You. The gods of many forms around me may try to lure me away, seeking my attention and demanding my worship, even settling for part of my heart, but You will not yield in this. You are jealous that I would love You with all my heart, all my soul, all my mind, and all my strength (Deuteronomy 6:5; Mark 12:30). Give me grace to honor You with my faithfulness to You alone—uncompromising and unadulterated. I choose again this day to have no other gods before You. In Jesus' name I pray, Amen.

Be encouraged today! In the Love of Jesus, *Tommy Hays*

"Truth is in Jesus"

Good morning, Lord Jesus. I lift my face and center my thoughts on You this day. ...

"For surely you have heard about Him and were taught in Him, as truth is in Jesus" (Ephesians 4:21).

As I rise and go out into the world today, I will hear and see many things. Let me filter it all through the cross and the blood of Jesus, as "truth is in Jesus." Sharpen my discernment. Sensitize my spirit. Give me Your wisdom to know to remember Your Word. Then I will not be deceived or confused, because I will be rooted and grounded in Your truth. In Jesus' name I pray, Amen.

Be encouraged today! In the Love of Jesus, *Tommy Hays*

Invocation

Good morning, Lord Jesus. By the Holy Spirit of the Living God living in me, I come to You, Father, through Jesus, Your Son. ...

"Be attentive to all that I have said to you. Do not invoke the names of other gods; do not let them be heard on your lips" (Exodus 23:13).

I invoke Your name, Lord Jesus. Your name is "the name that is above every name" (Philippians 2:9). Your name speaks of Your nature, and Your name means "the salvation of God." Thank You for saving me—saving me from the law of sin and death, saving me from the nature of my flesh and pride of self-centeredness, saving from the eternal torment of hell apart from You. "There is salvation in no one else, for there is no other name under heaven given among mortals by which we must be saved" (Acts 4:12).

As I invoke Your name, I welcome Your Holy Spirit, "the Spirit of Christ" living in me (Romans 8:9). Fill me Holy Spirit, possess me, Lord. Make me more like Jesus each day, conforming me into the image and nature of Christ (Romans 8:29). The Father and the Son are One, coming to abide in me and all the children of God by the Holy Spirit of the Living God. Your Spirit of Truth and Life comes to dwell in us, as Your life becomes our lives and we embrace Your possession of our lives each day. "Because I live, you also will live. On that day you will know that I am in My Father, and you in Me, and I in you" (John 14:19-20). In Jesus' name I pray, Amen.

Be encouraged today! In the Love of Jesus, *Tommy Hays*

Simply Yours

Good morning, Lord Jesus. I simply come and seek Your face. ...

> *I simply come and seek Your face,*
> *I simply bow and need Your grace.*
> *I simply praise Your name my King,*
> *I simply say You're my everything.*

"One thing I asked of the Lord, that will I seek after: to live in the house of the Lord all the days of my life, to behold the beauty of the Lord, and to inquire in His temple" (Psalm 27:4).

In all the busyness of this season, keep reminding me of the one thing that really matters most—my personal relationship with You. You are the "One Thing" I need most. As I seek you and seek You first, everything else comes into place. Then, everything else is covered by Your grace. Help me keep it simple. As I choose to be simply Yours. In Jesus' name I pray, Amen.

Be encouraged today! In the Love of Jesus, *Tommy Hays*

Lost and Alone*

"For the Son of Man has come to seek and to save that which was lost" (Luke 19:10).

A few days ago, my four year old son had his school Christmas party. I felt compelled to ask about the parakeets and even to volunteer to care for them over the holiday break. As I called for his teacher Peggy, I realized that I just didn't know much about birds. All I knew was that they were happier in pairs and I was so thrilled to see that she had found a friend for Walter. As she neared, I said, "It's so good that you got a second parakeet!" Peggy told me that there was a story behind it. I said, "Oh really! What's that?" She then told me this amazing story about how her neighbor had spotted a bright green bird in her chicken coupe one morning. He knew it was something exotic and went closer and discovered that it was a poor, starving parakeet. The parakeet was frantically eating with the chickens. Peggy's neighbor managed to catch the little bird and after looking him over, Peggy decided to put him in with her other parakeet named Walter. The children named him Kiwi and the two had been so happy together! Walter was happy, because he finally had a friend, and Kiwi was happy, because he was finally well fed and warm.

It really is quite amazing that a tropical bird could survive in the wild as Kiwi had done. God really impressed upon me the significance of Kiwi's life and how He had sustained him and brought him to a good place. It was as if He said, "Mary, this is how I care for the hurting and the lost."

There are times when we think there isn't a hope or a prayer for ourselves or others who are weak or lost. We may have wandered far and found it impossible to find our way back home. However, Christ in His mercy seeks us out and saves us. Not only does He save us, but He restores us! Psalm 113 says, "He raises the poor out of the dust, and lifts the needy out of the ash heap, that He may seat him with princes—with the princes of His people" (verse 7). Indeed, I had almost three weeks to marvel over this truth while I cared for Walter and Kiwi.

All praise and glory be to God! *Mary Margaret Adams*

---

* The following devotional was written by Mary Margaret Adams.

Needing Healing

Good morning, Lord Jesus. I seek You and I need You. I worship and adore You, then lay my needs before You. ...

"As the sun was setting, all those who had any who were sick with various kinds of diseases brought them to Him; and He laid His hands on each of them and cured them" (Luke 4:40).

Lord, I bring my youngest sons, Elijah and Josiah, to you. They are struggling with sickness that is stealing their peace and rest and ours. I'm asking You to lay Your hands on them and heal them. Drive all infirmity from them and restore them to health in Your created order, redeemed by Your blood and filled with Your Spirit. I praise You and thank You now for healing my children. It is already done in heaven, and it is in the process of being done here on earth as it is in heaven. "Bless the Lord, O my soul, and do not forget all His benefits—who forgives all your iniquity, who heals all your diseases" (Psalm 103:2-3). In Jesus' name I pray, Amen.

Be encouraged today! In the Love of Jesus, *Tommy Hays*

Hope Re-gifted

Good morning, Lord Jesus. I look to You and listen for the leading of Your voice. ...

"Guard what has been entrusted to you" (1 Timothy 6:20).

Thank You for entrusting to me the gift of a sure hope and confident faith in Your goodness and grace. "We have this hope, a sure and steadfast anchor of the soul" (Hebrews 6:19). You are faithful and true, worthy of all my trust. "Let us hold fast to this confession of our hope without wavering, for He who has promised is faithful" (Hebrews 10:23). This gift of hope is for me, but not for me to keep for myself. It is a gift to be given away—to be "re-gifted." Let me always be ready to share with others this gift of hope that is within me (1 Peter 3:15). I am both a child of the King and a servant of this gospel of hope in the good news of Your kingdom. Give me grace to both guard it in my heart and give it away for the hearts of others. In Jesus' name I pray, Amen.

Be encouraged today! In the Love of Jesus, *Tommy Hays*

Proclaim the Mighty Acts of God

Good morning, Lord Jesus. O Lord, my God, I praise You—Father, Son, and Holy Spirit. ...

"But you are a chosen race, a royal priesthood, a holy nation, God's own people, in order that you might proclaim the mighty acts of Him who called you out of darkness and into His marvelous light. Once you were not a people, but now you are God's people; once you had not received mercy, but now you have received mercy" (1 Peter 2:9-10).

Through faith, You have called me Your own. But I am called with a purpose—"to proclaim the mighty acts" of God. You have saved me and raised me up with You to be part of the people of God and to proclaim the power of God, by living a life transformed by God. Let me live my life this day by Your grace to display Your glory as one who has been touched and changed by the power of Your love. "To Him who loves us and freed us from our sins by His blood, and made us to be a kingdom, priests serving His God and Father, to Him be glory and dominion forever and ever" (Revelation 1:5-6). Let my life be a witness of the mighty acts of God this day. In Jesus' name I pray, Amen.

Be encouraged today! In the Love of Jesus, *Tommy Hays*

Commitment

Good morning, Lord Jesus. Before I rise and go about my day, I choose to first stop and wait and pray. ...

"Into Your hand I commit my spirit; You have redeemed me, O Lord, faithful God" (Psalm 31:5).

As I begin this new day, I have a choice. I can take this day into my own hands or I can commit it into Yours. Lord, You are faithful and worthy of my trust. So by Your grace, I commit myself and this day to You. I ask You to order my steps and guide my thoughts. Put Your thoughts in my mind and Your desires in my heart. I surrender all and entrust all to You. In Jesus' name I pray, Amen.

Be encouraged today! In the Love of Jesus, *Tommy Hays*

A Humble God

Good morning, Lord Jesus. As the Christmas song says, "O come, let us adore Him." I come this morning to adore You with the offering of my first thoughts and prayers this day. ...

"Joseph also went from the town of Nazareth in Galilee to Judea, to the city of David called Bethlehem, because he was descended from the house and family of David. He went to be registered with Mary, to whom he was engaged and expecting a Child. While they were there, the time came for her to deliver her child. And she gave birth to her firstborn Son and wrapped Him in bands of cloth, and laid Him in a manger, because there was no place for them in the inn" (Luke 2:4-7).

Lord Jesus, though You were "in the form of God," You humbled Yourself beyond our imagination and capacity to fully comprehend, "being born in human likeness" (Philippians 2:5-8). Not only humbling Yourself in human flesh, but being born to an unwed mother, displaced from her home, rejected from a place of security and shelter. You chose to be born in a stall made for animals, not even the poorest of humans. You are an awesome and a humble God (v. 2:8).

You continue to seek to dwell among the humble places—hearts humbled of our pride to seek You and welcome You as Lord of our lives. "For thus says the high and lofty One who inhabits eternity, whose name is Holy: I dwell in the high and holy place, and also with those who are contrite and humble in spirit, to revive the spirit of the humble, and to revive the heart of the contrite" (Isaiah 57:15). By Your grace, let my heart be a humble place for You to dwell. In Jesus' name I pray, Amen.

Be encouraged today! In the Love of Jesus, *Tommy Hays*

Tremble at the Word

Good morning, Lord Jesus. Help me wait for Your Word and listen for Your leading. ...

"Thus says the Lord: Heaven is My throne and the earth is My footstool; what is the house that you would build for Me, and what is My resting place? All these things My hand has made, and so all these things are Mine, says the Lord. But this is the one to whom I will look, to the humble and contrite in spirit, who trembles at My Word" (Isaiah 66:1-2).

Lord, let me never cease to tremble at Your Word. Though it may be written down into a book, though it may be packaged and sold in bookstores, though it may fill the shelves of my book cases, it is still the Word of God. It is holy and to be treated with reverence and awe in the fear of God.

They say familiarity breads contempt. Forgive me for any way my sensitivity to the privilege and honor of knowing You and hearing Your Word has grown dull.   The sons of Eli were priests who failed to tremble at Your Word. "They treated the offerings of the Lord with contempt" (1 Samuel 2:17). And they were judged for their sins with their lives. Lord, keep me mindful of the mystery of Your Word, revealed to us through Your Scripture and through Your Person. You are the Word of God (John 1:1, 14). By Your grace, I tremble before You. I welcome You to make my heart Your home, as I honor You and Your Word. In Jesus' name I pray, Amen.

Be encouraged today! In the Love of Jesus, *Tommy Hays*

Mighty Warrior God

Good morning, Lord Jesus. Strengthen my spirit in these morning moments of prayer. Gird up my heart in faith to face the battles I will face today for the sake of Your name. ...

"The Lord is my strength and my might, and He has become my salvation; this is my God and I will praise Him, my father's God, and I will exalt Him. The Lord is a warrior; the Lord is His name" (Exodus 15:2-3).

Moses and the people sang this song of praise as they stood in wonder at the shores of the Red Sea. Their enemies charged against them, shouting taunts of terror to melt their hearts in fear: "I will pursue, I will overtake, I will divide the spoil, my desire shall have its fill of them. I will draw my sword, my hand shall destroy them" (15:9). But it was Your hand that drew the sword of Your Word. "You blew Your wind, the sea covered them; they sank like lead in the mighty waters" (15:10). You defeated the enemies of Your people in the face of certain destruction. Then their hearts could not contain the songs of praise and shouts of joy for the strength and power of Your salvation. "Your right hand, O Lord, glorious in power—Your right hand, O Lord, shattered the enemy!" (15:6).

You are my strength and my might. Come in power to defeat the enemies of my soul. Stretch out Your mighty right hand, O Lord. Deliver me from destruction and establish me in the victory of Your salvation. You are love, but You are also a warrior—a mighty warrior who's love for Your people consumes our enemies and silences their taunts. Arise in Your power and let Your enemies be scattered. "This is my God and I will praise Him!" In Jesus' name I pray, Amen.

Be encouraged today! In the Love of Jesus, *Tommy Hays*

"Our Great God and Savior"

Good morning, Lord Jesus. Fill me with the hope and anticipation of Your presence in my life today. ...

"For the grace of God has appeared, bringing salvation to all, training us to renounce impiety and worldly passions, and in the present age to live lives that are self-controlled, upright, and godly, while we wait for the blessed hope and the manifestation of the glory of our great God and Savior, Jesus Christ. He it is who gave Himself up for us that He might redeem us from all iniquity and purify for Himself a people of His own who are zealous for good deeds" (Titus 2:11-14).

Lord Jesus, You are "our great God and Savior." I wait for "the blessed hope" of the manifestation of Your glory. Keep redeeming me from all iniquity, keep purifying me from all defilement of my sin and the sins of others against me, keep training me to renounce impiety and worldly passions. By Your grace and in Your power I want to live my life in a way that honors You—self-controlled, upright and godly. This is why You have appeared in the flesh, "bringing salvation to all." Help me embrace the fullness of Your salvation for me through the cleansing of Your blood and the power of Your Spirit to the glory of our Father. In Jesus' name I pray, Amen.

Be encouraged today! In the Love of Jesus, *Tommy Hays*

"Messiah is Coming"

Good morning, Lord Jesus. I welcome You, Lord God—Father, Son, and Holy Spirit—into my heart and my day. ...

"The woman said to Him, 'I know that Messiah is coming" (who is called Christ). 'When He comes, He will proclaim all things to us.' Jesus said to her, 'I am He, the One who is speaking to you' " (John 4:25-26).

Lord Jesus, You are the One who proclaims all things to us. You are *Yeshua HaMoshiach*—Jesus the Messiah, the Anointed One of God. You are "the Lord God, who is and who was and who is to come, the Almighty" (Revelation 1:8). You are still coming, still speaking, still proclaiming Your Word of truth and life to us. You are the Word made flesh—both exalted as Son of God and humbled as Son of Man—having no beginning and no end as Son of God, yet at the same time conceived by the Holy Spirit in the human womb of a virgin girl (John 1:14; Philippians 2:5-11).

" 'She will bear a Son, and you are to name Him Jesus, for He will save His people from their sins.' All this took place to fulfill what had been spoken by the Lord through the prophet: 'Look, the virgin shall conceive and bear a Son, and they shall name Him Emmanuel,' which means, 'God is with us' " (Matthew 1:21-23). Thank You for coming, and thank You for coming again soon. And in between these two great days, thank You for being with us, for being with me—this day and every day. In Jesus' name I pray, Amen.

Be encouraged today! In the Love of Jesus, *Tommy Hays*

The Messiah of Bethlehem

Good morning, Lord Jesus. I center my thoughts on You as I lift up my heart in prayer. ...

"But you, O Bethlehem of Ephrathah, who are one of the little clans of Judah, from you will come forth for Me One who is to rule in Israel, whose origin is from of old, from ancient days.... and He shall be the One of Peace" (Micah 5:2-5).

From everlasting to everlasting, You are Lord. You are the Messiah who has come forth to establish Your eternal throne in the hearts of all people (Revelation 11:15). You are the fulfillment of every prophecy of Your coming (Acts 3:18; 18:28). You are the "Ancient of Days" (Daniel 7:9). You are the "Prince of Peace" (Isaiah 9:6). You came in humility on the hay of a manger in Bethlehem and You are coming in glory in the hearts of Your people—all people who call upon Your name. Come and rule in Israel. Come and rule in me. In Jesus' name I pray, Amen.

Be encouraged today! In the Love of Jesus, *Tommy Hays*

Holy Habitation in Zion

Good morning, Lord Jesus. You are my Lord and my Savior. I bow before Your heavenly throne and welcome You here on to the throne of my heart. ...

"For the Lord has chosen Zion; He has desired it for His habitation: 'This is My resting place forever; here I will reside for I have desired it. I will abundantly bless its provisions; I will satisfy its poor with bread. It's priests I will clothe with salvation, and its faithful will shout for joy. There I will cause a horn to sprout up for David; I have prepared a lamp for My anointed One. His enemies I will clothe with disgrace, but on Him, His crown will gleam" (Psalm 132:13-18).

In this season of the celebration of Your first coming as the Christ Child, all the eyes of the world are turned toward Zion—the mountain of the city at the center of the land of Your birth, Your ministry, Your death, Your resurrection, and Your return. "Thus says the Lord God: This is Jerusalem; I have set her in the center of the nations, with countries all around her" (Ezekiel 5:5). As we think of Bethlehem and Jerusalem, Galilee and Nazareth, let us remember to pray for this land and its people at the center of the earth. Though there has been great rebellion, there will be great renewal. Though there has been great violence, there will be great victory. Though there have been great threats of great destruction, there will be great restoration.

So, I pray for the peace of Jerusalem, as Your Word commands us: "Pray for the peace of Jerusalem. May they prosper who love you" (Psalm 122:6). I pray for the people of "the city of God" to turn their eyes to You and behold their Messiah (Psalm 46:4). I pray for the day of peace that will come on the day of Your return to Your "resting place forever" as Your people declare, "Blessed is the One who comes in the name of the Lord" (Matthew 23:39). On that day, I will join all its faithful to "shout for joy" when Your "crown will gleam" by the praise of Your people. In Jesus' name I pray, Amen.

Be encouraged today! In the Love of Jesus, *Tommy Hays*

Blessed by Believing

Good morning, Lord Jesus. Before I face the stress of the season today, I wait in the silence of surrender before You now. ...

"Blessed is she who has believed that there will be a fulfillment of what was spoken to her by the Lord" (Luke 1:45).

Mary believed and received Your words of calling and destiny for her life. She was blessed, and in her obedience of faith, she blessed You. "And without faith it is impossible to please God, for whoever would approach Him must believe that He exists and that He rewards those who seek Him" (Hebrews 11:6). Mary pleased You because she believed You. Let my life please You. Give me grace and faith to believe You for the fulfillment of all You have spoken to me by Your Word and by Your Spirit. Like Mary, let me "accomplish all things" in Your power, according to the purpose and plan You have set for my life "before the foundation of the world" (Ephesians 1:3-14). In Jesus' name I pray, Amen.

Be encouraged today! In the Love of Jesus, *Tommy Hays*

Prepare Him Room

Good morning, Lord Jesus. I make room for You in my heart and welcome You into every area of my world this day. ...

"With the spirit and power of Elijah he will go before Him, to turn the hearts of parents to their children, and the disobedient to the wisdom of the righteous, to make ready a people prepared for the Lord" (Luke 1:17).

In the Christmas hymn *Joy to the World*, we sing, "Let every heart prepare Him room." Christmas Eve marks the time we prepare our hearts with great anticipation of Your coming. Like John the Baptist who came in the spirit of Elijah to prepare the way of the Lord, come Holy Spirit, and prepare the way of the Lord in my heart today. Fill me with anticipation and excitement to receive my Father's Christmas Gift—the gift of Christ the Lord into the world and into my heart. In Jesus' name I pray, Amen.

Be encouraged today! In the Love of Jesus, *Tommy Hays*

Happy Birthday, Jesus

Good morning, Lord Jesus. Happy Birthday! ...

"Then the angel said to them, 'Do not be afraid, for behold, I bring you good tidings of great joy which will be to all people. For there is born to you this day in the city of David a Savior, who is Christ the Lord. And this will be a sign to you: You will find a Babe wrapped in swaddling cloths, lying in a manger.' And suddenly there was with the angel a multitude of the heavenly host praising God and saying, 'Glory to God in the highest, and on earth, peace, goodwill toward men!" (Luke 2:10-14, NKJV).

Though the Word of God is from everlasting to everlasting, on this day we celebrate that "The Word became flesh and dwelt among us, and we beheld His glory, the glory as of the only begotten Son of the Father, full of grace and truth" (John 1:14, NKJV). Lord Jesus, You are the Word of God— eternal as One with the Holy Spirit and the Father, yet at the same time, humbling Yourself and "coming in the likeness of men" (Philippians 2:7, NKJV). Truly this was a miraculous sign and wonder—the Creator of heaven and earth humbling His Self to be born as a Babe in a manger.

"Fall on Your knees! Oh hear the angel voices!" I humble myself before You this day, Christ the Lord, my Savior. I praise You with all the heavenly host and all who call on Your name throughout all generations to celebrate the One who is "full of grace and truth." Glory to God in highest! And on earth, peace and goodwill toward men! In Jesus' name I pray, amen.

Be encouraged today! In the Love of Jesus, *Tommy Hays*

"No Returns, Please"

Good morning, Lord Jesus. With a thankful heart, I receive the gift of the grace of Your presence abiding in me and I abide in You. ...

"Do not, therefore, abandon that confidence of yours; it brings a great reward. For you need endurance, so that when you have done the will of God, you may receive what was promised. For yet 'in a little while, the One who is coming will come and not delay; but My righteous one will live by faith. My soul takes no pleasure in anyone who shrinks back.' But we are not among those who shrink back and are lost, but among those who have faith and so are saved" (Hebrews 10:35-39).

On the day after Christmas, the stores will be filled with people taking back their gifts. They may have expressed joy in the moment of unwrapping the gift, but down inside they did not really ever receive it. They may have appreciated the thought of the giver, but took no thought for the gift. So the gift is returned—once accepted, but no longer received.

But all Christmas gifts speak of the one true Gift. As God the Father, You humbled Yourself as God the Son, to be conceived in human flesh by God the Holy Spirit (Luke 1:35). You gave to us the greatest Gift we could ever receive, longing for us to embrace Your Gift of Grace with the joy of children on Christmas morning. "He came to what was His own, and His own people did not accept Him. But to all who received Him, who believed in His name, He gave power to become children of God" (John 1:11-12).

Father, thank You for Your Gift of Your Son through Your Spirit. I receive Your grace to embrace Your Gift—to never return it, never spurn it, never try to earn it—but simply to receive it with child-like faith and Christmas morning joy. In Jesus' name I pray, Amen.

Be encouraged today! In the Love of Jesus, *Tommy Hays*

A Life Lived in Christ

Good morning, Lord Jesus. I worship You and honor You. I entrust my life and this day to You. ...

"Whoever serves Me must follow Me, and where I am, there will My servant be also. Whoever serves Me, My Father will honor" (John 12:26).

Today we will celebrate and mourn the passing of one of Your servants and saints, Dora Caldwell. To her last day, she prayed with others and saw Your hand in her life. She knew You well and You knew her well. She followed You and served You in the grace and the light You freely gave her. On these days when we pause and look at the lives of others, it causes me to pause and look at my life as well:

> *When all is said and done,*
> *When at last my race is run,*
> *What will You think of me?*
>
> *When there's no room for regrets,*
> *When there's no time for amends,*
> *What will You think of me?*
>
> *When it doesn't matter what others say,*
> *When I won't have another day,*
> *What will You think of me?*
>
> *I'll be embarrassed of some things,*
> *I'll be glad of other things,*
> *But the most important thing,*
> *Will be what did I think of You.*
>
> *Did I trust You with my life,*
> *Did I receive Your sacrifice,*
> *Did I live my life for You?*
>
> *I can know this very day,*
> *What You'll think of me on that day,*
> *As I entrust my life to You.*
>
> *You'll see me through Your blood,*
> *You'll know me by Your love,*
> *And I'll spend my eternal life with You.*

In Jesus' name I pray, Amen.

Be encouraged today! In the Love of Jesus, *Tommy Hays*

Legacy of Faith

Good morning, Lord Jesus. I rise in my spirit to take Your hand and walk another day of the journey of faith with You. ...

"I am reminded of your sincere faith, a faith that lived first in your grandmother Lois and your mother Eunice and now, I am sure, lives in you" (2 Timothy 1:5).

Timothy lived a legacy of faith, passed down to him through the generations, as his grandmother and mother lived out that faith before him and taught him how to live out that faith for himself. As we celebrated the life of Dora Caldwell yesterday with her family, we saw the power and witness of a legacy of faith passed down and lived out through those she loved. She was a woman of prayer. And yesterday she must have been so pleased to see her prayers answered and her legacy live on as the name of her Savior and Best Friend was proclaimed from the lips and hearts from those she loved so much.

Lord, give me Your grace to live a life of prayer and faith that will live on in a legacy of faith in those I love. Let me not just live for today, but live for You. Her family said Mrs. Caldwell lived a life of "JOY"—Jesus first; others second; yourself last. Help me learn to live that way. Let Your legacy and hers live on in me. In Jesus' name I pray, Amen.

Be encouraged today! In the Love of Jesus, *Tommy Hays*

I will change Your Name*

"And you will be given a new name by the Lord's own mouth. The Lord will hold you in his hand for all to see—a splendid crown in the hand of God. Never again will you be called 'The Forsaken City' or 'The Desolate Land.' Your new name will be 'The City of God's Delight' and 'The Bride of God,' for the Lord delights in you and will claim you as his bride" (Isaiah 62: 2-4).

'For I am about to do something new. See, I have already begun! Do you not see it? I will make a pathway through the wilderness. I will create rivers in the dry wasteland' (Isaiah 43:19).

"To all who mourn in Israel, he will give a crown of beauty for ashes, a joyous blessing instead of mourning, festive praise instead of despair" (Isaiah 61:2).

Just the other day, a neighbor told me about a terrier that she had seen at the Humane Society. She was concerned and asked if I would look at the dog and consider adopting it. I really wasn't open to considering it, because I had two terriers already—neither of which were easy to care for. Terriers are very high energy pets that require lots of exercise and training.

A few minutes later, someone at Henry's school talked with me about wanting a dog so I went down to the Humane Society to look at the terrier my neighbor had mentioned thinking this person might take it. On the way, I reminded God that I couldn't possibly have another dog, especially a male terrier, but I wouldn't mind helping Him find the dog a home.

When I got there and found the dog, my heart sank. He was so skinny, dirty, and ill-behaved. The first thought that came to my mind was, "No one will ever adopt this dog!" And I knew in my heart that there was simply no way that the woman from Henry's school would take him.

I then quickly discovered why God had sent me there; He wanted *me* to adopt this dog! I walked away and prayed, "Please give me some sort of confirmation that I am to take him." God told me to go back and look at him again; this time through His eyes. I went back and this time I saw the little dog's potential. I knew I had seen his face before in a previous dog I owned. He was just as raggedy as my very first dog Maxwell and God reminded me of how quickly Maxwell had ruled my heart. God meant him as a gift. At that moment, we both knew he was going home!

---

* The following devotional was written by Mary Margaret Adams.

When I went to pay for my dog, the man at the checkout said he was deemed to be "un-adoptable." He had been there four months and no one had ever really considered him. He also told me that the dog had been named Diablo, which meant Devil in Spanish. It made me angry that someone had cursed him like that and so I asked God what his new name should be. God told me "Davey," which means "beloved."

With Davey's new name came a whole new identity and life. He was no longer cursed and desolate, unloved and unwanted. Within just a short period of time, he transformed from a scared, weak, sickly puppy with some pretty awful habits, into a beautiful dog. Although his transformation is not complete, it has brought me great joy to see all he has overcome and how he now has a loving family—including another terrier as his brother and best friend.

Like with Davey, God loves to redeem and restore our pasts and to give us a new identity. He will create streams in the deserts of our lives and transform us into something beautiful; all by His love for us. Although others may initially wonder what He sees in us or why He loves us, before long they will see the outcome of such a great love—a transformation so beautiful that others cannot help but to marvel at it.

Later, as I walked Davey through the neighborhood, people stopped to marvel at my beautiful Westie, not knowing and never guessing that he was once cursed as being of Satan, sick and unloved, imprisoned for months, and deemed un-adoptable.

All praise and glory be to God! *Mary Margaret Adams*

The Cost of a Soul*

"Those who trust in their wealth and boast in the multitudes of their riches, none of them can by any means redeem his brother, nor give to God a ransom for him—for the redemption of their souls is costly, and it shall cease forever—that he should continue to live eternally, and not see the Pit. . . . But God will redeem my soul from the power of the grave, for He shall receive me. . . . A man who is in honor, yet does not understand, is like the beasts that perish" (Psalm 49: 6-9, 15, 20).

I was reading Psalm 49 (the above passage) the other day and was struck by the value of each individual soul; something I had never really thought about before. I had always thought about us in another way; more the value of Christ, because He died for our pathetic souls. For me, this sort of undermined the value of our souls and how they could be redeemed by Christ. I never really thought my particular soul or body was of any importance what-so-ever to Christ!

Psalm 49 is actually more about looking to God for our security instead of putting our trust in our own wealth, power, or position. However, right in the middle of the psalm, there is a curious comparison between money and our souls, where the psalmist states that no one can redeem their brother, not even the richest man, because the redemption of their souls is costly. It struck me how costly it is to redeem our souls and how only God has the power to redeem and save souls. And He actually wants to redeem us and save us! 2 Peter 3:9 says, "The Lord is not slack concerning His promise, as some count slackness, but is longsuffering toward us, not willing that any should perish but that all should come to repentance."

Immediately, another verse in 1 Corinthians came to mind:

"For you were bought at a price; therefore glorify God in your body and in your spirit, which are God's" (1 Corinthians 6:20).

If I really understood the value of my particular soul and the souls of others to God, wouldn't I stop all self-destructive behaviors and want others to do the same? Wouldn't I feel my value from the inside—based on Christ's love for me—rather than looking for things on the outside to measure my worth? Wouldn't that free me up to be the person God really desires me to be? It's as if I hear God saying, "You were bought with a price, do not waste your life."

---

* The following devotional was written by Mary Margaret Adams.

How can I not waste my life? By accepting the following truths! First, our souls are of great value. Second, only God can redeem our souls and give us eternal live. Third, God wants to redeem our souls and give us eternal life. Fourth, God has redeemed us through Jesus Christ and His work on the cross. Fifth, Christ was our perfect, sinless example of how we are called to live. 1 Peter 2:21-24 says the following:

"For to this you were called, because Christ also suffered for us, leaving us an example, that you should follow His steps: 'Who committed no sin, nor was deceit found in His mouth'; who when He was reviled, did not revile in return; when He suffered, He did not threaten, but committed Himself to Him who judges righteously; who Himself bore our sins in His own body on the tree, that we, having died to sins, might live for righteousness—by whose stripes you were healed."

With all of this, surely I can grasp a bit of the depth of God's love for me and others and choose to submit my will to His care and control!

Lastly, Ephesians 3:14-21 sums up Christ's love for us, how we can be strengthened in the inner man (or on the inside) through His Holy Spirit, and the amazing redemptive work that He can do in us and through us. I will close with these verses. Please meditate on them.

"For this reason I bow my knees to the Father of our Lord Jesus Christ, from whom the whole family in heaven and earth is named, that He would grant you, according to the riches of His glory, to be strengthened with might through His Spirit in the inner man, that Christ may dwell in your hearts through faith; that you, being rooted and grounded in love, may be able to comprehend with all the saints what is the width and length and depth and height—to know the love of Christ which passes knowledge; that you may be filled with all the fullness of God. Now to Him who is able to do exceedingly abundantly above all that we ask or think, according to the power that works in us, to Him be glory in the church by Christ Jesus to all generations, forever and ever. Amen."

All praise and glory be to God! *Mary Margaret Adams*

"I Come to the End"

Good morning, Lord Jesus. You are the Alpha and the Omega, the Beginning and the End. You are my All in All. I watch and wait in surrender and silence for the leading of Your Spirit into the arms of my Father. ...

"In Your book were written all the days that were formed for me, when none of them as yet existed. How weighty to me are Your thoughts, O God! How vast is the sum of them! I try to count them—they are more than the sand; I come to the end—I am still with You" (Psalm 139:16-18).

I have come to the end of another year of the journey of faith in prayer with You. Morning by Morning, I have settled into my chair, opened my journal and my heart, lifted my face and spirit, and called on Your name to watch and wait in the silence of surrender for the leading of Your Spirit. "I come to the end—I am still with You." I come to the end, and You are still with me. You never leave me, nor forsake me. All that I endure, You have endured with me and within me by unending presence of Your Holy Spirit abiding in me as I abide in You.

Though You have not willed all that I have experienced this year, You have used it all as a means of Your grace to continue Your labor of love to conform me into the image of Christ (Romans 8:28-30). You have known every challenge that would come, every choice that would be made, and Your power to redeem all that would happen, no matter the source. I need not fear any of the things that are written in Your book of my days, because I know by faith the assurance of Your peace that my name is written in Your "book of life" (Revelation 20:12 and 21:27). Thank You for walking with me through this year. Thank You for being there to walk with me through the next. In Jesus' name I pray, Amen.

Be encouraged today! In the Love of Jesus, *Tommy Hays*

About the Author

Tommy Hays is a Spiritual Director, Teacher, and Prayer Revivalist. He serves as Executive Director of Messiah Ministries, the ministry he founded and leads for interdenominational teaching, preaching, equipping, and prayer ministries of inner healing, deliverance and spiritual formation. Tommy ministers throughout the diverse traditions of the Christian faith and is ordained as a United Methodist minister. He is also a member in covenant relationship with the MorningStar Fellowship of Ministries, an international prophetic teaching ministry. He holds a Master of Divinity from Asbury Theological Seminary and a Doctor of Jurisprudence from The University of Texas at Austin.

Tommy was called to ministry from his law practice as an attorney in Texas, and now offers personal prayer ministry and spiritual direction by private appointment through Messiah Ministries at their office in Lexington, Kentucky. He is a frequent speaker in conferences and churches of many traditions—leading teaching conferences, healing services, prayer retreats, ecumenical gatherings, spiritual renewal weekends, and prayer revivals inter-denominationally throughout the United States and the nations. His vision and the calling of Messiah Ministries is "Preparing the way of the Lord ... Ministering the Healing Love of God" by preparing the people of the Lord through the ministries of healing, wholeness, and sanctification to be trained and equipped to continue the ministry of the Lord throughout all the earth. His daily prayer devotional, "Morning by Morning" is sent to readers around the world every morning by email.

Tommy also leads a citywide, ecumenical service each month of prayer, praise and healing worship called "The Fountain" and teaches The Fountain School of Spiritual Ministry in a number of formats at home and by invitation to train and equip believers for spiritual ministry. Tommy is forty-seven years old, married to Tricia Hays, and the father of five wonderful children—Elizabeth, Zachary, Madison, Elijah, and Josiah Hays. They are members of Centenary United Methodist Church in Lexington, Kentucky, where the Messiah Ministries office is currently based. He continues to practice law on select matters from time to time as the Lord leads in the Lexington law firm of Troutman & Hays, as a minister in the marketplace and public square of the community.

Tommy's teaching and messages focus upon all aspects of spiritual renewal and revival through prayer, healing and wholeness, spiritual warfare, evangelism, and holiness, while equipping the Body of Christ to live out their identity and destiny in the ministry of the Kingdom of God. His ministry focuses on the process of healing form the inside out by bringing every area under the Lordship of Jesus Christ. Wounds of rejection, roots of bitterness, shadows of fear, walls of isolation, and shame of sin -- the unhealed pain and shame of life steals the blessings of abundant life Jesus makes available through the power of the Cross. Our unhealed wounds and brokenness block us from intimacy with God, divide us from loving one another, and imprison us from living out our destiny in Christ. We need healing from our wounds and deliverance from our bondage. We need to know our identity and our purpose. We need to know our gifting, our calling, and our destiny. Through ministries of healing and wholeness in the process of sanctification, we become free to be more like Jesus so we can continue the ministry of Jesus as the Body of Christ, filled with the Spirit of Christ, to a broken and hurting world.

Jesus came to bind up the brokenhearted and set the captives free as He proclaimed the coming of the Kingdom of God (Isaiah 61; Luke 4). Now, as the Father sent the Son, so the Son sends us in the power of the Holy Spirit to glory of God (John 20). This is the mission and ministry of Messiah Ministries as we do our part to "prepare the way of the Lord" in our generation.

Please contact Tommy Hays at Messiah Ministries to order our ministry resources or for invitations for speaking and ministry if we can come alongside you in the ministry of Jesus.

Tommy Hays
Messiah Ministries
2800 Tates Creek Rd.
Lexington, Kentucky 40502
859-422-1794
MessiahMin@aol.com
www.messiah-ministries.org

Printed in the United States
116202LV00005B/1-66/P

9 781598 586923